Study Guide

Essentials of Psychology
Concepts and Applications

Jeffrey Nevid
St. John's University

Prepared by

Marylou Robins
San Jacinto College

WADSWORTH
CENGAGE Learning

Australia • Brazil • Japan • Korea • Mexico • Singapore • Spain • United Kingdom • United States

ISBN-13: 978-1-111-30479-9
ISBN-10: 1-111-30479-3

Wadsworth
20 Davis Drive
Belmont, CA 94002-3098
USA

Cengage Learning is a leading provider of customized learning solutions with office locations around the globe, including Singapore, the United Kingdom, Australia, Mexico, Brazil, and Japan. Locate your local office at: **www.cengage.com/global**

Cengage Learning products are represented in Canada by Nelson Education, Ltd.

To learn more about Wadsworth, visit **www.cengage.com/wadsworth**

Purchase any of our products at your local college store or at our preferred online store **www.cengagebrain.com**

Printed in the United States of America
1 2 3 4 5 6 7 15 14 13 12 11

CONTENTS

To the Student...iii

Ch 1 – Introduction to Psychology and Methods of Research.................1

Ch 2 – Biological Foundations of Behavior......................................31

Ch 3 – Sensation and Perception..65

Ch 4 – Consciousness..95

Ch 5 – Learning...125

Ch 6 – Memory...151

Ch 7 – Thinking, Language, and Intelligence..................................177

Ch 8 – Motivation and Emotion..209

Ch 9 – Human Development...243

Ch 10 – Psychology and Health..287

Ch 11 – Personality...313

Ch 12 – Psychological Disorders..347

Ch 13 – Methods in Therapy..379

Ch 14 – Social Psychology..407

To the Student

Welcome to the *Study Guide* that accompanies your psychology text, Nevid's *Essentials of Psychology (3ⁿᵈ ed.)*. You are using a very insightful textbook, which will introduce you to an understanding of the inner self and those around us – the wonderful world of psychology. This study guide is intended to assist you in making the most of your textbook. It is not meant to be a textbook replacement.

The approach of this study guide is to parallel the material as it is presented to you in your textbook. Because the chapters in your textbook are divided into modules and each module presents a cohesive unit of information, the information included in this study guide has also been organized according to those units within each chapter. Study guide modules are broken down into sections that will help you focus more specifically on different segments of the material presented. Within each module, you will find (1) Learning Objectives, (2) an Outline, (3) a Summary of the module's contents, (4) Key Terms from that particular unit, and (5) a Self-Test Practice Quiz, which will help you assess your understanding of what you have learned in each module. This format is used for all study guide modules except those that correspond to the text's Application modules, which appear at the end of each chapter in your textbook. The Application modules in your textbook present helpful information that you could try out and make use of in your life outside the classroom. However, an objective, outline, and summary of each Application module are provided in this study guide as well. In a few cases, Key Terms and Self-Test Practice Quiz sections are also included in the study guide, depending upon the material presented in the textbook Application module. At the end of each chapter of the study guide, you will find an Application Exercise. This exercise, provided as part of your study guide review, is again geared towards not just conveying information to you but helping you take what you are learning and apply it to your own life.

Among the invaluable features of your textbook are the many opportunities for review. This study guide has been developed to complement those features. Following are some suggested procedures for making the best use of both your textbook and this study guide.

RECOMMENDED APPROACH FOR STUDY

Read the Textbook

It is recommended that you read through your assigned textbook material at least once before you begin to use this study guide. Much research has been done indicating the value of reading your textbook. Some of you have difficulty reading and/or comprehending the material or finding the time to read. If this is the case for you, do not attempt to read the entire chapter in one setting. Break the chapter down into paragraphs, highlight (finding the few words that state) what the paragraph is saying in summary. Get in the habit of taking your textbook and your highlighter with you. You will be surprised at the number of small opportunities you have throughout your day to read a paragraph at a time. As you continue to practice this process you will begin to add more than a paragraph, until you are reading a page at a time. The more you read (practice) the faster you become. Avoiding any reading task entirely and waiting for an instructor to "just tell me" results in your becoming dependent on others for your information and your success. Learning to read your textbook and making reading an important part of your life will open your world beyond the classroom. The study guide will be most effective if you already have some understanding of the material you will review. The study guide in no way incorporates every bit of information in the textbook, nor is it intended to. It is geared for your review once you have had some exposure to the textbook material. Your greatest success will come in using the textbook and the study guide in combination.

Highlight Important Features of the Textbook

As you read your textbook, take note of the most important information that it presents to you. What are the main concepts that are discussed? You will find these key concepts carefully presented and numbered in the margins of your textbook. However, restating all main concepts presented in the text in your own words will help with your understanding. The Concept Check sections in the textbook summarize and test the module material, but again, doing this on your own as well further facilitates retention of the material. Do take notes from the textbook, highlighting particularly important passages in the text. Stop and ask yourself periodically what you have learned. Lastly, you may do your own "self-test" by temporarily closing the book, taking a blank piece of paper, and writing down what you have learned so far. Writing information down from memory at this point will help you be clear on what you understand, what you did not retain, and what you need to look at further. Read and review the material presented in the textbook until you feel you have at least a basic grasp and understanding of the textbook information. You need not study a full chapter or even a full module's material at one time. Instead, use whatever units of textbook information you can comfortably master. As you progress with your studying, you will find you can review and retain larger and larger chunks of textbook material as you become increasingly familiar with the information through your efforts.

Turn to the Study Guide

At this point, you are ready to turn to this study guide for further help in mastering what is in your textbook. The study guide presents a summary of what is in the textbook. It reviews the material you have already read, conveys it to you in several different ways (module outline, module summary, and chapter overview) and helps you evaluate your level of understanding. The study guide is intended to strengthen your comprehension as well as aid you in assessing what you have mastered and what material needs further review.

Following is a more detailed description of each segment you will find for the modules in this study guide. Each module of the study guide, as was mentioned earlier, corresponds to the same-numbered module in your text. Thus, you will want to read the material assigned in your textbook once or twice, and then turn to the corresponding module in this study guide and begin to review further. Remember that the study guide is not a substitute for reading your textbook material, several times. For the maximum benefit from your study, it is recommended that you read the textbook material no fewer than three times over. Each time you read the textbook material, you will gain something further from it, and your understanding will be enhanced. When you feel that you have a sufficient level of mastery of the textbook material turn to the appropriate module(s) in the study guide and begin to review further. Below are the features presented in the study guide for each module (except for most of the last [Application] modules in each chapter in your textbook), along with a description of how best to use each of these features.

FEATURES WITHIN EACH MODULE OF THIS STUDY GUIDE

Learning Objectives

The learning objectives listed in each module of your study guide are derived from the survey questions highlighted in your textbook at the beginning of each module. For each module, there are several main topic areas that will be addressed throughout that particular section in your textbook. Keep these survey questions in mind as you read your textbook material. The learning objectives in the study guide reiterate the focus on these main topic areas. After you have read the information in the textbook, see if you can answer the textbook survey questions. The study guide will assist you in mastering the information corresponding to each learning objective. As with your textbook study, once you have finished reviewing the material in the study guide, go back to the learning objectives. Can you address each topic or area of focus emphasized by a particular learning objective?

Outline

Each module in your study guide contains a complete, detailed outline of the corresponding textbook module material. After you have read the textbook, go over the information in the study guide outline. What points do you remember accurately from having read the textbook? What points have you not remembered, or do you remember incorrectly? Make note of the points that you have not fully mastered. These sections of information will need further review.

Note the format of the overall presentation of the material, as evident in the organization of the module outline. What sections of information are presented together? What is the common theme in each section? Try, initially, to remember all the main points given in the outline for each module. Once you have mastered these, try to remember the sub-points presented under each main heading. When you find a unit of material in the module outline of which you do not feel confident, go back to the corresponding portion of the textbook and read the material again. Return to the study guide module outline once more and try to mentally list the points made under each heading. Follow this procedure until all information presented in the module outline is familiar to you.

Summary

Each module in this study guide includes a brief summary of all information presented in the corresponding textbook module. Read the summary once when you first begin your review of the textbook material, using this book as your guide. When you have finished using this book for study, read the study guide module summary again. Does the information in the summary now seem much more familiar? Be sure to read and review the module and chapter summaries presented in your textbook as well.

Key Terms

Each module in this study guide lists all the Key Terms given in the textbook for the material presented in the corresponding module. After you have read the textbook material, review the list of Key Terms, either at the back of your textbook chapter or in this study guide. Try to define each Key Term as you go through the list, and try to think of an example for each one. Clarify differences among related Key Terms. Which Key Terms are not familiar? Note the ones you cannot define and use accurately, and go back to the textbook and re-read the information related to those Key Terms. As a final step, again review the Key Term list, making sure you can define and appropriately apply each one.

Self-Test Practice Quiz

The objective of the Self-Test Practice Quiz in each study guide module is to allow you to evaluate your level of comprehension and mastery regarding the information presented in the corresponding module of the textbook. As such, you may wish to save the Self-Test Practice Quiz portion of your study guide review until you feel you have a good understanding of the material you have been studying. The Self-Test Practice Quiz will help you discover objectively just how complete your understanding of that relevant material is. For best results, it is recommended that you take the Self-Test Practice Quiz under the same conditions as if you were taking a real exam on the textbook material. That is, avoid looking at either the textbook or the related material in the study guide while you take the Self-Test Practice Quiz. If you find you are having difficulty with a number of the questions in the quiz, this suggests you need more review and study. Rather than complete the Self-Test Practice Quiz at that time, it is recommended that you return to the text and other portions of the study guide and review further. When you reach the point that you feel you have a very good mastery of the information for a given module, go back to the corresponding Self-Test Practice Quiz again. With your additional review and study you should be able to answer most, if not all, of the questions successfully. If not, this again is an indication that more review of the original material is needed. Continue this procedure until you can answer all or nearly all the Self-Test Practice Quiz questions correctly without referring either to the book or to other portions of the study guide.

The Self-Test Practice Quiz in each module of this study guide consists of matching and multiple-choice questions. Match the Key Terms in the right-hand column to the definitions in the left-hand column. *Please note!* For most study guide modules, matching alternatives for every Key Term are provided. However, where there are a very large number of Key Terms in a module, not every Key Term in that module has a corresponding matching definition. Some, but not all, of the Key Terms are used. In that case, please remember that, although not every Key Term is used in the Self-Test Practice Quiz, you do want to be sure that you can define, understand, and apply each Key Term listed. For any Key Term or matching item where you find you are uncertain regarding the meaning or definition, return to the corresponding portion of the textbook and read and study that material one more time.

For the multiple-choice questions in the Self-Test Practice Quiz, please choose the one alternative out of the four given which best completes or answers each question. Again, if you find you are having trouble with a number of the multiple-choice questions, stop your practice quiz and return to the textbook and other portions of the study guide for further review. Resume answering questions when you feel you have a very good mastery of the corresponding information. Evaluate how well you do on the Self-Test Practice Quiz. How many questions can you answer correctly (without looking at either the textbook or the related portions in the study guide)? Which questions were most difficult? Use these results as an indication of your level of mastery, and an indication of what areas in the corresponding textbook material you need to study further.

Essay Questions

In nearly all of the study guide modules, one or more essay questions relating to broader aspects of that module's information are provided. These are just sample essay questions; there may be more broad topics in the module you are studying that are suitable for essay-type questions as well. You might want to consider thinking up your own essay questions to prepare for in addition to studying for and answering the essay questions provided in this study guide.

Essay questions, of course, involve a different kind of testing and recollection than do multiple-choice questions. With essay questions, you bring information up from memory rather than having the correct alternative presented as one of four choices before you. Essay questions can often test deeper, more integrated, and more comprehensive levels of understanding. Follow the same procedures for answering essay questions as you do for the Self-Test Practice Quiz. Try to write a response to the essay question(s) without looking at either the textbook or related material in the study guide. If you find you are really stumped, consider going back to the textbook and other portions of the relevant material in the study guide and reviewing further before you continue. When you feel you have understood the essay question material in depth and have written a sufficiently complete short essay, evaluate the quality of the response you have written. Does it answer all portions of the essay question that was asked? Is your response clear and cohesive? Compare it to the sample answers to essay questions provided in the study guide module. How comprehensively were you able to answer the question? What points are made in the sample essay provided that you would like to include in your own response?

Answer Key

Answers to the Key Term matching questions, the multiple-choice questions, and the essay questions are provided at the end of each study guide module. As mentioned above, not every Key Term is used in the matching questions so be sure to review and master all Key Terms not used in the exercise as well as all of those that are. Check your answers against the answers to questions provided in the Answer Key. How well are you learning the material? Is the correct answer to most study guide questions fairly readily apparent to you? The Answer Key will help you objectively evaluate the degree to which you are absorbing and retaining the information presented in the text and study guide. If, when you go to check your answers, you find that more than a few of your responses are not correct, consider going back and studying the textbook material again more thoroughly before you continue. Once you have completed further review, again look at the study guide questions and reflect on the answers you have given. Are there any you would like to change in light of the more extensive information you have obtained? Evaluate your answers against those provided in the Answer Key. You will gain a fairly clear indication of how well you are mastering information provided in the textbook and study guide.

Sample Answers To Essay Questions

Nearly all study guide modules offer one or more essay questions to test your knowledge in addition to the matching and multiple-choice questions. Essay questions are always geared towards broader topics and more integrated and comprehensive responses. Be sure to write your answer to the essay question out first before you read the sample response given at the end of the study guide module. Evaluate what you have written in comparison to the sample answer provided in the study guide. How much is included in the same answer that you also incorporated in your own essay? What did you include that is not included in the study guide answer? While the sample answers to essay questions provided in this study guide are quite comprehensive, a good essay response does not have to precisely duplicate the sample answers you are given here. You may write your essay differently and include other points in addition to the necessary basic information and this would constitute a very good response. Always refer back to the appropriate section of the textbook to evaluate your answers as well to assure that they are accurate and complete. Remember that your instructor may ask essay questions other than what are presented in this study guide; each module has a number of potential essay question topics.

A Final Word

Learning is an opportunity and a great joy, and learning can change your life. There are few if any fields of study more relevant to very many aspects of your life than is psychology. The earnest wish of your study guide author is that you find this course in psychology an exciting adventure, with endless possibilities for application of what you learn to enhance your understanding and your experience as you journey through life.

CHAPTER 1

Introduction to Psychology and Methods of Research

In Chapter 1, you are introduced to the field of psychology and how we obtain what we know in this field. Although the term psychology has been around for centuries, modern-day psychology (beginning in the year 1879) is different in that it is much more scientific. Psychology is scientific because today we look for objective, empirical evidence to establish what we believe. Opinion, contemplation, tradition—these alone are not sufficient. What is commonly accepted may not necessarily be true.

Psychology traces back at least several thousand years to the Greeks; the word itself is Greek in origin, derived from *psyche* [mind] and *logos* [study or knowledge]. The Greeks were serious about the concept of knowing ourselves. In psychology today, we are still trying!

Perhaps the human has always wondered who we are, what human nature is like, and what our relationship is to this world we live in. Such are philosophical questions. Wise people throughout history have dwelled on these matters. Psychology as a modern scientific discipline is concerned with behavior and mental processes. The year 1879 is particularly important, and generally marks the start of psychology as we know it today because it is then Wilhelm Wundt began the first true psychological laboratory in Leipzig, Germany. Though now still a relatively young science, psychology has evolved rapidly and grown tremendously.

In this chapter, you will learn that there is not just one "psychology," but many, and also very many approaches to how we can research psychological questions. These varying explanations have enjoyed greater or lesser popularity through the years as the field of psychology has evolved—in part because society itself is constantly changing. Why should there be so many different ways to go about studying humans and so many different ideas as to what human nature is like? You are an exceedingly complex creature! And your environment can influence you to the extent that you may seem like a different person day to day—or even hour to hour! Different thoughts in your head and chemicals in your body can do the same. Other people standing right next to you may be different yet again from you. No wonder we have a challenging, and exciting, task ahead of us!

MODULE 1.1 FOUNDATIONS OF MODERN PSYCHOLOGY

LEARNING OBJECTIVES

After you have mastered the information in this unit, you will be able to:

1. Understand the basic meaning of psychology.

2. Know the origins of psychology, philosophical and scientific.

3. Name and describe the early schools of thought in the field of psychology.

4. Discuss six contemporary perspectives in psychology.

OUTLINE

I.   Origins of Psychology
  A.   No clear starting point – but traced at least as far back as Ancient Greek society
    1.   *Psyche:* Greek term for "mind"
    2.   *Logos:* Greek term meaning "study" or "knowledge"
    3.   Fundamentally a philosophical (rather than scientific) approach
  B.   Wilhelm Wundt, 1879—transition from philosophy to science
    1.   Considered the founder of modern psychology
    2.   Established first true psychological laboratory, in Leipzig, Germany
    3.   Teachings soon brought to United States by Englishman Edward Titchener
II.   Major Early Schools of Psychology
  A.   Structuralism (the school of Wundt and Titchener)
    1.   Research methodology was introspection (looking within)
    2.   Understand the mind by determining the components or building blocks of mental experience
  B.   Functionalism
    1.   Established by William James—founder of psychology in the United States
    2.   Trained as a medical doctor; contemporary of Wundt, Titchener and G. Stanley Hall
    3.   Basic focus was how the mind allows us to adapt to our environment
    4.   Understand the mind by understanding how it *functions*
  C.   Behaviorism
    1.   Founder was American John Watson—early 1900s
      a)   Limit study to only overt (observable, measurable) behavior
      b)   Experience, environment alone are what mold us
      c)   Rejected introspection; study *behavior*, not the mind
      d)   Famous for statement on "give me a dozen healthy infants…"
      e)   By 1920's behaviorism was dominant psychological school in U.S.
    2.   B.F. Skinner—operant conditioning—consequences are crucial to learning
      a)   Reinforcer—a pleasant consequence; increases behavior
      b)   Punishment—an unpleasant consequence; decreases behavior
      c)   Skinner further extended great popularity of behaviorism
      d)   Pigeons play the piano; rats learn bar-press
  D.   Gestalt psychology
    1.   Max Wertheimer—contemporary of Watson, but held much different perspective
    2.   Stemmed from his experience of "moving" scenery on a train
    3.   Unified, organized patterns provided by higher-level processes in the brain
    4.   Gestalt maxim: "Whole is greater than the sum of the parts"
    5.   Research on perception, with assistants Wolfgang Köhler and Kurt Koffka
  E.   Sigmund Freud and psychoanalysis
    1.   Austrian physician (early 1900s)
    2.   Focus on the unconscious
    3.   Sexual and aggressive impulses motivate behavior
    4.   Importance of early childhood experience
    5.   Dynamic conflict between unconscious impulses and acceptable behavior
    6.   Abnormal behavior stems from unconscious conflicts
    7.   Developed treatment method (psychoanalysis) for psychological disorders

III.   Contemporary Perspectives in Psychology
    A.   Behavioral perspective
        1.   Modeled after school of behaviorism, though original behaviorist approach too simplistic and limited
        2.   Focus still on observable behavior; emphasis on experience and learning
        3.   Traditional behaviorism, though influential, no longer dominant force in psychology
        4.   Broader variation preferred: social-cognitive theory
        5.   Behavior molded by environment *and* cognitive factors
        6.   Values, goals, and expectations important
        7.   Social-cognitivists suggest psychology include mental processes
        8.   Behavior therapy—applying learning principles to treat psychological problems
        9.   *Cognitive-behavioral therapy* addresses both maladaptive behaviors and thoughts
    B.   Psychodynamic perspective
        1.   Neo-Freudians expand emphasis to include self-awareness and choices
        2.   Reduced emphasis on basic drives such as sex and aggression
        3.   Focus remains on unconscious drives and early childhood experience
        4.   Wide-ranging acceptance of view that childhood, unconscious important
    C.   Humanistic perspective
        1.   Known as "third force" in psychology (besides psychodynamic and behavioral)
        2.   Prominence of perspective began in 1950's
        3.   Proponents Abraham Maslow, Carl Rogers opposed to deterministic views (that one's behavior determined independent of individual, either by environment or unconscious forces)
        4.   Each human being has unique abilities, traits and potential
        5.   Conscious experience important and worthy of study, even if subjective
        6.   Authenticity, self-awareness, free will, and personal choice: crucial aspects of this perspective
    D.   Physiological perspective
        1.   Examines relationship between biological processes and behavior
        2.   Many sources and scientists contribute to this perspective
        3.   Nervous system (especially brain) and body chemicals at root of human functioning
        4.   Heredity: an important consideration
        5.   Subfield: Evolutionary psychology
            a)   Behavioral characteristics (especially of a species) may have a genetic link, due to survival value for that species
            b)   Non-human and human species evolve by adapting to environmental demands
    E.   Cognitive Perspective
        1.   *Cognitio* means knowledge
        2.   Study of mental processes; acquiring knowledge of ourselves and the world
        3.   Includes how we learn, reason, solve problems, make decisions, and use language
        4.   May use computer information processing model to aid research
        5.   Scientific research principles can be successfully applied to mental experience
    F.   Sociocultural Perspective
        1.   Behavior and attitudes are influenced by culture and societal factors
        2.   Ethnicity, age, gender, income level and lifestyle have impact
        3.   Issues regarding diversity (many kinds) important for study
        4.   U.S. society becoming increasingly diverse; increase also in multiracial, multicultural, multiethnic individuals
        5.   Important that research (including psychological research) reflect these phenomena

SUMMARY

In this module, you learn the earliest beginnings of psychology. Very likely, reflecting on human nature and human behavior has been around just about as long as the species itself has been. While there is no precisely clear starting point, much credit goes to the Ancient Greeks, who not only considered psychological matters but also began written records of their thoughts, beliefs, and insights. The term psychology is derived from two Greek words: *psyche* and *logos*. Psychology for several thousand years, though, was not practiced in the manner we know the field to be today.

The psychological laboratory established by Wilhelm Wundt in 1879 in Leipzig, Germany, marks the beginning of modern psychology. Psychology today is *scientific*, which is why we distinguish it from its philosophical origins. No longer will we accept conjecture or long-standing beliefs as the ultimate determination of our view of human nature and human behavior. Scientific research means findings are based on objective, usually first-hand, evidence gathered in an atmosphere where bias and the influence of prevailing opinion are restrained. Reflection and contemplation certainly have a role, but their role is to evaluate fact and objective information insofar as we are able to obtain such.

Wundt had an associate in Germany, the Englishman Edward Titchener, who eventually brought Wundt's views and approach to the United States. Wundt's early psychology was known as structuralism. It was given this name because the objective (so it was thought!) was to discover, through careful, precise laboratory research, the fundamental building blocks (the structure) of the brain and mental experience. Introduced by William James, functionalism , expanded structuralism to look at how the mind helps us adapt to our environment. Sigmund Freud, originally trained as a physician in Austria, believed psychological issues stemmed from unconscious desires and conflicts within the human. He created the therapy known as psychoanalysis.

The early 1900s in America marked a shift in psychology; behaviorists came to the fore and insisted only observable behavior and experience were suitable for study. At about the same time, the school of Gestalt psychology was introduced, which has much to do with how we *perceive* the world. Both of these schools, for different reasons, objected to the structuralists' approach of studying the mind and attempting to break the mind into its component parts.

Contemporary perspectives in psychology include behaviorism and the Freudian or psychodynamic approach, modified somewhat from their earlier forms. Added to this list are humanism, with a focus on discovering one's true inner self, and the cognitive perspective, looking at how thoughts and mental processes influence our behavior. Other contemporary perspectives include the physiological approach (considering the brain and nervous system's influence on behavior) and the sociocultural view, reminding us that life experiences differ depending on the culture in which we are raised. Finally, another new movement is positive psychology, which explores the more positive elements of the human experience (love, altruism, hope, etc.).

KEY TERMS

Psychology

Psychophysics

Introspection

Structuralism

Functionalism

Behaviorism

Gestalt psychology

Gestalt

Unconscious

Psychodynamic perspective

Psychoanalysis

Behavioral perspective

Social-cognitive theory

Behavior therapy

Humanistic psychology

Humanistic perspective

Physiological perspective

Evolutionary psychology

Cognitive perspective

Sociocultural perspective

Positive psychology

SELF-TEST PRACTICE QUIZ

Match the following Key Terms and definitions (note: not every Key Term will be used):

1. _____ An approach within psychology that focuses on the impact of concept formation, reasoning, language, intelligence, problem-solving, and memory

2. _____ Part of Wundt's research methodology; involves "looking within"

3. _____ An approach within psychology based on the work of Sigmund Freud, emphasizing unconscious conflict, primitive sexual instinct and early childhood experiences

4. _____ A perspective within psychology that emerged as a reaction to the psychodynamic and behavioral approaches; emphasizes the uniqueness and self-awareness of every individual

5. _____ One of the more recently developed perspectives in psychology; it recognizes the influence of cultural heritage, gender/ethnic background, economic status, and lifestyle factors

a. Psychology

b. Psychophysics

c. Introspection

d. Structuralism

e. Functionalism

f. Behaviorism

g. Gestalt psychology

h. Gestalt

i. Unconscious

j. Psychodynamic perspective

k. Psychoanalysis

l. Behavioral perspective

m. Social-cognitive theory

n. Behavior therapy

o. Humanistic psychology

p. Humanistic perspective

q. Physiological perspective

r. Evolutionary psychology

s. Cognitive perspective

6. _____ A psychological school of thought that emerged in the early 1900s, suggesting that measurable overt behavior and experience were the only appropriate topics for study

7. _____ The study of behavior and of mental processes

8. _____ A school of psychology that examines how the brain interprets and organizes our experiences in the world so that what we perceive is a unified whole or pattern

9. _____ A contemporary perspective in psychology which advocates an expanded view of the principles that are the foundation of the school of behaviorism

10. _____ A contemporary movement within psychology that emphasizes the study of human virtues and assets, rather than weaknesses and deficits

11. _____ A movement within psychology based on the views of Charles Darwin, recognizing that genetic influences on behavior may serve to aid in the survival of the species

12. _____ A relatively recent expansion within the behavioral perspective, emphasizing that cognitions in addition to environmental experience shape behavior

13. _____ According to Freud, a region of the mind consisting of primitive urges and conflicts, and of which we are not aware

14. _____ A perspective within psychology where genetic, neurological and in particular brain functioning influences are researched

15. _____ An approach to psychological therapy developed by Sigmund Freud

16. _____ A psychological treatment approach based on the belief that maladaptive behaviors are learned

t. Sociocultural perspective

u. Positive psychology

17. Psychology's roots are in the ancient field of
    a. physiology.
    b. cognition.
    c. astronomy.
    d. philosophy.

18. Wundt's first psychological laboratory in Leipzig, Germany, in 1879, marked the transition of psychology from _____ to _____.
    a. humanism; behaviorism
    b. cognition; behaviorism
    c. philosophy; science
    d. psychoanalysis; physiological psychology

19. The "third force" in contemporary psychology (in addition to the behavioral and psychodynamic perspectives) is the
    a. sociocultural perspective.
    b. humanistic perspective.
    c. cognitive perspective.
    d. physiological perspective.

20. In what way is psychology still like philosophy? Both fields
    a. study questions related to behavior and the nature of the human being.
    b. take a scientific approach.
    c. research biological and genetic bases for behavior.
    d. are relatively new disciplines.

21. What was one criticism directed towards the school of behaviorism?
    a. There was too much emphasis on thought and inner experience.
    b. Animals were not believed to be useful research subjects.
    c. Psychology does not really fit the "scientific" model.
    d. Behaviorism did not deem the mind as appropriate for study.

22. Decision-making, the use of language, and reasoning processes are studied as part of the focus of the _____ perspective.
    a. behavioral
    b. physiological
    c. cognitive
    d. sociocultural

23. Freud was trained as a
    a. psychologist.
    b. physiologist.
    c. philosopher.
    d. physician.

24. Behavior therapy applies _____ principles to help individuals discover more adaptive ways to live.
    a. cognitive
    b. psychodynamic
    c. learning
    d. introspective

25. Which of the following psychologists is associated with humanism?
    a. Abraham Maslow
    b. B. F. Skinner
    c. William James
    d. John Watson

26.   The term "diversity" refers to differences in

   a.   race.
   b.   gender.
   c.   sexual orientation.
   d.   all of the above

27.   A psychologist associated with the _____ perspective would be most likely to be interested in the effects of brain damage on a wounded soldier's functioning.

   a.   humanist
   b.   physiological
   c.   psychodynamic
   d.   cognitive

28.   William James founded the school of

   a.   structuralism.
   b.   Gestalt psychology.
   c.   functionalism.
   d.   physiological psychology.

29.   Which psychological perspective is generally considered to be the most accurate?

   a.   Sociocultural
   b.   Cognitive
   c.   Physiological
   d.   None of the above—all perspectives have something valuable to offer.

30.   Which school of psychology attempted to break down mental experiences into their smallest possible component parts?

   a.   Structuralism
   b.   Functionalism
   c.   Gestalt psychology
   d.   Evolutionary psychology

31.   Sigmund Freud believed that much of our behavior is governed by

   a.   genetics.
   b.   rewards and punishments.
   c.   unconscious wishes and conflicts.
   d.   external forces.

ESSAY QUESTIONS

1.   Trace the history of psychology, from its earliest origins to the state of the discipline today.

2.   Why do we have multiple explanations regarding the nature of the human? Is one perspective more correct than another?

ANSWER KEY

1. Cognitive perspective
2. Introspection
3. Psychodynamic perspective
4. Humanistic perspective
5. Sociocultural perspective
6. Behaviorism
7. Psychology
8. Gestalt psychology
9. Behavioral perspective
10. Positive psychology
11. Evolutionary psychology
12. Social-cognitive theory
13. Unconscious
14. Physiological perspective
15. Psychoanalysis
16. Behavior therapy
17. d
18. c
19. b
20. a
21. d
22. c
23. d
24. c
25. a
26. d
27. b
28. c
29. d
30. a
31. c

SAMPLE ANSWERS TO ESSAY QUESTIONS

1.   The questions studied by psychologists have been around probably as long as thinking human beings have been around. Thus, the early Greeks and other ancients wondered about the inner nature of the human being and how we might best learn more about ourselves, our world, and how we function in our world. These questions have been around literally for millennia; however, they were not subjected to truly scientific study until the time of Wilhelm Wundt and his assistant Edward Titchener in the latter half of the 19th century. Wundt brought his scientific training as a physiologist to the long-standing questions about human nature. He established what is recognized as the first scientific laboratory in 1879 in Leipzig, Germany. Wundt took a very rigorous approach to learning about the human mind, using introspection. Titchener brought Wundt's approach to the U.S., and it became known as structuralism. William James looked at how the mind functioned to help us adapt to our environment, and behaviorists, beginning in the 1920s, promoted the idea that psychology is best served by concentrating on observable, measurable behavior. Gestalt psychology was introduced by Wertheimer, who emphasized higher-order organizational processes occurring within the brain. Sigmund Freud, in Austria, was a contemporary of most of the other pioneers in psychology. His emphasis, however, was quite unlike that of the other psychologists of his day. Freud believed the source of influence on our behavior lay out of our awareness, in the unconscious mind. A major contribution from Freud was the development of a treatment method for psychological disorders. The humanistic school emerged in the mid-20th century, emphasizing the uniqueness and self-determination of the human. Recent additions to the field of psychology include the cognitive, physiological, evolutionary and sociocultural perspectives.

2.   It is true that there are a number of approaches regarding human psychological functioning. Each perspective has a different emphasis, such as a focus on human thought, or on behavior, or on unconscious influences, or on our genetic heritage. The human being is quite a complex creature. Thus, it is no wonder that there are a variety of approaches utilized when examining human behavior and the human psyche. All of these aspects are influences as to why we behave the way we do, and each perspective makes a contribution towards human understanding. Each perspective has valuable information to offer; yet no one approach seems to adequately explain everything about human functioning. In addition, the various psychological perspectives really do not have distinct divisions. Social-cognitive theory, for example, is based on behavioral principles but adds considerations related to human thought and interpretation. Because the human being is so complex, we need a variety of different approaches that may focus on different aspects of the human. Together they begin to provide us with a clearer understanding about the nature and actions of the human being.

MODULE 1.2 PSYCHOLOGISTS: WHO THEY ARE AND WHAT THEY DO

LEARNING OBJECTIVES

After you have mastered the information in this unit, you will be able to:

1. Name and describe the major areas of specialization within the field of psychology.

2. Discuss the changing ethnic and gender characteristics of psychologists over time.

OUTLINE

I. Types of Research Psychologists Do
   A. Basic research—to expand knowledge and understanding
   B. Applied research—to address and find a resolution for a particular issue or problem
II. Traditional Major Specialty Areas of Psychology
   A. Experimental psychologists—use the experimental research method (to establish cause and effect) for study of behavior and mental processes
      1. Comparative—study animals and their behavior
      2. Physiological—study biological bases of behavior
   B. Clinical psychologists
      1. Study and treat individuals with psychological disorders
      2. May conduct research and teach future psychologists
      3. Largest number of psychologists within this specialty
      4. Function similar to psychiatrists but psychiatrists have medical degree
   C. Counseling psychologists—treat individuals with less severe adjustment problems
   D. School psychologists—work directly with children to aid in their school experience
   E. Educational psychologists—research and/or apply learning and instructional advances
   F. Developmental psychologists—study human growth and changes over the entire lifespan
   G. Personality psychologists—study unique personal characteristics and behaviors
   H. Social psychologists—focus on the individual as a member of a group
   I. Environmental psychologists—study the relationship between people's behavior and their physical environment
   J. Industrial/Organizational (I/O) psychologists—research and/or apply ways to improve the work setting
   K. Health psychologists—study the relationship between psychological factors and physical well-being
   L. Consumer psychologists—investigate people's purchases and reactions to advertising
III. Emerging Specialty Areas in Psychology
   A. Neuropsychologists—study the brain specifically for its relationship to behavior
   B. Geropsychologists—investigate the psychological impact of aging
   C. Forensic psychologists—work with individuals involved in the legal system
   D. Sport psychologists—study competition and ways to maximize athletic performance
IV. Professional Psychology: Becoming More Diverse
   A. Early psychologists (19th century)
      1. White male, European background
      2. Women and minorities faced many barriers
      3. Ph.D. not awarded to women, though doctoral work was completed
      4. 1920: first Ph.D. awarded to an African American

B.   Current demographics among psychologists
1.   Ethnic minorities in psychology slowly increasing
2.   Women now recipients of 2/3 of degrees in psychology

SUMMARY

Once psychology appeared in its modern, more scientific form, the field grew and expanded rapidly. Many psychologists conduct research: either basic, simply to expand our knowledge of a particular aspect within psychology, or applied, to determine new or better methods to address a particular problem. There are now many subfields, or specializations, within the profession of psychology. Individuals in these subfields may or may not conduct research as part of their day-to-day activities, but all attempt to stay current regarding research on relevant psychological topics. In addition, regardless of specialization, professionals within the field of psychology usually have adopted one or more of the psychological perspectives, such as cognitive, behavioral, humanistic, and the like. The perspective (or eclectic approach if a number of perspectives are utilized) tends to be reflected to an extent in how each professional undertakes his or her occupational activity.

Traditional specialty areas in psychology include experimental (always do research), clinical (study and provide therapy), counseling (treat less severe disorders), school (work directly with children), educational (try to improve teaching and learning), developmental (study whole lifespan), and personality (study unique human nature). Ongoing specialty areas also include environmental, I/O, health and consumer psychology. New areas in psychology include research on the brain, aging, sports, and legal concerns. Many more women now participate in psychology, and the role of ethnic minorities is increasing.

KEY TERMS

Basic research

Applied research

Experimental psychologists

Comparative psychologists

Physiological psychologists

Clinical psychologists

Psychiatrists

Counseling psychologists

School psychologists

Educational psychologists

Developmental psychologists

Personality psychologists

Social psychologists

Environmental psychologists

Industrial/Organizational (I/O) psychologists

Health psychologists

Consumer psychologists

Neuropsychologists

Geropsychologists

Forensic psychologists

Sport psychologists

SELF-TEST PRACTICE QUIZ

Match the following Key Terms and definitions (note: not every Key Term will be used):

1. _____ Psychologists who study human growth and changes over the life span

2. _____ Research aimed simply at furthering our knowledge and understanding

3. _____ Psychologists who study the relationship between psychological patterns and physical health

4. _____ Individuals with a medical degree who specialize in treating mental health disorders

5. _____ Psychologists who research criminal behavior and are involved with other aspects of the legal system

6. _____ Psychologists who research matters dealing with aging and the elderly

7. _____ Psychologists who conduct controlled research to establish cause and effect; usually carried out in a laboratory setting

8. _____ Psychologists who investigate genetic and other biological influences on behavior

9. _____ Research conducted in order to learn more about or solve a particular problem

10. _____ Psychologists who study brain structures, neurotransmitters and the like with regard to their impact on human functioning

a.   Basic research

b.   Applied research

c.   Experimental psychologists

d.   Comparative psychologists

e.   Physiological psychologists

f.   Clinical psychologists

g.   Psychiatrists

h.   Counseling psychologists

i.   School psychologists

j.   Educational psychologists

k.   Developmental psychologists

l.   Personality psychologists

m.   Social psychologists

n.   Environmental psychologists

o.   Industrial/Organizational (I/O) psychologists

p.   Health psychologists

q.   Consumer psychologists

r.   Neuropsychologists

s.   Geropsychologists

t.   Forensic psychologists

u.   Sport psychologists

11. _____ Psychologists involved in business or other organizational settings with the objective of optimizing the work experience for employees and administrators

12. _____ Psychologists investigating the influence of interpersonal contact and the actions of others on the behavior of individuals

13. _____ Psychologists who treat mental disorders by means of psychotherapy

14. _____ Psychologists involved with evaluating academic abilities and optimizing the learning experience

15. _____ Psychologists who study many other species besides the human to investigate similarities and differences

16. _____ Psychologists interested in the functioning of the individual and how individuals differ from one another

17. A professional who is permitted to prescribe drugs for psychological disorders is a(n)
    a. psychiatrist.
    b. clinical psychologist.
    c. experimental psychologist.
    d. all of the above

18. _____ psychologists study the relationship between the brain and behavior.
    a. Clinical
    b. Social
    c. Neuro
    d. Developmental

19. The subfield, or specialization, in psychology that has the greatest number of people working in it is _____ psychology.
    a. personality
    b. educational
    c. clinical
    d. industrial/organizational

20. A psychologist who does _____ research wants to help resolve a particular psychological issue.
    a. basic
    b. applied
    c. grant-funded
    d. humane

21. Unlike earlier years, _____ now make up the largest group of degree recipients in the field of psychology.

    a. men
    b. women
    c. African Americans
    d. Native Americans

22. Dr. Farleigh is studying the influence of birth-order position as individuals mature from childhood to adulthood. Most likely Dr. Farleigh's specialization within psychology is

    a. social psychology.
    b. educational psychology.
    c. clinical psychology.
    d. developmental psychology.

23. A personality psychologist is one who

    a. studies the impact of the environment on health and behavior.
    b. treats psychological disorders, such as anxiety and depression.
    c. investigates the unique characteristics of an individual.
    d. studies any of the above psychological topics.

24. If you were feeling dissatisfied, and unclear as to where you should be going with your life, most likely you would be advised to see a _____ psychologist.

    a. counseling
    b. forensic
    c. developmental
    d. consumer

25. _____ psychologists study such things as sensation, perception, and cognition.

    a. Developmental
    b. Experimental
    c. Educational
    d. Industrial/organizational

26. If you investigate such matters as interpersonal attraction, attitudes, aggression and conformity, you are most likely a _____ psychologist.

    a. social
    b. clinical
    c. developmental
    d. comparative

27. Though psychologists work in many settings, the greatest number of psychologists are employed

    a. in colleges and universities.
    b. in private practice and/or private (for-profit or not-for-profit) organizations.
    c. by government agencies.
    d. in schools.

28. The demand for _____ is increasing due to the increasing proportion of elderly adults in the population.

    a. personality psychologists
    b. comparative psychologists
    c. social psychologists
    d. geropsychologists

29. What type of psychologist would be most interested in studying how people's shopping choices are affected by product placement within a store?

    a. Neuropsychologist
    b. Developmental psychologist
    c. Consumer psychologist
    d. Industrial/organizational psychologist

30. A _____ psychologist might work with police departments to develop more effective ways of questioning suspects or witnesses in criminal cases.

    a. forensic
    b. social
    c. counseling
    d. physiological

31. Which of the following questions is most likely to be of interest to an environmental psychologist?

    a. How are young children affected by the death of a parent?
    b. Are office employees more productive when working in cubicles or in open areas?
    c. Why do people smoke even when they know it's bad for them?
    d. How are monkeys affected by pollution in rivers near where they live?

ESSAY QUESTIONS

1. If you were to choose a profession within the field of psychology, which area of specialization appeals most to you? Why?

2. What value or usefulness can there be in carrying out basic research?

3. How has the composition of people who become psychologists changed over the years?

4. What is the difference between a clinical psychologist, counseling psychologist, and psychiatrist?

5. Is someone who does research always an experimental psychologist? Explain.

ANSWER KEY

1. Developmental psychologists
2. Basic research
3. Health psychologists
4. Psychiatrists
5. Forensic psychologists
6. Geropsychologists
7. Experimental psychologists
8. Physiological psychologists
9. Applied research
10. Neuropsychologists
11. Industrial/organizational psychologists
12. Social psychologists
13. Clinical psychologists
14. Educational psychologists
15. Comparative psychologists
16. Personality psychologists
17. a
18. c
19. c
20. b
21. b
22. d
23. c
24. a
25. b
26. a
27. a
28. d
29. c
30. a
31. b

SAMPLE ANSWERS TO ESSAY QUESTIONS

1. Describe the psychology subfield that most interests you, and explain why it interests you.

2. Basic research explores psychological issues for the sake of knowledge. Of course, simply gaining that knowledge is useful. It may help expand our general understanding of human psychological functioning, and it may be interesting in its own right. Since funding sources are limited, however, we may not think of purely basic research as deserving of too much in the way of financial support. However, there is another advantage to basic research: even though it may have no apparent immediate application, it is entirely possible that at some time in the future the knowledge will help address a particular problem, or clarify advances we have made in related lines of research.

3. We are seeing more diversity among psychology professionals. Originally, psychologists were all white males of European descent. With time, however, the composition of people in psychology has changed. There has been a great increase in women taking professional roles in the field of psychology and some increase in the number of minorities. Presently, the greatest number of new undergraduate and Ph.D. degrees are awarded to women. The first female president of the American Psychological Association was Mary Whiton Calkins, in 1905, followed by the second woman president, Margaret Floy Washburn, in 1921. Gilbert Haven Jones was the first African American to receive a doctorate in psychology (in Germany, in 1909). Kenneth Clark was the first African American elected president of APA, in 1971. Richard Suinn was the first Asian American elected president of APA, in 1999.

4. There are some similarities between psychiatrists, clinical psychologists, and counseling psychologists because professionals in these three specializations all treat individuals with psychological disorders. However, clinical psychologists treat fairly serious mental health problems, such as schizophrenia and bi-polar disorder. Counseling psychologists treat the more everyday problems that people have. These more common problems include issues such as adjustment disorders, marital difficulties, and the considerations involved when making career decisions. Psychiatrists have medical degrees and usually are the only therapists permitted to prescribe drugs for treatment.

5. Psychological research may be carried out by almost any kind of psychologist. However, research does not always involve the procedures utilized by an experimental psychologist. Experimental psychologists always conduct research, and often on the same topics as Wundt and the other structuralists investigated in their early laboratories. Experimental psychologists also are more likely to carry out research with animals. Conducting experimental research (as opposed to other kinds of research) involves utilizing a very specific set of procedures that are particular to the experimental method. All experimentation, then, is a form of scientific research, but scientific research may involve methodologies in addition to those used by experimental psychologists. Other disciplines within psychology (social, developmental, educational, or clinical, for example) may conduct research using the experimental methodology, or other methodologies. Psychologists try to stay informed regarding current research findings even if they do not carry out the work themselves.

MODULE 1.3 RESEARCH METHODS IN PSYCHOLOGY

LEARNING OBJECTIVES

After you have mastered the information in this unit, you will be able to:

1. Describe the scientific method and its four general steps.

2. Identify the major research methods used in psychology, including their advantages and disadvantages.

3. Understand the role of ethics in psychological research, and explain the major ethical guidelines for treatment of research participants.

OUTLINE

I. The Scientific Method—a Search for Empirical Evidence
   A. Develop a research question
   B. Frame the research question in the form of a testable hypothesis
      1. Hypothesis—precise, testable prediction that forms the basis for a study
      2. Theory—summarizes/integrates large body of findings and may provide source for future research hypotheses
   C. Gather evidence to test the hypothesis
   D. Draw conclusions regarding the outcome
      1. Statistics—used to determine how likely the study outcome was simply due to chance (if not likely, research findings may meet criteria of *statistically significant*)
      2. Variable—a factor in a study that is capable of taking on a range of values
      3. Replication—crucial feature in research; comparable studies by others result in similar types of findings (research studies which fail replication are highly suspect)

II. Research Methods
   A. Case study—thorough, careful study of one or a few individuals
      1. Advantage: detailed and intensive information
      2. Disadvantage: lacks sufficient research control (and may not represent all individuals)
   B. Survey
      1. Information from target groups to reveal features of a population
         a) Population—entire group that comprise the individuals of interest
         b) Sample—small subset of population who are actually given survey (usually prohibitive to attempt to assess responses of whole population)
      2. Methodologies
         a) Structured interview
         b) Questionnaire
      3. To generalize accurately, sample must be representative (use random sampling)
      4. Truly representative sample for survey difficult to achieve
         a) Advantage: broad range of information if done correctly
         b) Disadvantage: variety of possible biases in participants' responses
   C. Naturalistic observation
      1. Studying humans (or animals) in familiar, everyday environment
      2. Researcher observing must be inconspicuous
      3. Advantage: greatest likelihood of genuine, authentic behavior; rich source of ideas
      4. Disadvantage: least amount of control over events that will take place

    D.   Correlational—relationship between two variables, represented mathematically (by *correlation coefficient*)

        1.   Advantages

            a)   Helpful for prediction—the stronger the correlation, the more precise the prediction

            b)   Suggests further study (e.g., relationship *may* be causal)

            c)   May identify at-risk populations

            d)   Enhances understanding of relationships between events

        2.   Disadvantage: does not establish causality, though may be (wrongly) interpreted as such

    E.   Experimental

        1.   Can truly establish cause and effect

        2.   Research design involves independent and dependent variables

            a)   Independent variable—suspected cause in a study; manipulated by researcher

            b)   Dependent variable—suspected effect in a study; measured to determine impact (if any) of level of independent variable

        3.   Control group helps establish causality

        4.   Random assignment helps assure no pre-existing differences between groups

        5.   Components of studies that help establish research control:

            a)   Placebo—has no effect, but fakes resemblance to potent variable

            b)   Single-blind study—participants not aware of experimental vs. control group membership

            c)   Double-blind study—neither researchers nor participants aware of experimental vs. control group membership

        6.   Advantages and disadvantages

            a)   Advantage: learn cause, why an effect actually happens—very important!

            b)   Disadvantage: expectations (e.g., placebo effect) may influence results

III.   Sample study utilizing experimental research methodology

    A.   Hypothesis: Participants would form trait impressions after viewing faces for only a tenth of a second

    B.   Procedure:

        1.   Participants were asked to make judgments about people after viewing faces for an unlimited time (control group) or short amount of time (experimental group)

        2.   Participants asked to judge each person's attractiveness, likeability, competence, trustworthiness, or aggressiveness

        3.   Also asked to rate their confidence in their impressions

    C.   Results:

        1.   Strong positive correlations between ratings under timed and untimed conditions

        2.   The longer participants viewed a picture, the more confident they were in their ratings

    D.   References cited, in American Psychological Association style

IV.   Ethical Principles in Psychological Research

    A.   Ethical standards to protect clients and research participants

    B.   Appropriate that humans protected from harm, free to make own choices

    C.   Review committees at institutions verify ethical procedures

    D.   Some basic ethical guidelines for research

        1.   Informed consent

            a)   Research participant knows what will happen in study

            b)   Willingly agrees, based on explanation given, to be part of study

            c)   Aware can withdraw from study at any time

        2.   Where deception (prohibits complete informed consent) used, stringent criteria

        3.   Confidentiality—keep records on clients and research participants private

    E.   Animal research
        1.   Animals used as subjects where use of humans impossible/unethical
        2.   Protect animal from harm unless no other research alternative
        3.   Controversial topic for public and psychologists alike
        4.   Ethics review panel must give permission
        5.   Benefits from such research must be substantial

SUMMARY

Because modern psychology is a science, information we gain in the field is through research. Researchers follow the scientific method. The objective of the scientific method is to obtain objective, empirical information and avoid bias. Each research study is founded upon a hypothesis—a testable prediction.

There are many different ways of conducting research in psychology. Each method has its particular advantages—but there are disadvantages, too. Participants in psychological research are now protected by ethical guidelines. Foremost among these guidelines are the notions of informed consent (the individual knows what he or she is about to experience and willingly agrees to participate) and confidentiality. Though less stringent, animals used in research are protected by ethical guidelines also.

The simplest research method is naturalistic observation. Naturalistic observation involves studying the research target in its familiar, everyday environment. This is an important methodology because we are most likely to get genuine, authentic behavior this way. When we utilize case study methodology we are investigating one, or only a few, individuals. We learn much about these few individuals through case study research, but bias may influence responses from case study participants. Nor can we assume these individuals are representative of humanity in general.

Correlation is a mathematical calculation showing that there is a link between two variables, or measures. Just because two factors are related, however, does not mean one causes the other. Surveys can collect large amounts of information that we hope reflects tendencies of the population, but the sample surveyed must be representative. Obtaining a truly representative sample is difficult, and usually expensive. The experimental methodology may be the most highly regarded research procedure. With it (and only with experimentation) we can establish the cause of some psychological phenomena. This is a very important achievement.

KEY TERMS

Empirical approach

Scientific method

Hypothesis

Theory

Statistics

Variable

Replication

Case study method

Survey method

Structured interview

Questionnaire

Population

Samples

Random sampling

Social desirability bias

Volunteer bias

Naturalistic observation method

Correlational method

Correlation coefficient

Experimental method

Independent variables

Dependent variables

Control groups

Random assignment

Placebo

Placebo effects

Single-blind studies

Double-blind studies

Ethics review committees

Informed consent

SELF-TEST PRACTICE QUIZ

Match the following Key Terms and definitions (note: not every Key Term will be used):

1. _____ A precise prediction about the outcomes of an experiment

2. _____ A subset from the population, used to test questions related to the entire population—for quality research, it must be representative of the entire population

3. _____ A research methodology which, through the use of a control group, can establish a causal relationship between independent and dependent variables

4. _____ Where there may be an effect from an intervention, but the effect is due to participants' hopes or expectations and not the treatment administered

a. Empirical approach

b. Theory

c. Variable

d. Scientific method

e. Hypothesis

f. Statistics

g. Replication

h. Case study method

i. Survey method

j. Structured interview

k. Questionnaire

l. Population

m. Samples

5. _____ A critical component in ethical research; the participant is aware of what he or she will experience as part of a research study, and willingly agrees to participate

6. _____ The result of many studies in a particular research area; the various confirmed and disconfirmed hypotheses are unified to provide a framework for understanding, interpretation, and direction for future research

7. _____ An important component in research; involves assuring that research findings are the result of direct observation and precise measurement

8. _____ All of the people about whom a research question is concerned (usually too many to test in their entirety, and subsets are used)

9. _____ An important research procedure that helps to control for possible preexisting differences among participants; each participant has equal likelihood of being placed in any of the study research conditions

10. _____ The suspected cause (it is proposed and manipulated by the researcher) in an experimental study

11. _____ A set of steps or criteria for research which help assure that the findings in the study were obtained objectively

12. _____ An important criterion in scientific research; similar results to a study are found when using the same methodology but conducted by a different researcher, with different participants, and often in a different location

13. _____ A research methodology where there is no intervention whatsoever by the researcher; participants are simply watched, without their awareness, in their familiar, comfortable, everyday habitat or environment

n. Random Sampling

o. Social desirability bias

p. Volunteer bias

q. Naturalistic observation method

r. Correlational method

s. Correlation coefficient

t. Experimental method

u. Independent variables

v. Dependent variables

w. Control groups

x. Random assignment

y. Placebo

z. Placebo effects

aa. Single-blind studies

bb. Double-blind studies

cc. Ethics review committees

dd. Informed consent

14. _____ A research methodology aimed at assessing the views of large numbers of people with regard to broad, general questions; to be done correctly a representative sample is crucial

15. _____ Components in a research study whose quantitative values can change (and these changes can be measured)

16. _____ The suspected effects (due to the independent variable) in an experimental research design

17. _____ A research methodology which indicates the degree to which measured behavior on one variable for individuals is related to scores obtained for those individuals on another variable

18. _____ A research methodology used in psychology where only one or a few individuals are studied, but they are researched in great depth

19. What was the independent variable in the "first impressions" study described in your text?

    a. Attractiveness of the faces
    b. Participants' assessment of their confidence in their ratings
    c. The people that participated in the study
    d. Length of time that participants viewed each face

20. An explanation that organizes large amounts of information resulting from research is called a(n)

    a. hypothesis.
    b. case study.
    c. theory.
    d. objective.

21. An important aspect of the scientific method is

    a. test every member of the relevant population.
    b. gather objective evidence with which to evaluate the hypothesis.
    c. use correlational findings to establish causality.
    d. all of the above

22. Statistics are used in psychological research in order to

    a. determine how likely it is that a given outcome occurred by chance.
    b. calculate correlation coefficients between two individuals.
    c. help assure that our observations are collected objectively.
    d. help assure that all research participants are treated ethically.

23. Questionnaires and interviews are part of the
    a. survey method.
    b. formation of the hypothesis.
    c. double-blind procedure.
    d. random sampling procedure.
24. What is a disadvantage of case study research?
    a. Memories of participants may have become distorted with the passage of time.
    b. The researcher may become biased from knowing the participant so well.
    c. We cannot legitimately generalize findings to other individuals.
    d. all of the above
25. Why must we be aware of the placebo effect?
    a. We don't want to risk a participant becoming ill during a study.
    b. A person's expectations can actually affect the outcome of a study; the result then is not entirely due to the independent variable or treatment intervention.
    c. In such cases, we cannot be sure our sample is representative.
    d. If the naturalistic observer is obvious, then participant behavior may not be truly authentic.
26. Which of the following correlation coefficients indicates the strongest relationship?
    a. +.85
    b. -.90
    c. +.61
    d. -.32
27. A researcher is surveying college students about their romantic relationships. One potential problem he faces is that people who are willing to talk about their love lives may be very different from those who are not willing. This is an example of_____.
    a. the social desirability bias
    b. a placebo effect
    c. volunteer bias
    d. experimenter bias
28. A researcher sits at a playground all day, making note of the length of time that girls vs. boys spend on the swings. What research method is she using?
    a. Naturalistic observation
    b. Case study
    c. Experimental method
    d. Survey method
29. Why is it important to make sure that a sample is representative of the population from which it is drawn?
    a. So that the results can be generalized
    b. To ensure random assignment
    c. To control for the social desirability bias
    d. To allow for replication
30. Generally speaking, people with more education tend to earn higher salaries. This is an example of a _____ correlation.
    a. negative
    b. perfect
    c. zero
    d. positive

31. When researchers study only some of the members of a population, this is called
    a. random assignment.
    b. a single-blind study.
    c. sampling.
    d. generalization.

32. Why is it important for experiments to include control groups?
    a. To control for the social desirability bias
    b. To make sure the sample is representative
    c. To make sure that statistics are properly analyzed
    d. To ensure that results are really due to the independent variable, rather than some other variable

33. A researcher conducts a study in which neither the researcher nor the participants know who got a drug and who got a placebo. This is a _____ study.
    a. double-blind
    b. single-blind
    c. ethical
    d. correlational

34. _____ means that researchers may not reveal participants' personal information without permission.
    a. Informed consent
    b. Confidentiality
    c. Random assignment
    d. Correlation

35. Which research method is the only one that allows researchers to determine cause and effect?
    a. Experimental method
    b. Case study
    c. Naturalistic observation
    d. Survey method

ESSAY QUESTIONS

1. How does the experimental method help determine the true cause of a psychological phenomenon?

2. What is the advantage for research in modern psychology to be scientific?

3. Why is it so important that sample groups studied via the survey method be representative of the larger population in which we are interested?

4. Discuss the term "ethics." What are some ethical guidelines we have for research in psychology?

5. Explain the idea of random assignment. How does this practice help us have more control in our psychological research (especially with regard to the experimental method)?

6. Why are there so many ways of doing research in psychology?

7. What are some ways a researcher conducting a naturalistic observation study can assure that he or she is unobtrusive? Why is this step so important?

ANSWER KEY

1. Hypothesis
2. Samples
3. Experimental method
4. Placebo
5. Informed consent
6. Theory
7. Empirical approach
8. Population
9. Random assignment
10. Independent variables
11. Scientific method
12. Replication
13. Naturalistic observation method
14. Survey method
15. Variable
16. Dependent variables
17. Correlational method
18. Case study method
19. d
20. c
21. b
22. a
23. a
24. d
25. b
26. b
27. c
28. a
29. a
30. d
31. c
32. d
33. a
34. b
35. a

SAMPLE ANSWERS TO ESSAY QUESTIONS

1. With the experimental research method, all conditions are kept the same between research groups except that which is expected to be the cause of some phenomena (this suspected cause is called the independent variable). If there is a difference in the dependent variable (that which is used to assess any effects of the independent variable), then that effect must be due to the independent variable—e.g., what was suspected by the researchers as the likely cause. Because of control in the experimental methodology procedures, there was no other difference between the two groups.

2. When we are scientific, we remain objective and do not allow our biases or expectations to enter into our investigating a research question. We attempt to carry out first-hand, empirical research, and let our experience and the objective evidence answer our research questions. It is thought, through being scientific, that psychologists are much more likely to discover real, unbiased truth, rather than being affected by expectations or preconceived notions.

3. A sample group must be representative of the population in which we are interested. That is, the small group we actually test with our research question(s) must be perfectly proportional to the larger population with whom we are actually concerned. Thus, the sample group must share proportionally the same socioeconomic, political, religious, educational, ideological, etc., characteristics as in the relevant population. Only when a sample is representative does it truly tell us what is going on with regard to the population.

4. "Ethics" conveys the notion that we should never put any other individual or group at risk or in jeopardy, and certainly not simply to further our own ends. Important ethical guidelines include:

    - No harm may come to participants, physically, psychologically, or in any other way.

    - A participant must give *informed consent;* that is, the participant knows the general nature of the study and willingly agrees to participate.

    - The participant is aware he or she is free to withdraw at any time.

    - All identities and information gained from the research study are kept anonymous and confidential.

5. Random assignment means any individual participating in a research study has equal likelihood of being put in any of the groups involved in the study. Thus, there is no pre-existing bias as to how the groups getting either the treatment or the control condition are formed. We assume any variation among humans participating in the study, which cannot be controlled for in any other way, is evened out through the random assignment. Such a practice is useful in experimental research. With sufficient numbers in each group, it is likely that research groups are fairly homogenous at the onset of a study. Any differences between groups at the conclusion of a study, then, would be due to the treatment variable (the independent variable), as all other features of the study were held constant.

6. There are many ways of doing research in psychology because (1) human beings are complicated and complex; (2) different perspectives may address different kinds of research questions more effectively depending on the nature of the question; and (3) we look for convergence among different research methods, which collectively help strengthen our confidence in our findings.

7. A researcher can be unobtrusive in naturalistic observation research by (1) using a one-way mirror; (2) blending into or hiding among surroundings; or (3) through time and exposure becoming a very familiar part of the surroundings, and thus inconspicuous.

    It is important to be unobtrusive because we do not want our observation targets to be aware they are being watched and/or to feel self-conscious. If they are aware of an observer, then their behavior may not necessarily be what they would naturally or ordinarily do. If the behavior exhibited by participants is not representative of what they typically do, then findings based on such research are in essence meaningless.

MODULE 1.4 APPLICATION: BECOMING A CRITICAL THINKER

LEARNING OBJECTIVE

After you have mastered the information in this unit, you will be able to:

1. Describe the key features of critical thinking.

OUTLINE

I. Critical Thinking
    A. Adopting a questioning attitude
    B. Willingness to challenge conventional thinking and "common knowledge"
    C. Objective is to get at *real* truth

II. Features of Critical Thinking
    A. Question everything
        1. Do not blindly accept claims
        2. Keep an open mind
    B. Look for clarification of terms
    C. Avoid oversimplifying
    D. Avoid overgeneralizing
    E. Maintain distinction between correlation and causality
    F. Consider assumptions made in report
    G. Carefully examine all sources for timeliness, credibility
    H. Question evidence—is it sound, rational, objective?
    I. As a precaution, think of other ways the findings might be interpreted besides the one presented

III. Thinking Critically About Online Information
    A. Anyone can create or post to Internet sites
    B. Not all information is accurate; retain critical thinking approach
    C. Best sources still scientific journals, credible and respected agencies and organizations
    D. Heavy recreational Internet use inversely related to student academic performance

SUMMARY

In this applications module, you learn about important critical thinking skills. Especially in this information age, there are untold numbers of sources where you can obtain opinions and findings on almost any topic. It is wonderful that we have access to so much information almost instantaneously. But now, perhaps more than ever, we need to be particularly wary about what we believe. Anyone can post just about any information or views to Internet sites. Just because something is presented in written form, even if it is presented repeatedly, does not make it true. For our own benefit, we can adopt critical thinking skills that will help us evaluate information. We can use these guides to critical thinking to evaluate the accuracy of information presented to us from any source.

A critical thinker keeps an open mind and a questioning attitude. Critical thinkers choose to be skeptical and avoid rushing to judgment. The objective is to wait until the facts and convincing evidence lead us to understand what is truly accurate. There may be times when the evidence that seems most legitimate does not correspond to existing popular views. A critical thinker needs to be comfortable challenging, if necessary, conventionally held beliefs.

Steps involved in critical thinking include questioning everything that comes your way; keep an open mind regardless of the sources of claims that you hear; when investigating, look for clarification of terms; make sure you and the communicator are in accord with regard to the meanings of terminology; avoid claims that oversimplify or overgeneralize, and refrain from doing these things yourself with information you have obtained; remember the distinction between correlation and causality. Just because there is a relationship between changes in one variable and changes in another does not mean that one variable causes another. These concepts are two entirely different things.

Clarify the assumptions made in the sources that you read or listen to. If the assumptions are inaccurate, then so are conclusions drawn from them. Check for the sources of the information you obtain. Are credible sources for all pertinent facts listed (such as in a citation)? Take note of dates of publication of all sources. Even once-accurate information may no longer be correct or relevant if considerable time has lapsed since the original investigation. Verify that claims are made on replicable, objective evidence. As a check for yourself, when you read an interpretation of some finding, try to think up alternate explanations. Focusing on alternative explanations at least long enough to come up with some will help you keep the claims you read or hear of in perspective. Despite the easy access to unlimited sources of information, it is probably best to rely on the most credible sources you can find wherever possible.

CHAPTER 1   APPLICATION EXERCISE

Choose an article reporting some new phenomena, either from an Internet resource or from a popular publication to which you have access.

Critique that article in terms of its scientific value. What findings does it report? How was the research carried out? Did the investigator(s) attempt to utilize the scientific method? Follow the steps listed above and in your textbook regarding critical thinking and evaluating informational sources. How does your article measure up based on these standards? Is this article or resource one that your critical evaluation suggests you should rely on? What are the differences between many popular publications and the way psychological research is carried out?

CHAPTER 2

Biological Foundations of Behavior

In Chapter 2, you are introduced to the biological processes that underlie much of human behavior. While we often think of behavior in a global sense (e.g. how your friend was acting yesterday afternoon or the excitement of spending a weekend at the beach), closer examination reveals that behaviors can be broken down to very small, physiologically based, increments of activity. In fact, in this chapter we look at behavior beginning with the unit of a single cell, the neuron. Perhaps if just a few cells or cell clusters fired differently in your brain, you would feel differently. Perhaps even just finding yourself experiencing different surroundings would lead to differing operations within your brain! Indeed, it is possible that all behavior can be traced to the firing of one nerve cell, eliciting a particular synapse, and then affecting one other neuron. As we will learn, the knee-jerk reflex is a visible behavior that involves just two cells in your nervous system.

Your nervous system, including your brain, is composed of nerve cells, also known as neurons. Neurons are cells that are specialized for rapid communication. You need communication both within your body to inform the brain and relevant organs of various body conditions, and with the outside world to allow you to absorb, process, and react to environmental events. The nervous system communicates quickly because it is predominantly electrical in nature. Neural impulses traveling within a nerve cell are electrical, but impulses must switch to chemical form in order to reach adjoining neurons. The tiny gap between nerve cells and the process of a neural message traveling through it is known as the synapse. Because transmission from cell to cell is chemical, neural messages at any time may be modified depending on the chemicals present in the region of the synapse. Your body contains billions and billions of neurons, most of them located in the brain. Think of all of these nerve cells, firing many times a second and interconnecting with thousands of other neurons; it is a process that is almost impossible to comprehend. However, in this chapter, at least we will begin to try!

Your body has another internal communication system, one that is slower than the nervous system and strictly chemical in nature. This is your system of glands, known collectively as the endocrine system. Your endocrine system is not independent of your nervous system, of course, and in fact the two work quite closely together. Workings of the brain determine to a great extent what happens with regard to glandular activity and hormones that are secreted. The hypothalamus is one of the most important brain structures to influence the endocrine system. Secretions from the hypothalamus (a part of the large brain structure known as the forebrain) stimulate the pituitary gland, which in turn secretes hormones affecting activity in many other glands.

The brain is so complicated—how can we study it? Because of technological advances, we now have a number of strategies available for brain research. Nearly all of these brain research techniques can be classified as noninvasive procedures. We are learning more about the role of genes and hereditary influences on behavior as well.

The nervous system has two divisions: the central and the peripheral. The central nervous system (CNS) consists of the brain and spinal cord. The peripheral nervous system has further divisions, with networks running throughout the body. Some bring information in, while others put responses from the brain into action. The entire nervous system is composed of nerve cells. A neuron is not a nerve; a nerve is made up of many, many nerve cells bundled together. Lucky for you, much of it operates without you having to think about it!

A tip as you start your travel through the wonder that is your brain: Keep in mind a small segment of your behavior—say perhaps just a few minutes' worth. When you finish reading the chapter, think back on that slice of behavior. What brain and peripheral nervous system components were involved in the activity? How much of the endocrine system was involved, if any? Genetic heritage? Were muscles activated? Were cognitions processed? The neurons in your body have been busy, indeed!

MODULE 2.1 NEURONS: THE BODY'S WIRING

LEARNING OBJECTIVES

After you have mastered the information in this unit, you will be able to:

1. Understand what a neuron is and how it functions within the body.

2. Know and describe the various parts of the neuron and their functions.

3. Explain the different types of neurons found within the nervous system.

4. Understand how neural impulses are generated and transmitted from one neuron to another.

5. Discuss the roles of neurotransmitters in psychological functioning.

OUTLINE

I.   The Structure of the Neuron
   A.   Basic building block of the nervous system
   B.   Cells specialized for rapidly communicating information
   C.   Neuron parts and functions
      1.   Soma (main body of cell)—houses nucleus, stores incoming impulses
      2.   Nucleus
         a)   Contains cell's genetic material
         b)   Carries out metabolic functions of cell
      3.   Axon—projection from soma; very short in brain, can be 2 or 3 ft. long in peripheral
         a)   Terminal buttons—knoblike vesicles at end of axon branches
         b)   Neurotransmitters—chemicals released from terminal buttons (to conduct impulses across synapse)
      4.   Dendrites
         a)   Branchings that project from one end of soma (opposite that of the axon)
         b)   Have receptor (docking station) sites that accommodate specific neurotransmitters
         c)   Receive chemical information emitted from adjoining neurons (or sensory receptors)
   D.   Types of neurons
      1.   Sensory neurons—bring information from outside world to your spinal cord and brain
      2.   Motor neurons—transmit responses from brain and spinal cord to muscles and glands
      3.   Interneurons
         a)   Connect neurons to other neurons
         b)   Join sensory and motor neurons in spinal cord
   E.   "Nerve"—NOT a neuron! Bundles of many, many axons
II.   Glial Cells
   A.   Most numerous cells within the nervous system
   B.   "Glue" to help hold neurons together
   C.   Assist and support activity of neurons

    D.   Form myelin sheath
        1.   Fatty, protective covering on many neuron axons
        2.   Nodes of Ranvier (gaps in myelin sheath)—neural impulse may jump from node to node

III. How Neurons Communicate
    A.   Ions involved: sodium, potassium, and chloride
    B.   Resting potential—neuron not activated; cell has slightly negative charge
    C.   Depolarization—stimulation leads sodium to enter cell; electrical charge now changed from negative to positive
    D.   Action potential—neuron fires down length of axon; called a neural impulse
    E.   Response is all-or-nothing; neuron fires completely or not at all
    F.   Refractory period—millisecond of time during which neuron cannot fire

IV. Neurotransmitters
    A.   Synapse is tiny gap between one neuron and the next
    B.   At synapse, the impulse changes from electrical to chemical
    C.   Neurotransmitters are these chemical messengers across synapse
    D.   Features in neural processing
        1.   Receptor site—dendrite/soma location to receive specific neurotransmitter
        2.   Incoming chemical message may excite or inhibit neural firing
        3.   Reuptake is reabsorption of unused neurotransmitter
        4.   Enzymes in synapse region may break down neurotransmitters (to keep stimulation in balance)
        5.   Neuromodulators from terminal buttons can influence sensitivity of receptor sites to incoming chemicals

V. Factors relating to neurotransmitters and neuron functioning
    A.   Antagonists—occupy receptor sites and thus block incoming chemical effect
    B.   Dopamine (neurotransmitter) as an example
        1.   Schizophrenia related to irregularities in brain utilization of dopamine
        2.   Antipsychotic drugs (antagonists) occupy dopamine-receiving sites
        3.   Parkinson's disease results from loss of dopamine-producing cells involved in body movement
    C.   Agonists—enhance effect of incoming chemical messages (such as stimulants, antidepressants)
    D.   Endorphins—neurotransmitters produced naturally by the body to inhibit pain, increase sense of well-being

SUMMARY

In this module, you learn about the structure and function of the neuron and accompanying glial cells. The neuron is one type of body cell, specialized for the very rapid communication of information. This information may be from the outside world (conducted to your spinal cord and brain by sensory neurons), from your brain back to your muscles and glands to help you act upon the world (via motor neurons), or completely within your body (most often conducted by interneurons). Glial cells support and nourish the activity of neurons.

The neuron is comprised of important components. The dendrites receive incoming information, and this is passed to the soma (cell body). The nucleus, in the center of the cell body, regulates the activity of the neuron, as it does in any of your body cells. Action potentials travel the length of the axon—that is when the nerve cell fires. Terminal buttons contain chemicals, the neurotransmitters. Axons may eventually become wrapped in the myelin sheath (composed of glial cells); this sheath speeds neural transmissions. Nerves are not neurons; nerves are bundles of many, many axons.

The neural impulse causes the release of chemicals into the synapse. When the neurotransmitters reach adjoining neurons, the impulse reverts to electrical form. The impact of brain chemicals can be enhanced or inhibited, such as by agonists or antagonists. Problems with the neurotransmitters and/or sending and receiving sites in the brain can be related to serious diseases, such as schizophrenia and Parkinson's disease.

KEY TERMS

Neurons

Brain

Soma

Axon

Terminal buttons

Neurotransmitters

Synapse

Dendrites

Sensory neurons

Motor neurons

Glands

Hormones

Interneurons

Nerve

Glial cells

Myelin sheath

Nodes of Ranvier

Ions

Resting potential

Depolarization

Action potential

All-or-none principle

Refractory period

Receptor site

Reuptake

Enzymes

Neuromodulators

Antagonists

Schizophrenia

Hallucinations

Delusions

Parkinson's disease

Agonists

Stimulant

Amphetamines

Antidepressants

Endorphins

SELF-TEST PRACTICE QUIZ

Match the following Key Terms and definitions (note: not every Key Term will be used):

1. _____ The fact that neurons fire down the complete length of the cell if a sufficient level of excitatory impulses are received

2. _____ The cell body, containing the nucleus

3. _____ Chemicals present in the brain that allow for message transmission among nerve cells

4. _____ Brain chemicals which moderate pain messages and produce feelings of pleasure

5. _____ Nerve cells

6. _____ Fibers extending out from the soma of the neuron; receive incoming messages from adjoining neurons

7. _____ Neurons in the peripheral nervous system that transport messages from spinal cord to muscles and glands

8. _____ Tiny gaps within the myelin sheath covering a nerve cell; may help speed impulses

9. _____ The connection between neurons where neural message becomes chemical (carried by neurotransmitters)

a. Neurons

b. Brain

c. Soma

d. Axon

e. Terminal buttons

f. Neurotransmitters

g. Synapse

h. Dendrite

i. Sensory neurons

j. Motor neurons

k. Glands

l. Hormones

m. Interneurons

n. Nerve

o. Glial cells

p. Myelin sheath

q. Nodes of Ranvier

r. Ions

s. Resting potential

t. Depolarization

u. Action potential

v. All-or-none principle

w. Refractory period

x. Receptor site

y. Reuptake

10. _____ The part of the neuron conducting messages down the length of the cell towards connections with other neurons; usually the longest part of a neuron

11. _____ A fatty protective layer that covers the axons of some nerve cells and helps speed transmission of neural impulses

12. _____ Chemical secretions from the endocrine system which regulate many body functions

13. _____ Neurons which receive messages from sensory receptors and transmit that information to the spinal cord

14. _____ Knobs on the ends of axon terminal branches which contain neurotransmitters

15. _____ Locations on neurons receiving incoming messages; neurotransmitters fit into these sites

16. _____ A number of axon fibers which are bunched together and relay neural information

z.   Enzymes
aa. Neuromodulators
bb. Antagonists
cc. Schizophrenia
dd. Hallucinations
ee. Delusions
ff. Parkinson's disease
gg. Agonists
hh. Stimulant
ii. Amphetamine
jj. Antidepressants
kk. Endorphins

17. The part of the neuron which receives incoming messages is the
    a. dendrites.
    b. axon.
    c. terminal buttons.
    d. myelin sheath.

18. What is the advantage of having axons be covered with a myelin sheath?
    a. It lessens the negative effects of antagonist drugs.
    b. It allows neurotransmitters to cross the synapse more effectively.
    c. It allows neural impulses to travel more quickly.
    d. It allows neurotransmitter reuptake to proceed more efficiently.

19. Transmission of a neural impulse travels from the _____ at the receiving end of the cell to the _____ at the other end of the cell (which will transmit messages to adjoining neurons).
    a. dendrites; terminal buttons
    b. terminal buttons; nucleus
    c. axon; terminal buttons
    d. axon hillock; myelin sheath

20. Neural messages become chemical in nature and are transmitted by neurotransmitters across the

    a. nodes of Ranvier.
    b. synapse.
    c. receptor site.
    d. terminal buttons.

21. _____ carry messages toward the spinal cord and brain.

    a. Sensory neurons
    b. Glial cells
    c. Endorphins
    d. Motor neurons

22. When sodium cells are concentrated outside a neuron, giving the cell a slightly negative charge, this is known as

    a. action potential.
    b. differential gradient.
    c. resting potential.
    d. the all-or-none principle.

23. Many medications work by increasing the availability of certain neurotransmitters. Such medications are known as

    a. antagonists.
    b. glutamates.
    c. amphetamines.
    d. agonists.

ESSAY QUESTION

1. How do neurons communicate with one another?

ANSWER KEY

1. All-or-none principle

2. Soma

3. Neurotransmitters

4. Endorphins

5. Neurons

6. Dendrites

7. Motor neurons

8. Nodes of Ranvier

9. Synapse

10. Axon

11. Myelin sheath

12. Hormones

13. Sensory neurons

14. Terminal buttons

15. Receptor site

16. Nerve

17. a

18. c

19. a

20. b

21. a

22. c

23. d

SAMPLE ANSWER TO ESSAY QUESTION

1. Neurons communicate with each other by means of neurotransmitters. Neurotransmitters are chemicals that travel across the synapse to adjoining neurons. Dendrites on receiving neurons have neurotransmitter receptor sites. Neurotransmitters bring either excitatory ("fire") or inhibitory ("don't fire") messages to a neuron. When the neuron is not active, the condition is known as the resting potential. During this time, sodium and potassium ions tend to be outside of the neuron, and chloride ions tend to be within it. When depolarization occurs (the electrical charge within a neuron shifts to become positive) and reaches a certain threshold, then the neuron fires. This is known as the action potential. The impulse within a neuron is electrical, but the transmission between neurons is chemical. The nucleus monitors nerve cell activity and makes the decision as to whether the cell will fire or not. Especially within the brain, a single neuron may exchange messages with thousands of other neurons.

MODULE 2.2 THE NERVOUS SYSTEM: YOUR BODY'S INFORMATION SUPERHIGHWAY

LEARNING OBJECTIVES

After you have mastered the information in this unit, you will be able to:

1. Understand how your body's nervous system is organized.

2. Explain the nature of spinal reflexes.

3. Describe the components and functions of the autonomic nervous system.

4. Explain the relationship between the sympathetic and parasympathetic divisions of the autonomic nervous system.

OUTLINE

I.   The Human Nervous System
    A.   Central nervous system—brain and spinal cord
        1.   Brain—major organ of nervous system and body's functioning
        2.   Spinal cord—thick column of nerves encased in bony spine
        3.   Spinal reflex—response to an external stimulus that does NOT involve action of the brain
    B.   Peripheral nervous system—components of nervous system other than brain and spinal cord
II.   Peripheral Nervous System
    A.   Somatic nervous system
        1.   Comprised of sensory and motor neurons
        2.   Links communication between central nervous system and sense organs, muscles
    B.   Autonomic nervous system (internal bodily processes)—two further divisions
        1.   Sympathetic nervous system
            a)   Prepares body to meet physical demands or stress
            b)   Increases heart rate, breathing, levels of blood sugar
        2.   Parasympathetic nervous system
            a)   Fosters bodily processes, such as digestion, to replenish/restore energy levels
            b)   Slows bodily activity, acts to conserves energy

SUMMARY

Module 2.2 discusses the basic organization of the human nervous system. Your nervous system has two major divisions: the central and the peripheral nervous systems. The central nervous system is composed of the brain and spinal cord. The peripheral nervous system composes the rest of your body's nervous system other than the brain and spinal cord.

The peripheral nervous system has two major divisions: the somatic nervous system and the autonomic nervous system. The autonomic nervous system has two further divisions: the sympathetic and the parasympathetic nervous systems. Though they have essentially opposite effects on the body, they act more or less in concert with each other. The sympathetic nervous system prepares you for stress or physical demands by speeding up your heart rate, increasing breathing, and giving you increased fuel in your bloodstream. The parasympathetic nervous system slows down the body again and allows for bodily activities that replenish your store of energy.

KEY TERMS

Nervous system

Central nervous system

Spinal cord

Spine

Reflex

Spinal reflex

Peripheral nervous system

Somatic nervous system

Autonomic nervous system

Sympathetic nervous system

Parasympathetic nervous system

SELF-TEST PRACTICE QUIZ

Match the following Key Terms and definitions (note: not every Key Term will be used):

1. _____ A part of the peripheral nervous system which regulates bodily processes such as breathing, heart rate, and digestion

2. _____ A part of the peripheral nervous system that works in tandem with the sympathetic nervous system; to restore the body's energy sources once they have been depleted

3. _____ A branch of the human nervous system that includes all components except the brain and spinal cord

4. _____ The part of the peripheral nervous system that controls voluntary movements

5. _____ The part of the human nervous system that encompasses the brain and spinal cord

6. _____ A branch of the autonomic nervous system that helps an organism respond to demands the organism faces from the environment

7. _____ A physical action by the body which does NOT initially involve the brain

a. Nervous system

b. Central nervous system

c. Spinal cord

d. Spine

e. Reflex

f. Spinal reflex

g. Peripheral nervous system

h. Somatic nervous system

i. Autonomic nervous system

j. Sympathetic nervous system

k. Parasympathetic nervous system

8. The _____ nervous system is made up of sensory and motor neurons.
    a. autonomic
    b. somatic
    c. central
    d. parasympathetic
9. The peripheral nervous system has two divisions, the _____ and _____.
    a. central; autonomic
    b. sympathetic; parasympathetic
    c. brain; spinal cord
    d. somatic; autonomic
10. The part of your nervous system that stimulates salivation, decreases breathing, stimulates digestion, and constricts the pupils is the _____ nervous system.
    a. central
    b. somatic
    c. sympathetic
    d. parasympathetic
11. The part of the body that encases the spinal cord is the
    a. spine.
    b. central nervous system.
    c. peripheral nervous system.
    d. spinal reflex.
12. The brain is part of the _____ nervous system.
    a. peripheral
    b. somatic
    c. central
    d. autonomic
13. When you run, your _____ nervous system controls your leg muscles.
    a. somatic
    b. parasympathetic
    c. autonomic
    d. sympathetic
14. What is the benefit of having spinal reflexes?
    a. They allow the sympathetic nervous system to function more efficiently.
    b. They allow us to respond more quickly to potentially dangerous situations.
    c. They permit the central and peripheral nervous systems to communicate.
    d. They speed up transmission of neural impulses.
15. Four-year-old Joey thought that he heard a monster under his bed. In response, his _____ nervous system prepared him to either fight or run away.
    a. somatic
    b. parasympathetic
    c. sympathetic
    d. central

ESSAY QUESTION

1. Trace the pathway of neural communication within your body from the instant an event occurs in your external environment until you have completed whatever response you will make to that event.

ANSWER KEY

1. Autonomic nervous system
2. Parasympathetic nervous system
3. Peripheral nervous system
4. Somatic nervous system
5. Central nervous system
6. Sympathetic nervous system
7. Spinal reflex
8. b
9. d
10. d
11. a
12. c
13. a
14. b
15. c

SAMPLE ANSWER TO ESSAY QUESTION

1. An event in the environment is detected by the sensory nervous system. The sensory nervous system is one of the two main divisions of the somatic nervous system, which in turn is a division within the peripheral nervous system. The sensory nervous system transmits the detected information to the spinal cord, where it is passed up to the brain. The brain and the spinal cord make up the central nervous system. The brain processes the environmental event and determines a response (if one is to be made). The message conveying the response travels outward from the brain, down the spinal cord, and to the motor nervous system (the other division in the somatic nervous system). The motor nervous system then activates muscles in the body, allowing you to make a physical response to the environmental event. If the event was at all threatening, the autonomic nervous system could be activated also. The sympathetic branch of the autonomic nervous system prepares you for meeting demanding challenges in the environment by increasing heart and breathing rates, and the like. When danger has past, the parasympathetic branch allows the body to be restored to normal functioning levels and replace energy reserves within the body that have been used.

MODULE 2.3 THE BRAIN: YOUR CROWNING GLORY

LEARNING OBJECTIVES

After you have mastered the information in this unit, you will be able to:

1. Discuss how the brain is organized and describe the functions of its various parts.
2. Explain the organization of the cerebral cortex.
3. Describe the major functions associated with the four lobes of the cerebral cortex.

OUTLINE

I.   The Brain
    A.   Hindbrain—lowest part of brain
        1.   Evolutionarily the "oldest"
        2.   Medulla—breathing, heart rate, swallowing
        3.   Pons—conducts information; influences wakefulness and sleep
        4.   Cerebellum—controls balance and coordination
    B.   Midbrain—above the hindbrain
        1.   Connects hindbrain with forebrain
        2.   Reticular formation
            a)   Neural network that connects to thalamus
            b)   Involved in attention, alertness and arousal
            c)   Filters out irrelevant information
    C.   Forebrain—largest part of the brain, located at top and front
        1.   Thalamus—relay station, routes information to appropriate cerebral cortex area
        2.   Basal ganglia—important for regulating voluntary body movement
        3.   Hypothalamus
            a)   Under the thalamus; size of a pea
            b)   Regulates hunger, thirst, body temperature
            c)   Involved in reproduction, emotional states
            d)   Directs activity of the endocrine system
        4.   Limbic system (also includes parts of thalamus and hypothalamus)—memory and emotional processing
            a)   Amygdala—aggression, rage and fear
            b)   Hippocampus—important role in formation of memories
II.   Cerebral cortex—relatively thin, but 80% of brain's total mass
    A.   Outer layer of largest part of the forebrain, the cerebrum
    B.   Convoluted surface; massive in size (compared to other brain components)
    C.   Two cerebral hemispheres, connected by corpus callosum
    D.   Each hemisphere—four lobes
        1.   Occipital lobes (back part of hemispheres)—processes visual information
        2.   Parietal lobes—above occipital
            a)   Includes somatosensory cortex
            b)   Touch, pressure, pain, external temperature, internal muscle/joint state
            c)   Area proportional to sensitivity of skin tissue
        3.   Frontal lobes
            a)   "Executive center"
            b)   Accesses stored memories to help in identification, decision-making
            c)   Used to solve problems, plan, reason, and carry out coordinated activities
            d)   Involved in emotional states
            e)   Motor cortex (directly across from parietal)—voluntary movement
        4.   Temporal lobes—hearing
    E.   Consists largely of association areas—for integration, higher mental functions

SUMMARY

In this module, you learn about the central nervous system. There are two divisions in the central nervous system: the brain and the spinal cord. The spinal cord runs through your spine (bony tissue which protects it), connecting your peripheral nervous system to the brain. Most of the neurons in your body are located in the brain.

The brain is divided into three major parts: the hindbrain, midbrain, and forebrain. The hindbrain includes the medulla, pons, and cerebellum and is responsible for the most basic life functions. The cerebellum is involved in controlling balance and coordination. The midbrain connects the hindbrain to the forebrain. The reticular formation runs from the hindbrain to the forebrain; it is responsible for filtering information and for alertness and arousal. The forebrain is the largest part of the brain. Parts of the forebrain include the thalamus (routes sensory information) and the hypothalamus (hunger and thirst, reproductive processes, internal body temperature, emotions). The amygdala (rage and fear) and the hippocampus (memories) are part of the limbic system. The cerebrum in the forebrain is covered with a thin layer known as the cerebral cortex. This cortex is divided into two hemispheres, and information passes between the two hemispheres by means of a thick connecting band of fibers called the corpus callosum. Each hemisphere is divided into four lobes; the function of the lobes differs somewhat depending on which of the two hemispheres they are located in. The occipital lobes are involved in vision; the parietal lobes process sensory information; the frontal lobes are the "executive center"; and the temporal lobes are involved in processing sound. Association areas in the cerebral cortex perform higher mental functions such as thinking and learning.

KEY TERMS

Hindbrain

Medulla

Pons

Brainstem

Cerebellum

Midbrain

Reticular formation

Forebrain

Thalamus

Basal ganglia

Hypothalamus

Limbic system

Amygdala

Hippocampus

Cerebral cortex

Cerebrum

Cerebral hemispheres

Corpus callosum

Occipital lobes

Parietal lobes

Somatosensory cortex

Frontal lobes

Motor cortex

Temporal lobes

Association areas

SELF TEST PRACTICE QUIZ

Match the following Key Terms and definitions (note: not every Key Term will be used):

1. _____ A network of neurons involved in regulating attention, alertness, and arousal

2. _____ A set of structures in the brain especially involved in the experience of emotion

3. _____ The lobes at the back of the head that process visual stimuli

4. _____ The part of the hindbrain involved in regulating vital life functions

5. _____ The lobes located at the top and front of the brain, most involved in higher-order functions

6. _____ The portion of the forebrain divided into two hemispheres

7. _____ The part of the limbic system most involved in the formation of memories

8. _____ A brain structure in the limbic system involved in many functions, including sexual reproduction, emotional reactions, and maintaining internal body temperature

9. _____ Lobes located in the upper back of the head; process information relating to touch, pressure, external temperature

10. _____ One component of the limbic system; particularly involved in the experiences of fear, aggression

11. _____ A forebrain structure which relays information on to different parts of the brain

12. _____ Lobes located on the sides of the head near the ear; primary function involves processing speech, sound

a. Hindbrain

b. Medulla

c. Pons

d. Brainstem

e. Cerebellum

f. Midbrain

g. Reticular formation

h. Forebrain

i. Thalamus

j. Basal ganglia

k. Hypothalamus

l. Limbic system

m. Amygdala

n. Hippocampus

o. Cerebral cortex

p. Cerebrum

q. Cerebral hemispheres

r. Corpus callosum

s. Occipital lobes

t. Parietal lobes

u. Somatosensory cortex

v. Frontal lobes

w. Motor cortex

x. Temporal lobes

y. Association areas

13. _____ The outer covering of the cerebrum

14. _____ A brain structure located in the back of the head; vital for balance and coordination

15. The _____ is in the hindbrain.
    a. hypothalamus
    b. occipital lobe
    c. pons
    d. reticular basal ganglia

16. The amygdala, hippocampus, and parts of the thalamus and hypothalamus make up the
    a. limbic system.
    b. reticular activating system.
    c. executive center.
    d. cerebral cortex.

17. The great majority of the cortex consists of
    a. the limbic system.
    b. the spinal cord.
    c. the corpus callosum.
    d. association areas.

18. The _____ makes up 80% of the brain's total mass.
    a. corpus callosum
    b. cerebral cortex
    c. medulla
    d. hippocampus

ESSAY QUESTION

1. Discuss the cerebral cortex in humans. Name, give the approximate location of, and describe the function of each of the four lobes in a human cerebral hemisphere.

ANSWER KEY

1. Reticular formation
2. Limbic system
3. Occipital lobes
4. Medulla
5. Frontal lobes
6. Cerebrum
7. Hippocampus
8. Hypothalamus
9. Parietal lobes
10. Amygdala
11. Thalamus
12. Temporal lobes
13. Cerebral cortex
14. Cerebellum
15. c
16. a
17. d
18. b

SAMPLE ANSWER TO ESSAY QUESTION

1. The cerebral cortex is the outer layer of the human cerebrum in the forebrain. Although it is relatively thin, most of the brain's neurons are in the cerebral cortex. Each hemisphere in the cortex contains four lobes. Located at the back of the brain, above the cerebellum is the occipital lobe. The primary function of the occipital lobe is to process visual information. Above the occipital is the parietal lobe; this lobe processes things that come in contact with our skin, such as touch, pressure, and external temperature. Over our ears is the temporal lobe—primarily used to process auditory information. Lastly, at the top and front of our heads is the frontal lobe. The frontal lobe directs our "executive" functions—the ability to think, reason, remember, analyze, make decisions, and feel emotion.

MODULE 2.4 METHODS OF STUDYING THE BRAIN

LEARNING OBJECTIVES

After you have mastered the information in this unit, you will be able to:

1. Discuss the recording and imaging techniques used to study brain functioning.

2. Describe the experimental methods used by scientists to study brain functioning.

OUTLINE

I.   Methods of Studying the Brain
    A.   Diseases and injuries affecting the brain
    B.   Recording and imaging techniques
        1.   EEG (electroencephalograph)—records electrical activity in the brain
        2.   CT (computed tomography) scan—measures reflection of an X-ray beam passing through body
        3.   PET (positron emission tomography) scan—radioactive isotope reveals more active parts of brain
        4.   MRI (magnetic resonance imaging)—gives picture of body's soft matter; disrupted atoms give signals as they realign
        5.   fMRI (functional magnetic resonance imaging)—pictures of the brain while in action; less invasive than PET
    C.   Experimental methods
        1.   Lesioning
            a)   Part of experimental animal's brain is destroyed
            b)   Researcher investigates effects of the brain tissue loss
        2.   Electrical recording—electrodes in neurons/brain tissue reveal changes
        3.   Electrical stimulation—observe results of mild electric current passed through brain

SUMMARY

In this module, you learn about methods for studying the brain. Initially, most of what we knew about the brain was due to natural occurrences; that is, individuals who suffered brain injury or disease showed corresponding losses in physical, mental, and psychological functioning. We learned, for example, that the left side of the brain controls the right side of the body and vice versa.

Today we have additional, often less invasive, techniques. Researchers may use either recording and imaging techniques or experimental methods. Technologies used include the EEG (to record brain waves), CT scans (X-ray beam reflection is measured), PET scans (reveals concentrations of radioactive isotope tracer), MRI (magnetic field aligns brain atoms which are then disrupted), and fMRI (can reveal the brain in action). Experimental methods include lesioning (cutting out part of a research animal's brain and observing results), electrical recording of neural activity, or electrical stimulation.

KEY TERMS

EEG (electroencephalograph)

CT (computed tomography) scan

PET (positron emission tomography) scan

MRI (magnetic resonance imaging)

Lesioning

Electrical recording

Electrical stimulation

SELF TEST PRACTICE QUIZ

Match the following Key Terms and definitions (note: not every Key Term will be used):

1. _____ Equipment that measures brain waves

2. _____ Electrodes in brain reveal brain changes

3. _____ Used to see the results of a radioactive isotope tracer

4. _____ Measures the reflection of an X-ray beam

5. _____ Passing a mild current through the brain

6. _____ Measures atoms as they realign

a. EEG (electroencephalograph)

b. CT (computed tomography) scan

c. PET (positron emission tomography) scan

d. MRI (magnetic resonance imaging)

e. Lesioning

f. Electrical recording

g. Electrical stimulation

7. Out of all the brain research techniques currently available, which is the only one that causes harm to the research animal?

    a. Lesioning
    b. Electrical recording
    c. Electrical stimulation
    d. MRI

8. Which method(s) allow researchers to study brain processes?

    a. MRI
    b. PET
    c. CT
    d. all of the above

9. What is the difference between MRI and fMRI?

    a. There is no difference between the two.
    b. MRI uses a magnetic field to create a picture of the brain, while fMRI involves measuring electrical activity in the brain.
    c. MRI is a type of X-ray, while fMRI involves physically cutting into a person's brain.
    d. MRI measures brain structure only, while fMRI also provides information about brain functioning.

ESSAY QUESTION

1. How does MRI (magnetic resonance imaging) produce an image of the brain?

ANSWER KEY

1. EEG (electroencephalograph)

2. Electrical recording

3. PET (positron emission tomography) scan

4. CT (computed tomography) scan

5. Electrical stimulation

6. MRI (magnetic resonance imaging)

7. a

8. b

9. d

SAMPLE ANSWER TO ESSAY QUESTION

1. Magnetic resonance imaging is conducted by having the brain placed within a device that creates a strong magnetic field. The magnetic field aligns atoms in the brain. These atoms are disrupted by radio waves, and the atoms again realign. The MRI is the result of signals the atoms emit while they are realigning. With computer technology, these signals can be put together to form an image of the brain.

MODULE 2.5 THE DIVIDED BRAIN: SPECIALIZATION OF FUNCTION

LEARNING OBJECTIVES

After you have mastered the information in this unit, you will be able to:

1. Describe the major differences between the left and right hemispheres.

2. Explain what determines handedness.

3. Discuss brain lateralization and research with "split-brain" patients.

4. Understand major causes of brain damage and how this damage impacts psychological functioning.

OUTLINE

I. The Brain at Work: Lateralization and Integration
   A. Lateralization
      1. Division of functions between left and right brain hemispheres
      2. Left hemisphere directs activity of right side of body; right hemisphere directs activity in left side of body
      3. Left brain (in most people): language, logical analysis, mathematical computations
         a) Broca's area (left frontal lobe): production of speech
         b) Wernicke's area (left temporal lobe): understanding meaning in language
         c) Aphasia: loss or impairment in language communication
      4. Right brain: spatial relations, recognizing faces, emotional expression
   B. Integration: Both hemispheres share work in performing most tasks

II.   Handedness—hand dominance related to hemispheric specialization
    A.   Left-handers may not follow typical pattern
    B.   Genetic factors seem to play a role
    C.   Prenatal hormones may also influence
    D.   Twice as many males as females are left-handed
III. Split-Brain Patients: Corpus Callosum Is Severed
    A.   Often a treatment for severe epilepsy
    B.   Left hand really may not know what right is doing
    C.   Hemispheres don't communicate but brain adapts
IV.   Brain Damage and Psychological Functioning
    A.   Head trauma or stroke
    B.   Surgical removal of severely damaged hemisphere
    C.   Brain plasticity—healthy part of brain may take over lost function

SUMMARY

In this module, you learn more about the two hemispheres of the brain. The hemispheres are connected by the thick band of nerve fibers known as the corpus callosum. In split-brain patients, however, the corpus callosum has been severed by physicians as a last resort treatment for brain diseases such as epilepsy. Thus, the two halves can no longer directly communicate. We have been able to learn more about specialization in the brain hemispheres due in part to research with split-brain individuals.

The left-brain hemisphere is usually the logical and analytical side, including processing for language functions and for mathematical computations. The right brain typically is more involved with communicating expression and emotion, with grasping spatial relations, and in appreciating music and art. It is important to note, however, that the hemispheres in most humans are highly integrated; that is, they have overlapping functions and share in most brain activities. The left side of the brain controls functioning in the right side of the body, and the right side of the brain controls the left side of the body.

Language functions are related to handedness. Nearly all right-handers have the language centers in the left brain; however, only about 70% of the left-handers do. The two vital language areas in the brain are Broca's area (for speech production) in the frontal lobe and Wernicke's area (for understanding word meanings) in the temporal lobe.

Though the brain may experience trauma, such as concussions, stroke, and even the removal in extreme cases of an entire hemisphere, it often can adapt and reorganize itself remarkably well. This is due to brain plasticity—the ability for brain cells that are still healthy to take over functions of brain tissue that has been injured or destroyed.

KEY TERMS

Lateralization

Broca's area

Wernicke's area

Aphasia

Epilepsy

Split-brain patients

Prefrontal cortex

Plasticity

SELF-TEST PRACTICE QUIZ

Match the following Key Terms and definitions:

1. _____ Individuals for whom the corpus callosum has been severed, due to brain illness

2. _____ A part of the brain, located on the temporal lobe, utilized in the processing of the meanings of speech

3. _____ The division of functions between the two hemispheres of the brain

4. _____ The ability of other brain cells to take over functions of damaged or destroyed brain tissue

5. _____ The part of the brain in front of the motor cortex; involved in judgments, reasoning and decision-making

6. _____ Loss or impairment of language function

7. _____ A part of the brain involved in the production of speech; located on the frontal lobe

8. _____ A neurological disorder involving tremendous bursts of electrical activity in the brain

a. Lateralization

b. Epilepsy

c. Broca's area

d. Split-brain patients

e. Wernicke's area

f. Prefrontal cortex

g. Plasticity

h. Aphasia

9. For right-handed people, the centers for language processing are typically located
   a. in the right hemisphere.
   b. in the left hemisphere.
   c. in the parietal lobe.
   d. above the brain stem.

10. Why is there some hope for recovery after strokes or other brain damage?
    a. Brain grafts are becoming increasingly successful.
    b. Dead brain cells can usually be revived.
    c. Spinal cord tissue takes over lost functions.
    d. Healthy brain cells may eventually assume some of lost functions.

11. An individual suffers from a severe brain disease, and as a last resort physicians sever the corpus callosum. Which of the following is NOT a likely characteristic of this individual after surgery?
    a. The individual will become one of the split-brain patients.
    b. The two hemispheres in his brain will be unable to communicate directly.
    c. When blindfolded, he will not be able to name an object in his left hand.
    d. He will never be able to function effectively again.

12. Brain plasticity is usually greatest among people who are
    a. young.
    b. male.

    c.   left-handed.

    d.   aphasic.

13.   Which part of Phineas Gage's brain was destroyed in his accident?

    a.   Temporal lobe

    b.   Motor cortex

    c.   Prefrontal cortex

    d.   Broca's area

ESSAY QUESTION

1.   Tell the story of Phineas Gage. In what ways was he different after his accident? What does this tell you about functions of the brain?

ANSWER KEY

1. Split-brain patients

2. Wernicke's area

3. Lateralization

4. Plasticity

5. Prefrontal cortex

6. Aphasia

7. Broca's area

8. Epilepsy

9. b

10. d

11. d

12. a

13. c

SAMPLE ANSWER TO ESSAY QUESTION

1. In the 1800s, while working on a railroad track, an inch-thick metal rod shot through Gage's brain, exiting out the top of his head. Despite the severity of his injuries, he survived, and his wounds healed in about two months. Gage was able to function; however, his personality was forever changed. One area of Gage's brain that was damaged in the blast was the prefrontal cortex. This region of the frontal lobe is responsible for reasoning, judgment, and maintaining appropriate restraints on impulsive behavior. Though Gage could speak and move (there was no damage to language or motor portions of his brain), he exhibited different personality characteristics than before the accident. Thus the brain is involved not only in physical and cognitive activities, but determines our personality and ability to make moral and social judgments.

MODULE 2.6 THE ENDOCRINE SYSTEM: THE BODY'S OTHER COMMUNICATION SYSTEM

LEARNING OBJECTIVES

After you have mastered the information in this unit, you will be able to:

1. Name the major endocrine glands, and describe the functions of the pituitary gland and the hypothalamus.

2. Understand the roles that hormones play in behavior.

OUTLINE

I. The Endocrine System—slower communication system; messages sent via hormones through blood vessels
   A. A grouping of glands
   B. Glands release hormone secretions

    C.   Regulates bodily processes such as growth, reproduction, and metabolism
    D.   Helps maintain homeostasis—an internally balanced state

II.   Important Glands
    A.   Hypothalamus—secretes releasing factors that act on pituitary gland (both located in brain)
    B.   Pituitary gland
        1.   "Master gland"—influences hormone activity of other glands
        2.   Also promotes physical growth via GH (growth hormone)
    C.   Pancreas
        1.   Produces the hormone insulin
        2.   Regulates concentration of glucose in the blood
    D.   Pineal gland
        1.   Secretes melatonin
        2.   Regulates sleep-wake cycles
    E.   Adrenal glands
        1.   Lie above the kidneys
        2.   Adrenal cortex
            a)   Secretes hormones which promote muscle development
            b)   Stimulates liver to release sugar in times of stress
        3.   Adrenal medulla—releases epinephrine and norepinephrine to deal with stress
        4.   Note some body chemicals function both as hormones and neurotransmitters
    F.   Gonads—sex glands
        1.   Ovaries in women
            a)   Produce egg cells for reproduction
            b)   Secrete female hormones estrogen and progesterone
        2.   Testes in men—produce sperm cells and male sex hormone testosterone

III. Hormones and Behavior
    A.   Testosterone levels linked to aggressive behavior
    B.   Thyroid hormones—influence metabolism; related to behavior
    C.   PMS—hormones appear to play a role

SUMMARY

In this module, you learn about the human endocrine system. The endocrine system is composed of glands that are distributed throughout the body. It is closely related to our nervous system and, like the nervous system, is a means for the body to communicate. Communication is slower than that of the nervous system because glands communicate chemically through the secretion of hormones. The hormones are released directly into the bloodstream. They lock into receptor sites just like neurotransmitters do.

Endocrine activity is under the control of the brain, particularly the autonomic nervous system. In addition, the hypothalamus secretes hormones that influence the "master gland," the pituitary gland. The pituitary is so-named because it influences, through hormones, the activity of many other glands. The pituitary gland also secretes the hormone promoting growth.

Other important glands include the pancreas (regulating blood sugar concentration), the pineal (important to sleep-wake cycles), the adrenal glands (help us face stress) and the gonads (promote sexual characteristics and capability for reproduction). The thyroid gland regulates metabolism, the rate at which the body turns our food into energy. Variations in thyroid hormone levels are associated with different behavioral patterns.

KEY TERMS

Endocrine system

Pancreas

Homeostasis

Pituitary gland

Pineal gland

Adrenal gland

Gonads

Ovaries

Testes

Germ cells

Thyroid gland

Premenstrual syndrome (PMS)

SELF-TEST PRACTICE QUIZ:

Match the following Key Terms and definitions (note: not every Key Term will be used):

1. _____ A system for regulating activities in the body by means of glandular secretions

2. _____ Glands in the body which secrete stress hormones

3. _____ Female reproductive gonads that secrete estrogen and produce egg cells

4. _____ Regulates body metabolism; different hormone levels associated with differing behavioral characteristics

5. _____ The cells which unite to create a new human organism

6. _____ An organ in the body which regulates blood sugar concentration

7. _____ Releases serotonin; involved in sleep-wake cycles

8. _____ The "master gland"—secretes hormones that impact the functioning of other glands

a. Endocrine system

b. Pancreas

c. Homeostasis

d. Pituitary gland

e. Pineal gland

f. Adrenal gland

g. Gonads

h. Ovaries

i. Testes

j. Germ cells

k. Thyroid gland

l. Premenstrual syndrome (PMS)

9. _____ Glands related to sexual characteristics and the processes involved in reproduction

10. _____ A balanced internal body state

11. _____ Male reproductive gonads that secrete testosterone and produce sperm

12. _____ A period of psychological and hormonal changes which occur a few days before the onset of the menstrual cycle

13. What is the difference between hormones and neurotransmitters?
   a. Hormones have more complicated chemical structures than neurotransmitters.
   b. Hormones only affect physical behavior, while neurotransmitters only affect emotions.
   c. Hormones lock on to receptor sites, but neurotransmitters do not.
   d. Hormones travel throughout the body, while neurotransmitters are found only in the nervous system.

14. The activity of the pituitary gland is most influenced by
   a. the hypothalamus.
   b. the pineal gland.
   c. the adrenal glands.
   d. blood sugar levels.

15. Homeostasis means
   a. the body maintains a balanced internal state.
   b. there is a shortage of insulin and excessive blood sugar.
   c. the quantity of chemicals secreted is equaled by the quantity of chemicals absorbed.
   d. endocrine glands are distributed rather uniformly throughout the body.

ESSAY QUESTION

1. Discuss the relationship between hormones and behavior.

ANSWER KEY

1.   Endocrine system

2.   Adrenal glands

3.   Ovaries

4.   Thyroid gland

5.   Germ cells

6.   Pancreas

7.   Pineal gland

8.   Pituitary gland

9.   Gonads

10.   Homeostasis

11.   Testes

12.   Premenstrual syndrome

13.   d

14.   a

15.   a

SAMPLE ANSWER TO ESSAY QUESTION

1.   Hormones do appear to influence human behavior. We know that variations in levels of thyroid hormones are related to different kinds of behavior. Excess levels of thyroid hormones are associated with anxiety, whereas deficient levels of the hormones are associated with sluggishness, weight gain, and retarded intellectual development in children. Hormones seem to play a role in premenstrual syndrome (PMS); levels of estrogen and progesterone change dramatically in the days just preceding the start of a woman's period. In addition, testosterone may be one factor associated with aggression, and low levels of testosterone lead to loss of sexual desire for both males and females.

MODULE 2.7 GENES AND BEHAVIOR: A CASE OF NATURE AND NURTURE

LEARNING OBJECTIVES

After you have mastered the information in this unit, you will be able to:

1.   Understand the roles genetic factors play in behavior.

2.   Describe the methodologies used in researching genetic influences on behavior.

OUTLINE

I.   Genes
   A.   Composed of deoxyribonucleic acid (DNA)
   B.   Linked together on long strands called chromosomes
   C.   Found in cell nucleus

  D. A child receives 23 chromosomes from each parent
  E. Human genome now completely mapped
  F. Only twins share identical genetic code
 II. Genetic Influences on Behavior
  A. Nature-nurture problem still a debate in psychology
  B. Genotype dictates features and traits; phenotype determines whether they are expressed
  C. Many psychological characteristics may be polygenic traits
  D. Genetic factors establish a predisposition; characteristics may not necessarily appear
  E. Clear that genetic factors interact with environment
 III. Kinship Studies
  A. Familial association studies
   1. Closer genetic links related to more similar traits and behaviors
   2. Higher incidence of schizophrenia as genetic commonality increases
   3. Note people sharing close genetic links often share similar environment
  B. Twin studies
   1. Monozygotic (identical) twins—identical genetic inheritance
   2. Dizygotic (fraternal) twins—genetic commonality-like siblings
   3. Concordance rates suggest genetic contribution
   4. Identical twins more similar than fraternal twins on sociability, some psychological disorders
   5. Note identical twins may share greater environmental similarity
  C. Adoptee studies
   1. Adopted children compared to biological and adoptive parents
   2. Genetically identical (monozygotic) twins, reared apart
    a) Rare event, but a natural experiment
    b) Heredity seems to play major role in personality development
    c) Still cannot discount some shared-environment and/or personal contact influence

SUMMARY

In this module, you learn of the genetic influences on behavior. Nature refers to what we have inherited (the genetic code); nurture means our experiences as a result of our environment. Genes are composed of DNA and are linked together on chromosomes. This genetic information is carried in the nucleus of every typical body cell. Mapping of the human genome has been completed, and additional research is ongoing. We now know the precise chemical arrangement that comprises human DNA. The genetic code (genotype) is the basic blueprint of the characteristics a human may have. However, traits included in the genotype do not necessarily manifest themselves unless they become part of the phenotype—the features and traits we actually see in a person. The phenotype is the result not only of genetic inheritance but also of other factors, such as environmental experiences. Many psychological characteristics are complex and thus probably polygenic; that is, they result from a cluster of genes.

How can we study genetic influence more precisely? We use kinship studies, and especially studies involving individuals with an identical genetic heritage (monozygotic twins, triplets, and so forth). Familial association studies do tell us that the more genes there are in common, such as among close family members, the more similar traits and behaviors are likely to be. It is true, however, that close family members usually share the same or similar environment as well. Children who have been adopted are compared with both their adoptive and their biological parents. In the rare case where identical twins have been raised apart, evidence suggests that many personality characteristics and traits have a genetic basis.

KEY TERMS

Genotype

Genes

Deoxyribonucleic acid (DNA)

Chromosomes

Nature-nurture problem

Phenotype

Polygenic traits

Familial association studies

Identical twins

Zygote

Fraternal twins

Twin studies

Concordance rates

Adoptee studies

SELF-TEST PRACTICE QUIZ

Match the following Key Terms and definitions:

1. _____ An organism's observable traits

2. _____ Twins produced when one fertilized egg splits

3. _____ Comparing adopted children with biological and adoptive parents

4. _____ Underlying set of instructions determining organism's possible characteristics

5. _____ The challenge in distinguishing between influences due to environmental experience and those due to genetic inheritance

6. _____ The chemicals within chromosomes which determine genetic heritage

7. _____ A single-celled organism resulting from the union of an egg and a sperm

8. _____ The percentage of cases where both twins share the same trait or disorder

a.   Genotype

b.   Genes

c.   Deoxyribonucleic acid (DNA)

d.   Chromosomes

e.   Nature-nurture problem

f.   Phenotype

g.   Polygenic traits

h.   Familial association studies

i.   Identical twins

j.   Zygote

k.   Fraternal twins

l.   Twin studies

m.   Concordance rates

n.   Adoptee studies

9.   _____ Basic units of heredity; composed of DNA

10.   _____ The genetic source for many psychological characteristics

11.   _____ Twins who develop from different eggs fertilized by different sperm; no more genetically alike than other siblings

12.   _____ Long strands of genetic instructions found in the nuclei of cells

13.   _____ Genetic commonality is compared with exhibited traits

14.   _____ Investigating behavioral similarities between twins

15.   If a trait is largely due to genetics, then we would expect the highest concordance rate to be among
    a.   siblings who are not twins.
    b.   identical twins.
    c.   adopted children and their adoptive parents.
    d.   fraternal twins.

16.   Examining the relationship between close family members and their common behaviors is involved in
    a.   human genome mapping.
    b.   polygenetic traits.
    c.   familial association studies.
    d.   predisposition studies.

ESSAY QUESTIONS

1.   Why is it helpful to study identical twins raised separately when investigating genetic influences on behavior?

2.   When examining genetic influences on behavior (e.g., by looking at family members, identical and fraternal twins), what is a problem we nearly always encounter?

ANSWER KEY

1. Phenotype
2. Identical twins
3. Adoptee studies
4. Genotype
5. Nature-nurture problem
6. Deoxyribonucleic acid (DNA)
7. Zygote
8. Concordance rates
9. Genes
10. Polygenic traits
11. Fraternal twins
12. Chromosomes
13. Familial association studies
14. Twin studies
15. b
16. c

SAMPLE ANSWERS TO ESSAY QUESTIONS

1. It is helpful to study identical twins, especially those reared apart, because monozygotic twins share an identical genetic heritage. If they are raised in different environments, it is assumed that behaviors that remain similar or alike in both twins must be due to heredity. Anything influenced by environment would theoretically be different because each twin experienced a different environment. It should be remembered, however, that even though twins have been separated from birth or shortly thereafter and not raised in the same environment, the individual environments that they did experience may not have been that fundamentally different after all.

2. We examine genetic influence on behavior by looking at various family members. Family members, of course, share many of the same genes. Thus, we look for similar behavior traits where there are many genes in common. The problem that we encounter, however, is that very often genetically close family members reside in the same, or similar, environments. Once again, it becomes difficult to separate nature from nurture.

MODULE 2.8 APPLICATION: BIOFEEDBACK TRAINING: LEARNING BY LISTENING TO THE BODY

LEARNING OBJECTIVE

After you have mastered the information in this unit, you will be able to:

1. Understand the nature and the applications of biofeedback training.

OUTLINE

I.   Biofeedback Training (BFT)
  A.   Monitoring equipment provides information about internal bodily functions
  B.   Tones indicate changes in heart rate, brain wave patterns and the like
  C.   Individuals learn to adjust their physiological processes
  D.   Example: Relieving headaches
    1.   EMG feedback can aid in tension headaches
    2.   Thermal biofeedback can help with migraine headaches
    3.   Information is provided about forehead muscles, or blood flow

SUMMARY

In this Application module, you learn one way to apply the knowledge we have gained from physiological research. Biofeedback works on the principle that individuals can learn to listen to their body and thus help control some bodily processes. Monitoring equipment attached to an individual provides information regarding these processes; a tone may be used, for example. People learn when they are changing a physiological process by hearing changes in the tone. Biofeedback is particularly used to help reduce pain and other undesirable symptoms.

CHAPTER 2   APPLICATION EXERCISE

Take a five-minute slice of time from your day during waking hours. Write down everything that you do for those five minutes. Now, analyze the components of your body utilized during each of the activities you listed (it might almost be easier to list the components not used! You can see how very integrated our whole physiological system is). What part of your nervous system was involved? What particular brain structures were used? Do you think your glandular system was part of your activity for those five minutes? If so, how? Can you think of any neurotransmitters that might have been particularly involved? What pathways, and what directions did your neural transmissions travel? Did you attempt in any way to control or modify your various physiological processes?

CHAPTER 3

Sensation and Perception

In Chapter 3, you are introduced to the basic concepts that comprise the processes of sensation and perception. Sensation and perception are two different things. Sensation occurs at the level of your senses and includes all the information impinging on your sensory receptors. Note that there are very many stimuli in the world that can constantly bombard you—triggering reactions in your eyes, ears, nose, and skin, for example. Suppose all of this information traveled all the way to the cerebral cortex in your brain? You would be on overload, indeed!

Fortunately, much of the information that your senses can detect is filtered out, and only a small portion is transmitted to your brain where it can be further processed. Perception occurs in the brain, and the process of perception involves the brain receiving the incoming stimuli, then organizing and making meaningful interpretations of it. The brain may process in either a top-down or bottom-up fashion. Gestalt principles are important in perception, helping us understand how the brain can determine what we perceive as meaningful wholes. Clearly, the brain's understanding of current phenomena has much to do with information stored from prior experiences.

Information about the world is transmitted via your sensory nervous system. This process begins with your sensory receptors, the nerve cells specialized to detect stimuli in the environment. For vision, the retina of the eye contains the rods and cones (called rods and cones because that is what each looks like). These sensory receptors detect wavelengths of light energy that enter the eye. Each wavelength corresponds to what we would perceive as a color. It is important that the wavelengths land directly on the fovea in the retina. This aids in color vision and visual acuity. For the sense of hearing, wavelengths create vibrations in the ear, which, like visual input, are converted to neural signals. These impulses are transmitted by the auditory nerve to the brain. Hearing loss is occurring largely as a result of years of living loudly. Several theories exist for how we detect color, and also how we determine the pitch of a sound. For both processes it seems to take more than one theory to explain how they occur.

Smell and taste are both conveyed by means of chemical molecules. A chemical molecule from the environment must fit one of the sensory receptors in the nose or tongue region—otherwise the stimulus is not detected. Skin sense receptors are distributed throughout your body. Your skin responds not only to touch, but to pressure, pain, cold, and warmth. With all your senses, the human body is very sensitive—but only to a certain range of stimuli. That is, for vision for example, there are many, many electromagnetic energy frequencies zipping around in your world. Your receptors, however, can detect only a certain amount of these. For color, as conveyed by light, the wavelengths to which we are sensitive make up the visible spectrum; our sensory receptors simply cannot detect other wavelengths in the environment. This phenomenon is true for all your senses. Unless a receptor exists for a certain wavelength, vibration, chemical molecule or the like, you will not be able to detect that stimulus. It's a little spooky to consider that there are things in our environment we cannot perceive!

All stimuli impinging on your senses must reach a certain minimum threshold in order to be detected. To a degree, this minimum is affected by how sensitive, alert, healthy and attuned an organism is. Once sensory information is received, we use perceptual cues to organize and interpret this information. Visual perception, for example, utilizes both monocular (one eye is sufficient) and binocular cues from the environment. Monocular cues include linear perspective and relative size. Binocular cues usually incorporate the phenomenon known as retinal disparity—the fact that each eye sends the brain a slightly differing image. The brain then integrates and interprets this information.

Sometimes we are misled by the perceptual cues we rely on, as in the case of visual illusions. Scientists have studied subliminal perception and paranormal phenomena, such as ESP. There is some evidence that subliminal perception does indeed occur. On the other hand, as yet, reliable and replicable scientific evidence does not exist for extrasensory perception. At least at present, it's likely no one can read your mind!

MODULE 3.1 SENSING OUR WORLD: BASIC CONCEPTS OF SENSATION

LEARNING OBJECTIVES:

After you have mastered the information in this unit, you will be able to:

1. Define and explain the process of sensation.

2. Describe the difference between absolute threshold and difference threshold.

3. Know the factors that contribute to signal detection.

4. Discuss the concept of sensory adaptation.

OUTLINE

I.   Sensation
    A.   Process by which we receive, transform, and process stimuli presented to sensory organs
    B.   Information converted to neural impulses for the brain to process into meaningful impressions
    C.   Begins with sensory receptors
        1.   Found in sensory organs (vision, hearing, taste, smell, touch, joints, muscles and skin)
        2.   Detect and transform stimuli from the outside world
    D.   Psychophysics
        1.   How we experience such physical stimuli
        2.   Begun with work of Gustav Fechner
            a) Some historians believe his publication in 1860 signaled the beginning of the scientific approach to psychology

II.   Absolute and Difference Thresholds
    A.   Absolute threshold
        1.   Smallest amount of stimulus reliably detected
        2.   Variation in sensitivity among individuals
    B.   Difference threshold
        1.   Just-noticeable difference (jnd)
        2.   Weber's law – studied the smallest differences between stimuli that people were able to perceive
        3.   Must change stimulus by a constant proportion for change to be detected
        4.   Constants are given for various senses
            a) People are more sensitive to changes in pitch than changes in volume

III.   Signal Detection
    A.   Signals are stimuli impinging on organism
    B.   Threshold for detection depends on:
        1.   Intensity of signal
        2.   Background stimulation or noise
        3.   Individual sensitivity and physical condition
        4.   Attention (fatigue or alertness) and motivation (example – hunger) of receiver

IV. Sensory Adaptation
   A.   Becoming less sensitive to unchanging stimuli
   B.   Will not happen when stimulus is very, very strong
        a) Very strong depends on the receiver – example a person working in the stock yards eating lunch outside on the property

SUMMARY

In this module, you learn how the process of detecting what is going on in the outside world actually begins. First, information must be sensed—that is, received by sensory receptors within our sense organs. Our sense organs are our eyes, nose, mouth, etc., and also body muscles, joints, and skin. Sensory receptors receive physical inputs from the world and convert them into a form your body can use—into the neural impulses with which your brain and the rest of your nervous system communicates. Thus, once signals are converted, your nervous system can use this information.

Not all stimuli in the world can be detected. A stimulus must be present in a sufficient amount to reach the absolute threshold for detection relevant to that particular sense. This minimum amount that can be reliably detected is known as the absolute threshold. There also must be a sufficient increase or decrease in the amount of stimulus presented in order for an individual to determine that there has been a change. This amount for detection of change is known as the just-noticeable difference (jnd), and for each sense it is a constant proportion (Weber's law). Detection of signals (sensory stimuli) is governed by stimulus intensity, background factors, sensitivity, one's overall physical condition, and how alert and attuned the receiving individual is. Repeated presentations of unchanging stimuli can lead to sensory adaptation where sensitivity decreases, but not if the stimulus is extremely strong.

KEY TERMS
Sensation

Sensory receptors

Psychophysics

Absolute threshold

Difference threshold

Weber's law

Signal-detection theory

Sensory adaptation

SELF-TEST PRACTICE QUIZ
Match the following Key Terms and definitions (note: not every Key Term will be used):

1. _____ The amount of stimulus change that can be detected is a constant

2. _____ The process by which we receive, transform and process impinging stimuli

3. _____ Factors related to the human's ability to detect a stimulus

a.   Sensation

b.   Sensory receptors

c.   Psychophysics

d.   Absolute threshold

e.   Difference threshold

f.   Weber's law

g.   Signal-detection theory

4. _____ The minimum amount of stimulus we can reliably detect

5. _____ Nervous system cells specialized to detect outside stimuli

6. _____ Reduced sensitivity to an unchanging stimulus

7. _____ The minimum amount of stimulus we can reliably detect

8. _____ 1860 publication signaling the beginning of the scientific approach to psychology

h.   Sensory adaptation

i.   Gustav Fechner

9. The very first step in understanding behavior and mental processes is understanding the process of

    a.   sensory adaptation.
    b.   signal detection.
    c.   perception.
    d.   sensation.

10. _____ is the study of how we experience physical stimulation.

    a.   Weber's law
    b.   Psychophysics
    c.   Sensory adaptation
    d.   Neurometrics

81. The minimum amount of a stimulus necessary for a human to detect that that stimulus is present is known as the

    a.   minimum threshold.
    b.   absolute threshold.
    c.   difference threshold.
    d.   just-noticeable difference.

92. Physical stimuli impinging upon our senses are first detected by

    a.   sensory receptors.
    b.   perceptual mechanisms in the brain.
    c.   sensory adaptation mechanisms.
    d.   the visual and auditory channels.

103. Information from the environment must take a(n)_____ form in order for the nervous system to utilize the information.

    a.   auditory
    b.   visual
    c.   neural impulse
    d.   somatosensory

114. When you first put on a shirt, you are aware of the change in pressure, but after a short while you usually cease to notice the weight of the shirt. This illustrates the concept of

    a.   signal detection.
    b.   the absolute threshold.
    c.   the just-noticeable difference.
    d.   sensory adaptation.

125. At low volumes, people are sensitive to even small changes in loudness, while at higher volumes the same small change may not even be noticeable. This is an illustration of
    a.   Weber's Law.
    b.   the absolute threshold.
    c.   a sensory receptor.
    d.   signal-detection theory.

136. Which concept explains why you are more likely to notice a person's voice if you were specifically trying to listen for that particular person?
    a.   The difference threshold
    b.   Signal-detection theory
    c.   Weber's Law
    d.   Psychophysics

ESSAY QUESTION

1.   Certainly, how intense a stimulus is and how frequently it is presented to you are factors related to whether you will detect that stimulus or not. Based on signal-detection theory, what other considerations are there with regard to the human detection of physical energies?

ANSWER KEY

1. Weber's law

2. Sensation

3. Signal-detection theory

4. Absolute threshold

5. Sensory receptors

6. Sensory adaptation

7. Difference threshold

8. i

9. d

10. b

11. b

12. a

13. c

14. d

15. a

16. b

SAMPLE ANSWER TO ESSAY QUESTION

1. Signal-detection theory also considers other features in the process of sensation. These features include characteristics of the background, such as how noisy and/or distracting the setting is. Whether or not a stimulus is detected also depends on physical and psychological characteristics of the receiver, as well as general health, the acuity of the sense organ, state of alertness and degree of motivation.

MODULE 3.2 VISION: SEEING THE LIGHT

LEARNING OBJECTIVES

After you have mastered the information in this unit, you will be able to:

1. Explain how the eyes process light.

2. Describe feature detectors and the role they play in visual processing.

3. Know the two major theories of color vision.

4. Identify the two major forms of color blindness in humans.

OUTLINE

I. Light: The Energy of Vision
    A. Physical energy is the source – the brain interprets
    B. Electromagnetic radiation
        1. Visible spectrum is a small portion of entire spectrum
        2. Wavelengths correspond to the experience of different colors – order of colors Roy G. Biv – Red, Orange, Yellow, Green, Blue ,etc.

II. The Eye: The Visionary Sensory Organ
    A. Contains the sensory receptors to detect light
    B. Parts of the eye
        1. Cornea—transparent covering on the surface of the eye
        2. Iris
            a) Muscle surrounding pupil; adjusts to permit entry of light
            b) Adjustment in reaction to light is reflexive
        3. Pupil—size of opening is controlled by iris
        4. Lens—changes shape to adjust to distance of object (accommodation)
        5. Retina
            a) Receives the image created by light striking it
            b) Contains photoreceptors (receptor cells that are sensitive to light) —rods – 120 million – more sensitive to light – peripheral vision and vision in dim lights and cones – 6 million – allow us to detect colors and to discern fine details of objects under bright illumination
                1. Some animals, including certain birds, have only cones in their eyes – they see only during daylight hours when the cones are activated
        6. Bipolar cells—interconnecting cells
        7. Ganglion cells—each projecting axon is one nerve fiber
        8. Optic nerve
            a) Large bundle of ganglion nerve fibers
            b) Transmits visual information to the brain
            c) Creates blind spot
        9. Fovea
            a) Contains only cones
            b) Site for sharpest vision
            c) Nearsightedness (unusually close to see) and farsightedness (far away to see) result from abnormalities in the shape of the eye

III. Feature Detectors: Getting Down to Basics
    A. Nerve cells in visual cortex
    B. Respond to specific features of the visual stimulus

      C.   Higher order brain processes must integrate these individual messages – long way from understanding how the brain transforms sensory stimulation into the visual world

IV. Color Vision: Sensing a Colorful World

      A.   Color receptors (cones) transmit different messages to the brain—depending on wavelength

      B.   Hermann von Helmholtz—trichromatic theory
           1.   Three types of color receptors—for red, green, and blue-violet
           2.   Other colors result from combinations of these three

      C.   Ewald Hering—opponent-process theory
           1.   Afterimages—image seen on neutral surface after other visual stimulation
           2.   Three sets of color receptors that work in either-or pairs – example, red is the afterimage of green, white of black and blue of yellow

      D.   Both theories correct regarding some parts of vision

      E.   Color blindness due to missing one or more types of cones
           1.   Trichromats—people with normal color vision who can see full color spectrum
           2.   Monochromats—have only one of the cones; see only in black and white
           3.   Dichromats—have two of the three cones; can't distinguish between certain color types
           4.   Red-green color blindness appears to be a sex-linked genetic defect that is carried on the X sex chromosome – 8% of men and 17% of women have some form of color blindness (Bennett, 2009)

SUMMARY

In this module, you are presented with basic information regarding how the process of vision works. Vision begins with light, which occurs in our environment in the form of electromagnetic energy. This energy enters our eyes as wavelengths. Not all of electromagnetic radiation is visual information we can detect; only a small portion of these wavelengths (those ranging from 300 to 750 nanometers) falls within the visible spectrum. The shortest wavelength we can detect corresponds to what we see as violet; the longest wavelength corresponds to what we see as red. The Roy G. Biv acronym we may have learned refers to the colors of the visible spectrum, arranged in order of decreasing wavelength.

Light enters the eye through the pupil, the diameter of which is controlled by the iris. If light is very bright, the iris makes the pupil small; conversely, when there is little light the iris widens the pupil, which allows us to see more clearly. The lens changes shape in order to best direct incoming light to the retina, where it will be processed by photoreceptors. Cones can detect color and provide acuity, but need bright light to work well. Rods, the other photoreceptors, function well in dim light, but cannot process color. Rods also provide our peripheral vision. Very specific features of a visual stimulus are conveyed by neurons known as feature detectors. The visual cortex in the brain combines incoming information to yield meaningful visual patterns.

There are two theories explaining how a human detects color, and both seem to account for parts of this process of vision. Helmholtz's trichromatic theory proposes that three different types of photoreceptors (cones) process one of three basic colors: red, green, and blue-violet. According to this theory, all other colors result from combinations of these three. The opponent-process theory, proposed by Hering, suggests that there are three photoreceptors in the retina but each works as a pair of receptors—when "on" for one color in the pair, the receptor is "off" for the other. This latter theory helps explain some visual phenomena, such as afterimages. Evidence does show there are three kinds of cone receptors, and cells that process color vision information sent from the cones do operate as Hering described. Color blindness is caused by a genetic defect where one or more type of photoreceptor is lacking.

KEY TERMS

Cornea

Iris

Pupil

Lens

Accommodation

Retina

Photoreceptors

Rods

Cones

Bipolar cells

Ganglion cells

Optic nerve

Blind spot

Fovea

Feature detectors

Trichromatic theory

Afterimage

Opponent-process theory

Trichromats

Monochromats

Dichromats

SELF-TEST PRACTICE QUIZ

Match the following Key Terms and definitions (note: not every Key Term will be used):

1. _____ Part of the retina with a concentration of cone cells; color processing and acuity most effective here

2. _____ Color vision theory proposing that each photoreceptor processes one basic color; other colors are a combination of these three

3. _____ Photoreceptors that process color and provide sharpness of image

a.   Cornea

b.   Iris

c.   Pupil

d.   Lens

e.   Accommodation

f.   Retina

g.   Photoreceptors

h.   Rods

4. _____ A transparent covering on the eye's surface

5. _____ The changing of the shape of the lens to help direct an incoming image onto the retina

6. _____ Hering's view that the three photoreceptors are pairs of receptors; stimulation of one color on pair leads to inhibition of processing of the other color

7. _____ The black opening in the center of the iris; light enters the eye this way

8. _____ Neural mechanism that transmits visual information from the retina to the brain; creates blind spot on retina

9. _____ The eye structure which, using the process of accommodation, helps incoming light to land on the retina

10. _____ Individuals lacking one of the three types of cones used in visual color processing

11. _____ Specialized neurons in the visual cortex; they respond to very specific visual stimuli

12. _____ Colored muscle surrounding the pupil; adjusts to amount of available light

13. _____ The lining on the back inner surface of the eye; contains photoreceptors

14. _____ Photoreceptors for peripheral vision and visual activity in dim light

15. _____ Axons of these cells are the nerve fibers in the optic nerve

16. _____ Specialized cells in the eyes retina which are sensitive to light

i.   Cones

j.   Bipolar cells

k.   Ganglion cells

l.   Optic nerve

m.   Blind spot

n.   Fovea

o.   Feature detectors

p.   Trichromatic theory

q.   Afterimage

r.   Opponent-process theory

s.   Trichromats

t.   Monochromats

u.   Dichromats

17. How much electromagnetic radiation can we see?
   a.   All of it
   b.   Most of it
   c.   Some of it
   d.   None of it

18. Wavelengths entering our eyes are measured in terms of
    a. nanometers.
    b. feet.
    c. inches.
    d. centimeters.
19. Which type of color blindness is most common?
    a. Monochromatic color blindness
    b. Blue-yellow color blindness
    c. Red-green color blindness
    d. all of the above
20. The blind spot in our vision occurs because
    a. receptors cannot work in very dim light.
    b. the wavelengths we are processing have landed on the fovea.
    c. there are no receptors in the visual cortex.
    d. it corresponds to the position of the optic nerve in the retina.
21. Photoreceptors best used when we want sharp vision are
    a. densely concentrated in the region known as the fovea.
    b. called cones because that is the appearance of their shape.
    c. only really effective when operating in bright light.
    d. all of the above are correct.
22. When the eyeball is too long, or the cornea is very curved, an individual experiences
    a. tunnel vision.
    b. nearsightedness.
    c. farsightedness.
    d. monochromatism.
23. At night, we often see better using peripheral vision than if we look at an object directly. This is because _____ are more densely packed at the periphery of the retina.
    a. cones
    b. rods
    c. ganglion cells
    d. bipolar cells
24. The existence of afterimages can be explained by the _____ theory.
    a. dichromatic
    b. feature detector
    c. trichromatic
    d. opponent-process

ESSAY QUESTIONS

1. Briefly explain how feature detectors work. Where are they located?
2. Compare and contrast the two theories of color vision. Give at least one example of visual phenomena that support each point of view.

ANSWER KEY

1.   Fovea
2.   Trichromatic theory
3.   Cones
4.   Cornea
5.   Accommodation
6.   Opponent-process theory
7.   Pupil
8.   Optic nerve
9.   Lens
10. Dichromats
11. Feature detectors
12. Iris
13. Retina
14. Rods
15. Ganglion cells
16. Photoreceptors
17. c.
18. a
19. c
20. d
21. d
22. b
23. b
24. d

SAMPLE ANSWERS TO ESSAY QUESTIONS

1.   Feature detectors are specialized neurons within the visual cortex in the brain. They respond to very specific features of visual stimuli, such as particular angles, various orientations of lines, and stimuli following particular patterns of movement. These neurons respond only when the specific stimulus characteristics are presented.

2.   One theory of color vision, proposed by Helmholtz, says that there are three photoreceptors (cones), and each cone responds to a particular color wavelength. These colors are red, green, and blue-violet, and all other detected colors result from combinations of these three. This view proposed by Helmholtz is known as the trichromatic theory. Indeed, we do experience other colors (such as yellow) from combinations of the basic three.

A second theory of color vision, suggested by Hering, also confirms that there are three photoreceptors to process stimuli for color. This second theory, called the opponent-process theory, proposes that each photoreceptor has two components. Color processing occurs as the photoreceptor components work in pairs—when a receptor for one color is active, the paired receptor is inhibited. Suggested color pairings are red-green, blue-yellow, and black-white. The experience of afterimages supports the opponent-process view. Research overall suggests portions of both theories are correct.

MODULE 3.3 HEARING: THE MUSIC OF SOUND

LEARNING OBJECTIVES

After you have mastered the information in this unit, you will be able to:

1. Describe how the ear processes sound.

2. Understand what determines the perception of pitch.

3. Identify the main types and causes of deafness.

OUTLINE

I.   Sound: Sensing Waves of Vibrations – converted into electrical signals that are sent to the brain
    A.   Audition (hearing) is detecting energy that travels in waves (vibrations)
    B.   Unlike light (that can travel through the empty outer space), sound must have a medium such as air liquids, gases or even solids in order to exist - light travels faster than sound – see lightening and 5 seconds later you hear the sound
    C.   Characteristics
        1.   Amplitude (loudness)—the height of a wave
        2.   Frequency—number of complete waves, or cycles, per second
        3.   Travels much more slowly than light
        4.   Measured in decibels (dB), an indication of perceived loudness
        5.   Perception of pitch is related to wave frequency – shorter equals higher pitch
II. The Ear: A Sound Machine
    A.   Sound waves are captured and converted to neural form
    B.   Ear components
        1.   Eardrum— tight membrane that vibrates in response to sound waves
        2.   Ossicles—three tiny bones in middle ear that transmit vibration further
            a)   Hammer (*malleus*)
            b)   Anvil (*incus*)
            c)   Stirrup (*stapes*)
        3.   Oval window—membrane connecting to inner ear
        4.   Cochlea—fluid-filled snail-shaped bony tube
        5.   Basilar membrane—vibrates within the cochlea
        6.   Organ of Corti—gelatinous structure lined with hair cells
        7.   Hair cells—auditory receptors (bend in response to movement of basilar membrane)
        8.   Auditory nerve—transmits auditory messages to brain's auditory cortex
    C.   Determining source of sound
        1.   Location (direction) of sound determined by disparity between two ears' messages
        2.   More distant sounds—softer, also aids in determining location
III. Perception of Pitch: Perceiving the Highs and Lows
    A.   Place theory – high frequency sounds
        1.   Developed by Hermann von Helmholtz

      2.   Perceived sound related to vibration location on basilar membrane
      3.   High frequencies—vibration near oval window
      4.   Low frequencies—further down basilar membrane
   B.   Frequency theory
      1.   May best account for perception of lowest-frequency sounds
      2.   Basilar membrane vibrates at same frequency as sound wave
      3.   Limitations – neurons cannot fire more frequently than 1,000 times per second
   C.   Volley principle (alternating successions) —helps explain how mid-range sounds are detected – those sounds that are from 1000 – 4000 cycles per second
IV.   Hearing Loss –birth defects, disease, advanced age (not inevitable), injury, exposure to loud noise
   A.   Conduction deafness
      1.   Damage to middle ear—eardrum or ossicles
      2.   Hearing aids may help this problem
   B.   Nerve deafness—damage to hair cells or to auditory nerve
   C.   For protection avoid excessive noise, wear earplugs -
   D.   Expectations for future hearing loss because of years of living loudly, a by-product of listening to earsplitting music on personal music devices, (Noonan, 2006) the clamor at most bars and clubs and attending rock concerts

SUMMARY

In this module, you learn about the sense of hearing. Sound, like light, travels in the form of waves, though sound travels much more slowly. The waves are vibrations, reflecting changes in pressure of air or water. Unlike the process of vision, however, sound must have a medium through which to travel. This is why we can hear even through a wall or through water. Characteristics of a sound wave include amplitude, which conveys loudness, and frequency—how many complete waves, or cycles, per second. These waves must be converted into neural impulses in order to be used by your body.

The outer ear is shaped to help capture sound waves. Waves next go to the eardrum, which vibrates and passes the message to the ossicles. These little bones vibrate in turn, and the last passes the vibration on to the oval window. The cochlea, basilar membrane, organ of Corti, and auditory nerve complete the chain for the transmission of sound. Both place theory and frequency theory help explain the perception of pitch, along with a combination of the two called the volley principle. Deafness is due to failures in sound wave transmissions, either from middle ear damage, which can be rectified to a degree, or from more serious damage, such as to the auditory nerve. Many types of auditory damage can be prevented.

KEY TERMS

Audition

Pitch

Eardrum

Ossicles

Oval window

Cochlea

Basilar membrane

Organ of Corti

Hair cells

Auditory nerve

Place theory

Frequency theory

Volley principle

Conduction deafness

Nerve deafness

SELF-TEST PRACTICE QUIZ

Match the following Key Terms and definitions (note: not every Key Term will be used):

1. _____ Auditory receptors triggered by basilar membrane vibration

2. _____ A bony tube in the inner ear, filled with fluid

3. _____ The neural mechanism by which auditory messages are transmitted to the brain

4. _____ Deafness due to damage to hair cells, or the auditory nerve

5. _____ How high or low a sound is (related to frequency)

6. _____ The process of hearing

7. _____ An explanation for hearing which best accounts for higher-pitched sounds

8. _____ The little bones in the middle ear: the hammer, anvil, and stirrup

9. _____ A structure within the cochlea

10. _____ A gelatinous structure, lined with hair cells

11. _____ The membrane to which the stirrup is attached

12. _____ A tight membrane receiving sound waves from the outer ear

a. Audition

b. Pitch

c. Eardrum

d. Ossicles

e. Oval window

f. Cochlea

g. Basilar membrane

h. Organ of Corti

i. Hair cells

j. Auditory nerve

k. Place theory

l. Frequency theory

m. Volley principle

n. Conduction deafness

o. Nerve deafness

13. Place theory best explains pitch perception for
    a. high-frequency sounds.
    b. mid-range sounds.
    c. low-frequency sounds.
    d. mid-range to high frequency sounds.

14. In what way is audition much like the process of vision?
    a. Information is transmitted by means of wavelengths.
    b. Information travels at about the same rate.
    c. A unified theory explains how each sense operates.
    d. Both need a medium in which to exist.

15. Loudness is conveyed by the _____ of a sound wave.
    a. length
    b. height (amplitude)
    c. frequency
    d. duration
16. According to your text, approximately what percentage of American teens report having at least one symptom of hearing loss?
    a. 0%
    b. 10%
    c. 50%
    d. 90%
17. A sound of 20 decibels is _____ louder than a sound of 10 decibels.
    a. two times
    b. five times
    c. ten times
    d. twenty times
18. Loss of hearing due to damage to the eardrum or ossicles
    a. is known as nerve deafness.
    b. cannot be remedied through the use of hearing aids.
    c. leads to greater vibration in the oval window.
    d. is known as conduction deafness.
19. The actual sensory receptors in the process of audition are
    a. the middle ear bones.
    b. the hair cells in the organ of Corti.
    c. found in various locations along the basilar membrane.
    d. found in all parts of the ear.
20. How does your brain determine where a sound is coming from?
    a. By comparing how long it takes for sound to reach each ear
    b. By analyzing the frequency of sound waves
    c. By vibrating the basilar membrane
    d. none of the above

ESSAY QUESTIONS

1. Put the following in order to reflect the sequence in which a sound vibration is transmitted: organ of Corti, eardrum, ossicles, outer ear, oval window, hair cells, and basilar membrane.

2. Why are women's voices perceived as higher in pitch than men's?

3. How does the volley principle explain shortcomings in the place and frequency theories?

ANSWER KEY

1. Hair cells
2. Cochlea
3. Auditory nerve
4. Nerve deafness
5. Pitch
6. Audition
7. Place theory
8. Ossicles
9. Basilar membrane
10. Organ of Corti
11. Oval window
12. Eardrum
13. a
14. a
15. b
16. c
17. c
18. d
19. b
20. a

SAMPLE ANSWERS TO ESSAY QUESTIONS

1. The order in which these organs in the ear will experience incoming sound waves is: outer ear, eardrum, ossicles, oval window, basilar membrane, organ of Corti, and hair cells.

2. Women's vocal cords are shorter and thus vibrate at a greater frequency. The frequency of the occurrence of sound waves entering the ear is related to the pitch that is perceived by a listener. In general the greater the frequency, the higher the pitch that a listener hears. Since women have shorter vocal cords and shorter vocal cords have a higher frequency of vibration, women's voices are perceived as having a higher pitch. The same holds true, for example, with a harp.

3. Several theories thus far are needed to explain the process of hearing. The place theory (location on the basilar membrane) best explains our hearing of high-pitched sounds. Frequency theory (vibration of the membrane in accord with the actual sound wave) best accounts for low-pitched sounds. The volley principle is needed to explain how we detect mid-range (1,000 – 4,000 cycles/sec) waves. Groups of basilar membrane neurons fire in rotation, detecting these sounds.

MODULE 3.4 OUR OTHER SENSES: CHEMICAL, SKIN, AND BODY SENSES

LEARNING OBJECTIVES

After you have mastered the information in this unit, you will be able to:

1. Describe how odors are sensed.

2. Explain how tastes are sensed.

3. Discuss the skin senses and the sensation of pain.

4. Describe the kinesthetic and vestibular senses.

OUTLINE

I.   Other Senses in the Human Body
   A. Human has more than the five usually thought of senses (sight, hearing, smell, taste and touch)
   B. Receptors include chemical, skin and body senses
II. Olfaction: What Your Nose Knows
   A. Chemicals in the air that the nose can respond to – critical to our survival
   B. Lock-and-key fitting of molecules into odor receptors
   C. Olfactory nerve—transmits odor information to brain
   D. Olfactory bulb—brain destination; odor information does not travel through thalamus
   E. Aroma actually crucial to the experience of taste
   F. Smell intensity related to number of receptors stimulated simultaneously
   G. Pheromones—chemical substances that play a role in behavior in animals but in humans there is not enough evidence; note close relationship between odors and emotional memories
III. Taste: The Flavorful Sense – important role in adaption and survival
   A. Four basic tastes: sweet, sour, salty, and bitter
   B. Flavors are a result of combinations of these tastes, along with aroma, texture, temperature
   C. Taste cells—nerve cells that are taste receptors, located in taste buds
   D. Taste buds—pores or openings on tongue (and surrounding area)
   E. Taste receptors regenerate quickly, since they are frequently destroyed [by very hot food]
   F. Taste preferences, sensitivity—partly genetic, probably some cultural influences
   G. Supertasters (overly sensitive to some tastes – one in four people more women than men (Goode, 2001a) —have a very dense network of taste buds
   H. People with no tongues can sense taste through taste receptors on the roof of the mouth, inside the cheeks and the throat
   I. Cultural background play a part in taste preferences – spicy foods activate receptors that detect warmth (Aamodt & Wang, 2008); brain senses produce a natural sweating response
   J. Genetic factors influence a preference for sugary foods (Eny et al., 2008)
IV. The Skin Senses: Your Largest Sensory Organ
   A. Code information regarding touch, pressure, warmth, cold, and pain
   B. Sensory receptors distributed throughout body
   C. Somatosensory cortex—brain region processing skin sense information
   D. Specific receptors for warmth and cold
   E. Pain messages important—a signal that something is wrong located not only in the skin but in other parts (muscles, joints, ligaments and pulp of the teeth); acute pain in fingers and face

F.   Gate-control theory of pain—pain messages may be regulated via a neural gateway
G.   Acupuncture may release endorphins—natural painkillers
H.   First sharp pangs of pain cannot be blocked out – ice packs produce sensations of cold that help create a bottleneck at the gate in the spinal cord
V.   The Kinesthetic and Vestibular Senses: Of Grace and Balance
  A.   Kinesthesis tells us about body position and body movement
  B.   Vestibular sense monitors body position in space
    1.   Aids in keeping one's balance
    2.   Informs whether we are moving quickly, slowly, or reverse
    3.   The ear's semicircular canals—movement of fluid relates body position information
    4.   Dizziness: semicircular canal fluid still moving though we have stopped

SUMMARY

In this module, you learn about your other body senses: smell, taste, and skin senses. Your skin sense conveys more than just touch; it also relays information about pain, pressure, warmth, and cold. Senses discussed in this module also include the kinesthetic and vestibular senses, which tell you about your body movement, direction, speed, and balance.

The senses of smell and taste are both based on chemical molecules, which may or may not fit into receptors in your nose and mouth. We can only sense, in terms of taste or smell, what we have receptors for. Odor receptors are located in the nose. Taste receptors are imbedded within the taste buds, most of which are on the tongue but which also can be found in mouth regions near the tongue.

Detecting a taste or an odor depends on whether the chemical molecule fits, like a key into a lock, the sensory receptor it reaches. If so, then information about that particular molecule is passed on to the brain. Information about odors is relayed directly to the olfactory bulb; unlike other sensory input, this information does not first pass through the thalamus. If many receptors are stimulated at once, flavors or smells are more intense. Our sense of smell has a lot to do with our experience of taste.

The skin is your body's largest organ, and information from skin receptors is processed in the brain's somatosensory cortex. You have sensory receptors for skin information distributed throughout your body. Pain messages in the body may be monitored via the gate-control theory, suggesting that factors influence whether the pain message is relayed or not. The body produces endorphins, which are natural painkillers. The vestibular sense helps you keep your balance, know where your body is in space, and if and how it is moving through space. Your kinesthetic sense helps you know about movement of your various body parts, and what position they are in relative to one another. Your sense of balance is related to the movement of fluid in the semicircular canals within your inner ear.

KEY TERMS

Olfaction

Olfactory nerve

Olfactory bulb

Pheromones

Taste cells

Taste buds

Skin senses

Gate-control theory of pain

Acupuncture

Kinesthesis

Vestibular sense

Semicircular canals

Vestibular sacs

SELF-TEST PRACTICE QUIZ

Match the following Key Terms and definitions:

1. _____ Sensory receptors for taste

2. _____ Chemical substances that may play a role in human behavior

3. _____ Inserting thin needles into the body and rotating them—to aid healing

4. _____ Transmits information about odors to the brain

5. _____ Fluid-filled portion of inner ear; relay information about movement

6. _____ Receptors that convey information about touch, pressure, warmth, cold, and pain

7. _____ A sense that monitors position and movement of the body in space; aids balance

8. _____ Openings in the tongue; contain taste cells

9. _____ The sense of smell

10. _____ Structures in the ear that connect the semicircular canals; also relay information about head position and movement

11. _____ A brain structure that processes information about odors

12. _____ The sense of body movement and interrelation of body parts and positions

13. _____ The notion that neural messages from the spinal cord may not be passed on to brain

14. Which of these is NOT one of the four basic tastes?

    a. Sweet
    b. Sour
    c. Salty
    d. Spicy

a. Olfaction

b. Olfactory nerve

c. Olfactory bulb

d. Pheromones

e. Taste cells

f. Taste buds

g. Skin senses

h. Gate-control theory of pain

i. Acupuncture

j. Kinesthesis

k. Vestibular sense

l. Semicircular canals

m. Vestibular sacs

15. Which is the largest sense organ in your body?
    a. Skin
    b. Kinesthetic
    c. Vestibular
    d. Visual
16. The _____ sense allows you to know whether or not your arms are raised, even when your eyes are closed.
    a. olfactory
    b. skin
    c. vestibular
    d. kinesthetic

ESSAY QUESTIONS

1. How do we detect odors and tastes to which we are exposed?

2. What are pheromones, and what role might they play in human and animal behavior?

3. Briefly explain the gate-control theory of pain.

ANSWER KEY

1. Taste cells
2. Pheromones
3. Acupuncture
4. Olfactory nerve
5. Semicircular canals
6. Skin senses
7. Vestibular sense
8. Taste buds
9. Olfaction
10. Vestibular sacs
11. Olfactory bulb
12. Kinesthesis
13. Gate-control theory of pain
14. c
15. a
16. d

SAMPLE ANSWERS TO ESSAY QUESTIONS

1. Odors and tastes are both transmitted by means of chemical molecules. We have sensory receptors for only some of the chemical molecules to which we are exposed. If a chemical molecule fits one of our sensory receptor sites, its presence is then detected and such information is relayed to the brain.

2. Pheromones are chemical substances that species emit, which may then play a role in behaviors exhibited among members of that species. Pheromones emitted by animals are involved in mating behavior, marking territory, obtaining food, establishing dominance, and managing aggression. Human pheromones and organs for detection have not been found.

3. The gate-control theory of pain suggests that we may or may not feel all the pain messages that are produced in our nervous system. Nerve fibers that conduct pain messages through neural gateways in the spinal cord are thinner and slower than other nerve fibers, which conduct messages about touch, or warmth and cold. Thus, the signals carried on the thicker, faster nerve fibers may block the gate, helping to inhibit neural messages about pain.

MODULE 3.5 PERCEIVING OUR WORLD: PRINCIPLES OF PERCEPTION

LEARNING OBJECTIVES

After you have mastered the information in this unit, you will be able to:

1. Define and explain the process of perception.

2. Describe how perception is influenced by attention and perceptual set.

3. Describe the two general modes of processing visual stimuli.

4. Discuss the Gestalt principles of perceptual organization.

5. Explain perceptual constancy, and describe the cues used to perceive depth and movement.

6. Describe visual illusions.

7. Discuss whether or not subliminal perception exists.

8. Consider whether evidence supports the existence of ESP.

OUTLINE

I. Perception—The Brain Organizes and Interprets Sensations
    A. Perception help us make sense of the world but it may not accurately reflect external reality
II. Attention: Did You Notice That?
    A. Attention—the first step in perception
    B. Selective attention—limit attention to certain stimuli (e.g., driving and cell phone use)
    C. Habituation—results from exposure to a constant stimulus
    D. We pay more attention to stimuli that are meaningful or emotionally significant
III. Perceptual Set: Seeing What You Expect to See (Expectations Guide Interpretations)
IV. Modes of Visual Processing
    A. Bottom-up processing—begin with specific features of shapes in environment
    B. Top-down processing—begin with knowledge and experience about patterns
V. Gestalt Principles of Perceptual Organization
    A. Figure and ground—figures have shapes; ground does not
    B. Gestalt laws of grouping: proximity, similarity, continuity, closure, and connectedness
VI. Perceptual Constancies
    A. Shape constancy—shape seen as the same across various perspectives
    B. Size constancy—size perceived as same regardless of variations on retina
    C. Color constancy—color perceived the same despite changes in lighting
    D. Brightness constancy—brightness seen as the same though illumination may change
VII. Cues to Depth Perception
    A. Binocular cues—need both eyes
        1. Retinal disparity—slightly differing image relayed to brain from each eye
        2. Convergence—muscle tension relating to both eyes turning to look at visual object
    B. Monocular cues—one eye sufficient
        1. Relative size: larger objects perceived as closer
        2. Interposition: obscured object perceived as farther away
        3. Relative clarity: distant objects are blurrier
        4. Texture gradient: closer objects appear coarser, more detailed
        5. Linear perspective: parallel lines appear to converge in distance
        6. Shadowing: light and dark are cues to projections and indentations

VIII. Motion Perception
- A. Projected image of object moves across retina
- B. Changing size of object

IX. Visual Illusions: Do Your Eyes Deceive You?
- A. Perceptual cues may lead to misinterpretation (Müller-Lyer, Ponzo illusions)
- B. Relative-size hypothesis—amount of space around perceived object
- C. Stroboscopic movement—the movement in motion pictures

X. Cultural Differences in Perceiving Visual Illusions
- A. Experience plays a role in visual perception
- B. Carpentered-world hypothesis—an environment dominated by straight lines and angles

XI. Controversies in Perception
- A. Subliminal perception
  1. Perception of stimuli presented below the threshold of awareness
  2. Two-thirds of Americans believe subliminal suggestions do work
  3. Does seem to occur in some cases – researchers report is yes; influence is subtle, may be minimal
- B. Extrasensory perception
  1. Perception that occurs without benefit of the known senses
  2. Parapsychology—study of these paranormal phenomena
     a) Telepathy—the ability to exchange thoughts without use of the senses
     b) Clairvoyance—the perception of events that are not available to the senses
     c) Precognition—the ability to foretell the future
     d) Psychokinesis—the ability to move objects without touching them
  3. As yet no reliable, replicable findings of ESP that have withstood scientific scrutiny

SUMMARY

In this module, you are introduced to basic concepts regarding perception. Perception is different from sensation in that perception occurs in the brain. With perception, sensory information transmitted to the brain is interpreted; that is, it is compared to past experience and given meaning. With visual illusions, such as presented in this module, interpretation is difficult because perceptual cues may be conflicting.

The process of perception begins with giving our attention to some stimulus. Selective attention means we are limiting ourselves to certain stimuli and not attending to others. Thus we are able to focus our attention and avoid being bombarded by the many events and distractions in our environment. Past experience very much directs how we tend to interpret certain situations. Our expectancies (perceptual set) regarding what we are going to see or hear may shape our actual experience of these events.

Visual processing may be top-down (the brain is aware of meaningful wholes and does not first process individual parts) or bottom-up (the brain begins by attending to specific features in the environment). We organize what we see by grouping and determining what is figure and what is ground. Both monocular (one eye needed) and binocular (two eyes needed) cues help us interpret depth. Perceptual constancy means objects continue to appear the same to us even though they may change in orientation, illumination, and proximity. Visual illusions help us learn more about how the process of perception works. Studies have shown that there are cultural differences in perception. Once again, past experience plays a role. Perceptual experience in differing environments leads members of various cultures to perceive the world differently.

Two controversies within the field of perception involve whether subliminal perception and extrasensory perception (ESP) exist. Subliminal perception is the perception of stimuli presented below the threshold for conscious awareness. Extrasensory perception is the ability to perceive without using any of the known senses. It is easier to test for the effects of subliminal perception than for ESP. Laboratory researchers can test for the presence of subliminal perception by exposing individuals to a stimulus at such a rapid rate that these individuals are not consciously aware the stimulus was present. Yet, a subtle influence due to such exposure can sometimes be found. Researchers testing paranormal phenomena—telepathy, clairvoyance, psychokinesis, and precognition—have yet to come up with reliable, replicable scientific evidence that supports the existence of ESP.

KEY TERMS

Perception

Selective attention

Habituation

Perceptual set

Bottom-up processing

Top-down processing

Laws of perceptual organization

Proximity

Similarity

Continuity

Closure

Connectedness

Perceptual constancy

Shape constancy

Size constancy

Color constancy

Brightness constancy

Binocular cues

Retinal disparity

Convergence

Monocular cues

Visual illusions

Stroboscopic movement

Carpentered-world hypothesis

Subliminal perception

Extrasensory perception

Parapsychology

Telepathy

Clairvoyance

Precognition

Psychokinesis

SELF-TEST PRACTICE QUIZ

Match the following Key Terms and definitions (note: not every Key Term will be used):

1. _____ Perceptual grouping based on how alike stimuli are

2. _____ The brain attends to specific features in order to yield an overall pattern

3. _____ Limiting attention to certain stimuli and filtering out other stimuli

4. _____ Information from both eyes is needed to interpret stimuli

5. _____ An object is perceived as the same size even though the image on the retina changes

6. _____ The ability to perceive information without using the known senses

7. _____ The ability to foretell the future

8. _____ The brain receives slightly differing image from each eye

9. _____ Features of a stimulus are perceived as remaining the same even though sensory input changes

10. _____ Perceptual grouping based on how near stimuli are to each other

11. _____ Becoming accustomed to constant exposure to a stimulus

12. _____ The study of events that cannot be explained by known physical, psychological, or biological mechanisms

13. _____ Perceiving stimuli presented below the level of conscious awareness

14. _____ Expectations or preconceptions that influence what we perceive

a. Perception

b. Selective attention

c. Habituation

d. Perceptual set

e. Bottom-up processing

f. Top-down processing

g. Laws of perceptual organization

h. Proximity

i. Similarity

j. Continuity

k. Closure

l. Connectedness

m. Perceptual constancy

n. Shape constancy

o. Size constancy

p. Color constancy

q. Brightness constancy

r. Binocular cues

s. Retinal disparity

t. Convergence

u. Monocular cues

v. Visual illusions

w. Stroboscopic movement

x. Carpentered-world hypothesis

y. Subliminal perception

z. Extrasensory perception

aa. Parapsychology

15. _____ How people assemble bits of sensory stimuli into meaningful wholes

16. _____ Muscular tension produced by both eyes turning inward

     bb. Telepathy

     cc. Clairvoyance

     dd. Precognition

     ee. Psychokinesis

17. With _____ the image presented to the brain from each eye differs slightly.
    a. binocular cues
    b. monocular cues
    c. perceptual set
    d. retinal disparity

18. When songs are played backward, people are more likely to perceive "hidden messages" if they were told what to listen for in the first place. This illustrates the principle of
    a. perceptual set.
    b. bottom-up processing.
    c. perceptual constancy.
    d. Gestalt formation.

19. Bottom-up processing is directed mostly by
    a. patterns existing in the brain.
    b. specific features of the stimulus.
    c. visual illusions.
    d. all of the above

20. When we see the letter "O," we usually perceive it as a circle even if the person writing it did not make the ends of the circle touch. This illustrates the Gestalt principle of
    a. similarity.
    b. closure.
    c. proximity.
    d. connectedness.

21. Perception differs from sensation in that perception
    a. occurs in the brain, where information about stimuli are interpreted.
    b. consists of all information transmitted by sensory receptors.
    c. necessitates binocular cues, while monocular cues are sufficient for sensation.
    d. does not utilize cues such as linear perspective and interposition.

22. Which of the following is a binocular cue for depth perception?
    a. Relative size
    b. Convergence
    c. Interposition
    d. Linear perspective

23. The ability to read other people's minds is known as
    a. clairvoyance.
    b. telepathy.
    c. precognition.
    d. psychokinesis.

24. What does research on subliminal perception indicate?
    a. Participants in subliminal perception studies often become ill.
    b. Research on subliminal perception has been discontinued.
    c. There is some scientific evidence to suggest the phenomenon does exist.
    d. Subliminal perception cannot be tested scientifically.

ESSAY QUESTIONS

1. How do we perceive motion, such as when we watch movies?
2. Explain visual illusions. Why do they occur?

ANSWER KEY

1. Similarity
2. Bottom-up processing
3. Selective attention
4. Binocular cues
5. Size constancy
6. Extrasensory perception
7. Precognition
8. Retinal disparity
9. Perceptual constancy
10. Proximity
11. Habituation
12. Parapsychology
13. Subliminal perception
14. Perceptual set
15. Laws of perceptual organization
16. Convergence
17. d
18. a
19. b
20. b
21. a
22. b
23. b
24. c

SAMPLE ANSWERS TO ESSAY QUESTIONS

1.   We perceive motion in various ways. One way is simply that the image moves across the retina corresponding to how the stimuli move in our field of vision. Another way is that objects change size; for example, we perceive that an object has moved away from us if the retinal image grows smaller. Motion that appears to occur (as in motion pictures) but actually does not is stroboscopic motion. Here, illuminated images that are projected are still. However, they are presented in a progression and at such a rapid rate that they are perceived as displaying movement.

2.   We cannot fully explain why visual illusions occur. However, it is probably related to our reliance on perceptual cues. These cues come from our experience with the environment. The cues may trigger one perception. Actual objective measurement of the stimuli involved, however, may produce different, and more accurate, information.

MODULE 3.6 APPLICATION: PSYCHOLOGY AND PAIN MANAGEMENT

LEARNING OBJECTIVE

After you have mastered the information in this unit, you will be able to:

1.   Describe what psychologists have learned about controlling pain.

OUTLINE

I.   Gaining Control Over Pain
   A.   Pain does protect us from danger
   B.   Endorphins produced by body can help diminish experience of pain
II.   Pain Management Strategies
   A.   Distraction—directing attention away from pain
   B.   Bottleneck pain at neurological gate—rubbing, heat and cold may block gateway
   C.   Changing thoughts and attitudes—remain positive, focus on what can help; negative thinking can lead to perceptions of lack of control and produce feelings of helplessness and hopelessness
   D.   Obtaining accurate information—about pain source and treatment
   E.   Meditation—focused attention yields a relaxed, contemplative state
   F.   Biofeedback training—learning to control tension and other responses by the body
   G.   Hypnosis—using an altered state of consciousness

SUMMARY

In this Application module, you learn what psychologists have discovered about pain. True, pain does help us in that it makes us aware of harm. The body has some defense against pain; this is the naturally-occurring production of endorphins. Pain management strategies include maintaining positive and informed thoughts and a relaxed state, directing attention to other activities, and some physiological activities that may block the pain message or help us lessen tension and stress.

CHAPTER 3   APPLICATION EXERCISE

Which of your senses do you tend to rely on the most? That is, which one seems to provide you with the most information during the course of a typical day? How does that information come into your awareness? Can you distinguish the sensory information from what you then perceive? How much different is what you sensed from how your mind later interpreted it? What do you think influenced those interpretations?

How do your thoughts and feelings affect what you perceive? Can you think of an example where you were processing information from the environment? It is happening all the time, of course! How did the stimuli from the environment catch your attention? What frame of mind were you in? Evaluate how, if at all, your mental set and/or emotional state affected what it was that you perceived.

CHAPTER 4

Consciousness

In Chapter 4, you learn about the many different states of consciousness a human being can experience, sometimes all within a day's time. Conscious states range from being alert and aware, perhaps particularly focused, to sleeping, dreaming, altered states of awareness, and the deep unconsciousness due to brain injury or anesthesia. Much of our state of consciousness is in our own hands—either through where we choose to focus our attention, when we decide to lie down and sleep, or via altered mental functioning we have induced through meditation or the use of drugs.

Some states of consciousness can be helpful. We can prime our minds to be particularly alert and aware, absorbing the maximum amount of information from whatever stimuli we have chosen to attend to. We can allow ourselves sufficient time to sleep, thus increasing the likelihood that we will awake alert, refreshed, and most able to do our best. Drifting consciousness (the mind is free to wander) or meditation both provide opportunities for the mind to contemplate new ideas, and the body is likely to be in a natural, more relaxed state. Hypnosis, again an altered state where no drugs are used, may be of therapeutic value in treating physical or psychological disorders, and in helping an individual adopt more desirable behavior patterns such as losing weight or stopping smoking.

We not only must sleep to allow the body to restore and replenish itself, but we must also dream. Individuals who obtain enough sleep, but who are prevented from dreaming, show learning and memory impairments even though they may not experience fatigue. We can tell when an individual is dreaming during sleep by observing that individual's eyes. The state of dreaming is associated with REM sleep—that is, rapid-eye-movement sleep, where the eyes are moving under the eyelids as if the person were watching a movie. Everyone dreams every night, though the dreams may not be remembered. Sleeping during the night tends to occur in stages, with Stages 1 and 2 being associated with lighter sleep, and Stages 3 and 4 with deeper sleep. Dreaming tends not to occur during any of these stages, but rather usually after an individual has been in Stage 4 sleep and is cycling out of it (reversing through Stage 3 and then Stage 2, respectively). Each stage of sleep corresponds to a different pattern of brain waves, which can be measured electrically. Waking states are associated with beta waves, early phases of relaxation with alpha waves, and the deepest stages of sleep with delta waves. Influences on when we sleep include the amount of available light hitting our eyes, regular bodily patterns for activity and rest, which are known as circadian rhythms, and a brain structure that secretes the hormone melatonin, making us feel sleepy.

Our state of consciousness may also be altered through the use of chemical substances. These chemicals include the most widely used and abused drug, alcohol, and also include a number of other legal and illegal substances. All of the mind-altering substances are classified according to the effect they have on the body. Depressants lower the activity of the central nervous system; an individual will feel relaxed, calm, and may experience a sense of euphoria. Depressants include alcohol, barbiturates, tranquilizers, and opioids (also called opiates). Some of these have legitimate uses in the medical field. Stimulants make us more alert and aware, as they increase the activity level of the central nervous system. Stimulants include amphetamines, cocaine, MDMA (Ecstasy), nicotine, and caffeine. Stimulants may be sought after because they can produce a "rush" or a psychological "high." They may create intense feelings of pleasure that, once a user is hooked, become hard to resist. These feelings of pleasure drive the user to desire more and more of the drug, and often a user then becomes addicted. Addictions may be psychological, physiological, or both. Physiological dependency means the mental chemistry of the brain actually has been changed due to repeated use of the drug. A third class of mind-altering drugs is the hallucinogens, which include marijuana (the most widely used illicit drug), LSD, PCP, and similar drugs. Mind-altering drugs may be naturally-occurring or may be synthesized in a laboratory-type setting. Many have serious consequences from their prolonged use, and can and do result in death.

MODULE 4.1 STATES OF CONSCIOUSNESS

LEARNING OBJECTIVE

After you have mastered the information in this unit, you will be able to:

1.   Describe the various states of consciousness.

OUTLINE

I.   States of Consciousness
    A.   William James
        1.   Father of American psychology – first psychology lecture he ever attended was the one he gave himself (Hothersall, 1995)
        2.   Interested in the nature of consciousness ("stream of thoughts")
    B.   State of awareness of ourselves and that around us
        1.   Frequently shifts during the day
        2.   Changing levels of awareness from focused awareness to divided consciousness to drifting consciousness
        3.   Negative ways of thinking act like mental filters slanting how we react to life events
    C.   Focused awareness
        1.   Wide awake, fully alert; engrossed in present task
        2.   Distraction limited from other stimuli
    D.   Drifting consciousness
        1.   Focused awareness difficult to maintain long term
        2.   Mind may start to drift from thought to thought
        3.   Daydreaming—a waking state but of dreamy thoughts (relatively few have sexual themes) (Klinger, 1987)
    E.   Divided consciousness
        1.   We may perform two different tasks simultaneously—both demand level of attention
        2.   Automatic pilot—performing mechanical tasks while part of mind remains free – example: driving a car
        3.   Excessive multitasking [e.g., cell phone and driving] – Drivers who talk on a cell phone are four times more likely to have an accident, about the same level of increased risk as drivers who are legally drunk (Parker-Pope, 2009)
        4.   Reduced concentration—increased risk for accident
    F.   States of unconsciousness
        1.   Relatively unaware of our external surroundings—as in sleeping and dreaming
        2.   Still responsive to personally meaningful stimuli
        3.   Deep unconsciousness—as from trauma, anesthesia or coma
        4.   Altered states of consciousness (outside world fades away)
            a)   State of awareness unlike normal waking state
            b)   Daydreaming, meditation, hypnosis, influence of mind-altering drugs
            c)   Also may result from repetitive physical activity

SUMMARY

In this module, you learn about states of consciousness. In the early history of psychology, both Wilhelm Wundt and William James were interested in studying consciousness, but the behaviorists who followed them suggested this effort be abandoned. Among other things it was thought that studying something so unobservable and subjective was simply too difficult. However, recently, especially with advances in technological equipment, studying varying types of consciousness is back in the fore.

Consciousness is a state of awareness of ourselves and of the world around us. Consciousness can shift from alert arousal to a deep unconsciousness as in sleep. Focused awareness is a heightened state of alert wakefulness, where extraneous stimuli are filtered out. Drifting consciousness means the mind moves away from focused awareness to a mental wandering from thought to thought. Drifting consciousness can lead to daydreaming. Divided consciousness involves doing more than one mental activity at a time. Often one of the activities is a mechanical one, which when well learned frees us to simultaneously contemplate something else, such as meeting a friend for a baseball game or ruminating about a romantic relationship. Dividing our focus in this fashion works to an extent, but presents hazards if the second task (cell phones, children who need attention, heated discussions or arguments) becomes too distracting. Distraction during driving is related to greatly increased risk of accident.

Unconsciousness means we are relatively unaware of our surroundings, such as during sleep or when dreaming. States of awareness unlike our typical waking state are known as altered states of awareness. They are likely to occur when we daydream, meditate, or as a result of using mind-altering drugs.

KEY TERMS

Consciousness

States of consciousness

Focused awareness

Drifting consciousness

Daydreaming

Divided consciousness

Unconsciousness

Altered states of consciousness

SELF-TEST PRACTICE QUIZ

Match the following Key Terms and definitions:

1. _____ Attention given to two tasks at the same time

2. _____ When the mind wanders to dreamy states or fantasies

3. _____ Heightened alertness, full attention directed to the task at hand

4. _____ A state of awareness of ourselves and of the world around us

5. _____ Range of consciousness, from alert wakefulness to unconsciousness

a.   Consciousness

b.   States of consciousness

c.   Focused awareness

d.   Drifting consciousness

e.   Daydreaming

f.   Divided consciousness

g.   Unconsciousness

h.   Altered states of consciousness

6. _____ States of awareness that are unlike the typical waking state

7. _____ When thoughts meander from one to the next

8. _____ A lack of awareness

9. William James felt that consciousness was

    a. similar to being on automatic pilot.
    b. where the mind drifts from thought to thought.
    c. a continuous process of thinking, like water flowing down a river.
    d. mental states not typical of our everyday wakefulness.

10. When we are completely engrossed in the task at hand and ignore stimuli, such as traffic or background noise from a fan, we are displaying

    a. an altered state of consciousness.
    b. focused awareness.
    c. drifting consciousness.
    d. divided consciousness.

11. When we are asleep, we

    a. are at the lowest levels of consciousness.
    b. are functioning outside of conscious awareness.
    c. are in a state of deep unconsciousness.
    d. may still be responsive to some kinds of stimuli.

12. The state of deep unconsciousness may be induced by

    a. repetitive physical activities.
    b. trauma to the head, or general anesthesia.
    c. prolonged meditation or hypnosis.
    d. mind-altering drugs such as alcohol or marijuana.

13. Daydreaming occurs during states of _____ consciousness.

    a. drifting
    b. focused
    c. divided
    d. all of the above

14. How can people lower the risk associated with talking on a cell phone while driving?

    a. Use speaker phone
    b. Use a hands-free headset
    c. Make the volume louder
    d. none of the above

15. Which of the following is an example of an altered state of consciousness?

    a. Dreaming
    b. Hypnosis
    c. Meditation
    d. all of the above

ESSAY QUESTIONS

1. Why did the behaviorists object to studying consciousness? Give some pros and cons with regard to the study of this subject.

2. Discuss situations where our use of divided consciousness can be an advantage. Discuss situations where its use can become hazardous.

ANSWER KEY

1. Divided consciousness

2. Daydreaming

3. Focused awareness

4. Consciousness

5. States of consciousness

6. Altered states of consciousness

7. Drifting consciousness

8. Unconsciousness

9. c

10. b

11. d

12. b

13. a

14. d

15. d

SAMPLE ANSWERS TO ESSAY QUESTIONS

1. The behaviorists objected to studying consciousness because it involved internal and subjective phenomena, thus quite difficult to measure. What would studying such a vague concept accomplish? Behaviorists' research focus was simply on observable behavior, and they believed that all human characteristics were derived solely from the environment and experience. An advantage to studying consciousness is that, indeed, at least some of the human psyche can be traced to inner, rather than external, workings. A disadvantage is that consciousness is more difficult to measure—but innovations in research methodology are helping with that problem.

2. Dividing the focus of our attention, as in divided consciousness, can be helpful in that we can accomplish more than one task at a time. In addition, devoting our full attention to a task that is easy and/or which we know well often is not necessary, and may in fact lead to feelings of boredom. Conversely, if we are attempting more than one task at a time, such as driving while using a cell phone, eating, or putting on makeup, and that secondary task becomes demanding of more and more of our attention, we put ourselves (and others) at serious risk.

MODULE 4.2 SLEEPING AND DREAMING

LEARNING OBJECTIVES

After you have mastered the information in this unit, you will be able to:

1. Explain how sleep-wake cycles are regulated.

2. Discuss the stages and function of sleep.

3. Discuss alternate explanations for the purpose of dreams.

4. Describe common sleep disorders.

OUTLINE

I.   Sleeping and Dreaming
    A.   Why do we sleep? Why do we dream? Answers are uncertain
    B.   Dreaming not bound by physical reality

II. Sleep and Wakefulness: A Circadian Rhythm
    A.   One-third of human life is spent sleeping
    B.   Circadian rhythm—daily pattern for sleep-wake cycles (about 24 hours in length)
    C.   Suprachiasmatic nucleus (SCN) in hypothalamus regulates sleep
    D.   Melatonin is a hormone that makes us feel sleepy – exposure to darkness stimulates the brain's production
    E.   The human eye is sensitive to light, input to SCN
    F.   Jet lag—local time conflicts with internal body clock resulting in irritability, fatigue and difficulty concentrating

III. Stages of Sleep – sleep cycles repeat about every ninety minutes
    A.   EEG (tracks brain waves) one source to provide information
        1.   Awake: fast, low-amplitude *(beta)* waves
        2.   Relaxing for sleep: slower, rhythmic *(alpha)* waves
        3.   Sleeping: passing through various stages
    B.   Stage 1
        1.   Brain waves small and irregular, varying frequencies
        2.   Light sleep; sleeper is easily awakened – may not realize they have been asleep
    C.   Stage 2
        1.   Onset two minutes after Stage 1 sleep
        2.   Bursts of brain wave activity: sleep spindles
        3.   More than half of sleep time is Stage 2
    D.   Stage 3—Deep sleep; 50% or fewer of brain wave patterns are delta waves (slow wave sleep)
    E.   Stage 4—Deep sleep; 50% or more of brain wave patterns are delta waves
    F.   REM (rapid-eye-movement) sleep
        1.   Stage of sleep most associated with dreaming
        2.   Eyes dart about under eyelids
        3.   Follows Stages 3 and 2 after reverting from deep sleep
        4.   High level of brain activity; body movement blocked
        5.   Sleep cycles repeat about every 90 minutes
        6.   Amount of REM sleep increases as sleep goes on; Stage 4 sleep eventually disappears
        7.   Also called paradoxical sleep – despite activity of the brain muscle activity is blocked person is practically paralyzed
        8.   Lack of REM impairs learning ability and memory (Greer, 2004)
        9.   REM helps boost creative problem solving ability (Mednick et al., 2009)

IV. Why We Sleep
    A.   Species' average length of sleep time varies
    B.   Universal need for sleep suggests survival necessity
    C.   Sleep serves a variety of functions—restores, preserves, protects, and conserves energy and memory consolidation function; newly learned material may be better retained when you have a chance to sleep on it
    D.   Reduces chances of catching the common cold and bolsters the body's ability to defend

V.   Dreams and Dreaming
    A.   Why do we dream?
        1.   No explanation entirely certain
        2.   May help consolidate memories and new learning

3.   Dreaming may help provide solutions to everyday problems
4.   Activation-synthesis hypothesis—cerebral cortex tries to integrate experiences generated by random electrical brain impulses (possibly creates a "story line")
5.   Brain stem activated, but area for logical thought less active during dream state
6.   Activation-synthesis hypothesis—attempt by the cerebral cortex to make sense of random discharges of electrical activity in the brain during REM sleep (Hobson, 1999)

B.   What do dreams mean? Sigmund Freud: wish fulfillment
1.   Dreams interpreted usually as sexual or aggressive
2.   The "royal road" to the unconscious
3.   Manifest content—events that actually occur in a dream
4.   Latent content—what the dream really means, since dreams are symbolic

C.   Dream interpretation not verified objectively
D.   Lucid dreams: dreamer is aware of dreaming

VI.   Sleep Deprivation
A.   Normally need 7 to 9 hours of sleep per day, but some apparently less – many in their 60's and 70's require only 6 hours
B.   Infants and children require more sleep: more time proportionally in REM sleep
C.   Insufficient sleep
1.   Slows reaction times
2.   Impairs concentration, memory, problem-solving ability, and more difficult to retain newly acquire information
3.   Harder to retain newly acquired information
4.   Impairs academic performance
5.   Common cause of highway accidents
6.   Chronic sleep deprivation is a concern
7.   Increases risk of developing hypertension (high blood pressure) (Bakalard, 2006; Egan, 2006; Motivala & Irwin, 2007)
D.   Need sufficient REM sleep as well

VII.   Sleep Disorders
A.   Insomnia
1.   Most common sleep disorder
2.   Inability to fall asleep, remain asleep, or return to sleep after being awakened
3.   Array of causes
a)   Substance abuse, physical illness
b)   Psychological disorders—depression, worry
c)   Sleep is a natural function that cannot be forced
B.   Narcolepsy—falling asleep suddenly ("sleep attacks") during the day afflicting some 150,000 Americans (Seigel, 2004)
1.   REM sleep usually begins almost immediately after onset of a narcoleptic attack
2.   Sleep scientists believe it is caused by a loss of brain cells in an area of the hypothalamus (Dauvilliers, Arnulf, & Mignot, 2007)
C.   Sleep apnea—frequently stopping breathing during sleep time
1.   More common in men and obese people
2.   Increased risk of stroke and hypertension (high blood pressure) (Yaggi et al., 2005)
3.   Snore very loudly
D.   Nightmare disorder—frequent, disturbing nightmares; occurs during REM sleep
1.   More susceptible when under stress, high fever or sleep deprivation
E.   Sleep terror disorder
1.   More likely to affect children, especially boys
2.   More intense than nightmares

3.   Does not occur during REM sleep—occurs during deep sleep period
4.   Begins with a panicky scream
F.   Sleepwalking
1.   Also more often in children than adults; if persistent, a disorder
2.   Sleeping individual walks about, eyes open, expressionless
3.   No harm in wakening sleepwalker

SUMMARY

In this module, you learn about our remarkable experiences of sleeping and dreaming. Sleep appears to be fundamentally necessary both to our physical well-being and survival and for our effective mental functioning. Most people need between seven and nine hours of sleep a night in order to feel truly refreshed and alert. Sleep deprivation endangers our health and impairs our functioning.

Why do we sleep? There are a variety of reasons. Circadian rhythms direct many body patterns of activity, and the sleep-wake cycle is one of them. The human sleep cycle corresponds roughly to the 24-hour clock. The eye is sensitive to the presence or absence of light, and that plus the production of melatonin in our body (the hormone that makes us feel sleepy) help explain why we sleep and wake when we do. Of course, sleep time is an opportunity for our body to restore itself. Energy in our cells can be replenished, and some wear-and-tear in the body and brain can be repaired. Insufficient sleep appears to suppress the immune system. Animal species (probably true for our forebears also) are afforded protection by sleeping at night when predators roam.

Sleep is not a consistent state; our sleep time goes through cycles, from very light sleep (Stage 1, where we may not even realize we are asleep) to the deep sleep of Stage 4. Brain wave patterns change with each sleep stage, and humans typically experience four or five sleep cycles during a night. Most of our sleep time is spent in Stage 2 sleep, during which the brain experiences bursts of wave activity known as sleep spindles.

We need not only to sleep but also to dream, although the actual purpose of dreaming is not entirely known. We do know that individuals who get enough sleep in terms of hours still are cognitively impaired if they are deprived of REM sleep. REM (rapid-eye-movement) sleep occurs when an individual is dreaming; the eyes are actually moving under the eyelids, as if the individual were watching a movie. REM sleep is usually a separate period of sleep, not corresponding to any of the sleep stages, and usually occurs after an individual is reversing the sleep stages following the deep sleep period. The majority of dreams are about our day's activities. These dreams may help us consolidate in the brain what we have learned during the day, and/or help us work on various solutions to problems we face. Sigmund Freud felt that dreams represent a way to fulfill unconscious wishes. Still others believe that dreams are merely the byproduct of random bursts of electrical activity in the brain.

Not everyone goes to sleep easily or sleeps soundly at night. There are various sleep disorders, including narcolepsy, where individuals will fall asleep suddenly even though they have just been actively involved in daytime events. Insomnia may be caused by substance abuse or physical pain; other possible causes are psychological disorders and simple worry. We can even become anxious about not sleeping, and that keeps us awake more! Sleep disorders can be treated with sleep medication, but can lead to physiological dependence; use medication briefly, possibly a few weeks at most (Pollack, 2004a). Cognitive-behavioral therapy focused on changing problem sleep habits is just as effective as medication in treating insomnia (Dolan et al., 2010; Ebben & Spielman, 2009; Perlis et al., 2008; Pollack, 2004a; Roy-Byrne, 2007).

It is most often children who have nightmares (which occur during REM sleep) and night terrors (which occur during a deep-sleep phase). Usually most of a nightmare can be remembered, but with the more intense night terror little is usually remembered. Children also are more prone to sleepwalking. Fortunately, most of these disorders lessen as a child grows older.

KEY TERMS

Circadian rhythm

Jet lag

Rapid-eye-movement (REM) sleep

Activation-synthesis hypothesis

Lucid dreams

Insomnia

Narcolepsy

Sleep apnea

Nightmare disorder

Sleep terror disorder

Sleepwalking disorder

SELF-TEST PRACTICE QUIZ

Match the following Key Terms and definitions:

1. _____ The stage of sleep most closely associated with dreaming

2. _____ Temporary cessation of breathing during sleep

3. _____ A disruption of sleep-wake cycles due to long-distance air travel

4. _____ The notion that the brain creates dreams to help make sense of random electrical brain activity during sleep

5. _____ Difficulty falling asleep, remaining asleep, or returning to sleep after being awakened

6. _____ A disorder involving frequent, disturbing nightmares

7. _____ Rather frequent occurrence of walking about while sound asleep

8. _____ Fluctuations in bodily processes that occur regularly each day

a. Circadian rhythm

b. Jet lag

c. Rapid-eye-movement (REM) sleep

d. Activation-synthesis hypothesis

e. Lucid dreams

f. Insomnia

g. Narcolepsy

h. Sleep apnea

i. Nightmare disorder

j. Sleep terror disorder

k. Sleepwalking disorder

9. _____ Dreams in which the dreamer is aware that he or she is dreaming

10. _____ Repeated episodes of intense fear during sleep

11. _____ Sudden, unexplainable "sleep attacks" that occur during the day

12. Why do some people have difficulty falling or staying asleep?

    a. They may be suffering from psychological problems, such as depression.
    b. They have worries or concerns that they take to bed with them.
    c. They may be experiencing pain.
    d. all of the above

13. The hormone secreted by our body that tends to make us feel sleepy is

    a. dopamine.
    b. serotonin.
    c. acetylcholine.
    d. melatonin.

14. The part of the hypothalamus in the brain that helps regulate sleep-wake cycles is the

    a. ventromedial lobe.
    b. superior olive.
    c. suprachiasmatic nucleus (SCN).
    d. reticular formation.

15. How can we tell when individuals are dreaming?

    a. They tend to thrash about and talk in their sleep.
    b. They exhibit REM sleep, where their eyes under the eyelid are moving.
    c. They tend to get up and walk around the room or house.
    d. all of the above

16. Circadian rhythms are largely regulated by

    a. alarm clocks.
    b. exposure to sunlight.
    c. sheer habit.
    d. the frontal lobe of the brain.

17. Which sleep disorder is most common?

    a. Sleep apnea
    b. Narcolepsy
    c. Insomnia
    d. Sleepwalking

18. We spend most of our time in

    a. Stage 1 sleep.
    b. Stage 2 sleep.
    c. Stage 3 sleep.
    d. Stage 4 sleep.

19. Delta waves are associated with

    a. Stage 1 sleep.
    b. sleep Stages 1 and 2.
    c. sleep Stages 2 and 3.
    d. sleep Stages 3 and 4.

20. About how long does the typical human sleep cycle last?
    a.   20 minutes
    b.   40 minutes
    c.   60 minutes
    d.   90 minutes
21. Which statement best describes Sigmund Freud's view of dreams?
    a.   Dreams have no meaning—they're just the byproduct of random electrical discharges.
    b.   Dreams have underlying meanings which represent our unconscious wishes, desires, and fears.
    c.   Dreams are useful because they allow us to work out problems that have been bothering us.
    d.   Dreams represent messages from the spirits of dead ancestors.
22. If an individual is deprived of REM sleep, but otherwise spends sufficient time sleeping, that individual
    a.   shows no particular cognitive impairments.
    b.   tends to spend more time sleeping during the next few nights.
    c.   tends to spend less time sleeping during the next few nights.
    d.   shows learning and memory impairments, and will dream (REM sleep) more proportionally when allowed uninterrupted sleep.
23. How do sleep patterns typically change over the course of a night?
    a.   The amount of REM sleep increases, and the amount of deep sleep also increases.
    b.   The amount of deep sleep decreases, and the amount of REM sleep increases.
    c.   Sleep cycles get longer.
    d.   Lucid dreams become more common.
24. REM sleep is called paradoxical sleep because
    a.   our dreams may be disturbing or difficult to interpret.
    b.   though we are asleep, we are getting very little actual rest.
    c.   the brain is very active but muscles are essentially paralyzed.
    d.   dreaming is not really helpful if the dreamer experiences nightmares.
25. What is the difference between nightmares and night terrors?
    a.   It is safe to wake someone from a nightmare, but not from a night terror.
    b.   Nightmares occur during REM sleep; night terrors occur during deep sleep.
    c.   Nightmares are normal; night terrors indicate that something is seriously wrong with a child.
    d.   Nightmares are more common in adults; night terrors are more common in children.

ESSAY QUESTIONS

1. Briefly describe the typical sleep pattern of a human during the night. What sleep stages does this individual go through? How does the sleep cycle change? When do we dream?

2. In what ways does sleeping help our body function?

3. What are some causes of insomnia?

4. What were some of Freud's views on dreaming?

ANSWER KEY

1. Rapid-eye-movement (REM) sleep
2. Sleep apnea
3. Jet lag
4. Activation-synthesis hypothesis
5. Insomnia
6. Nightmare disorder
7. Sleepwalking disorder
8. Circadian rhythm
9. Lucid dreams
10. Sleep terror disorder
11. Narcolepsy
12. d
13. d
14. c
15. b
16. b
17. c
18. b
19. d
20. d
21. b
22. d
23. b
24. c
25. b

SAMPLE ANSWERS TO ESSAY QUESTIONS

1. Sleep begins with our relaxation, and the beta brain waves shift to slower alpha waves. We slip into Stage 1 sleep, where brain waves become small, irregular, and of varying frequencies. All of these brainwave patterns may be measured by an electroencephalograph (EEG). Stage 2 sleep begins two minutes after Stage 1, and brainwave patterns are characterized by bursts of activity known as sleep spindles. In both Stage 1 and Stage 2 sleep we can easily be awakened. In deeper sleep (Stages 3 and 4) the brain exhibits a large, slow (delta) wave pattern. In Stage 3 sleep, delta waves constitute 50% or less of the brainwave pattern; in Stage 4 sleep, delta waves comprise more than 50%. REM sleep is not associated with any of these sleep stages; generally it occurs as a person is coming out of deep sleep, reversing the pattern through Stages 3 and 2. What follows then is the REM sleep period. These full sleep cycles typically last about 90 minutes, and an individual probably experiences four or five of these cycles each night. As our sleep period continues, Stage 4 sleep basically disappears, so we reach the REM sleep phase more quickly.

2.   It is apparent that sleep is necessary to preserve and protect our body. During sleep, our body restores and replenishes itself. Wear and tear from daily experiences and activity can be remedied. Research on individuals deprived of sleep shows that they experience impairment in both cognitive and motor functions. Obviously, then, sleep helps keep our body, particularly the brain and the rest of the nervous system, in top working order. Lack of sleep also weakens our immune system, so sleeping helps protect our health as well. We need not only to sleep, but to be able to experience REM sleep as needed through the night.

3.   Insomnia may have physical or psychological causes, or may simply result from poor sleeping habits. Substance abuse or physical pain may inhibit our ability to relax and to sleep. Psychological depression is known to be associated with sleep problems. Sleep must come naturally and cannot be forced.

4.   Freud was one of the first major figures in psychology to study and write extensively about dreams and dream interpretation. In keeping with his other views on the human psyche, Freud believed that dreaming was symbolic. Dreams represent wishes that we would like to have come true in our lives. Most of these wishes, according to Freud, dealt with sexual or aggressive desires.

Dreaming, to Freud, had two layers: the outer layer (the manifest content), which was what the dream appeared to be, and the inner layer (latent content), which represented the true underlying meaning of the dream. The true meaning of the dream was hidden to disguise our perhaps unacceptable desires even to ourselves. Freud believed that dreaming helped us remain asleep. By disguising our underlying feelings through the use of symbols, our sleep would not be disturbed. If the actual content of our inner desires was apparent in our dreams, it might be sufficiently emotionally upsetting to awaken us. Freud's views have not garnered notable research support.

MODULE 4.3 ALTERING CONSCIOUSNESS THROUGH MEDITATION AND HYPNOSIS

LEARNING OBJECTIVES

After you have mastered the information in this unit, you will be able to:

1.   Explain the process and purpose of meditation.

2.   Describe the nature of hypnosis.

3.   Discuss the major theories of hypnosis.

OUTLINE

I.   Meditation
    A.   Focused attention; relaxed, contemplative state
    B.   Narrow attention to a single object or thought
    C.   Transcendental meditation—repeat a phrase or sound (mantra)
    D.   Mindfulness meditation—focus on simple moment-to-moment experience
    E.   Individual is relaxed but alert
    F.   May help:
        1.   Expand consciousness
        2.   Achieve a state of pure awareness or inner peace
        3.   Relieve stress and chronic pain
        4.   Treat psychological disorders
II. Hypnosis
    A.   An altered state of consciousness

    B.   Focused attention, deep relaxation, and heightened susceptibility to suggestion

    C.   Experiences under hypnosis:

        1.   Hypnotic age regression—reliving past events (usually childhood)

        2.   Hypnotic analgesia—loss of awareness of pain

        3.   Posthypnotic amnesia—inability to recall what happened during hypnosis

        4.   Posthypnotic suggestion—planting a suggestion during hypnosis that individual follows (usually without awareness) after trance

        5.   Distortions of reality

            a.   Positive hallucination – seeing, hearing, or feeling something that is not present

            b.   Negative hallucination – NOT perceiving something, such as a pen or a chair, that really does exist

III.   Theories of Hypnosis

    A.   No consensus as to what hypnosis is or does

    B.   Possibly just role-playing (but most evidence does not support this notion)

    C.   Ernest Hilgard: neodissociation theory

        1.   Altered state of consciousness—consciousness splits or divides

        2.   Split off portion follows hypnotist's suggestions

        3.   "Hidden observer" part of mind still monitors all events

    D.   Hypnosis has therapeutic value; much depends upon type of individual being hypnotized – hypnotic suggestions may have more to do with the effort and skills of the people who are hypnotized than those of the hypnotist

SUMMARY

In this module, you learn about states of consciousness that are unlike our typical everyday awareness. Meditation and hypnosis are both altered states of consciousness brought about through focusing attention and no other (chemical, for example) means. In meditation, the individual focuses his or her attention on a single object, spoken word, or thought. All other thoughts are removed from consciousness, and the result is a relaxed, contemplative state. Unlike hypnosis, the meditative individual is still alert and aware. Meditation is thought to be helpful in expanding awareness, achieving a state of inner peace, relieving stress, and aiding in the treatment of physical and psychological disorders.

Hypnosis comes from the Greek word for sleep, although hypnotized individuals are not actually sleeping. Researchers are still not quite certain as to what hypnosis is or how it works; also, not everyone can be truly hypnotized. As with meditation, hypnosis involves focusing attention, but usually on the hypnotist's voice. When the individual is deeply relaxed, the hypnotist gives suggestions. These suggestions may guide the individual through unusual experiences (age regression, distortions of reality), reduce awareness of pain, or lead to certain responses once the individual reawakens.

Theories about the nature of hypnosis include that it is a trance state, where the individual is particularly susceptible to suggestion. Others believe hypnosis is simply role-playing—the individual is not really affected or "under" hypnosis at all. Evidence does support the notion that hypnosis is more than just pretense. Ernest Hilgard has proposed the neodissociation theory regarding hypnosis. According to this theory, hypnosis is an altered state of consciousness, and the hypnotized individual splits off part of the consciousness. It is this part that is impacted by the hypnotist's suggestion. Another part of the brain remains detached from the experience, but monitors what is going on. Though the actual nature of hypnosis still remains unclear, it has established itself as useful in treating a range of physical and psychological problems.

KEY TERMS

Meditation

Transcendental meditation (TM)

Mindfulness meditation

Mantra

Hypnosis

Hypnotic age regression

Hypnotic analgesia

Posthypnotic amnesia

Posthypnotic suggestion

Neodissociation theory

Hidden observer

SELF-TEST PRACTICE QUIZ

Match the following Key Terms and definitions (note: not every Key Term will be used):

1. _____ Loss of feeling or responsiveness to pain as a result of hypnosis

2. _____ According to Hilgard, the part of consciousness that is detached from hypnotic influence

3. _____ Re-experiencing past events in one's life due to hypnosis

4. _____ Meditation where the focus is moment-to-moment experience

5. _____ An inability to recall what happened during hypnosis

6. _____ A process of focused attention that induces a relaxed, contemplative state

7. _____ A hypnotic suggestion about behavior once an individual reawakens

8. _____ A sound or phrase chanted repeatedly

9. _____ An altered state of consciousness, involving focused attention, deep relaxation, and heightened susceptibility to suggestion

a. Meditation

b. Transcendental meditation (TM)

c. Mindfulness meditation

d. Mantra

e. Hypnosis

f. Hypnotic age regression

g. Hypnotic analgesia

h. Posthypnotic amnesia

i. Posthypnotic suggestion

j. Neodissociation theory

k. Hidden observer

10. A state where an individual remains alert and awake, but is focused, relaxed, and contemplative, is known as

    a. hypnosis.
    b. neodissociation.
    c. meditation.
    d. hypnotic stupor.

11. In transcendental meditation, it is typical that someone practicing it uses a mantra, which is

    a. a word or phrase.
    b. a type of hallucinogenic drug.
    c. incense.
    d. a type of musical instrument.

12. In hypnosis,

    a. one is asleep.
    b. one is susceptible to suggestion.
    c. one is alert and focused.
    d. the hypnotist directs all behavior of the hypnotized individual.

13. Evidence regarding hypnosis

    a. verifies that it really is just role-playing.
    b. has demonstrated that hypnotized individuals share the same experiences as non-hypnotized individuals.
    c. shows that it has no lasting therapeutic value.
    d. does not substantiate any of the above.

14. Which of the following is NOT a characteristic of individuals who are more easily hypnotized?

    a. Possesses a vivid imagination
    b. Has a positive view of hypnosis
    c. Possesses excellent memory skills
    d. Has a well-developed fantasy life

15. Which of the following statements best describes neodissociation theory?

    a. People who claim to be hypnotized are faking.
    b. Hypnosis splits consciousness into two parts, one of which is called the "hidden observer."
    c. Hypnosis is really just a type of elaborate pretending.
    d. Hypnosis is a type of trance state.

ESSAY QUESTIONS

1. What have we learned regarding the value of meditation?

2. What are some experiences one may have while under hypnosis?

ANSWER KEY

1. Hypnotic analgesia
2. Hidden observer
3. Hypnotic age regression
4. Mindfulness meditation
5. Posthypnotic amnesia
6. Meditation
7. Posthypnotic suggestion
8. Mantra
9. Hypnosis
10. c
11. a
12. b
13. d
14. c
15. b

SAMPLE ANSWERS TO ESSAY QUESTIONS

1. Meditation, unlike hypnosis, is something everyone can do. Also, unlike hypnosis, meditation does not take the presence of another individual (the hypnotist) in order to be practiced, and the phenomenon is fairly well understood. Meditation involves deep relaxation combined with focused attention and an alert awareness. Such complete relaxation has both physical and psychological health benefits. In addition, meditation aids in reducing the experience of pain and stress, and in treating psychological disorders such as anxiety and some addictions. As is often cited with regard to meditation, it is credited with expanding awareness and creating a state of inner peace.

2. Hypnosis is an altered state of consciousness where the individual is very relaxed, is focused on the hypnotist's voice, and is more susceptible to suggestion. Not everyone can be hypnotized, but those who are may be helped with problems they are facing. Under hypnosis an individual may experience an age regression (going back to re-live earlier childhood events) or hypnotic analgesia (reducing experience of pain). Hypnotic suggestion may aid individuals who wish to quit smoking or lose weight, and it appears to relieve pain and boost immunological functioning. Hypnosis is best used in combination with other traditional therapeutic treatments.

MODULE 4.4 ALTERING CONSCIOUSNESS THROUGH DRUGS

LEARNING OBJECTIVES

After you have mastered the information in this unit, you will be able to:

1. Understand the distinction between drug use, drug abuse, and dependence.

2. Describe the different types of psychoactive drugs and their effects.

3. Discuss the factors that contribute to alcohol and drug abuse problems.

4. Know the various treatment alternatives available to help people with drug problems.

OUTLINE

I.   Psychoactive Drugs
   A.   Chemical substances impacting brain and emotional states
   B.   Affect mood, thought processes, perceptions, and behavior
   C.   Used for many reasons; *illicit* drugs are illegal
II. Drug Abuse
   A.   Repeated use causes or aggravates personal, occupational, or health-related problems
   B.   Maladaptive or dangerous use of a chemical substance
   C.   Impairs one's health or ability to function
III. Drug Dependence
   A.   Individual compelled to use or unable to resist a drug despite its harm
   B.   Physiological (chemical) dependence—body chemistry has been changed due to repeated use
      1.   Withdrawal syndrome (abstinence syndrome) —painful symptoms when drug use abruptly stopped
      2.   Tolerance—need to increase the amount of drug taken to achieve same effect
      3.   Drug addiction—chemical addiction; physiological dependence involved
   C.   Psychological dependence—individual unable to control reliance on drug, but no physiological dependence involved
IV. Depressants—reduce activity of central nervous system and thus body processes; high doses can kill and can be dangerous or lethal if overdose or when mixed with other drugs
   A.   Alcohol
      1.   Intoxicant—chemical substance that produces drunkenness
      2.   Females intoxicated at lower doses than males – the less people weigh the less alcohol it takes to produce intoxication
      3.   Impairs judgment, concentration, attention, depth perception, and ability to evaluate consequences of behavior
         a.   Consuming even one alcoholic drink impairs driving ability
      4.   Disinhibits—may lead to aggressive or impulsive behavior
      5.   Alcoholism—chemical dependence on alcohol
         a)   Few alcoholics fit "skid-row bum" stereotype
         b)   Very heavy use—body, especially liver (cirrhosis of the liver), severely damaged
         c)   Moderate use of alcohol appears to have health benefits
      6.   Binge-drinking—large quantity of alcohol consumed on one occasion – 5 or more drinks for men and 4 or more for women on one occasion (Wechsler & Nelson, 2008)
         a)   Linked to increased risks of alcohol dependence, alcohol overdoses, unsafe or unplanned sex, and driving while impaired

      b)   Associated with increased health risks, including death from overdose – place people at risk of coma, blackouts and seizures

      c)   Depressant effects on central nervous system interfere with the normal vomiting response; vomit accumulates in the air passages and can lead to asphyxiation and death

    7.   Maternal use of alcohol during pregnancy can cause fetal alcohol syndrome – leading cause of mental retardation

NOTE: a person who is unresponsive or unconscious should not be left alone DO NOT assume they will sleep it off

B.   Barbiturates
1. Calming or sedating drugs
2. Legitimate medical uses such as managing high blood pressure, block pain, and control epilepsy
3. Highly addictive: street drugs that induce state of euphoria, relaxation
4. Include pentobarbital, phenobarbital (Quaalude is similar)
5. Induce drowsiness, slurred speech; impair motor activity and judgment
6. Should withdraw under careful medical supervision – abrupt withdrawal can cause convulsions and even death

C.   Tranquilizers
1. Depressants used to treat anxiety, insomnia
2. Less toxic than barbiturates
3. Dangerous in high doses, especially when combined with alcohol or other drugs
4. Include Valium, Xanax, and Halcion
5. Potentially physiologically and psychologically addictive

D.   Opioids (narcotics)
1. Highly addictive drugs; have pain-relieving and sleep-inducing properties
2. Include morphine, heroin, codeine, Demerol, and Percodan
3. Produce a "rush" of euphoria, reduce awareness of problems
4. Legitimate medical use to treat pain
5. Similar to endorphins naturally produced by body

V.   Stimulants—heighten activity of central nervous system, in some cases producing a high; used therapeutically in treatment of attention-deficit hyperactivity disorder

A.   Amphetamines
1. Synthetic chemical form only
2. Increase heart rate, breathing, blood pressure
3. Low doses: heighten alertness, reduce feelings of fatigue
4. High doses: intense, pleasurable rush
5. Boost brain neurotransmitters dopamine and norepinephrine
6. Include Benzedrine ("bennies") and methamphetamine ("speed", "ice", "crystal meth")
7. High doses may cause brain damage, amphetamine psychosis, coma, and death

B.   Cocaine
1. Natural stimulant from coca plant
2. Increases brain levels of norepinephrine and dopamine
3. Increases arousal, feelings of extreme pleasure
4. High is shorter than that produced by amphetamines
5. Regular use damages heart, other organs – prolonged use may lead to psychological problems (anxiety, irritability, and depression)
6. Highly physically addictive; produces intense cravings
7. In 1886 Coca-Cola contained cocaine marketed as "the ideal brain tonic"

    C.   MDMA (Ecstasy)
1. Produces mildly euphoric and hallucinogenic state
2. Increases bodily arousal; undesirable psychological and cognitive effects
3. Physical consequences; high doses may cause death
4. Psychological effects – can lead to depression, anxiety, insomnia, states of paranoia, or psychotic symptoms; heavy use is associated with cognitive deficits, including problems with memory functioning, learning ability, and attention (Buchert et al., 2004; Eisner, 2005)

    D.   Nicotine
1. Mild stimulant, highly addictive
2. Increases physiological arousal, but also feelings of calmness and relaxation – means of coping with stress
3. Physiological and psychological dependence – can begin within the first few weeks
4. Addiction responsible for many deaths due to cancer (responsible for 1 in 3 cancer deaths)
5. Major contributor to cardiovascular disease (heart and artery), the biggest killer of all (Teo et al., 2006)
6. Leading cause of premature death – doubles the risk of dying during middle age (before 70) (Doll et al., 2004)

    E.   Caffeine
1. Mild stimulant, found in coffee, tea, chocolate
2. Physiological dependence, but most can be controlled; "hooked" – feel on edge or have headaches when going without
3. Enhances alertness; may pose risk to pregnancy, jitters at higher doses
4. Associated with health risks during pregnancy

VI. Hallucinogens
    A.   Alter sensory perceptions (psychedelics)
    B.   May induce relaxation, but also paranoia or panic in others
    C.   Psychological but not physical dependence
    D.   LSD ("acid") —"trip" (a "trip" may last as long as twelve hours) produces vivid hallucinations and other sensory distortions – may eventually have flashbacks
    E.   Mescaline, Psilocybin, PCP ("angel dust") – produced delirium (mental confusion characterized by excitement, disorientation and difficulty focusing attention)
    F.   Marijuana
1. Alters perceptions, may induce hallucinations
2. Lower doses: relaxation, heightened awareness of bodily sensations, which can create anxiety or panicky feelings in some cases
3. Higher doses: nausea, disorientation, and paranoia
4. Most widely used illicit drug in Western world – nearly half of American adults admit to using at some point in their lives (SAMHSA, 2006)
5. Psychological but not physiological dependence
6. Increases cardiovascular and other risks
7. Impairs motor performance and coordination, may lead to problems with learning and memory (Messinis et al., 2006; Puighermanal et al., 2009; Yucel et al., 2008)
8. Introduces cancer causing agents and increases risk of respiratory diseases (Zickler, 2006)
9. Linked to later use of harder drugs such as heroin and cocaine (Kandel, 2003)

VII. Understanding Drug Abuse
    A. Social and behavioral context
        1. Pleasurable effects, peer pressure, modeled behavior, and avoiding withdrawal pain
        2. Unemployment
        3. Cultural norms and attitudes
    B. Physical factors
        1. Genetics
        2. Neurotransmitters and endorphins – habitual users quit and find little aches and pains magnified until the body resumes adequate production of endorphins
    C. Psychological factors
        1. Hopelessness, sensation-seeking (easily bored people) – escape troubling emotions
        2. Self-medication, to relieve anxiety
    D. Cognitive factors: positive expectations and attitudes
VIII. Drug Treatment
    A. Most effective programs use a variety of approaches
    B. Detoxification—clear body of addictive drugs
    C. Professional counseling to confront underlying psychological problems
    D. May use therapeutic drugs (such as methadone) as well

SUMMARY

In this module, you learn of other ways our consciousness may be altered—in this case via chemical means, using legal and illegal drugs. Most drugs do not affect our mental state; however, psychoactive drugs do. These are chemicals that literally act on the brain and change how it functions. Psychoactive drugs affect neurotransmitter activity in the brain. They may also occupy or otherwise impact the neurotransmitter sending and receiving sites. Emotions, cognitions, and behavior are all impacted.

Essentially everyone uses drugs; we drink coffee, tea, or colas, and many individuals still smoke despite the demonstrated health risks. Alcohol, of course, is very widely used. Some drugs are vital to the treatment of physical disorders. They may control pain, treat epilepsy, or anesthetize a patient during surgery. Drug use becomes drug abuse when obtaining and using a drug becomes the focus of one's existence. All other aspects of one's life—occupation, personal health, relationships with loved ones—take second place. At this point, the individual is physically or psychologically addicted. Physiological dependency means the body's chemistry and chemical functioning literally have been changed as a result of repeated use of a drug. Psychological dependency means an individual is unable to cope with life without relying on the drug, though no true chemical dependency is present. Some drugs are strictly psychologically addictive; others have both physiologically and psychologically addicting capacities. Drug addiction means an individual is both compulsive about obtaining and using a drug and is chemically dependent upon it.

Legal and illegal drugs are categorized in various classifications, depending upon the effect the particular drug has. Some drugs decrease arousal; these are classified as depressants. Some drugs increase arousal and activity; these are known as stimulants. A third category of drug classification is that of hallucinogens. Hallucinogens change sensory perceptions. They will create, as the name implies, hallucinations—the world perceived by the individual using these drugs is not as it actually exists. Sensory input is distorted.

Depressants include alcohol, barbiturates, tranquilizers, and opioids. They reduce the activity of your central nervous system; in other words, your body slows down. Depressants typically have a calming effect, inducing feelings of relaxation and perhaps relief. Heart rate, breathing, and other bodily activities are reduced. These drugs can be quite dangerous because, in sufficient quantity, vital bodily processes are halted altogether. Depressants typically are highly addictive. They also are especially lethal when combined with other drugs. Drug users are drawn to depressants because they calm an individual and may create feelings of euphoria.

Stimulants arouse the body and increase the rate of physiological processes. The appeal of stimulants is that they create a "rush." The individual using stimulants may feel a physiological "high"—they feel particularly alert, focused, and unusually sharp or perceptive. Interestingly, others around a drug user may not share this view! The class of stimulants includes amphetamines (methamphetamine or "speed" is one example), cocaine, and MDMA (Ecstasy). Legal stimulants include both nicotine (found in tobacco products) and caffeine in our coffee, cola, and chocolate foods and drinks.

Hallucinogens include LSD, marijuana, and PCP. These drugs may create states of delirium, or vivid hallucinations. Hallucinogens are also known as psychedelic drugs because the user feels particularly attuned to what is perceived as revealing sensory phenomena. Though these drugs are psychologically addicting, there is no evidence that they are also physically addictive. They often create sensations of calmness and relaxation, but the use of hallucinogens is also associated with feelings of paranoia or panic. Marijuana is the most widely used illicit drug in the Western world. Cocaine is the second most frequently used.

There are many problems associated with drug use beyond the fact that many mentioned here are illegal and are controlled substances. Chronic drug use plays havoc with the body, disrupting and harming physiological organs and processes. It impacts the very functioning of the brain, changing the levels of naturally-occurring neurotransmitters and affecting neural transmissions. High doses of drugs, and/or drugs taken in combination with other substances, can lead to permanent physical damage, coma, or death. There are psychological effects as well. Drug use may produce feelings of anxiety or paranoia. Users of LSD report flashbacks—sometimes many years later. Because the human body develops a tolerance when drugs are used regularly, increasing amounts of the drug must be taken in order to achieve the same effect. Drug use can easily become dependency, disrupting the functioning of all other facets in one's life.

It is thought that drug dependency is the result of a number of factors. Some of these include genetic predisposition, social pressures, and self-medication. Very often substance abuse is a symptom of more serious underlying difficulties. To treat the drug abuse problem, the psychological precipitating factors must be addressed. Typically, a chemically-dependent individual must undergo detoxification (addictive drugs are cleared from the body) before other therapies are undertaken. Drugs are addictive, sometimes highly addictive. The potential for physical and psychological harm is great.

KEY TERMS

Psychoactive drugs

Drug abuse

Polyabusers

Drug dependence

Physiological dependence

Withdrawal syndrome

Tolerance

Drug addiction

Psychological dependence

Depressants

Intoxicant

Alcoholism

Narcotics

Stimulants

Hallucinogens

Delirium

Detoxification

SELF-TEST PRACTICE QUIZ

Match the following Key Terms and definitions:

1. _____ Clearing drugs or toxins from the body

2. _____ Chemicals that reduce the activity of the central nervous system; induce relaxation and euphoria

3. _____ A severe drug-related problem involving compulsive use of and reliance on a drug

4. _____ Drugs that alter or distort sensory input

5. _____ Drugs that increase the activity of the central nervous system; increase alertness and arousal

6. _____ Lack of control over use of and physiological dependence on alcohol

7. _____ Body adjusts to regular drug use; increasing amounts of drug are needed to achieve same effect

8. _____ Maladaptive or dangerous use of a chemical substance; causes physical or personal harm

9. _____ Painful symptoms associated with abrupt cessation of use of a drug

10. _____ People who abuse more than one drug at a time

11. _____ Physical dependence on a drug due to repeated use that changes body chemistry

a.   Psychoactive drugs

b.   Drug abuse

c.   Polyabusers

d.   Drug dependence

e.   Physiological dependence

f.   Withdrawal syndrome

g.   Tolerance

h.   Drug addiction

i.   Psychological dependence

j.   Depressants

k.   Intoxicant

l.   Alcoholism

m.   Narcotics

n.   Stimulants

o.   Hallucinogens

p.   Delirium

q.   Detoxification

12. _____ Chemical substances that affect functioning of the brain; change mental state

13. _____ Confusion, disorientation, inability to focus attention; may result from use of a hallucinogen

14. _____ Chemical substance that induces a state of drunkenness

15. _____ Compulsive use of and reliance on a drug; no physiological dependence is apparent

16. _____ Addictive drugs that relieve pain, induce feelings of drowsiness; also called opioids

17. _____ Drug use involving both physiological and psychological dependency; cessation would result in withdrawal symptoms

18. LSD and marijuana are in the class of
    a. stimulants.
    b. depressants.
    c. barbiturates.
    d. hallucinogens.

19. Which of the following drugs can lead to physiological dependence?
    a. Alcohol
    b. LSD
    c. Marijuana
    d. none of the above

20. Psychoactive drugs are
    a. illegal substances.
    b. legal medications.
    c. street drugs.
    d. drugs that act on the brain, affecting moods of the user.

21. The difference between drug use and drug abuse is that, in drug abuse, use of substances
    a. interferes with the ability to function effectively.
    b. causes physical damage to the user's body.
    c. puts one's employment and/or emotional relationships in jeopardy.
    d. all of the above

22. Chemical dependence is also known as
    a. psychological dependence.
    b. physiological dependence.
    c. chemical addiction.
    d. drug addiction.

23. Compulsive behaviors such as gambling, sexual addiction, and the like, are known as _____ dependencies.
    a. disruptive
    b. non-chemical
    c. behavioral
    d. abusive

24. The most widely used and abused depressant is
    a. marijuana.
    b. caffeine.
    c. alcohol.
    d. cocaine.

25. Drugs that calm or sedate, and have a number of legitimate medical uses, are
    a. barbiturates.
    b. amphetamines.
    c. derived from the cannabis plant.
    d. endorphins.

26. The psychoactive substance in marijuana is
    a. ethanol.
    b. THC.
    c. opiates.
    d. MDMA.

27. Why is binge drinking so dangerous?
    a. It may lead people to engage in other risky behaviors such as drunk driving.
    b. It is a strong predictor of later alcoholism.
    c. Large doses of alcohol can lead to coma or death.
    d. all of the above

28. High doses of depressants can kill because they
    a. destroy large areas of brain tissue.
    b. can stop functioning of vital bodily processes altogether.
    c. lead to aggressive behavior where an individual is likely to be physically attacked.
    d. lead to the use of other substances in large quantities.

29. Which of the following is NOT a risk factor for drug abuse?
    a. Unemployment
    b. Social pressures
    c. Genetic predisposition
    d. A sense of hope

30. An individual may use stimulants because of chemical properties that
    a. provide a sense of relaxation and relief.
    b. increase a sense of alertness or euphoria.
    c. decrease levels of dopamine and epinephrine in the brain.
    d. numb the awareness of pain or grief.

31. The most widely used illicit substance in the Western world is
    a. marijuana.
    b. cocaine.
    c. heroin.
    d. methamphetamine.

32. Opioids (opiates) are also known as
    a. psychedelics.
    b. narcotics.
    c. intoxicants.
    d. hallucinogens.
33. In the past, whenever Jake was tired he could drink one cup of coffee and feel much better. But now he has found that he needs *two* cups of coffee to get the same effect. What concept does this illustrate?
    a. Psychological dependence
    b. Polyabuse
    c. Tolerance
    d. Detoxification
34. Which of the following is NOT a stimulant?
    a. Marijuana
    b. Caffeine
    c. Cocaine
    d. Nicotine
35. Narcotics occupy the same brain receptor sites as
    a. dopamine.
    b. acetylcholine.
    c. endorphins.
    d. all of the above

ESSAY QUESTIONS

1. Why are individuals drawn to use and abuse mind-altering substances?

2. What are some of the harmful effects of drug abuse and dependency?

3. What are the most effective methods we have for treating drug addictions?

ANSWER KEY

1. Detoxification
2. Depressants
3. Drug dependence
4. Hallucinogens
5. Stimulants
6. Alcoholism
7. Tolerance
8. Drug abuse
9. Withdrawal syndrome
10. Polyabusers
11. Physiological dependence
12. Psychoactive drugs
13. Delirium
14. Intoxicant
15. Psychological dependence
16. Narcotics
17. Drug addiction
18. d
19. a
20. d
21. d
22. b
23. b
24. c
25. a
26. b
27. d
28. b
29. d
30. b
31. a
32. b
33. c
34. a
35. c

SAMPLE ANSWERS TO ESSAY QUESTIONS

1. Individuals may be drawn to drug use for a variety of reasons. Depending in part on the individual's physiological and psychological characteristics, drug use may turn into drug abuse and dependency. The initial pull to try drugs or continue to use them may be social, in that if one's peers use drugs then such use may help make one more a part of the group. Drugs are often used as an escape to provide relief from psychological or emotional problems. They may help reduce feelings of anxiety and in fact help one feel more at ease and socially adept. Because drugs not only relieve pain, dull awareness of problems, create a "rush" or a "high," induce temporary feelings of euphoria, and yield the perception of heightened awareness, once used the desire to experience such feelings again may become quite strong. In addition, it appears that there is a genetic predisposition regarding substances. Some individuals are more likely than others to become compulsive about drug use, and exhibit addictive behaviors and patterns of use.

2. Drug use and dependency can negatively impact every facet of a person's life. Chronic drug use causes physical harm to the user's body, affecting bodily organs (such as the liver or heart) and various life-sustaining systems such as respiration. Brain functioning also is affected, and physiological dependency literally means that one's brain chemistry has been changed. Should an individual try to stop using drugs, there may be a period of severe withdrawal where the body, which has grown used to the presence of the chemical(s), readjusts to functioning without such drugs. When one becomes addicted, obtaining and using the drug(s) of choice becomes the focus of existence. Personal integrity and values, employment obligations, family and social matters, and even physical health take a back seat to compulsive behavior regarding the drug. Thus, all of these latter issues are neglected and tend to suffer. Drug use itself can cause death, either directly through very high doses or via drugs that become lethal in combination with other drugs—or indirectly, in that functioning is impaired and one is more at risk for automobile accidents and the like. Also, when one is addicted, such an individual engages in behaviors (stealing, prostitution, and worse) where there is a high risk of physical harm or legal consequences.

3. To treat individuals with drug addiction, usually the most important first step is detoxification; that is, getting rid of all drugs that may be present in the user's system. Since this process is difficult and painful, often it takes place in an institution such as a hospital. Though chemical dependency may be the most obvious problem, typically there are underlying psychological difficulties that must be addressed if the individual is to become truly well. Following detoxification, persons with addictions usually begin therapy with professional counselors. The objective is not simply to get off drugs, but to stay off drugs. Therapy is intended to help the individual face the psychological problems leading to drug use and drug abuse; psychological difficulties often involve problems with depression and self-esteem. In some cases, therapeutic drugs (like methadone for heroin users) may be used in combination with psychological counseling to help individuals resist falling back into old patterns of drug use.

MODULE 4.5 APPLICATION: GETTING YOUR Z'S

LEARNING OBJECTIVE

After you have mastered the information in this unit, you will be able to:

1. List suggestions for developing healthier sleep habits.

OUTLINE

I. Suggestions for Developing Healthier Sleep Habits (not caused by underlying physical or psychological problems)
    A. Adopt a regular sleep schedule (go to bed and get up at about the same time every day)
    B. Allow yourself to wind down naturally before trying to sleep – don't try to force sleep
    C. Have a routine before going to bed
    D. Use your bed primarily for sleeping; not, for example, for reading or studying
    E. If you can't sleep, get up and go somewhere else to relax
    F. Avoid daytime naps
    G. Don't bring problems to bed
    H. Use relaxing mental imagery
    I. Engage in regular exercise during the day – **several** hours before sleep
    J. Avoid caffeine and nicotine, especially in the afternoon
    K. Think positively about your ability to sleep and to cope

SUMMARY

In this Application module, you learn about ways to combat insomnia and get a restful night's sleep. We must remember that sleep cannot be forced. It is helpful to engage in sufficient exercise during the day and avoid napping so we will be more prone to sleep at night. Following a routine before bedtime and reserving our bed primarily for sleep will help make sleep come more naturally. We can create a good sleep habit by going to bed and getting up at approximately the same time each day. It is important not to bring worries and concerns to bed, and, if one cannot sleep, it is better to get up, go elsewhere to relax, then return to bed when relaxed and try again. Caffeine and nicotine are stimulants so they are to be avoided, especially late in the day, if one has sleep problems. We need a positive attitude about sleeping and our ability to sleep. Above all, worrying about lack of sleep only makes the condition worse. It is important to remember that we can get through a day and function, whether or not we have been able to get all the sleep we would like.

CHAPTER 4   APPLICATION EXERCISE

Observe a television, theater, Internet, or video production where one or more characters in the cast have drug addictions. What are some of the behaviors they exhibit? Has their substance abuse been long-term and chronic, or has it begun recently? Briefly describe the setting of the program you have viewed, then consider the following:

(1) Is the drug use or abuse glamorized? (2) What seem to be precipitating factors leading to the drug use? (3) Do cultural or social norms in the setting seem to support, tolerate, or frown upon the substance use and abuse? (4) Is the user seeking treatment? If so, what does that treatment consist of? (5) How might you help a friend with a substance abuse problem?

CHAPTER 5

Learning

In Chapter 5, you are introduced to processes that are vital to human and animal survival. These processes involve the ability to learn. If humans were not able to learn from experience—to assess, contemplate, adapt to, and make best use of our environment—our time on this planet would be short indeed!

Learning involves a relatively permanent change in behavior, due to experience. Usually learning is adaptive; that is, it makes our behavior and existence more conducive to survival. However, this beneficial end-product of learning is not always the case. We may learn things that are not helpful, or in fact are detrimental. Why would we learn such things when they are not truly productive? Probably because there is some stimulus, some reinforcer in the environment, which can keep even maladaptive behaviors going. If we learn about learning, we can think more in depth about what we do and why we do it. If learning comes from experience, we can learn better ways to function in our world. Perhaps we behave in some ways that truly are not helpful. Learning why this behavior occurs can help us alter or eliminate it. Since much of learning does enhance and improve our well-being, understanding how the processes occur will help us maximize the experience.

Learning is generally thought to come from three basic sources. Fundamental to our understanding of learning is the premise that environment and experience play a tremendous role. In fact, early well-known psychologists, such as John Watson and B. F. Skinner, insisted that only observable behaviors should be studied. They chose to disregard any processes that were not visible to the eye. Not surprisingly, then, two of the three major categories regarding learning deal strictly with experiences relating to the external environment. These two categories are classical conditioning and operant conditioning. A third source for learning is that due to cognitive processes. The first two sources are, of course, easier to study. The impact of experience with the environment is clear. The latter process, cognitive learning, is harder to study, because such learning takes place almost entirely within the mind. Some behaviorists argue that cognitive learning does not really occur. The debate continues and is difficult to settle. This state of affairs is likely to continue since, at least at present, we cannot see the actual process that is the subject of contention!

Classical conditioning was first discovered and introduced by Ivan Pavlov. He was not a psychologist and was not researching learning—but in his digestion studies he found that dogs used secreted saliva when he did not expect them to. Why would they salivate when no food was actually present? Pavlov's work is a fine example of how some of our most worthwhile advances are discovered by accident. The animals had learned (just like you and your pets might!) that a food dish, or the handler, or even certain sounds, were associated with the presence of food. The neutral stimulus (the dish or a tone) was perceived as having characteristics like the unconditioned stimulus (the food), and thus, with time, came to elicit a response from the organism. If you have a dog or a cat how do they know when you are about to feed them? One way could be the sound of the door opening, if that is where the food is kept.

Operant conditioning is best known as the work of B. F. Skinner. Skinner built upon the earlier findings of Edward Thorndike. In operant conditioning, consequences of behavior have everything to do with whether that behavior will be learned. Simply put, we adopt and exhibit behaviors that (based on past experience) we know will lead to pleasant outcomes. We minimize the appearance of behaviors when we have learned they likely will have unpleasant consequences. Note that classical conditioning tends to be built upon reflexive, or wired-in, behaviors. It deals predominantly with the learning of feelings and emotions. Operant conditioning is a more conscious experience; the learner here is more actively and intentionally involved. An example would be when little Albert turned his head to avoid seeing the white rat (out of sight out of mind). Through operant conditioning we learn a huge array of different skills. In general the voluntary motor nervous system is involved.

Cognitive learning, mentioned above, deals with unseen mental processes. These include such activities as thinking, problem solving, and mental imagery. Human beings are able to learn much, both from experience and from reasoning. How very fortunate we are that we have this great capacity to learn! How fortunate, also, that so many enriching learning opportunities come our way.

MODULE 5.1 CLASSICAL CONDITIONING: LEARNING THROUGH ASSOCIATION

LEARNING OBJECTIVES

After you have mastered the information in this unit, you will be able to:

1.   Define and understand the nature of learning.

2.   Discuss the process of classical conditioning.

3.   Discuss the roles of extinction, spontaneous recovery, reconditioning, stimulus generalization, and stimulus discrimination in classical conditioning.

4.   Describe the stimulus characteristics that strengthen conditioned responses.

5.   Discuss the cognitive perspective on classical conditioning.

6.   Describe examples of classical conditioning in daily life.

OUTLINE

I.   Principles of Classical Conditioning
   A.   Work of physiologist Ivan Pavlov—learning by association
   B.   Unconditioned stimulus (US)—stimulus that elicits a response from an organism with no learning needed
   C.   Unconditioned response (UR)—a response by an organism to a stimulus that is based on reflexive behavior (no learning is needed)
   D.   Neutral stimulus (NS)—a stimulus from the environment around the organism that does not initially elicit the response in question
   E.   Conditioned stimulus (CS)—a previously neutral stimulus; through pairing with unconditioned stimulus comes to elicit conditioned response
   F.   Conditioned response (CR)—a learned response; through pairing of CS with US becomes the reaction to an initially neutral stimulus
   G.   Extinction—conditioned (learned) response disappears when CS repeatedly presented without pairing with the US
      1.   A therapy technique called gradual exposure makes use of the principle of extinction to help people overcome phobias
   H.   Spontaneous recovery—conditioned response (CR) may reappear briefly if CS again presented at a later time
   I.   Reconditioning—the quicker relearning of a conditioned response after extinction
   J.   Stimulus generalization—CR elicited; is in response to stimuli similar to CS
      1.   Example when you walk into a room and suddenly feel very uncomfortable or anxious for no apparent reason

2. An explanation of déjà-vu (feeling of having experienced something before that you didn't actually experience) may apply here

K. Stimulus discrimination—CR not elicited; stimuli presented are unlike CS
1. Allows us to differentiate between threatening and nonthreatening stimuli

L. Strengthening conditioned responses
1. Frequency of pairings—the more often the CS is paired with the US, the stronger the CR will be
2. Timing—for strongest CR, CS must be presented first and remain during entire presentation of US
3. Intensity of US—stronger level of US will result in quicker conditioning than weak presentation of US

II. Cognitive Perspective on Classical Conditioning
A. Learning not just via NS/US pairing
B. Rescorla's research shows CS must be able to reliably predict occurrence of US (thus a cognitive component in classical conditioning – holds that conditioning depends on the informational value)
1. Organisms learn to anticipate events based on cues, called conditioned stimuli, that come to reliably predict the occurrence of these events
2. Classical conditioning as a kind of built-in early warning system

III. Examples of Classical Conditioning
A. Study of "Little Albert" (conditioning of fear response)
1. Eleven-month-old boy used as subject (Watson & Rayner, 1920)
2. Initially not afraid of a white rat presented to him
3. Did respond naturally with fear to a loud noise
4. Rat (CS) presented with loud noise (US)—eventually Albert feared the white rat
5. Albert's fear generalized to other furry stimuli – such an acquired fear response is called conditioned emotional reaction (CER)
   a) Exposing a child to intense fear, even with the parents' permission, fails to adhere to the responsibility investigators have to safeguard the welfare of research participants
   b) Watson and Rayner made no attempt to undo or extinguish Albert's fears, as ethical codes would now require. The original conditioning experience may be lost to memory, but consideration needs to be given to the process of spontaneous recovery. Could "Big" Albert (as a grown man) one day be affected by his past experience?

B. Phobias
1. Excessive fears
2. May be acquired through classical conditioning
3. Behavior therapy—psychological treatment (such as for phobias) based on classical conditioning principles

C. Positive emotions—these also may be learned via association (classical conditioning)
D. Drug cravings—environment (such as a bar, party, or drug-using friends) may trigger desire for drug due to learned association
E. Taste aversions—learned avoidance (such as of a food) due to prior unpleasant experience with it (e.g., nausea or vomiting)

IV. Conditioning the Immune System—investigators have found that even immune-system responses can be classically conditioned; animals learned to suppress their own immune system response (CR) when they drank a CS previously paired with an immune response suppressing drug (US)
A. May be used to give the immune system a boost in its fight against disease
B. May be used in people who receive organ transplants – when the body's immune system would normally attack the foreign object

SUMMARY

In this module, you learn one of the ways our environment teaches us through pairings of neutral stimuli with things that we naturally (usually reflexively) already respond to. Your pets are a perfect example. Does your cat know where you keep the can opener? Does your dog respond to his leash, or when you tear open a package that sounds like the dog treat bag (its food)? Notice these learnings (these responses) did not occur initially. Your dog or cat first was enthusiastic just about the food itself. However, after repeated pairings (the can opener is always kept in the same drawer; you have to open the drawer to open the food tin; to your dog the leash comes to mean "Hurray! We are going out!"), these originally neutral stimuli come to signify the unconditioned stimulus—the food your pet will eat or the wonderful walk in the park. These are learnings of positive emotions. Classical conditioning can teach us both positive or negative associations. Your dog or cat may usually be very enthusiastic about the car (the car has come to signify an exciting trip with you, which may include many marvelous smells!). However, once that car is used to take the pet to the vet—where your pet may receive a shot or experience perhaps painful surgery—the car is no longer exciting. In fact, at least for a few trips, you might have to work hard to coax your pet back into the car. The car, a conditioned stimulus (CS), now has come to represent something unpleasant (the pain of a veterinarian visit) rather than something pleasant (you, that trip, and those wonderful smells…!).

Humans also learn much through classical conditioning. Typically, classical conditioning involves the learning of feelings or emotions. Generally it involves our autonomic nervous system—responses or reflexes that are already "wired in" to our functioning. The conditioning occurs when these naturally-eliciting stimuli are paired (usually repeatedly) with a stimulus to which at first we have a different, or no, reaction to. However, when the naturally-eliciting stimulus (maybe a very good meal or social pleasures shared with warm and wonderful friends) is paired repeatedly with this neutral stimulus—eventually the neutral stimulus becomes a conditioned stimulus (CS)—it takes on the characteristics of the unconditioned stimulus (US). The unconditioned stimulus is the one to which we responded from the beginning. No learning was necessary. Notice that learning (experiencing the association of the CS with the US) is necessary for classical conditioning to occur. We may come to respond to the sight of that restaurant which serves such delicious meals, or is the place where we always congregate with friends very dear to us. Advertising tries to sell us on products by combining a given product or logo with something we already like. Do you respond with feelings of interest and anticipation when you simply see the box from your favorite pizza shop?

The terms needed to understand classical conditioning are (1) the US (a stimulus from the environment around the organism which elicits a naturally-occurring reaction); (2) the UR (a naturally-occurring response from the organism; the response is to the presentation of the US); (3) the CS (a stimulus from the environment where the reaction of the learning organism was initially neutral); and (4) the CR—a learned response that now is elicited by the CS, though this reaction was not present prior to the CS/US experience.

We become classically conditioned to many things. If your room is a place where you are comfortable and experience many pleasant things, you have a positive response to it now (a CR) even though you may not have felt that way originally. If your sweetheart broke up with you on a warm summer evening in June down by the ocean, you may feel more despondent than charmed for a while by your summer ocean experiences. With time (due to the classical conditioning phenomenon known as extinction) the seashore and summer evenings will come to enchant you again. Would spontaneous recovery one day briefly bring the feeling back? Phobias (excessive fears) may have their roots in classical conditioning, in that an early terrifying experience may become associated with the setting where the experience occurred. If you were in a serious car accident, for example, you may forever feel tense and clammy when you pass the location where that accident occurred. Taste aversions and the like also can be learned via classical conditioning.

It is important to remember that the environment and experience do teach us. For example, if you offer a baby a cookie or a bottle of juice or milk, the baby will take the food that is in your one hand, rather than the $100 bill in your other hand! Notice our response to money (or even the sight of it) is learned through classical conditioning. Fortunately, what we know about classical conditioning also helps us undo learned behaviors that actually are detrimental to us. Understanding the factors that cause us to learn by means of classical conditioning also helps us understand influences on our behavior. If we choose to, we can eliminate or change these behaviors.

KEY TERMS

Learning

Classical conditioning

Unconditioned response (UR)

Unconditioned stimulus (US)

Neutral stimulus (NS)

Conditioned response (CR)

Conditioned stimulus (CS)

Extinction

Spontaneous recovery

Reconditioning

Stimulus generalization

Stimulus discrimination

Conditioned emotional reaction (CER)

Phobias

Behavior therapy

Conditioned taste aversions

Immune system

SELF-TEST PRACTICE QUIZ

Match the following Key Terms and definitions:

1. _____ Excessive fears of objects or situations

2. _____ The quicker relearning of a conditioned response following extinction

3. _____ A relatively permanent change in behavior due to experience

4. _____ Aversions to particular tastes; acquired via classical conditioning

5. _____ A learned response to an originally neutral stimulus (which has been paired with an unconditioned stimulus)

6. _____ A previously neutral stimulus; comes to elicit a learned response due to repeated pairing with an unconditioned stimulus

7. _____ The diminishing and disappearance of a conditioned response when the CS is no longer ever paired with the US

8. _____ An emotional response to a particular stimulus resulting from classical conditioning

9. _____ A stimulus that elicits a response from an organism where no learning or conditioning is necessary

10. _____ The spontaneous return of a conditioned response following extinction

11. _____ A therapeutic application of principles regarding conditioning and learning

12. _____ Learning, usually involving affective states, due to the pairing of a neutral stimulus with an unconditioned stimulus

13. _____ A response by an organism to an unconditioned stimulus

a. Learning
b. Classical conditioning
c. Unconditioned response (UR)
d. Unconditioned stimulus (US)
e. Neutral stimulus (NS)
f. Conditioned response (CR)
g. Conditioned stimulus (CR)
h. Extinction
i. Spontaneous recovery
j. Reconditioning
k. Stimulus generalization
l. Stimulus discrimination
m. Conditioned emotional reaction (CER)
n. Phobias
o. Behavior therapy
p. Conditioned taste aversions
q. Immune system

14. _____ The ability to differentiate, and not respond to, stimuli that are unlike a conditioned stimulus

15. _____ A stimulus that initially does not elicit a response; one may be learned later through conditioning

16. _____ An organism responds to a stimulus because it is similar to the original conditioned stimulus

17. _____ The system that protects the body from disease

18. Part of the concept of learning is that any change in behavior resulting from it is

    a. adaptive.
    b. relatively permanent.
    c. innovative.
    d. healthful.

19. Classical conditioning was first discovered by

    a. B.F. Skinner.
    b. John Watson.
    c. Sigmund Freud.
    d. Ivan Pavlov.

20. Watson and Rayner's "Little Albert" experiment was so important because it was the first experiment in which it was shown that

    a. it is possible to classically condition a taste preference.
    b. it is possible to classically condition an emotional response.
    c. organisms can learn to discriminate between different stimuli.
    d. classical conditioning only works if the CS is a reliable predictor of the US.

21. In order to stop her cat from jumping on the sofa, Crystal squirts the cat with water, which the cat hates. After a while, the cat becomes afraid just at the sight of the water bottle. What is the unconditioned stimulus in this scenario?

    a. The sofa
    b. The water bottle
    c. Fear
    d. Being sprayed with water

22. The love of your life drives a silver Volkswagen. Prior to meeting her you could care less about Volkswagens, no matter what color they were. Now when you see a silver Volkswagen, your pulse quickens and your heart leaps. Your positive feelings for silver Volkswagens are

    a. conditioned stimuli.
    b. conditioned responses.
    c. unconditioned responses.
    d. foolishness.

23. Through classical conditioning, it is possible to affect a person's

    a. immune system.
    b. food preferences.
    c. fears.
    d. all of the above

24. The stimulus that becomes the CS was initially a(n)
    a. unconditioned stimulus.
    b. conditioned stimulus.
    c. neutral stimulus.
    d. random behavior.

25. The relationship between an unconditioned stimulus and response is
    a. based on an organism's life experiences.
    b. elicited without prior learning.
    c. a matter of willpower.
    d. inconsistent.

26. Michael is a young boy who has been physically abused by his father who has a heavy beard. As a result, Michael now exhibits fear around any man with a beard. This is an example of
    a. spontaneous recovery.
    b. extinction.
    c. stimulus discrimination.
    d. stimulus generalization.

27. Research by Robert Rescorla (1967, 1988) demonstrates that there is a cognitive component to classical conditioning—that is, not just any stimulus can be paired with a US and come to elicit a conditioned response. Rescorla's findings indicate that the CS must
    a. be familiar to the learning organism.
    b. be easy to discriminate.
    c. reliably predict the US.
    d. all of the above

ESSAY QUESTIONS

1. Briefly explain how the process of classical conditioning works.

2. From each of the following two episodes, pick out the US, the UR, the CS, and the CR. For each episode, explain why you made the choices that you did:

    a. Every summer Alan went up to the lake cottage with his family and friends. He left his work and worries at home. He and his friends would often fish, swim, or go boating. They had many good times and many good meals at the cottage. Alan has taken pictures of the lake and cottage and has them posted around his office. Whenever he looks at the pictures, he feels peaceful and happy.

    b. Your mother was quite sick during much of your childhood. She often was hospitalized, and you would visit her there. Your mother was uncomfortable in the hospital and many pieces of medical equipment were in the room and attached to her body. Eventually she died while she was at the hospital. To this day, you despise hospitals and feel sick and full of dread whenever you go near one.

3. There are several features of the classical conditioning process that can help speed up or strengthen the learning of the conditioned response. What are these? Explain each.

ANSWER KEY

1. Phobias

2. Reconditioning

3. Learning

4. Conditioned taste aversions

5.   Conditioned response
6.   Conditioned stimulus
7.   Extinction
8.   Conditioned emotional reaction (CER)
9.   Unconditioned stimulus
10. Spontaneous recovery
11. Behavior therapy
12. Classical conditioning
13. Unconditioned response
14. Stimulus discrimination
15. Neutral stimulus
16. Stimulus generalization
17. Immune system
18. b
19. d
20. b
21. d
22. b
23. d
24. c
25. b
26. d
27. c

SAMPLE ANSWERS TO ESSAY QUESTIONS

1.   In classical conditioning, we learn to have an affective response of some kind to a stimulus that did not elicit that type of response earlier. The response (a conditioned response) is learned because the one stimulus, originally known as the neutral stimulus, comes to represent the unconditioned stimulus because the two have been paired. We learn to associate the conditioned stimulus (CS) with the unconditioned stimulus (US), since they have occurred together. Such learning, or classical conditioning, takes place best if the CS and US are paired together repeatedly. This learning may happen to us (as in the learning of phobic reactions) without our intentionally taking part in the process. If the CS is presented many times without being combined with the US, extinction will occur—that is, the learned response (CS) will eventually disappear. We may respond also to stimuli similar to the CS (stimulus generalization) and not respond to stimuli that are sufficiently unlike the CS (stimulus discrimination).

2.

    a.   US: good food, pleasant social times; UR: happiness and peace in response to the good food and pleasant social times; CS: pictures of the lake and cottage where the pleasant times occurred; CR: happiness and peace in response to looking at the lake and cottage pictures.

    b.   US: Suffering, death and loss of mother; UR: child's unhappiness in response to this loss. CS: Hospital where death and loss took place; CR: unhappiness now experienced in response to seeing the hospital.

3.   Classically conditioned responses may be strengthened by (a) frequent pairings of US and CS; (b) timing; and (c) using a greater intensity of US. In other words, the more often an organism experiences the pairing of a US with a CS, the stronger the learning (as evidenced by the CR) will be. Also, it is quite important that the CS be presented first and followed rather promptly by the US. The CS must be present during the entire time the US is administered in order for maximal learning to take place. The stronger the intensity of the US presented, the more quickly classical conditioning will take place.

MODULE 5.2 OPERANT CONDITIONING: LEARNING THROUGH CONSEQUENCES

LEARNING OBJECTIVES

After you have mastered the information in this unit, you will be able to:

1.   Explain Thorndike's Law of Effect.

2.   Discuss the process of operant conditioning.

3.   Discuss the different types of reinforcers.

4.   Describe schedules of reinforcement and their typical effects.

5.   Explain escape learning and avoidance learning.

6.   Define punishment, and discuss why psychologists are concerned about its use.

7.   Discuss applications of operant conditioning.

OUTLINE

I.   Other Types of Learning (Besides Classical Conditioning)

II.   Thorndike and the Law of Effect – first systematic attempt to describe how behavior is affected by its consequences

    A.   Used animals for research because they were easier to study

    B.   Proposed learning occurs only through trial and error

    C.   No cognitive component; consequences "stamped in" successful responses

    D.   Law of Effect: Environment important—pleasant consequence increases likelihood behavior will be repeated; unpleasant consequence decreases; and modern psychologists call the first part reinforcement and the second part punishment

III.   B. F. Skinner and Operant Conditioning – a more formal model also called instructional learning

    A.   Limit study to observable behavior

        1.   Skinner was a strict behaviorist believing that psychologists limit themselves to observable behavior – thoughts and feelings, cannot be observed and have no place in scientific account of behavior – the mind was a "back box" whose contents cannot be illuminated by science

B.   Radical behaviorism—all behavior (human and animal) determined exclusively by genetics and environment
C.   Free will is an illusion, myth
  NOTE - both radical behaviorism and free will were very controversial
D.   Skinner box—for testing operant conditioning principles with animals
E.   Operant conditioning (also called instrumental learning)—consequences of a behavior determine probability of its recurrence
F.   Reinforcer—pleasant/desirable outcome; increases likelihood behavior will occur again
G.   Superstitious behavior—learned when random behavior is coincidentally paired with a reinforcing consequence – always use the same pencil because you once got an A using that pencil

IV.   Principles of Operant Conditioning
A.   Positive reinforcement—desirable stimulus introduced after response occurs
  1.   Examples include food, money, and good grades
B.   Negative reinforcement—undesirable stimulus removed after response occurs
  1.   A response is strengthened when it leads to the removal of an "aversive" (unpleasant or painful) stimulus- loud noise, cold, pain, child's crying; aversive stimulus is removed
  2.   It does NOT imply punishment
  3.   Helps account for the avoidance of fearful stimuli or situations in people with phobias
  4.   May have an undesirable effects in some situations – child throws a tantrum –child is positively reinforced while parent is negatively reinforced because tantrum stops
C.   Discriminative stimuli—signals reinforcement is available if correct response produced by organism
  1.   A time to ask a favor – clue: observe the person's face to see how receptive they may be
D.   Primary reinforcer—intrinsically reinforcing; satisfies a basic need – biological needs or reward value
E.   Secondary reinforcer—reinforcing value (such as money) learned through association
F.   Shaping—application of successive approximations method – learning in small steps
G.   Method of successive approximations—reinforcing broad or general attempts first; then reinforcing closer and closer steps toward ultimate desired behavior
H.   Extinction—learned behaviors (responses) disappear if not ever paired with a reinforcer

V.   Schedules of Reinforcement
A.   Continuous reinforcement
  1.   Every desired response is followed by a reinforcer
  2.   Behaviors are learned most quickly with continuous reinforcement
  3.   Learned behaviors also most quick to extinguish this way – likely to return once reinforcement is reinstated
B.   Partial reinforcement (ratio = number of responses; interval = passage of time)
  1.   Fixed-ratio (FR) schedule—reinforcement given after a set number of responses (after every third, or sixth, or the like)
    a)   An example, piecework – works are paid according to a number produced – quality may suffer if quantity alone is the only determining factor
  2.   Variable-ratio (VR) schedule
    a)   Reinforcement based on number of responses; actual number varies
    b)   Targeted number of responses is an average
    c)   Example of VR schedule: slot machine
  3.   Fixed-interval (FI) schedule—reinforcement given for desired response produced after a set amount of time has passed

    4.   Variable-interval (VI) schedule
        a)   Reinforcement based on passage of time; actual length of time varies
        b)   Targeted passage of time is an average
        c)   Example of VI schedule: "pop" quizzes in class
        d)   More resistant to extinction

VI.   Escape Learning—organism learns a behavior in order to escape an aversive stimulus

VII. Avoidance Learning—organism learns a behavior in order to avoid an aversive stimulus

VIII. Punishment
    A.   Something unpleasant follows a behavior
    B.   Introduce an aversive stimulus or remove a pleasant one
    C.   Objective: decrease occurrence of undesirable behavior(s)
    D.   Drawbacks of punishment
        1.   May suppress but does not eliminate undesirable behavior
        2.   Does not teach more preferable behavior
        3.   Can create anger, fear, lowered self-esteem, and/or strong negative emotions toward the punisher
        4.   Used frequently, may become out of control becoming abusive
        5.   Does not model desirable behaviors for children (they learn force is an acceptable way of resolving interpersonal issues)
        6.   Milder punishments include controlled verbal reprimand, removal of a reinforcer and time out
    E.   Best approach is to reinforce desirable behaviors

IX.   Applications of Operant Conditioning
    A.   Biofeedback training – thinking calming thoughts
    B.   Behavior modification—target desired behaviors; strengthen through operant conditioning (may use a token economy program)
    C.   Programmed instruction—reinforce each step in a learning task
        1.   Computer-assisted instruction – computer guides the learner through increasingly more challenging information

SUMMARY

In this module, you learn about another kind of conditioning—operant conditioning. Whereas classical conditioning involves mostly reflexive, "wired-in" behaviors, operant conditioning involves learning where the organism is much more an active and knowing participant. Operant conditioning includes the many behaviors we as humans have learned in order to navigate our way through the world. These behaviors range from the simplest, such as tying a shoe or jotting down notes, to more complex, such as a complicated dance step, driving a car, building a house, or preparing for your Ph.D. For example, your ability to speak, feed and dress yourself, ride a bike, use the microwave, participate in a classroom, study for an exam, behave in social settings, find your way to Paris or to the movie theater were all learned predominantly through operant conditioning. Notice these behaviors almost entirely involve motor skills. Thus, operant conditioning makes extensive use of the voluntary nervous system. Animals, too, learn by the same means as you, and they were the most used research subject when early studies on operant conditioning began.

Edward Thorndike (1874–1947) was the first to study operantly-learned responses. He used animals for his research because they were less complex than humans. Based on his work with animals, Thorndike concluded that all learning was trial and error. When an organism happened to stumble upon an appropriate behavioral response (such as running the correct pathway in a maze), the animal was more likely to utilize that behavior in the future because it met with a desirable outcome (the food reward at the end of the maze). Thorndike did not believe that the animals had any insight or cognitions regarding this learning process. Rather, it was his view that the pleasurable outcome "stamped" the behavior pattern into the brain.

To fully understand operant conditioning, you must be aware of the great impact of consequences. Behaviors (conditioned responses) learned through classical conditioning depend mostly upon how frequently the CS is paired with the US. This pairing comes before the learned response is made. For responses learned through operant conditioning, the outcome of any behavior (even if the behavior is random) influences heavily whether that response will be made again. Psychologically well-adjusted people generally like pleasant outcomes, and most prefer them to other, more unpleasant outcomes. We learn from our earliest days to perform or exhibit the behaviors that have pleasurable consequences for us. These consequences might be a smile, praise, or a cookie when we've managed to say the word correctly. A behavior that we learn that leads to something unpleasant is not a behavior we are likely to repeat any time soon. Thus, via experiences with our environment, much of our long-term behavior is shaped. It should be noted that, in the ideal world, "good" behaviors would result in positive outcomes, and poor or harmful behaviors would result in unpleasant consequences. That is the ideal world. However, unfortunately in our world, good behavior, or even very good behavior, sometimes goes unnoticed and unappreciated. In contrast, undesirable behavior (disrupting class, knocking over a lamp, harming innocent people) may inadvertently be encouraged, due to all the attention it receives. Parents need to make very clear exactly what behavior is being punished and what the child can do differently.

B. F. Skinner built upon Thorndike's ideas and noted that the organism *operates* on the environment; hence, the term operant conditioning. Good outcomes are called reinforcers because they literally strengthen a behavior (like reinforced concrete). Where the consequence of a response is pleasant, the response is more likely to occur again. Both positive and negative reinforcers increase the likelihood that a behavior will occur again. However, a positive reinforcer is better! Positive reinforcers mean something good is introduced into the environment for you. A negative reinforcer is still a good thing to have; it is removing something from your environment that has been unpleasant for you. Punishment is a term with which you are already familiar, and its meaning in operant conditioning is similar to what you already know. Punishment is an unpleasant consequence, and its intended impact is to reduce the likelihood that the behavior it follows will occur again. We must be careful in our use of punishment. Also, reinforcers are most effective if, once a response is learned, they occur on a partial, rather than a continuous, schedule. Behavior modification is one very useful application of operant conditioning.

KEY TERMS

Law of Effect

Radical behaviorism

Skinner box

Operant conditioning

Operant response

Reinforcer

Superstitious behavior

Positive reinforcement

Negative reinforcement

Discriminative stimulus

Primary reinforcers

Secondary reinforcers

Shaping

Method of successive approximations

Schedules of reinforcement

Schedule of continuous reinforcement

Schedule of partial reinforcement

Escape learning

Avoidance learning

Punishment

Behavior modification (B-mod)

Token economy program

Programmed instruction

Computer-assisted instruction

SELF-TEST PRACTICE QUIZ

Match the following Key Terms and definitions (note: not every Key Term will be used):

1. _____ Increases the likelihood that a behavior will occur again by removing an unpleasant stimulus

2. _____ A process of learning where consequences are crucial in determining whether or not a response will occur again

3. _____ A system of reinforcement where some, but not all, responses are reinforced

4. _____ A kind of programmed instruction, guiding and reinforcing the student step by step

5. _____ Reinforcers that gain their reinforcing power through being associated with a reinforcer that meets a basic need

6. _____ Behavior acquired because a random act was accidentally reinforced by a pleasant outcome

7. _____ A consequence designed to decrease the likelihood that the behavior it follows will occur again

8. _____ Increases the likelihood that a behavior will occur again by introducing a desirable stimulus following the emitted response

9. _____ Thorndike's principle regarding why learned behaviors reoccur

10. _____ Reinforcing increasingly more accurate manifestations of a learned response

11. _____ Applying operant conditioning principles in a systematic fashion to help improve behaviors

12. _____ A reinforcement schedule where every desired response from an organism is reinforced

a. Law of Effect
b. Radical behaviorism
c. Skinner box
d. Operant conditioning
e. Operant response
f. Reinforcer
g. Superstitious behavior
h. Positive reinforcement
i. Negative reinforcement
j. Discriminative stimulus
k. Primary reinforcers
l. Secondary reinforcers
m. Shaping
n. Method of successive approximations
o. Schedules of reinforcement
p. Schedule of continuous reinforcement
q. Schedule of partial reinforcement
r. Escape learning
s. Avoidance learning
t. Punishment
u. Behavior modification (B-mod)
v. Token economy program
w. Programmed instruction
x. Computer-assisted instruction

13. _____ Responses an organism learns in order to avoid experiencing an unpleasant stimulus

14. _____ The belief that only environment and genetics determine behavior

15. _____ An apparatus designed by B.F. Skinner in order to study and test the impact of operant conditioning principles on learning

16. What kind of learning is NOT explained by classical conditioning?

    a. The learning of modern-day musical themes
    b. The learning of voluntary responses such as motor skills
    c. The learning of feelings and affective responses
    d. Various responses elicited by a conditioned stimulus

17. Radical behaviorism encompasses the notion that

    a. all behavior can be traced to genetic and/or environmental influences.
    b. every human organism is rightfully granted free will.
    c. cognitive activities like reasoning are an important influence on behaviors.
    d. all of the above

18. Watson and Skinner both believed that

    a. vicarious conditioning was best researched by neurological lesioning.
    b. cognitive influences were the most complete explanation for instrumental learning.
    c. it was not appropriate to study if a behavior could not be seen by the human eye.
    d. behaviors were often likely to reappear even though no reinforcer was administered.

19. What is the difference between punishment and negative reinforcement?

    a. Punishment occurs after a response, while negative reinforcement occurs before a response.
    b. Punishment decreases the odds of a behavior reoccurring, while negative reinforcement increases those odds.
    c. Punishment involves removing a stimulus, while negative reinforcement involves adding a stimulus.
    d. There is no difference—"punishment" and "negative reinforcement" are two terms for the same thing.

20. According to operant conditioning theory, superstitious behavior most likely occurs because

    a. parents and grandparents hand down family beliefs.
    b. parents and grandparents hand down cultural beliefs.
    c. random behaviors are inadvertently preceded by reinforcers.
    d. random behaviors are inadvertently followed by reinforcers.

21. When an organism is first learning a response, it is most effective if that organism is reinforced under a _____ schedule of reinforcement.

    a. fixed-interval
    b. fixed-ratio
    c. partial
    d. continuous

22. When parents are trying to instill manners in their children, they don't start out expecting perfection. Instead, they first reinforce the child for simple actions such as saying "thank you." Later on, that is not enough to earn praise—the child must exhibit more advanced social skills. This illustrates the principle of
    a.   negative reinforcement.
    b.   extinction.
    c.   shaping.
    d.   escape learning.

23. Extinction in operant conditioning is likely to occur when
    a.   a CS is promptly followed by a US.
    b.   learned behaviors no longer have a reinforcer as a consequence.
    c.   the CS is rarely or never paired with the US.
    d.   a species has experienced no learning for a considerable length of time.

24. Which schedule of reinforcement is *most* resistant to extinction?
    a.   Fixed-ratio (FR)
    b.   Variable-ratio (VR)
    c.   Fixed-interval (FI)
    d.   Variable-interval (VI)

25. Brittany is baking cookies. The recipe says to bake them for 8–10 minutes. At some point, Brittany will be reinforced when the cookies are finished and she can eat them. What schedule of reinforcement is she on?
    a.   Fixed-ratio (FR)
    b.   Fixed-interval (FI)
    c.   Variable-ratio (VR)
    d.   Variable-interval (VI)

26. Which of the following could be an example of a primary reinforcer?
    a.   Money
    b.   An A in your psychology course
    c.   A hug
    d.   Being complimented on your clothing

27. Behavior modification programs
    a.   utilize operant conditioning strategies.
    b.   identify desirable behaviors that will be strengthened through reinforcement.
    c.   may make use of a token economy system.
    d.   all of the above

28. A problem with fixed-ratio schedules of reinforcement for piecework (e.g., as in a factory) is
    a.   workers are not very motivated to produce.
    b.   quality may suffer if only quantity is rewarded.
    c.   absenteeism rates are likely to increase.
    d.   the very high level of resistance to extinction.

ESSAY QUESTIONS

1.   How does a negative reinforcer influence the occurrence of a behavior? Give an example.

2.   Why is a Skinner box particularly useful for studying operant conditioning?

3.   Why do positive reinforcers tend to increase the likelihood that a behavior will occur again?

4.   What are some concerns we have regarding the use of punishment?

ANSWER KEY

1. Negative reinforcement
2. Operant conditioning
3. Schedule of partial reinforcement
4. Computer-aided instruction
5. Secondary reinforcers
6. Superstitious behavior
7. Punishment
8. Positive reinforcement
9. Law of Effect
10. Shaping
11. Behavior modification
12. Schedule of continuous reinforcement
13. Avoidance learning
14. Radical behaviorism
15. Skinner box
16. b
17. a
18. c
19. b
20. d
21. d
22. c
23. b
24. b
25. d
26. c
27. d
28. b

SAMPLE ANSWERS TO ESSAY QUESTIONS

1. A negative reinforcer influences behavior the same way any reinforcer would. A reinforcer is a stimulus that follows an organism's response, increasing the likelihood that this response will occur again. Both positive and negative reinforcers strengthen (that is, increase the likelihood of future occurrence) learned behaviors. Any reinforcer is considered a desirable outcome. This is the fundamental notion of operant conditioning—that consequences shape what we do and how we do it. Unlike a positive reinforcer, however, a negative reinforcer influences the occurrence of

future behavior by taking away something unpleasant. A rather gruesome example would be an individual who is confined or beaten until he reveals national secrets. The behavior that is desired from the organism is giving up the information. The negative reinforcer is that the unpleasant experience will be removed as soon as this occurs. Such behavioral responses (revealing the secret information) are likely to increase due to the available negative reinforcer.

2. A Skinner box is particularly useful for studying operant conditioning phenomena because the environment in the box can almost be completely controlled by a researcher. All other stimuli except for the intended reinforcer(s) may be eliminated from the chamber. The organism in the box has no other access to food (the typical reinforcer used in a Skinner box), and probably is hungry. There is little else in the apparatus except the mechanism (usually a lever or bar) allowing for the learned behavioral response. With no other distractions, the animal is bound to soon exhibit the desired behavior (in this case, bar-pressing) even if purely by accident. The organism's response rate to the bar can be precisely measured. A researcher can vary reinforcement schedules easily in this highly structured environment. In the real world, there would be too many other uncontrollable events taking place.

3. A positive reinforcer increases the likelihood that the response it follows will occur again because gaining a positive reinforcer is a pleasant experience. The notion of working extra hard to experience something pleasant and discontinuing a behavior if it leads to an unpleasant consequence, forms the very basis of Thorndike's Law of Effect. Humans (and animals) like pleasurable things. Once we learn that that pleasant outcome is a possibility, we will do what is within our means to make that experience occur again.

4. Punishment is an aversive or unpleasant consequence to a behavior. It is administered with the intention of decreasing that behavior's occurrence. The organism being punished has an unpleasant experience following a response from that organism. It is true that the behavioral concept of punishment does have some usefulness in the shaping of how organisms act. Problems with the use of punishment include that it doesn't really eliminate undesirable behavior, nor does it teach an individual what behavior is more preferred. Parents who punish, especially with physical punishment, are modeling aggressive behavior. They are conveying to their children that "might makes right," the bully wins. The child who is punished may come to resent the parent who is punishing her. And a frequently punished child starts to feel that he is not good or worthwhile. Anger and fear may be created, and the child's level of self-confidence is lowered.

MODULE 5.3 COGNITIVE LEARNING

LEARNING OBJECTIVES

After you have mastered the information in this unit, you will be able to:

1. Define and discuss cognitive learning.
2. Describe insight learning.
3. Discuss the process of latent learning.
4. Describe the process of observational learning.

OUTLINE

I.   Cognitive Learning
   A.   Mental processes that cannot be directly observed
   B.   Involves thinking, information processing, problem solving, and mental imaging
   C.   Learning without the experience of actual performance, direct reinforcement
II.   Types of Cognitive Learning
   A.   Insight learning
      1.   Kohler's (1927) research with chimpanzee Sultan—Sultan joins sticks to reach bananas
      2.   Problem solving did not occur with step-by-step approximations
      3.   Involves the sudden realization of the solution to a problem (the "Aha!" phenomenon) may occur by restructuring or reorganizing a problem in your mind from different angles
      4.   The behaviorist view "insight" is neither sudden nor free of prior reinforcement – nothing more than the chaining of previously reinforced responses
   B.   Latent learning ("hidden" learning)
      1.   Tolman and Honzik (1930) for 10 days do not reward some rats placed in a maze
      2.   Eleventh day: now with a food reward, these rats run the maze with even fewer errors than rewarded rats
      3.   Apparent that unrewarded rats learned even though not reinforced
      4.   Learning only evident when reinforcement provided later
      5.   Cognitive map—mental representation of surrounding world (formed without actual reinforcement)
   C.   Observational learning (vicarious learning or modeling)
      1.   Learn from simply watching the behavior (and consequences) of others—use imitation
      2.   Practice and aptitude still very important
      3.   Learning most likely to occur when model is similar to learner
      4.   Learning most likely to occur when learner witnesses model's behavior being reinforced
      5.   Social – cognitive theorists – psychologists Albert Bandura believed that children learn to imitate aggressive behavior they observe, like exposure to violence on TV

SUMMARY

In this module, you learn about a learning process that seems to take place almost entirely within the mind; that is, no direct or overt interaction with the environment appears necessary. With operant conditioning, the learner absorbs and uses behaviors because the environment directs that he should do so. The learned behaviors are manifested because they lead rather reliably to pleasurable outcomes. Other behaviors are suppressed or not manifested because in the past they have been ignored—or worse, they met are with consequences that were unpleasant. Thus, with operant conditioning, experience with and feedback from the environment is crucial. Cognitive learning is different in that the learner comes up with or adopts new behaviors without any apparent direct reinforcement. Cognitive learning involves a learning process that is not outwardly visible. The results of the learning may, of course, be visible, but the process itself is not.

Cognitive learning consists of three basic types. The first is insight learning—the individual (or organism) may work and work with a problem, and no solution is immediately available. However, eventually, there is a flash of understanding (of insight), and the solution to the problem comes to the individual all at once. The problem has perhaps been restructured in the head, and the learner suddenly comes to look at it in a different way. The second type of learning, latent learning, occurs where it seems the individual is making no effort to learn whatsoever. This type of learning was well demonstrated by Tolman and Honzik (1930). Rats placed in a maze for 10 days in a row where no reinforcer (food reward) was provided then ran the maze better than rats that had been rewarded (during those 10 days) once a reinforcer was provided to the previously non-rewarded rats. Tolman suggested that individuals create cognitive maps—a representation of the surrounding world created in the head of the organism. The last type of cognitive learning discussed in this section involves observational learning—that is, learning simply by watching the behavior (and behavior outcomes) of others. This is also known as vicarious learning (or modeling), and those whom we learn from are models. We are most likely to model the behaviors of individuals to whom we can relate, and where we can see that given behaviors result in (at least for our model) desirable consequences.

KEY TERMS

Cognitive learning

Insight learning

Latent learning

Cognitive map

Observational learning

SELF-TEST PRACTICE QUIZ

Match the following Key Terms and definitions:

1. _____ A mental representation of our surroundings that helps us find our way

2. _____ Learning by an organism that occurs without apparent direct reinforcement

3. _____ Mentally working through a problem until the solution suddenly comes to us

4. _____ Also known as vicarious learning, it is learning through watching the behavior (and behavioral consequences) of others

5. _____ Learning that occurs without reinforcement or apparent intent; the learning is only evident when reinforcement for it is provided later

a. Cognitive learning

b. Insight learning

c. Latent learning

d. Cognitive map

e. Observational learning

6. The type of learning that seems to take place entirely in the head, and involves reasoning, information processing, problem solving and mental imagery is

    a. active intellectual contemplation.
    b. classical conditioning.
    c. operant conditioning.
    d. cognitive learning.

7. When Sultan, the chimp, was faced with bananas outside of his cage which he could not reach with his stick, he

    a. signed to his keeper that he needed the bananas.
    b. tried repeatedly and unsuccessfully with the stick to reach the bananas.
    c. combined his stick with another stick, thereby reaching the bananas.
    d. ate the apples and mangoes that were already available in his cage.

8. The type of learning evidenced by the chimp Sultan when he wanted the bananas he could not reach with his stick is

    a. latent learning.
    b. observational learning.
    c. insight learning.
    d. rational learning.

9. If you study a map of your destination (even though you may never have been there), then upon arriving are better able to navigate this new environment, you are making use of

    a. latent learning.
    b. observational learning.
    c. insight learning.
    d. territorial learning.

10. You have been invited to dinner with the governor of your state. You have no idea how to act, so you watch what other attendees around you do. The type of learning you are utilizing is

    a. latent learning.
    b. observational learning.
    c. insight learning.
    d. etiquette learning.

11. What is one argument that behaviorists present to dispute the existence of insight learning?

    a. The past history of reinforcement relative to the new learning must be considered.
    b. Insight learning really is another form of observational learning.
    c. Insight learning really is another form of latent learning.
    d. Insight learning does not involve trial and error in the head.

12. You are in a department store, when suddenly the fire alarm goes off. Other customers in the store nonchalantly ignore the sound. You remember reading that crowds may misinterpret situational cues, so you go heading for the door. Soon you are safe outside. The type of learning you are utilizing is

    a. latent learning.
    b. observational learning.
    c. insight learning.
    d. rational learning.

13. You are more likely to imitate the behavior of a model who

    a. is younger than you.
    b. is very different from you.
    c. is reinforced for the behavior in question.
    d. all of the above

14. Children who are physically punished for engaging in aggressive behavior often become even *more* aggressive as a result. This occurs because

    a. the parent should have instead reinforced the child for behaving aggressively.
    b. the parent didn't punish the child severely enough.
    c. punishment is never an effective means of changing behavior.
    d. the parent is serving as a model of aggressive behavior.

ESSAY QUESTIONS

1. A key feature to cognitive learning is that, if the process truly exists, it involves learning by an organism without first having the experience of performing the learned behaviors (perhaps randomly or inadvertently) and/or being reinforced for them. What evidence can you think of that supports the notion that cognitive learning is a genuine phenomenon? What evidence can you think of that refutes this concept?

2. What is the most helpful thing you have learned through observational learning? Have you experienced insight or latent learning in your life? If so, relate what you learned and how you learned it.

ANSWER KEY

1. Cognitive map

2. Cognitive learning

3. Insight learning

4. Observational learning

5. Latent learning

6. d

7. c

8. c

9. a

10. b

11. a

12. a

13. c

14. d

SAMPLE ANSWERS TO ESSAY QUESTIONS

1. Evidence in support of cognitive learning includes the studies reported in this module (Kohler reporting Sultan's insight to combine both sticks; Tolman and Honzik's research with rewarded and unrewarded rats in a maze). Evidence also includes the many things we learn simply through thought or mental analysis. Behaviorists argue that the insight is not really a learning process in and of itself. Rather, they point out that the "insight" may be nothing more than the final step in a long process of trial-and-error efforts (with consequences for each). Behaviors leading up to the "insight" are the cumulative product of previous reinforcement and punishment.

    Cognitive learning really does exist, although it is not, of course, independent of past experience. Those of us who have labored long to arrive at a solution (and the solution is just not presenting itself at the time) know that there is a difference between having all the pieces of the puzzle and grasping how that puzzle fits together. Further trial and error simply does not help, though knowing what has worked in the past does. The mind reorganizes and reworks relevant aspects. Nothing new is added; rather, what is needed is a different or fresh way of looking at the same information. This new understanding is appropriately termed *insight*. Unlike operant conditioning, a solution gained through insight may mentally appear even when we are not actively working on the problem. Latent and observational learning, too, occur without any particular effort on the part of the learner. This is in contrast to operant conditioning, where the learner *operates* on the environment. With latent and observational learning, we may not even know we have gained new information until the opportunity to use it presents itself later. Ultimately, much of learning is not a discrete experience. All components mentioned in this chapter play a part.

2.   You may relate important personal examples of each of the three cognitive learning types. Experiences that fit insight, latent, and observational learning categories must be distinguished from each other.

MODULE 5.4 APPLICATION: PUTTING REINFORCEMENT INTO PRACTICE

LEARNING OBJECTIVE

After you have mastered the information in this unit, you will be able to:

1.   Describe guidelines for applying basic reinforcement principles.

OUTLINE

I.   Applying Reinforcement—establish clear contingency (connection) between desired behavior and reinforcement; contingency contracting exchange of desirable reinforcers (two people in a relationship list the behavior of the other that they would like changed – they then agree to reinforce each other)
   A.   Identify specifically the target behavior you wish to strengthen
   B.   Make sure requests and instructions are clear
   C.   Choose a reinforcer that is meaningful to the individual you are working with
   D.   Explain how the reinforcer (contingency) will be used once the behavior occurs
   E.   Administer the reinforcer
      1.   If the desired behavior appears, reward it immediately
      2.   If the individual does not perform the behavior, demonstrate and help
      3.   Pair the reinforcer with praise
   F.   Track the pattern of the desired behavior—how often does it occur?
   G.   Gradually wean the individual from the reinforcer, but continue to give praise
II. Tips for Giving Praise Effectively to Children—(Praise is a powerful social reinforcer)
   A.   Make eye contact, smile, give hugs
   B.   Connect praise to specific behavior; praise effort
   C.   Avoid using same words each time
   D.   Keep statements positive, don't end with a negative comment
   E.   Reward the effort not the outcome

SUMMARY

In this Application module, you learn how to shape and influence the behavior of others, especially children. Though intentional application of learning principles may seem manipulative, in fact the environment gives such encouraging or discouraging feedback to us hundreds of times each day. In addition, children (and adults!) function much better when their efforts are noticed and appreciated. We feel more capable of performing a behavior if we have received praise and recognition for it previously. Much of our ability to learn is, indeed, related to our beliefs and expectations regarding our abilities.

Those beliefs predominantly come from feedback from the environment. The conscientious and effective application of reinforcement principles can do much to optimize the behaviors of individuals with whom you come in contact.

CHAPTER 5   APPLICATION EXERCISE

Is there a behavior you would like to change about yourself? Why do you think this behavior occurs? Where did it come from? What seems to keep the behavior going (what reinforces it)?

What would work for you as a different effective reinforcer? We have discussed conditioning others—it is also possible to condition oneself! See if you can alter your own behavior, using principles discussed here. Set up a reinforcement schedule and give yourself two or three weeks to change.

CHAPTER 6

Memory

In Chapter 6, you are introduced to the many facets of our memory. There is much that we know about memory, and much we still have to learn. Memory can be compared to an information processing system. We need to get information in (encoding), store it (the specific phases of memory) and then get the information back out again when we need it (retrieval). Have you ever tried hard to learn something, but didn't? Did you ever think you'd never forget something—but you did? Certainly our memory is far from perfect! But, considering how complex and comprehensive our memory system is, it is remarkable that it works as well as it does!

Memory is the system by which we are able to retain information and bring it to mind. Encoded information comes from any of our senses, but most typically takes the form of visual or auditory representations. The first stage of memory is the sensory storage phase. Here all input is kept very briefly in the sensory register. Sensory memory is fleeting—visual mental images last a fraction of a second. The auditory stimuli input (echoes) may last as long as 3 or 4 seconds. Though much information in sensory storage is transmitted no further, some is moved on into short-term memory (STM). Short-term memory is often also referred to as *working memory,* because information in STM includes things we are "working on." These are things the brain is actively processing, mulling over, and so forth. Capacity in STM is actually rather limited. Research indicates we can retain about seven items, plus or minus two. We say "items" or "units" with regard to STM storage capacity, rather than a more specific term (like "words"), because information in STM can be chunked; that is, larger amounts of information may be broken up into convenient, perhaps more familiar units (chunks), and thus more information may be retained. For example, perhaps you had to remember the numbers: 0-7-8-1-2-1-9-0-7-6-5-7. That's more than seven, and looks a little cognitively demanding. How about if you recoded these numbers—into, let's say, 1776, 1987, 2005. Make things a little easier for you? Also recall Roy G. Biv for the colors of the rainbow.

The duration for short-term memories is also rather brief, although it is longer than sensory memory. STM information may be retained typically up to about 30 seconds, unless one begins to practice the information (called maintenance rehearsal) by repeating it over and over again (for example, what you do when you've just looked up a telephone number or the correct spelling of a word you need to use).

Most information, even if initially visual, is retained in STM in auditory form. Notice that the telephone number or word that you looked up was presented to you in the visual channel. Yet, to retain it in STM, you repeat the word or number to yourself (an auditory function). Converting even visual information to auditory form means we can recreate the stimuli for ourselves (we can repeat it), aiding our memory. Information is moved from short-term memory to long-term memory by a process called consolidation. Consolidation seems to occur in, or be regulated by, the brain structure known as the hippocampus. Without the hippocampus each new experience would never be recalled. Memories are stored in brain cell units called neural networks.

Long-term memory (LTM) has features unlike either sensory storage or STM. Obviously, duration is much different—long-term memories can last a lifetime. Capacity is different as well, and it is believed that LTM capacity is essentially unlimited. We store many different kinds of information in LTM, such as how to do things (procedural memory), who and what we know (declarative memory), and our own personal story (episodic memory). Information in LTM tends to be retained on the basis of semantics, or meaning (note in STM it was on the basis of sound).

Maybe it is easier to get information into LTM than to get it back out again. We have an array of theories regarding forgetting, among them decay theory, which suggests that we forget because information has not been used for some time. There is evidence for this theory, but there also is substantial evidence for interference theory—that other information, particularly if it is similar to what was originally learned, makes remembering more difficult. A lack of retrieval cues or failure to actually encode the original information are also some of the explanations for forgetting. One important thing to remember about memory is that our recollections may not be exact. This fact must be considered when evaluating eyewitness testimony or recovered repressed childhood memories. Why do we remember things that never took place yet forget things that did take place? There are steps we can take to help our memories work better!

MODULE 6.1 REMEMBERING

LEARNING OBJECTIVES

After you have mastered the information in this unit, you will be able to:

1. Describe the basic processes, stages, and types of memory.

2. Explain the constructionist theory of memory.

3. Describe flashbulb memories.

4. Discuss factors that influence the accuracy of eyewitness testimony.

5. Evaluate whether recovered memories of childhood sexual abuse are credible.

OUTLINE

I.   Human Memory as an Information Processing System
    A.   Memory—the system by which we retain information and bring it to mind
        1.   You are more likely to remember information when you make a conscious effect to understand what it means then relying on repeating the information verbatim.
    B.   Memory encoding—taking information in
        1.   Converting information into a form we can store
        2.   Acoustically—encoded by sound
        3.   Visually—encoded by mental image (tends to fade more quickly than auditory coding)
        4.   Semantically—encoded by meaning
    C.   Memory storage—retaining information in memory (see Memory Stages, below)
    D.   Memory retrieval
        1.   Accessing stored information to make it available to our consciousness
        2.   Availability may be a function of retrieval cue
II.   Memory Stages—Three-Stage Model
    A.   Sensory memory
        1.   Very brief sensory information storage (few seconds at most)
        2.   Iconic memory
            a)   Holds very clear sensory visual images
            b)   Lasts fraction of a second
        3.   Eidetic imagery (photographic memory) – rare in adults, 5% of young children (Haber, 1979) disappearing before age 10
        4.   Echoic memory
            a)   Holds sensory auditory input—mentally "echoes"
            b)   Lasts three or four seconds maximum – longer than visual images

B.   Short-term (working) memory—STM
1.   Holds information up to 30 seconds
2.   Most information stored acoustically
3.   "Working memory" because we are actively processing
4.   "Magic number": 7 ± 2 units can be stored
5.   Chunking—more remembered when restructured into units
6.   Maintenance rehearsal—repeating information to keep longer in STM

C.   Long-term memory (LTM)
1.   Retains information for a longer period of time
2.   Essentially unlimited in capacity
3.   Consolidation
   a)   Converting less stable STM information into LTM
   b)   The first twenty-four hours after information is acquired are critical for consolidation to occur (Ellenbogen, 2008; Fenn et al, 2009; Tucker & Fishbein, 2008)
   c)   Increase chances of retaining the information by getting a good night's sleep
4.   Information stored on basis of meaning (semantically)
5.   Elaborative rehearsal—focus is on meaning of material
6.   Semantic network model
   a)   Leading model regarding LTM organization
   b)   Information held via interlinking concepts
   c)   Spreading activation—one concept triggers recall of related others (rippling effect)
   d)   Provided the inspiration for the structure of the World Wide Web
7.   Levels-of-processing theory
   a)   Information held best when processed at a "deeper" level - encoded on the basis of its meaning
   b)   Elaborative rehearsal more effective than maintenance rehearsal

III.   The Contents of Long-Term Memory
A.   Declarative memory (explicit memory)
1.   "Knowing that"
2.   Takes conscious effort to bring to mind
3.   Categories (organized by type or time frame):
   a)   Semantic memory—memory of facts – better remembered when they are retrieved and rehearsed
   b)   Episodic memory—personal experiences, personal "story"
   c)   Retrospective memory—memory of past events
   d)   Prospective memory—keeping in mind future events – memory of intentions
B.   Procedural memory
1.   "Knowing how"
2.   Engaged without conscious effort
3.   Less easy to explain verbally
4.   Involves motor or performance skills
5.   Types of procedural memory:
   a)   Implicit memory—memory evoked without intentional effort (e.g., pleasant memories when hearing a favorite song)
   b)   Explicit memory—intentional effort needed to bring it to mind (e.g., remembering the capital of a state or country)

IV. The Reliability of Long-Term Memory
  A. Constructionist theory
    1. Memories not a verbatim copy of past experience
    2. Memories created from integrated pieces of stored information
    3. Possibility that memories can be distorted – brain may invent details to weave a more coherent story – in some cases outright false
    4. Negative stereotyping can influence perceptions and attitudes consistent with their existing concepts or schemas (set of beliefs about the world)
  B. Flashbulb memories
    1. Vivid, lasting, highly detailed memories
    2. Derived from extremely stressful or emotional past events (i.e., where were you on 9/11?)
    3. Also may be inaccurate, distorted (like other LTM)
  C. Eyewitness testimony
    1. Possible that it is inaccurate, distorted
    2. Misinformation effect—suggestions lead to inaccuracies in recall; our memory of events can be altered by later exposure to misleading information
    3. Elizabeth Loftus a leading expert in eyewitness testimony points out inaccuracies resulting in wrongful convictions
    4. Accuracy involves the following factors:
      a) Ease of recall—slower response indicates less accurate
      b) Degree of confidence—more confident eyewitness not necessarily more accurate
      c) General knowledge about a subject—more knowledgeable witness is more accurate regarding that particular subject
      d) Racial identification—more errors made when identification crosses racial lines
      e) Types of questions—leading, suggestive questions result in more errors from witnesses than open-ended questions
      f) Facial characteristics—distinctive features make faces more recognizable
  D. Recovery of repressed memories
    1. May be a lack of corroborating evidence; possible some are induced
    2. Some memories may be genuine; some surely are false or distorted
    3. Very difficult to differentiate between false vs. true – may be distorted, even when the person believes them to be true

SUMMARY

In this module, you learn about remembering. All that we learn would not be very helpful to us if we could not retain it, retrieve it, and use it over time. This is the role of memory.

There seem to be different kinds of memory. You yourself know that some things you forget instantly, while others you remember seemingly forever. In fact, our memory does have stages—there are different kinds of memory storage, and each has its own characteristics and properties.

Before we can store information, we first must get it into our awareness. This is known as encoding. Our ability to remember is much like an information processing system. Sensations from the world (transmitted to us by our sensory receptors, thus providing sensory input) must be encoded before they can become a part of our memory. Once information is encoded, it is processed further, then it is stored (this is the memory phase), and then, in order to use it again, information must be retrieved. If no information was ever stored (there is, in fact, no memory), it can never be retrieved.

Our memory storage also has three phases, or components. The first, corresponding to the encoding process mentioned above, is sensory memory. All our sensory input arrives here. Most information is in the form of visual (iconic) or auditory (echoic) memory. Visual memory lasts a fraction of a second; auditory input lasts no more than three or four seconds. It is a good thing that auditory memory lasts as long as it does! Because we speak in sentences (and thus information enters our brain in a linear fashion, one auditory unit after another), we need to be able to retain earlier tidbits of information while continuing to process current input. If our auditory memory were not three or four seconds long, we would forget the beginning of a sentence before our speaker arrived at the end! Notice that with visual input this longer storage capacity is not necessary. Visual images are presented all at once.

The second phase of memory storage is short-term memory, often abbreviated as STM. Short-term memory is also known as *working memory* because it is what we are actively using, or working on. It contains everything we are conscious of at the moment—but we may be attending to only a small portion of all that is available. This ability to selectively attend to what we will process keeps us from being overloaded by all the sensory input coming our way. Short-term memory lasts, obviously, longer than sensory memory—about 30 seconds, unless we use maintenance rehearsal to keep information in storage longer. Capacity for STM is not large—about seven units of information, give or take. Seven units are so typical of regular STM storage that it is known as the "magic number," or "Magic 7." We say "units" rather than words because information may be chunked; that is, we may take a larger amount of information and recode it into units (U-T-A-A-S-W may be recoded as USA TWA, for example), and thus we can retain much more in STM. Information in short-term memory tends to be stored on the basis of sound.

The third and last phase of memory storage is long-term memory, abbreviated LTM. Long-term memory again has its own very unique characteristics. While STM memory capacity is very limited, LTM storage capacity is essentially unlimited. STM information tends to be stored acoustically; in LTM, it is stored semantically (on the basis of meaning). STM storage is brief; LTM information may be stored indefinitely. Information moves from STM to LTM by a process known as consolidation. Interestingly, consolidation occurs some time after (as much as 24 hours or more) the information is first learned. REM (rapid-eye-movement) sleep seems to play a very important role in the consolidation process. Elaborative rehearsal (practicing information by focusing on its meaning) seems a better strategy than maintenance rehearsal to move information from STM to LTM.

There are many aspects of long-term memory. It stores all kinds of things—from what we know (declarative memory) to knowing how to do things (procedural memory). We may have to work to invoke certain memory processes (such as semantic or explicit memory), but others may happen effortlessly (such as procedural or implicit memory). Though our long-term memory is remarkable, as is indeed the entire memory process, LTM is not entirely flawless. Research suggests that, rather than being a precise, exact record of all we have experienced, LTM is more piece-meal in how information is stored. When we want to retrieve information (call upon a memory), research suggests the LTM information is *reconstructed*—that is, the bits and pieces are recalled, and in remembering we integrate these pieces to form a coherent whole. According to research, the whole that is remembered is not necessarily exactly what happened during the actual event or experience remembered. Thus, as evidenced by this research, eyewitness accounts and recovered repressed childhood memories can be fallible. Both, for example, may be influenced by how requests for the remembered information may be phrased. If the request contains some cues suggesting either directly or indirectly what happened, these suggestions can and do impact what is recalled. We also remember things that never took place and forget things that have taken place.

KEY TERMS

Memory

Memory encoding

Memory storage

Memory retrieval

Retrieval cues

Three-stage model

Sensory memory

Sensory register

Iconic memory

Eidetic imagery

Echoic memory

Short-term memory (STM)

Chunking

Maintenance rehearsal

Long-term memory (LTM)

Consolidation

Elaborative rehearsal

Semantic network model

Levels-of-processing theory

Declarative memory

Semantic memory

Episodic memory

Retrospective memory

Prospective memory

Procedural memory

Implicit memory

Explicit memory

Constructionist theory

Flashbulb memories

Misinformation effect

SELF-TEST PRACTICE QUIZ

Match the following Key Terms and definitions (note: not every Key Term will be used):

1. _____ Storage phase of memory that holds initial input when first encoded; very brief

2. _____ A belief that how well information is stored is a function of the mental depth at which it is processed

3. _____ Possible memory distortion due to suggestions made during retention interval

4. _____ STM information retained longer because the information is intentionally repeated

5. _____ Sensory storage component that very briefly holds visual images

6. _____ Also called *working memory*; holds 7 ± 2 units of information

7. _____ Memory of facts and personal information that requires a conscious effort to bring to mind

8. _____ The memory phase where an unlimited amount of information may be stored, perhaps indefinitely

9. _____ The system that allows us to retain information and bring it to mind

10. _____ Sensory storage component that very briefly holds auditory input

11. _____ Retaining more information in STM by recoding it into manageable units

12. _____ Transferring information from STM to LTM by focusing on the meaning of the information

13. _____ The view that LTM is not infallible; memory is only a representation of the past

14. _____ The process of accessing information stored in memory and bringing it into conscious awareness

a. Memory

b. Memory encoding

c. Memory storage

d. Memory retrieval

e. Retrieval cues

f. Three-stage model

g. Sensory memory

h. Sensory register

i. Iconic memory

j. Eidetic imagery

k. Echoic memory

l. Short-term memory (STM)

m. Chunking

n. Maintenance rehearsal

o. Long-term memory (LTM)

p. Consolidation

q. Elaborative rehearsal

r. Semantic network model

s. Levels-of-processing theory

t. Declarative memory

u. Semantic memory

v. Episodic memory

w. Retrospective memory

x. Prospective memory

y. Procedural memory

z. Implicit memory

aa. Explicit memory

bb. Constructionist theory

cc. Flashbulb memories

dd. Misinformation effect

15. _____ Converting short-term information into LTM; takes 24 hours or more after learning

16. _____ Our memory of how to do things— involves motor or performance skills

17. _____ The conversion of information acoustically, visually or semantically to be stored in memory.

18. In the three-stage model of memory, which stage comes first?

    a. Short-term memory
    b. Sensory memory
    c. Declarative memory
    d. Semantic memory

19. If you remember someone's phone number by combining pieces of information (such as by remembering the last four digits as "twenty-forty" rather than "2-0-4-0"), then you are engaging in

    a. chunking.
    b. eidetic memory.
    c. maintenance rehearsal.
    d. misinformation.

20. In order for information to enter our memory storage, it first must be

    a. encoded.
    b. selectively attended to.
    c. retrieved.
    d. recalled.

21. The part of our memory system that is also known as working memory is the _____ phase.

    a. encoding
    b. sensory
    c. STM
    d. LTM

22. Though some memories come to mind spontaneously, others are helped by

    a. hypnotic suggestion.
    b. eidetic imagery.
    c. retrieval cues.
    d. the central executive.

23. Short-term memory

    a. consists of auditory and visual input.
    b. stores information on the basis of meaning.
    c. holds approximately seven units.
    d. all of the above

24. In the sensory memory phase of memory storage, which type of information is retained the longest?

    a.   Visual imagery
    b.   Semantic input
    c.   Echoes
    d.   Procedural input

25. When Kayla studies for her psychology classes, she makes a point of trying to relate concepts from class to ideas and concepts from other classes and from her life in general. Kayla is using a process called

    a.   episodic buffering.
    b.   chunking.
    c.   maintenance rehearsal.
    d.   elaborative rehearsal.

26. REM (rapid-eye-movement) sleep may play a very important role in the process of

    a.   encoding.
    b.   retrieval.
    c.   consolidation.
    d.   selective attention.

27. Levels-of-processing theory is useful in explaining

    a.   the constructionist model of memory.
    b.   how knowledge is sorted into either declarative or procedural memory.
    c.   how information gets from short-term memory to long-term memory.
    d.   why elaborative rehearsal is generally superior to maintenance rehearsal.

28. The part of our long-term memory that contains our personal story, like an autobiography, is _____ memory.

    a.   semantic
    b.   episodic
    c.   retrospective
    d.   implicit

29. In which part of your memory would you store the knowledge that Washington, DC, is the capital of the United States?

    a.   Semantic
    b.   Procedural
    c.   Implicit
    d.   Flashbulb

30. Remembering vivid details long after an intense emotional experience is known as a(n) _____ memory.

    a.   declarative
    b.   episodic
    c.   retrospective
    d.   flashbulb

31. Which statement about eyewitness testimony is most accurate?

    a.   Eyewitnesses are usually accurate, so long as they are motivated to cooperate.
    b.   Eyewitnesses are more likely to be accurate in identifying someone of their own race than in identifying someone of another race.
    c.   Eyewitness memories can be affected by information learned after the event occurred.
    d.   Both B and C are accurate statements.

ESSAY QUESTIONS

1. What is the misinformation effect? How can it impact the testimony of eyewitnesses?

2. What are repressed memories? How accurate can we assume recovered repressed memories to be?

ANSWER KEY

1. Sensory memory

2. Levels-of-processing theory

3. Misinformation effect

4. Maintenance rehearsal

5. Iconic memory

6. Short-term memory (STM)

7. Declarative memory

8. Long-term memory (LTM)

9. Memory

10. Echoic memory

11. Chunking

12. Elaborative rehearsal

13. Constructionist theory

14. Memory retrieval

15. Consolidation

16. Procedural memory

17. Memory encoding

18. b

19. a

20. a

21. c

22. c

23. c

24. c

25. d

26. c

27. d

28. b

29. a

30. d

31. d

SAMPLE ANSWERS TO ESSAY QUESTIONS

1.   The misinformation effect occurs when an individual is trying to recall a past experience. It can happen, actually, any time between when the experience occurred and when the individual attempts to recall it some time later. The misinformation effect involves the introduction, intentionally or accidentally, of features or characteristics that were not actually present when the event or experience occurred. These features may be introduced (usually through the use of words) by an interviewer or other person who asks questions about the remembered experience. Research by Loftus and her colleagues (1978, 1997) revealed that when individuals are given misleading information (such as whether a yield sign is present at an intersection), this misinformation tends to create distortions in the memories recalled. When an incorrect feature or descriptor is suggested, that feature may find its way into the recalled memories. Thus, at least portions of recalled information can be false. Although eyewitness testimony is often viewed as highly credible, we must remember that errors and mistakes in such memories can and do occur.

2.   Repressed memories are usually memories of traumatic childhood events. However, the early experiences may have been so painful that the experience is no longer actually remembered. It is thought that very disturbing memories are too emotionally disruptive to keep in conscious awareness. Thus, the individual represses the memory—he or she "forgets" that the events ever occurred. With time, especially as the individual gets older, the individual may experience flashbacks—brief glimpses or recollections of these painful past events. A psychotherapist or hypnotist may be consulted to help gain more information about these flashbacks. In this setting, many more repressed memories may be recovered. On the basis of these recovered memories, sometimes with no other corroborating evidence, a person may be accused and convicted of serious sexual crimes. It is true that at least some recovered repressed memories are accurate, and we want the perpetrator of such crimes to be appropriately punished. However, as with eyewitness testimony, we must remember that distorted and false memories can be created. Investigators and interviewers must be careful to ask only open-ended questions and not plant suggestions through either words or nonverbal behavior.

MODULE 6.2 FORGETTING

LEARNING OBJECTIVES

After you have mastered the information in this unit, you will be able to:

1.   Describe major theories of forgetting.

2.   Understand how recall is related to the methods used to measure it.

3.   Discuss amnesia and its causes.

OUTLINE

I.   Why Do We Forget?
  A.   Some people more forgetful than others
  B.   Variety of explanations for normal forgetting
II.   Decay Theory
  A.   Belief that memory is a trace that fades over time
  B.   Hermann Ebbinghaus (1885) used nonsense syllables (to eliminate any earlier association to the material to be remembered) to test himself and memory
  C.   Ebbinghaus forgetting curve—most information lost shortly after learning (66% in first day – nearly 80% after a month)
  D.   Savings method—much less time to relearn forgotten information

E.   Massed (crammed) vs. spaced practice effect—more information retained when learning sessions spread out over time; mental fatigue interferes with learning and retention with crammed sessions, which is useful to keep in mind when training (i.e., use shorter sessionsj)

F.   Weakness in decay theory:
1.   Forgetting over time is quite uneven
2.   Seems to be related to meaningfulness of original material – more distinctive or unusual information tends to be remembered

III. Interference Theory
A.   Belief that memory loss is due to occurrence of other similar events – greater the similarity the greater the risk
B.   Retroactive interference—what learned now interferes with previous learning
C.   Proactive interference—what learned now interferes with what will be learned in the future
D.   Steps to minimize memory disruption from interference:
1.   Sleep after learning
2.   Practice (repeat) new information when first learned (may want to over learn)
3.   Schedule breaks between learning sessions (such as between classes) – try not to schedule one class directly after another
4.   Avoid studying similar topics in close succession
E.   Serial position effect
1.   Tendency to recall first and last items in a list best
2.   Interference most likely to occur with items in middle – items compete with one another
3.   Primacy effect—recalling items best when they are given first
4.   Recency effect—recalling items best when they are given last
a)   As the delay between information learned and test period increases, primacy effect become stronger where as recency effect becomes weaker (Knoedler, Hellwig, & Neath, 1999)

IV. Retrieval Theory
A.   Forgetting results from breakdown in retrieving stored memories
B.   Encoding failure
1.   Memory cannot be retrieved because information was never originally stored (never encoded)
2.   We encode only as much information as we need
3.   Distinct, unique events tend to be remembered
4.   Similar events tend to be encoded as a group (based on common features) so more difficult to distinguish among these
C.   Lack of retrieval cues
1.   Information encoded but not accessible
2.   Insufficient distinctive cues to help us retrieve
3.   Tip-of-the-tongue phenomenon—partial recall, which may be associated with general word retrieval difficulty; tends to increase in later life
4.   Recalling proper names – they have no built-in association

V.   Motivated Forgetting
A.   Sigmund Freud—memories are not forgotten, just kept hidden (repression); a belief that if it were not for repression we would be flooded with overwhelming anxiety
B.   Repressed information is threatening or unpleasant
1.   Problem with this concept is that people who are traumatized tend to retain vivid if somewhat fragmented memories of these experiences and find it difficult putting these thoughts out of their minds
C.   Repression—defense mechanism that helps protect from overwhelming anxiety
D.   Concept is controversial since there is evidence that refutes

VI.   Measuring Memory
    A.   What is remembered may in part depend on how it is assessed
    B.   Recall task—reproduce information that has been stored in memory
        1.   Free recall—remember as much as possible; order does not matter
        2.   Serial recall—recall items or numbers in a particular order
        3.   Paired-associates recall—after word pairs are memorized, one word is presented (must retrieve associated word)
    C.   Recognition task
        1.   Select correct answer from among choices given (like a multiple-choice test)
        2.   Recognition memory nearly always better than recall
VII.   Amnesia—Severe Type of Memory Loss
    A.   Types of amnesia
        1.   Retrograde amnesia
           a)   Loss of memory regarding past events
           b)   May involve disruption of consolidation process
           c)   Loss is greatest for more recent events
        2.   Anterograde amnesia—difficulty or inability to store new memories
    B.   Causes of amnesia—physical or psychological
        1.   Physical causes
           a)   Blows to the head (interferes with memory consolidation), degenerative brain diseases (such as Alzheimer's)
           b)   Blood vessel blockage, infectious diseases, alcoholism
           c)   Early detection critical to successful treatment
        2.   Psychological causes (dissociative amnesia)—memory is traumatic, too disturbing for conscious awareness

SUMMARY

In this module, you learn about the various theories for forgetting. Everyone forgets things at one time or another, though there is wide variation among human beings of all ages as to how often this experience occurs. Several explanations for forgetting have been proposed. The first seems like an obvious one: decay theory. This theory suggests that we forget information we once knew simply because we have not used it in so long. The view is derived from the notion that memories leave a trace in the brain. If left dormant, or unused, this trace will fade and eventually disappear.

Though the decay theory of forgetting seems to have many obvious applications, there are some phenomena that it does not explain well. For example, information we have had in our memory at one time may be forgotten very quickly, while other tidbits or recollections stay with us essentially indefinitely. It appears that not just frequency of use but meaningfulness of information affects memory. Secondly, if we go to relearn "forgotten" information, much less time is needed to relearn in comparison to time needed in our first attempt. So information we thought had decayed and was no longer there actually is.

A remarkable person in the history of psychology provided much of what we know about memory and forgetting. This individual was Hermann Ebbinghaus (1850–1909), and what is perhaps more remarkable is that he used only himself as his research subject! Ebbinghaus would study and memorize information. He would investigate how long it took him to learn information to the point where it could be recalled perfectly. He also gave us what is now known as the Ebbinghaus forgetting curve. He recorded how much information, once memorized, he forgot, and over what span of time the forgetting of learned material occurred. Most information, he discovered, is forgotten rather promptly, beginning immediately after it is learned. Wisely, Ebbinghaus knew he could not use ordinary words and concepts as memorization material. There would be too many associations relating to familiarity with words;

thus he could not be sure he was truly testing pure memory. Instead, Ebbinghaus cleverly devised three-letter nonsense syllables (such as *lef* and *nuz*). Because they were not true words, no prior associations or familiarity with these terms existed to confound memory research.

A second explanation for forgetting is interference theory. This theory proposes that we forget because we are exposed to massive amounts of other information as well. The more this information is similar to what we have already learned, or memorized, the more it is likely to cause problems (interfere) with our attempts at recollection. Retroactive interference means what we learn now makes it harder to remember information learned earlier. Proactive interference means what we learn now will likely make it more difficult to absorb and remember information presented in the future. Though we can do things to combat the effects of interference, it is clear that this phenomenon can "get" us coming and going! Actively practicing (repeating) learned material, sleeping after studying, and spacing learning and study times can help us retain more of the material we have learned.

A third possible explanation for why we forget is retrieval theory. This theory places emphasis on our attempts to get information back out of memory (to retrieve it). One reason we may not be able to get information back out of our memory is that it was never entered into memory storage in the first place! This is known as encoding failure. We all have had this experience. We may stare and stare at the printed words on the page. We may be staring at those words for some length of time! But unless we are actually attending to the words, actively processing them and their meanings, the information is not really going into our heads. We have stared at the words, but the material does not get encoded. Come test time, we cannot bring the information back out for our use. Why? It never entered our memory in the first place! Another component in retrieval theory is noting that lack of helpful, distinctive cues is a factor in forgetting. Memories are triggered by cues that bring them to mind. If there is a dearth of such retrieval cues, it is much harder to bring information out of our memory store. Certainly, how questions are asked (e.g., there are more cues in a recognition task than in memory recall) is related to what and how much we can remember. Physical and/or psychological trauma also impacts our ability to remember.

KEY TERMS

Decay theory

Massed vs. spaced practice effect

Interference theory

Retroactive interference

Proactive interference

Overlearning

Serial position effect

Primacy effect

Recency effect

Retrieval theory

Tip-of-the-tongue (TOT) phenomenon

Repression

Free recall

Recognition task

Savings Method

Amnesia

Retrograde amnesia

Anterograde amnesia

Dissociative amnesia

SELF-TEST PRACTICE QUIZ

Match the following Key Terms and definitions (note: not every Key Term will be used):

1. _____ The view that forgetting is due to similar memories that interfere with each other

2. _____ Loss of memory of past events

3. _____ A defense mechanism proposed by Freud; threatening information is kept out of conscious awareness

4. _____ The tendency for better recall for items learned first

5. _____ Information is retained better when learning sessions are spread out over time

6. _____ An explanation for forgetting based on the notion that information in memory will fade and disappear if not used for an extended period of time

7. _____ What we learn now will interfere with information we store from future learning

8. _____ What we learn now interferes with information we have stored in memory earlier

9. _____ A memory task where an individual must choose the correct answer among alternatives

10. _____ The tendency to recall items at the beginning and ending of a list; memory is less good for items in the middle of the list

11. _____ The theory that forgetting occurs because there is difficulty in accessing stored memories

12. _____ Loss of memory due to traumatic psychological experiences; no underlying physical cause

a. Decay theory
b. Massed vs. spaced practice effect
c. Interference theory
d. Retroactive interference
e. Proactive interference
f. Overlearning
g. Serial position effect
h. Primacy effect
i. Recency effect
j. Retrieval theory
k. Tip-of-the-tongue (TOT) phenomenon
l. Repression
m. Free recall
n. Recognition task
o. Amnesia
p. Retrograde amnesia
q. Anterograde amnesia
r. Dissociative amnesia

13. _____ A recall task where an individual just needs to remember as much information as possible

14. _____ Practice continued beyond what is needed to remember information completely; helps with memory recollection in future

15. The theory of forgetting that involves the inability to access information because it was never really encoded into memory is the _____ theory.
    a. decay
    b. interference
    c. retrieval
    d. proactive

16. Which statement about Ebbinghaus's research findings is true?
    a. Most of what we forget is forgotten very soon after it is learned.
    b. The best way to remember lots of information is to study it all at one time.
    c. Once information is forgotten, it will take just as long to learn it the second time as it did the first time.
    d. none of the above

17. The inability to remember information we have stored in memory previously due to information we are storing in memory now is called
    a. failure to encode.
    b. retroactive interference.
    c. proactive interference.
    d. the serial position effect.

18. In order to study memory and avoid prior associations due to familiarity with words, Ebbinghaus used
    a. family names.
    b. nonsense syllables.
    c. words that were all of equal difficulty.
    d. words that all contained the same number of vowels and consonants.

19. One way to help reduce the effects of interference on our ability to remember is to
    a. avoid studying topics in close succession, especially when they are very similar to each other.
    b. try to sleep for some length of time soon after a period of studying.
    c. practice or repeat newly memorized information, perhaps to the point of overlearning.
    d. all of the above

20. The tendency to best remember words at the beginning and end of a list, and remember less well the words in the middle of a list, is known as
    a. the primacy effect.
    b. the recency effect.
    c. the serial position effect.
    d. proactive interference.

21. One reason that decay theory is an incomplete explanation for forgetting is that
    a. the more that time passes, the more information we tend to forget.
    b. how meaningful information is to us is related to how long we remember it.
    c. we tend to remember the words in the middle of a list less well than other words at the beginning or end.
    d. failure to remember information may occur because it was never encoded.

22. When events occur regularly in our lives, it is harder to distinguish among them because
    a. repetitiveness of these events makes us less alert and aware.
    b. information is lost due to the serial position effect.
    c. such events tend to be encoded on the basis of common features.
    d. there is a greater likelihood for retrograde amnesia.

23. Sigmund Freud's theory of repression has been criticized because
    a. it is difficult to test empirically.
    b. it does not account for everyday forgetfulness.
    c. many victims of trauma find they are unable to forget what has happened.
    d. all of the above

24. Which of the following is *not* helpful for improving memory?
    a. Overlearning
    b. Massed practice
    c. Getting a good night's sleep
    d. Rehearsal

25. Which of the following is an example of a recognition task?
    a. A paired-associates task
    b. A free-answer test question
    c. Reciting from memory the capitals of all 50 states
    d. Picking a suspect out of a lineup

26. Which of these is a potential cause of amnesia?
    a. Repression
    b. Alcoholism
    c. Degenerative brain diseases
    d. all of the above

ESSAY QUESTIONS

1. It is important to keep in mind that how much an individual shows he or she can remember is in part a function of how memory is measured. In most cases, an individual is more successful (that is, the person remembers more) using recognition memory than at free recall tasks. Why would this be? Can you think of any instance where a recognition task might lead to lesser amounts of information remembered in comparison to a recall task on the same material?

2. What is the massed vs. spaced practice effect? Apply this concept to how you have scheduled your classes and the pattern you typically follow when you study.

ANSWER KEY

1.   Interference theory
2.   Retrograde amnesia
3.   Repression
4.   Primacy effect
5.   Massed vs. spaced practice effect
6.   Decay theory
7.   Proactive interference
8.   Retroactive interference
9.   Recognition task
10. Serial position effect
11. Retrieval theory
12. Dissociative amnesia
13. Free recall
14. Overlearning
15. c
16. a
17. b
18. b
19. d
20. c
21. b
22. c
23. d
24. b
25. d
26. d

SAMPLE ANSWERS TO ESSAY QUESTIONS

1.   Recognition tasks are almost always easier than recall tasks when people are being tested for what they remember. A main reason for the greater success rate at recognition tasks is that many retrieval cues are present—indeed, they are right before your eyes. The recognition task is easier in that the test-taker simply must choose the response that has the most (and the most relevant) retrieval cues of all. The only real difficulty is selecting which set of retrieval cues is most complete and relevant, including eliminating choices where the retrieval cues do not apply. With recognition memory, it is not necessary to generate a response entirely out of the head, as is the case with any of the different recall tasks. Recall tasks have fewer or no retrieval cues available.

Serial recall tasks have the added demand that not only must the information itself be remembered but the order in which it was presented must be remembered as well.

An exception to the above may be when plausible suggestions are made, either before or during the recognition task session that is closely related or similar to information already in memory storage. As with eyewitness testimony, for example, plausible suggestions may create their own mental images, which possibly are integrated when memories are reconstructed. Unless information is extremely well learned, and in great detail (such as with overlearning), these inaccurate but plausible features may be incorporated into what an individual thinks he or she remembers. Thus, due to the power of suggestion, a recognition memory task may become more difficult than a recall task. In the latter, there are few retrieval cues, but on the other hand the individual is free to pull from memory what the experience or information was. With typical recall-type questions, at least no distracting or misleading information is given.

2. The massed vs. spaced practice effect relates to the fact that trying to cram much information into memory, especially within a very short period of time, creates mental fatigue. This fatigue interferes with the ability to learn and remember. Research has shown (Payne & Wenger, 1996) that more information is retained when sessions for learning are spaced over time. We learn and remember better when the mind is fresh and rested. In addition, as we have seen, the process of consolidation (moving information from STM to LTM) takes some time to complete. It is suggested that at least 24 hours, at a minimum, is necessary. Thus, studying large amounts of information, in a short period of time and with insufficient opportunity to make the information really a part of long-term memory is less effective! It produces undue mental strain and is necessarily less successful for true learning.

At this point, you should reflect on your schedule and study patterns. How effective are they in light of what we know about memory and forgetting?

MODULE 6.3 THE BIOLOGY OF MEMORY

LEARNING OBJECTIVES

After you have mastered the information in this unit, you will be able to:

1. Discuss how memories are stored in the brain, including the role of the hippocampus.

2. Describe long-term potentiation and the role it plays in memory formation.

3. Discuss what scientists have learned about the genetic basis of memory.

OUTLINE

I. Brain Structure in Memory: Where Do Memories Reside?
    A. Karl Lashley (early 20th c.)—search for engram
        1. Believed to be the physical trace or etching in the brain
        2. Research on rats—removing portions of cortex
        3. Rats still retained memory, regardless of what removed
        4. Conclusion is memory is stored throughout brain
    B. Neuronal networks—current technology reveals memory stored in intricate circuitry of neural constellations (in brain)
    C. Hippocampus (seahorse-shaped structure in the forebrain) —storage bin
        1. Portion of limbic system in brain
        2. Responsible for converting STM into long-term declarative (semantic, episodic) memory
        3. Is not involved in procedural memory processes

4.   Probably temporary storage only of new declarative memories
5.   Does not appear to be the final destination for new memories (Stickgold & Wehrwein, 2009); no one part of the brain is entirely responsible for memory information
6.   Play a role in remembering the context in which fearful responses were experienced
   D.   Other brain structures
      1.   Thalamus—if damaged, results in amnesia
      2.   Amygdala—helps encode emotional experiences
II.   Strengthening Connections Between Neurons: The Key to Forming Memories
   A.   Research on sea snail (*Aplysia*) by Eric Kandel (1995)
      1.   Shows memory formation involves biochemical changes (at level of synapse, the connection between neurons)
         a)   Neurotransmitter amount increased as animal learned response
         b)   Synapses became stronger; more capable of transmitting messages
   B.   Long-term potentiation ("strengthening") (LTP)
      1.   Repeated electrical stimulation also results in stronger synaptic connections
      2.   Stronger synaptic connections mean neuron communication easier
      3.   LTP believed to be a factor in STM to LTM conversion
      4.   Cells that "fire together wire together" (Abraham 2006)
      5.   Newly formed memories may need to be strengthened by elaborating upon the meaning of the material
III.   Genetic Bases of Memory
   A.   STM-LTM transformation in brain requires various proteins
   B.   Production of these proteins regulated by certain genes
   C.   Manipulate gene—enhance learning and memory skills

SUMMARY

In this module, you are learning about structures in the brain that are related to the processes of memory. Since the technology allowing us to investigate these questions is quite new, we have by no means learned everything there is to know about how the brain functions during learning, remembering, and forgetting. Research is ongoing and much more will be added to our store of knowledge. We continue to study and investigate further these fascinating processes.

The earliest notion about memory was that there must be a physical trace (called an engram) in the brain that corresponds to the memories an individual has. Karl Lashley investigated this concept in the early 20th century. Laboratory rats were first trained to run a maze; thus, they would have a memory for the layout of the maze and how most rapidly to get to the food reward. Lashley then surgically removed a portion of a research rat's brain in the region of the cortex. The cortex is responsible for higher function activities, which would include learning and memory. The rat was again put in the maze and tested. Lashley did his work with a variety of rats, removing all different portions of the cortical region. No matter what portion of the cortex Lashley removed from a rat—the rat still showed memory for the maze. Lashley had to conclude (we now know correctly) that there was no specific region in the brain corresponding to memory.

Happily, we have become more sophisticated in our research on the brain. We have learned that any memory does not reside in one or a few particular brain cells. Rather, it is believed that memories are stored in constellations of neurons, which then are connected in a very elaborate circuitry. The circuits are known as neural (or neuronal) networks.

Certain brain structures are clearly involved in memory. One such structure is the hippocampus, a component of our limbic system. The most crucial role of the hippocampus seems to be in the transfer of information from STM to LTM. We learn much about brain functioning when an area of brain damage or destruction corresponds to a loss in how a human functions. Damage to the hippocampus interferes with, or prevents, the formation of long-term memories. Thus it is reasonable to conclude that this STM-LTM movement is carried out by the hippocampus. However, the hippocampus is involved in the transfer of declarative memory information only, not procedural. And it appears that storage at the site of the hippocampus is temporary. Long-term storage of declarative memories probably occurs elsewhere. In addition, other brain structures have a role in memory. We know that if the thalamus in the brain is damaged amnesia can result. The amygdala is involved in the storage of emotional experiences related to fear and rage, and appears to work closely with the hippocampus.

We still have much to learn regarding the brain's functioning; neural activity is exceedingly complex. However, research on a large sea snail, *Aplysia,* (Eric Kandel, 1995) revealed that, when learning occurs, levels of the relevant neurotransmitter are increased, and the synaptic connections among brain cells are strengthened. Stronger connections result in quicker transmissions. Repeated electrical stimulation of brain cells also strengthens neural connections. This is known as long-term potentiation (LTP). Synapses occur more easily and more quickly when the neural network has undergone potentiation. It appears that the STM-LTM conversion depends upon the production of LTP. LTP may well result from the repeated stimulation of brain cells, a consequence of the learning/rehearsal effort.

Lastly, genetic research has impacted what we know about memory because certain proteins influence memory functions in the brain. Production of these proteins is directed by gene activity. If a relevant gene is manipulated, then learning and memory functions are affected as well. We have no scientific evidence that any drug or supplement available today can enhance memory in normal individuals.

KEY TERMS

Engram

Neuronal networks

Long-term potentiation (LTP)

SELF-TEST PRACTICE QUIZ

Match the following Key Terms and definitions:

1. _____ Strengthening neural connections within a neural network; occurs as a result of repeated stimulation

2. _____ The term for the original idea that memories would have a corresponding physical trace in the brain

3. _____ Our current view of memory in the brain, consisting of units of neurons combined into neural circuits

a. Engram

b. Neuronal networks

c. Long-term potentiation (LTP)

4. Lashley researched the brain site for memories by
   a. training rats on increasingly complex mazes.
   b. removing portions of a rat's cortex to see if memory had disappeared.
   c. conducting microscopic examination of rat brain tissue.
   d. comparing tissue from rat cortexes to that of other organisms.

5. The part of the brain that seems to be involved in the movement of information from short-term memory to long-term memory is the

   a. hippocampus.
   b. hypothalamus.
   c. thalamus.
   d. amygdala.

6. The current belief about memory is

   a. memories are etched into particular brain cells.
   b. learning and memory processes are unrelated.
   c. the hippocampus is responsible for procedural memory processes.
   d. memory storage is in clusters of brain cells known as neuronal networks.

7. The amygdala appears to be involved in

   a. the long-term destination for declarative memories.
   b. encoding intense emotional experiences.
   c. the sudden occurrence of dissociative amnesia.
   d. the sudden occurrence of anterograde amnesia.

8. What does LTP stand for?

   a. Left-track processing
   b. Long-term processing
   c. Long-term potentiation
   d. none of the above

9. Research with the sea snail *Aplysia* revealed that

   a. memory storage is closely related to memory capacity.
   b. memory was better for fish than for scorpions.
   c. synaptic connections can be strengthened through repeated stimulation.
   d. all of the above

10. Long-term potentiation (LTP) occurs because

    a. synaptic connections are flooded with greater amounts of relevant neurotransmitters.
    b. neural connections cannot really function well as a unit.
    c. training in mazes is only partially reinforced.
    d. salt water is most conducive to the transmission of neural (electrical) impulses.

11. Which part of the brain is the repository for human memory?

    a. Hippocampus
    b. Amygdala
    c. Frontal lobe
    d. none of the above

12. Why might an altered gene produce, for example, a smarter mouse?

    a. Intelligence increases as the number of genes increases.
    b. Altered genes increase the occurrence of LTP.
    c. Genes produce the proteins that are involved in learning and memory.
    d. The altered gene allowed for the introduction of human cortical tissue.

ESSAY QUESTIONS

1. Why was Lashley unable to find the brain site for memories?

2. How is long-term potentiation (LTP) related to research on the sea snail *Aplysia*?

ANSWER KEY

1. Long-term potentiation (LTP)
2. Engram
3. Neuronal networks
4. b
5. a
6. d
7. b
8. c
9. c
10. a
11. d
12. c

SAMPLE ANSWERS TO ESSAY QUESTIONS

1. Lashley conducted his research believing that there would be a trace, or engram, in the brain where memory was located. As such, his approach was to remove various portions of the brain (in the cerebral cortex) and see if research rats then lost their memory of a maze on which they had been trained. No matter what portion of the rat's brain Lashley removed, the rats never lost their memory for the maze. Because Lashley was looking for a specific location for memory, his endeavors were unsuccessful. However, his research has led us to understand that memory does occur in clusters of cells and networks throughout the brain.

2. The *Aplysia* is a small enough and simple enough animal that its neurological processes can be studied. It has a few simple reflexes (such as withdrawing gills) that can be trained through simple conditioning procedures. Thus, the sea snail is able to "learn" to respond to a conditioned stimulus (a squirt of water in the research by Kandel). Kandel noted that the quantity of neurotransmitter increased as the animal learned the response. Synaptic connections were strengthened (LTP) as a result, and stronger connections are related to increased learning and memory ability.

MODULE 6.4 APPLICATION: POWERING UP YOUR MEMORY

LEARNING OBJECTIVE

After you have mastered the information in this unit, you will be able to:

1. Discuss methods for strengthening memory ability.

OUTLINE

I. Using Mnemonics to Improve Memory
   A. Mnemonic—device for improving memory
   B. Types of mnemonics
      1. Acronyms and acrostics—make a word or verse using first letters of memory information; acronym HOMES helps to remember the names of the Great Lakes: Huron, Ontario, Michigan, etc.
      2. Popular sayings and rhymes (such as "30 days hath September…")

3.   Visual cues, visual imagery—leave a visual note or create an associated visual image

4.   Chunking—recombine larger amounts of information into a useable or familiar unit

II.   General Suggestions for Improving Memory

A.   Pay attention—focus on task, avoid distractions

B.   Practice—especially with elaborative rehearsal; strengthen retention of material

C.   Use external memory aids—a reminder note is fine!

D.   Link time-based tasks to external cues – you need to take medication each evening; link it to dinner

E.   Mentally rehearse—plan and visualize your tasks in advance

F.   Control stress (stress interferes with learning and memory)

G.   Adopt healthy habits—healthy diet, sleep and exercise help memory

1.   Avoid studying on an empty stomach or eating too much

2.   Using alcohol and other drugs does not mix with mental alertness

H.   Spaced practice is more effective than crammed practice

I.   Break it down by sections or parts and rehearse your knowledge of each part

SUMMARY

In this Application module, you learn very helpful ways to improve your memory. These range from simple specific memory strategies, known as mnemonics, to more general tips like keeping the mind healthy and focusing attention. Practice, whether it is repeating information or visualizing in advance what one will do, is crucial to effective memory. Making use of mnemonics (acronyms, everyday rhymes and sayings) or just leaving ourselves notes are easy steps to improving memory.

KEY TERMS

Mnemonic

Acronym

Acrostic

SELF-TEST PRACTICE QUIZ

Match the following Key Terms and definitions:

1.   _____ A verse or saying in which the first letter of each word stands for something else

2.   _____ A device or strategy for improving memory

3.   _____ A word made up of the first letters of words one needs to remember

a.   Mnemonic

b.   Acronym

c.   Acrostic

4.   The mnemonic where one takes larger amounts of information and recasts them into more familiar, manageable units is known as

a.   the method of loci.

b.   chunking.

c.   rehearsal.

d.   using an acrostic.

5. "I before E except after C" is an example of a(n)
   a. mnemonic device.
   b. acrostic.
   c. acronym.
   d. visual cue.

6. SCUBA (which stands for "Self Contained Underwater Breathing Apparatus") is an example of
   a. chunking.
   b. an acrostic.
   c. an acronym.
   d. a visual cue.

7. Using the phrase "Some People Can Fly" to remember the order of Piaget's stages of cognitive development (sensorimotor, preoperational, concrete operational, formal operational) is an example of
   a. chunking.
   b. an acrostic.
   c. an acronym.
   d. a visual cue.

ESSAY QUESTION

1. What are some general things you can do to help improve your memory?

ANSWER KEY

1. Acrostic
2. Mnemonic
3. Acronym
4. b
5. a
6. c
7. b

ANSWER TO SAMPLE ESSAY QUESTION

1. There are many general things we can do to help our ability at memory tasks, and many of them can help our lives overall as well! The first is to adopt a healthy lifestyle, which includes sleep, sufficient exercise, and an appropriate, nutritious diet. In addition, we need to manage the stress in our lives so that it is not excessive. We can avoid distraction and make use of the many memory aids available. There is no embarrassment in making use of prominently displayed sticky notes, hand-held memory devices, writing things down, and so forth. For memory, we usually need all the help we can get! We certainly need to pay attention to important events or information, and mentally practice or rehearse what we will do or what we need to remember. Lastly, we can be forgiving of ourselves if we cannot remember everything all of the time! We can be equally forgiving of others, as well, who may forget things on occasion, too! By this point, we know that memory is a complex process!

CHAPTER 6 APPLICATION EXERCISES

1. Recall the clever work Hermann Ebbinghaus did regarding memory and how much we have learned from his work.

    Take on the role of Hermann Ebbinghaus. Make up for yourself lists of nonsense syllables, and see how long it takes you to memorize them all. How many words can you remember easily in short-term memory? How long can you remember all the words in your list perfectly? When do you start to forget, and how much do you forget? Are there some syllables that you remember longer than others?

2. Think of an occasion when you forgot something—something really important. What was it that you forgot? Why do you think you forgot it? What was the frame of mind you were in at the time? How were you feeling physically?

    At what point did you remember what you had forgotten? How did you feel at that time? What do you think triggered that memory?

CHAPTER 7

Thinking, Language, and Intelligence

In chapter 7, you are introduced to the ways humans (and maybe some animals) think, use language, and demonstrate intelligence. Study on this whole realm within psychology did not really begin until the 1960s and later, because prior to that time anything "inside the head" was not considered acceptable subject matter by many psychologists. Because it was necessarily more vague, with a process not immediately visible, cognition and related topics were not viewed as sufficiently scientifically rigorous. You may remember that, beginning with the early 20th century, the behavioral perspective was a dominant force within the field of psychology. Behaviorism would deal only with observable behavior. Behaviorists thought that everything anyone learned and manifested was directly due to reinforcement (a consequence that involved a pleasant or desirable outcome) or punishment (a consequence that involved a painful or unpleasant outcome).

Research began in earnest on mental processes in part because we gained the technological resources needed for in-depth and accurate study. In addition, psychologists acknowledged that not everything important in human functioning dealt just with observable environmental factors or behavior. Cognitive psychology has become a substantial scientific discipline.

How do we think? An important component to thinking is creating mental representations of objects and/or experiences from the environment. We form concepts regarding our mental representations; these are mental categories to which we believe the object or experience belongs. Because we can manipulate these representations, and manipulate concepts, we can turn these things and ideas about in our heads. We can try physical, intellectual, or other rotations of these ideas mentally, very quickly, and without the tedious stimuli needed were we to actually try them out in the environment. Concepts may be logical (category membership is clear) or natural (we seem to know what fits in a category, and the associated probability that it does, but cannot actually state clearly what the rules of category membership are). We learn concepts through experience with the environment. Problem solving is an important part of thinking. By using algorithms (standard step-by-step procedures), heuristics (handy rules of thumb), or analogies (drawing on experience with previous similar situations), we may solve a problem more quickly or effectively. Creativity is one kind of thinking (in which we combine information in new ways that provide useful solutions to problems), but high creativity does not necessarily mean an individual is highly intelligent, or vice versa. Everyone has some creative ability. Intelligence seems to encompass a number of different components, and in fact there probably are a number of different types of intelligence. Certainly it is related to thinking processes. Heredity and environment are both vitally important factors in intelligence.

Could we think if we did not have language? There are varying opinions on this question. While language tremendously advances and streamlines our ability to think, it is apparent that our thinking may take effective forms other than language-based. Einstein, for example, reported that his creativity was visually based. Clearly, though, language greatly increases our ability to communicate with each other.

What makes a true language? The most basic unit of sound in a language is a phoneme. Then phonemes are combined to make morphemes, the most basic unit of meaning in a language. Not just any morphemes or words can be strung together. Word order is governed by syntax—the proper ordering to give an utterance meaning. Also, the meaning of words (referred to as semantics) can change, depending upon how words are used in a sentence. Rules of grammar govern how all of this language composition takes place. Whether animals can acquire language is still under debate.

Children in all cultures learn language so quickly, so easily, and when they are very young; it seems as if they come into the world "prewired" to absorb the components necessary to communicate whatever language it is that they are exposed to. This notion was given a name by a well-known linguist, Noam Chomsky. He called this innate ability to quickly pick up speech a language acquisition device. It does not really exist, neurologically (as far as we know), but it represents the recognition that the language learning process is very fast and is universal in sequence and timing among the world's children. The marvelous skills of language, thinking, and intelligence certainly do much to make us human.

MODULE 7.1 THINKING

LEARNING OBJECTIVES

After you have mastered the information in this unit, you will be able to:

1. Define cognitive psychology.

2. Discuss the concept and process of thinking, including the use of mental images.

3. Describe the major types of concepts and how they are organized.

4. Explain steps that can be taken for more efficient problem solving.

5. Discuss cognitive biases and their influence on decision making.

6. Describe the cognitive processes that underlie creative thinking.

OUTLINE

I.   Cognitive Psychology
    A.   Not considered appropriate for study in psychology until 1960s
    B.   Includes how we think, form concepts, use language, process information, solve problems – how we acquire knowledge about the world
    C.   A return to the study of mental experience
II. Thinking
    A.   The mental representation and manipulation of information
    B.   Solving problems, making decisions, and engaging in creativity
III. Mental Images
    A.   We represent information in the mind
    B.   Representations are images, words, or concepts
    C.   Mental image
        1.   Mental picture (representation) of an object or event, like remembering directions
        2.   A reconstruction of the object or event from memory
        3.   Uses similar parts of visual cortex as those for actually seeing the object
        4.   Advantage is mental representation can be manipulated—allows for many cognitive tasks
        5.   Gender differences in mental imagery abilities
            a)   Women—more vivid imagery of past experiences and greater use of imagery to remember past experiences
            b)   Men—greater use in problem solving; better at visualizing moving objects
        6.   Behavior therapists used mental imagery in treating phobic individuals by having them engage in exercises in which they imagine confronting a series of fear-inducing stimuli

7.   Albert Einstein's many creative insights arose from personal thought experiments – did not play any role in his creative thought
8.   Not limited to visual images; sensory experience such as "hearing": try listening to your favorite song using only you mind; people generally have an easier time forming visual images than images of other sensory experiences
9.   Some information is better represented by words and concepts – justice, respect etc.

IV. Concepts
   A. Mental categories used to group objects, events, and ideas according to their common features
   B. Categorization based upon common features or properties
   C. Adaptive for organizing, functioning in our world
   D. Types of concepts
      1. Logical concepts—clearly defined rules for membership
      2. Natural concepts (much more common)
         a) Include objects (such as fruit), activities, and abstractions
         b) Rules for membership understood and applied, but less clear
         c) Membership for category based on *probability* that item fits

V. Problem Solving
   A. A cognitive process—mental strategies are used to solve problems
   B. Previously discussed methods are insight, trial and error – may be tedious and require a long wait
   C. Useful problem-solving strategies
      1. Algorithms
         a) Step-by-step set of rules for solving a problem
         b) None may apply specifically to given problem
      2. Heuristics
         a) A rule of thumb that aids in problem solving and decision making – does not guarantee a solution
         b) Backward-working heuristic—start from solution and see if it fits problem
         c) Means-end heuristic—compare current situation and desired end result; create steps to connect or resolve difference
         d) Creating subgoals heuristic—divide objective into smaller units and solve each individually
      3. Analogies
         a) Use and apply knowledge from similar problems solved in the past
         b) Effective unless past and present problems not really very similar
      4. Incubation periods
         a) Take a break from attempting to solve problem
         b) Passage of time may actually help in seeing problem clearly
   D. Mental roadblocks to problem solving
      1. Mental set
         a) Relying on strategies that worked well in previous situations
         b) May lead to quick solution to current problem
         c) Hinders ability to find solution when prior method not effective
      2. Functional fixedness—inability to see how familiar objects can be used in new ways
      3. Irrelevant information—attending to this distracts from truly relevant factors
   E. Mental roadblocks in decision making
      1. Decision making—problem solving where one course of action is selected from among alternatives
      2. Not always arrived at completely objectively or logically

3.   Examples of decision-making roadblocks – cognitive biases:
      a)   Confirmation bias—sticking to initial approach despite evidence that does not support (preference is to confirm existing belief, ignore facts that might necessitate reconsideration) ; "Don't confuse me with the facts" is an example of failure to reconsider decisions even when strong contradictory evidence is presented
      b)   Representativeness heuristic—assuming given sample is like all other cases; no true basis for believing this is so; in other words, judge people by first impression
      c)   Availability heuristic—basing decision on information that most readily comes to mind (e.g., buying a particular brand); judgments we make about the risks we face

VI. Creativity
    A.   Thinking that leads to original, practical, and meaningful solutions
    B.   Thinking that generates new ideas or artistic expressions
    C.   Everyone has potential for creativity; some show more than others
    D.   Creative people have at least average intelligence – people at the higher echelons of intelligence are not necessarily any more creative than those of average intelligence
    E.   Creativity is distinct from general intelligence
    F.   Measuring creativity
      1.   Variety of tests (one is Alternate Uses Test)
      2.   Most typically measure *divergent thinking* (finding new ways to view situations or familiar objects)
      3.   *Convergent thinking* not considered a measure of creativity (looks at finding the one "correct" solution only)
    G.   Cognitive processes that underlie creative thinking – creativity involves using cognitive processes to manipulate or act on stored knowledge
      1.   Metaphor and analogy
        a)   Metaphor—one object or concept is seen as like another – likening the actions of the heart of those of a pump
        b)   Analogy—comparing two things having similar features or properties
      2.   Conceptual combination—uniting two or more concepts into one novel result (e.g., "veggie burgers")
      3.   Conceptual expansion—extending a familiar concept to novel application (e.g., chef's variation)
    H.   Ability to take what we know and modify and expand on it is one of the basic processes

SUMMARY

In this module, you learn about the incredible process of human thinking. The study of thinking is part of the endeavors of the branch of psychology known as cognitive psychology. Cognition, of course, means thinking. Though much research currently is carried out by cognitive psychologists, it was not always so. For the greater part of the 20th century (when a dominant force in psychology was that of the behaviorists), anything going on inside the head—whether it be thought or, worse, emotion!—was not considered appropriate subject matter for study. Such topics were considered soft, not scientific nor rigorous enough. However, as time went on (and the technology allowing more study of the brain and mental functioning was developed) cognition eventually became a suitable and respectable research area. In part, we were beginning to be aware of the incredible role thinking and other mental processes had with regard to behavior. In part, too, by the 1960s behaviorism had been around for some 40 years. Despite behaviorists' tremendous contributions to psychology and our understanding of behavior, the limitations of the field (ignoring what was going on within the human psyche) were becoming apparent.

How do we think? Most thinking is done by creating mental representations (of objects, events, and concepts) in the mind, then mentally moving them around, sometimes with an intended objective (such as problem solving). Interestingly, mental images (that mental picture we have) use most of the same parts of the visual cortex in the brain as actually viewing the object does. Though mental images typically are of visual stimuli, other representations (such as of smells or auditory experiences) may be formed also.

A major goal of thinking is to solve problems, big and small, which arise in our lives every day (and sometimes, it seems, all the time!). We also are faced with various avenues and alternatives, and must arrive at decisions by choosing from among these. Both activities take mental work. Though trial and error, and insight, as methods of problem solving have already been discussed, other problem-solving strategies are presented in this unit that we also rely on for effective solutions. These include the use of algorithms (a set of step-by-step rules), heuristics (standard rule-of-thumb guidelines), analogies (considering solutions from prior similar situations), and an incubation period (taking a break to allow inspiration or a fresh look).

Roadblocks to good problem solving include being unable to move beyond an existing mental set (a past successful way of approaching a problem), functional fixedness (the inability to see new uses for familiar objects), and being distracted by irrelevant stimuli or information. Roadblocks to successful decision making include having a confirmation bias (a preference for prior notions despite new, perhaps disconfirming, information), relying too much on heuristics (believing whatever is handy or most obvious, without more thorough examination), and being swayed by how various outcomes are described instead of considering the deeper meanings and implications.

Lastly, this module deals with one application of thinking, which is creativity. There is some relation between creativity and intelligence, in that creative individuals typically have average or higher levels of intelligence. However, there is no correspondence between high levels of intelligence and high levels of creativity—having one is unrelated to whether an individual has the other. Creative people seem to possess the ability for divergent thinking—being able to see and use everyday items and experiences in new ways. Metaphor, analogy, conceptual combination and conceptual expansion also are key cognitive processes related to creativity. All people have the potential for creativity to some extent.

KEY TERMS

Cognitive psychology

Thinking

Mental image

Concepts

Logical concepts

Natural concepts

Positive instance

Negative instance

Problem solving

Algorithm

Heuristic

Analogy

Incubation period

Mental set

Functional fixedness

Decision making

Confirmation bias

Representativeness heuristic

Availability heuristic

Creativity

Divergent thinking

Convergent thinking

Metaphor

Conceptual combinations

Conceptual expansion

SELT-TEST PRACTICE QUIZ

Match the following Key Terms and definitions (note: not every Key Term will be used):

1. _____ A problem-solving strategy where knowledge gained from solving prior similar problems is applied to the current situation

2. _____ Mental categories for classifying events, objects, and ideas on the basis of their common features

3. _____ A rule of thumb for making a decision based on the assumption that the given sample is representative of all cases

4. _____ The ability to come up with new ways of viewing familiar situations and objects

5. _____ A branch of psychology that focuses on thinking, problem solving, use of language, and the like

6. _____ An experience that teaches that a given object does belong to a particular concept

7. _____ A set of step-by-step rules for solving a problem

8. _____ Taking a break from problem-solving attempts, may allow for a fresh perspective

9. _____ The process of mentally representing information and manipulating these representations

10. _____ The tendency to rely on past successful strategies that worked in prior situations but that may not be effective in current situation

11. _____ A mental picture or representation, usually visual

12. _____ Concepts with clearly defined rules for membership

13. _____ Combinations of two or more concepts, resulting in one novel idea or application

14. _____ A type of thinking where the attempt is simply to find the "correct answer"

a. Cognitive psychology
b. Thinking
c. Mental image
d. Concepts
e. Logical concepts
f. Natural concepts
g. Positive instance
h. Negative instance
i. Problem solving
j. Algorithm
k. Heuristic
l. Analogy
m. Incubation period
n. Mental set
o. Functional fixedness
p. Decision making
q. Confirmation bias
r. Representativeness heuristic
s. Availability heuristic
t. Creativity
u. Divergent thinking
v. Convergent thinking
w. Metaphor
x. Conceptual combinations
y. Conceptual expansion

15. _____ An inability to conceive of novel uses for familiar objects

16. _____ Originality in thinking that tends to result in new, practical, and useful solutions or approaches

17. _____ The type of problem solving where one must choose a course of action from among the available alternatives

18. The form of thinking where we come up with original ways of conceiving of objects or concepts that result in useful solutions or applications is

    a. convergent thinking.
    b. creativity.
    c. analogy.
    d. mental imagery.

19. The study of cognition in the field of psychology did not really begin until the 1960s because

    a. we lacked the techniques to study mental processes.
    b. other issues in psychology had not been fully investigated.
    c. reinforcers for thinking and problem solving were not well defined.
    d. the topic was not considered sufficiently scientific.

20. When we represent information in our heads so we can make use of it, we form a(n)

    a. analogy.
    b. metaphor.
    c. mental image.
    d. heuristic.

21. As we learn more about the world, we classify information into categories based on commonalities. These classifications are known as

    a. concepts.
    b. algorithms.
    c. mental images.
    d. heuristics.

22. If you solve a problem by starting with a solution and then seeing if the solution fits the data, you are using

    a. a confirmation bias.
    b. a mental map.
    c. the backward-working heuristic.
    d. an incubation period.

23. Solving a math problem that has only one correct answer requires the use of _____ thinking.

    a. divergent
    b. convergent
    c. creative
    d. conceptual

24. With regard to mental imagery, men show a superiority for

    a. mentally rotating or visualizing moving objects.
    b. vividness of images of past experiences.
    c. greater use of imagery in recalling past experiences.
    d. forming mental representations of still objects.

25. Samantha wanted to hammer a nail into a wall, but had no hammer. She did not realize that she could use a shoe or heavy book to hammer the nail into the wall. Samantha fell victim to
   a. confirmation bias.
   b. functional fixedness.
   c. the representativeness heuristic.
   d. mental set.

26. Trying to decide what makes someone "a good friend" is an example of a _____ concept.
   a. logical
   b. natural
   c. subordinate
   d. divergent

27. Most people greatly overestimate the odds of winning the lottery because lottery winners make big news. This is an example of the _____ heuristic.
   a. algorithm
   b. availability
   c. representativeness
   d. confirmatory

28. A disadvantage in using trial and error or insight for problem solving is that both
   a. are relatively inefficient and take a fair amount of time.
   b. cancel out the beneficial effects of other problem-solving methodologies.
   c. make creativity in thought and divergent solutions less likely.
   d. none of the above

29. Confirmation bias in decision making means we
   a. tend to be distracted by irrelevant information.
   b. have difficulty in making a decision and then sticking to it.
   c. have a preference for information that is consistent with our existing beliefs.
   d. rely on information that most easily comes to mind.

ESSAY QUESTIONS

1. What are some characteristics of creative people? Use Arthur Fry and George deMestral as examples. Does everyone have the potential to be creative, or is it limited to a select few?

2. Why are mental representations important in effective thinking processes?

ANSWER KEY

1. Analogy
2. Concepts
3. Representativeness heuristic
4. Divergent thinking
5. Cognitive psychology
6. Positive instance
7. Algorithm
8. Incubation period
9. Thinking
10. Mental set
11. Mental image
12. Logical concepts
13. Conceptual combinations
14. Convergent thinking
15. Functional fixedness
16. Creativity
17. Decision making
18. b
19. d
20. c
21. a
22. c
23. b
24. a
25. b
26. b
27. b
28. a
29. c

SAMPLE ANSWERS TO ESSAY QUESTIONS

1. Creative people can be anyone, and all individuals possess some creative ability. Intelligence is related to creativity to an extent, in that creative people typically have at least average levels of intelligence. Highly intelligent people, however, are no more likely to be highly creative than any other individuals possessing a moderate degree of intelligence.

Both Arthur Fry and George deMestral show a creative mind at work. Fry had developed a compound through his research that was only mildly adhesive, and his company, 3M, saw no immediate use for it. However, Fry had a problem that needed a solution—pieces of paper, which he used to mark his place in his hymnal, tended to fall out from among the pages. He was able to take a new compound, which had no apparent use, and apply it (literally!) to solve his problem, in a way that had not been done before. This is evidence, among other things, of conceptual combination. DeMestral took an everyday, and in fact annoying, experience of getting burrs stuck to his clothing and his dog and applied these long-known circumstances to a new and very beneficial use (Velcro). Both individuals show divergent thinking—coming up with fresh new ways of seeing events, objects, and components that already existed. The ingredients for deMestral's creative breakthrough have been around as long as there have been burrs, dogs, and outdoor clothing. However, it took deMestral's ability to look further (in this case, he examined the phenomenon microscopically) and see a new application for a very familiar experience that led to the now widespread use of his creative insight. For both Fry and deMestral, the tools they utilized in their creativity were already available (for a short time and a long time, respectively). The spark of creativity was all in how these individuals viewed already-existing phenomena.

2.   Mental representations make our thinking process far more efficient and quick. We are able to create representations in our mind, which we then can manipulate, unlike the ponderous task of manipulating actual objects and situations in the real world. Also, by using mental representations, we are able to attempt solutions or recombinations that might not even be possible in our current environment. Mental representations allow us to play out possible new applications (divergent thinking), draw on past similar experiences (analogies), and extend existing concepts (conceptual expansion) without the time and materials needed to actually try these out. We can come up with helpful new solutions that, at least for the time being, exist only in the world of our imagination.

MODULE 7.2 LANGUAGE

LEARNING OBJECTIVES

After you have mastered the information in this unit, you will be able to:

1.   Define the major components of language.

2.   Describe how language develops.

3.   Explain the linguistic relativity hypothesis.

4.   Discuss whether species other than humans can use language.

OUTLINE

I.   Language
   A.   A system of communication composed of symbols
   B.   Symbols are arranged according to a grammar
   C.   Grammar—a set of rules governing the proper use of words, phrases, and sentences to express meaning
   D.   Communication (in some form) crucial to human existence – when there is no one to talk with, people talk to themselves, their dog and even to plants
II.   Basic Components of Language
   A.   Phonemes—basic units of sounds in a language (single letters and letter units)
   B.   Morphemes
      1.   Formed by combinations of phonemes
      2.   Smallest units of meaning in a language

    3.   Include simple words (car, ball) but also prefixes and suffixes ("un," "ed")
  C.   Syntax—rules of grammar that determine how words are ordered in a sentence (or phrase) to form meaningful expressions
  D.   Semantics—the set of rules governing the meaning of words
III.   Language Development
  A.   Children develop language in the same stages, at the same ages, universally
    1.   About 6 months of age, infants are limited to nonlinguistic forms of communications – crying and cooing
    2.   Progressing through stages of one- and two-word phrases
    3.   2 – 3 years begins developing more complex speech patterns
  B.   Language acquisition in young children usually occurs very easily and naturally
  C.   Language acquisition device—suggested by Chomsky; human is "prewired" to acquire a language
  D.   Both nature and nurture necessary to learn language – help child develop language skills by talking (using proper language) and reading to them <u>frequently</u>
  E.   Close relationship between language and thought
  F.   Scientists are beginning to locate genes involved in the development of brain mechanisms responsible for speech and language (Lichtenbelt et al., 2005; Vargha-Khadem et al., 2005)
IV.   Culture and Language
  A.   Is the language one speaks related to how one thinks?
  B.   Linguistic relativity hypothesis (Whorfian hypothesis)
    1.   Proposes that language we use determines how we think
    2.   Proposes that language we use determines how we perceive reality
    3.   Research (e.g., by Rosch et. al., 1972) does not support this notion
    4.   Dani tribe just as capable as English-speaking participants at distinguishing colors
    5.   There is support for notion that language and culture influence how we think – we used to use he not he/she when writing, females might have gotten the notion that it did not include them (e.g., police<u>men,</u> fire<u>men,</u> etc.)
V.   Is Language Unique to Humans?
  A.   Apes taught American Sign Language (ASL) or another artificial language
  B.   Washoe, Sarah, Kanzi findings give evidence of communication, basic grammar
  C.   Debate is whether this communication is actually use of true "language"
  D.   Possibly just product of imitation, reinforcement
  E.   Ultimate conclusion depends on how "language" is defined

SUMMARY

In this module, you learn about the fascinating concept of language. Although language generally makes us think of speech, communication may take other forms as well (such as sign language). Language is a communication system based on symbols. These symbols must be used and arranged in a certain way to allow for meaningful exchange. Rules guiding this use and arrangement are known as grammar.

The most basic units in language are phonemes. These are the simplest, single sounds (like "d," "th") a language has. Morphemes, the smallest units of meaning in a language, are made up of phonemes. Syntax involves the rules of grammar that govern how words are sequenced in order to create meaningful expressions. Semantics relates to the actual meaning of words—the meaning of the same word can change depending upon how it is used in a communication.

People learn language universally, and children learn language remarkably easily. Children grasp the same concepts, at the same ages, worldwide. Why might this be? Noam Chomsky, a famous linguist, suggests that humans come into the world "prewired"—the brain, due to its structure, is already prepared to absorb a language. Experience just needs to supply what the specific words are to be. In other words, according to Chomsky, the neural circuitry for language already exists. He calls this particular readiness for language the language acquisition device. The device is not an actual brain structure—the term represents the notion of the neural "blueprint" or circuitry readiness. Since language acquisition in children does occur so easily, readily, consistently, and universally, some explanation for this phenomenon seems desirable. There is opposition to Chomsky's viewpoint, however. Predominantly, this opposition emphasizes that no real brain structure exists precisely corresponding to the language acquisition device.

The linguistic relativity hypothesis (also called the Whorfian hypothesis) proposes that our language determines how we think and how we perceive the world. If we lack the term for a certain concept in the world—can we then truly know and contemplate that concept? In fact, research (Rosch et. al., 1972) does not provide much support for the linguistic relativity hypothesis. The Dani tribe, who have almost no words in their language for color, were just as able to distinguish among plastic chips of different colors as were English-speaking participants (with 11 different terms for color). Our language may to an extent *influence* how we think; there is some evidence that people from different cultures do think differently (Goode, 2000).

For several decades, researchers have been investigating human-animal communication. Gorillas and other apes do show some facility for human language. Since apes lack the vocal structures needed to form human sounds, sign language (ASL, for example) or other artificial languages are taught. Washoe, Sarah, and Kanzi (all chimpanzees) seemed to grasp the notions of the language they were taught, including something of a basic grammar. They were able to create sentences for communication, and put the subject, verb, and object of their communication in the proper order to reflect what they wanted to convey. (Washoe, for instance, knew the difference between "Washoe tickle you" and "You tickle Washoe," depending upon how she wanted the tickling to occur!) There is criticism regarding ape-human communication—perhaps these communication exchanges are really just the result of imitation and reinforcement. It is difficult, fundamentally, to make a clear distinction as to whether the animals truly use and understand language, or whether they are simply repeating actions of their trainers that they have seen and have been rewarded for. Whether animals can communicate with humans via language ultimately depends in part upon how stringently the term "language" is defined.

KEY TERMS

Language

Grammar

Phonemes

Morphemes

Syntax

Semantics

Language acquisition device

Linguistic relativity hypothesis

SELF-TEST PRACTICE QUIZ

Match the following Key Terms and definitions:

1. _____ The notion of an inborn neural preparedness, suggested by Noam Chomsky, which explains why children learn language so easily and in a universal pattern

2. _____ The smallest units of meaning in a language

3. _____ A system of communication involving symbols that are arranged according to a set of rules to yield meaningful expressions

4. _____ Rules of grammar that govern how words are sequenced within sentences or phrases in order to result in meaningful communications

5. _____ The view that the language we use determines how we think and how we perceive the world

6. _____ The most basic units of sounds within a language

7. _____ Rules that govern the meaning of words

8. _____ The set of rules regarding how symbols within a given language are to be used in order to form meaningful expressions

a. Language
b. Grammar
c. Phonemes
d. Morphemes
e. Syntax
f. Semantics
g. Language acquisition device
h. Linguistic relativity hypothesis

9. A system of communication, using symbols whose ordering is governed by a grammar, is known as
   a. linguistics.
   b. language.
   c. syntax.
   d. semantics.

10. Language is absorbed and used so easily by children, and in a pattern that is universal across all cultures, that Noam Chomsky has suggested the existence of
    a. private speech.
    b. one innate universal language.
    c. a language acquisition device.
    d. neural prewiring that is identical in apes and humans.

11. In the word "cars," the "s" is a
   a. syntax.
   b. phoneme.
   c. morpheme.
   d. both B and C are correct

12. When we put words in the correct order in a sentence so that the sentence is meaningful, we are using rules of grammar called
   a. syntax.
   b. semantics.
   c. morphemes.
   d. linguistic relativity.

13. The sentence "I love to pizza eat" violates the rules of
   a. semantics.
   b. syntax.
   c. punctuation.
   d. phonemes.

14. Evidence regarding the linguistic relativity hypothesis leads us to conclude that
   a. language precedes thought.
   b. thought precedes language.
   c. language determines how we perceive the world.
   d. language influences how we think.

15. _____ are formed from combinations of _____.
   a. Syllables; vowels
   b. Universals; constants
   c. Phonemes; morphemes
   d. none of the above

16. Based on research evidence, which statement about the linguistic relativity hypothesis is correct?
   a. Language may affect thinking, but it does not completely determine thinking.
   b. It is impossible for people to conceive of ideas that they do not have words for.
   c. Language has no effect on cognition.
   d. The linguistic relativity hypothesis holds true for animals such as gorillas, but not for humans.

17. One argument against the idea that chimpanzees and gorillas can communicate with humans using a version of our language is that
   a. American sign language (ASL) is not a true language.
   b. trainers tend to be biased due to their emotional attachment to their animals.
   c. gorillas and other apes do not have the vocal structures necessary to use our language.
   d. ape "communication" with humans is really just imitating behaviors that they have seen their trainers do; animals repeat the behaviors because they have been reinforced for doing so.

18. When Kanzi, a male pygmy chimp, was with his mother while she learned a communication system using geometric symbols, he
   a. ignored the training and played with extra geometric shapes.
   b. was trained on a smaller keyboard, using the same kinds of symbols.
   c. was given no specific training, but seemed to pick up the communication system anyway.
   d. never fully grasped how to order symbols correctly.

ESSAY QUESTIONS

1. Discuss the concept of the linguistic relativity hypothesis (the Whorfian hypothesis), and the evidence presented in the text for and against it. How is the former use of the pronoun "he" in language (to represent all humans) a way that language can influence thinking?

2. It is difficult to conclude whether animals can communicate using language, because ultimately the answer lies with how "language" is defined. What are some ways we can define language? Evaluate the findings regarding animal communication in light of these definitions.

ANSWER KEY

1. Language acquisition device
2. Morphemes
3. Language
4. Syntax
5. Linguistic relativity hypothesis
6. Phonemes
7. Semantics
8. Grammar
9. b
10. c
11. d
12. a
13. b
14. d
15. d
16. a
17. d
18. c

SAMPLE ANSWERS TO ESSAY QUESTIONS

1. The linguistic relativity hypothesis suggests that language determines both how we think and how we perceive the world. Despite some logic in this approach (if a word does not exist for a concept, how can we think about it?), evidence does not fully support Benjamin Whorf's view. Research by Rosch on distinguishing colors, for example, found no differences between results from study participants who did and did not have words for many different colors. Research by Goode (2000) and Nisbett (2000, 2001) support the notion that there is cultural variation in how people think, and language, while not a total determinant, does have some influence. Using a term such as "he," even for all speakers of the same language, can impact how such a communication is perceived. Though intended, in its past use, to represent all humans, "he" still conveys that the information presented really relates more to, or is more appropriate for, males.

2. If a definition of language includes the concept simply of communication by means of symbols, then Washoe, Kanzi, Sarah, and other animals indeed are communicating effectively. They seem

to understand proper placement of subjects and objects in sentences, and are able to learn and communicate their wishes. If, however, our definition of language includes an understanding and use of complex syntax and grammatical structures, then the animal communication presented is not sufficient to meet these criteria. Language use in the chimpanzee examples given in the textbook material may be similar to the early communication forms exhibited by young children.

MODULE 7.3 INTELLIGENCE

LEARNING OBJECTIVES

After you have mastered the information in this unit, you will be able to:

1. Define intelligence and explain how it is measured.

2. Discuss the features of a good intelligence test.

3. Discuss special issues in intelligence: misuse of intelligence tests, gender differences, and extremes of intelligence.

4. Outline the major theories of intelligence.

5. Evaluate the roles of heredity and environment with regard to intelligence.

OUTLINE

I. Intelligence
    A. Difficult to define—may be many components, different types
    B. David Wechsler (1975): "…the global capacity of the individual to act purposefully, to think rationally, and to deal effectively with the environment"
    C. Theorists suggest multiple intelligences, or many different forms of intelligence
    D. Some theorists believe that the ability to recognize and manage emotions is a form of intelligent behavior called emotional intelligence
II. How Is Intelligence Measured?
    A. Alfred Binet (French)
        1. Commissioned (1904) by school officials in Paris to identify intellectually at-risk children
        2. Binet and Theodore Simon developed an intelligence test (1905) – Simon developed an intelligence test consisting of memory tasks and other short tasks representing everyday problems for children (counting coins), scaling the tasks according to the age the child should be able to perform
        3. Test items scaled to what typical child of a given age could do
        4. Mental age—age level of work a child could do
    B. IQ (Intelligence Quotient)
        1. Suggested by William Stern, (1912)
        2. IQ = MA (mental age) divided by CA (chronological age) x 100
    C. Lewis Terman (at Stanford University, USA)
        1. Adapted Binet-Simon test for use in United States, added many test items
        2. Established norms for comparison of scores
        3. Revised test known as the Stanford-Binet Intelligence Scale (SBIS, 1916) – establishing criteria (norms) for comparing individual scores with those of the general population
    D. Most widely used intelligence tests today: created by David Wechsler
        1. Developed for pre-school children, school age children, and adults
        2. Score consists of a deviation IQ (how different from norm for that age group)

3.   Test based on idea that intelligence is a variety of abilities
4.   Test includes verbal and performance subtests

III. Characteristics of Good Intelligence Tests
    A.   Standardization
        1.   Establishing norms by administering test to large numbers of people (standardization sample)
        2.   Sample must be representative of population to which it refers
        3.   IQ score is based on difference (deviation) from norm
        4.   Mean (average score) is 100
        5.   2/3 of scores from general population range from 85 to 115
        6.   Uniform procedures must be followed when administering test
    B.   Reliability
        1.   Consistency of test scores over time
        2.   Some methodologies are test-retest and alternate-forms – when the method is used, subjects are given a parallel form of the test
    C.   Validity—when a test measures what it is supposed to test
        1.   Example: math test indeed tests math ability, not verbal or mechanical skills or success at following directions
        2.   Predictive validity—test's accuracy for projecting future behavior, performance
    D.   Misuses of intelligence tests
        1.   Parents and teachers may lose hope for children with low IQ scores
        2.   Low expectations can become self-fulfilling prophecies
        3.   Children may give up on themselves; accept label
        4.   Too much emphasis may be placed on IQ scores—other measures of assessment should also be considered
        5.   Tests may be biased against those not in majority culture
        6.   Culture-fair tests have been developed, but not as good predictors of academic performance as well as standard IQ tests
            a)   May be impossible to develop a purely culture-free IQ test because the skills that define intelligence depends on the values of the culture in which the test is developed (Benson, 2003b)
            b)   Nor should we assume that all people have the same experience with test-taking skills or familiarity with the types of material used on the test; at best, culture-reduced test not tests which are entirely culture-fair (Sternberg & Grigorenko, 2008)

IV. Gender Differences in Cognitive Abilities
    A.   No differences with regard to general intelligence, learning and problem-solving abilities – no evidence that one sex is smarter than the other
    B.   Females show superiority for activities involving verbal skills such as reading writing and spelling
    C.   Males: greater incidence of reading difficulties, show superiority for math, visual-spatial – map reading and mental rotation of 3-D figures
        1.   Girls tended to have less confidence in their math skills but no less ability than boys

V.   Extremes of Intelligence
    A.   Mental retardation—not just IQ score
        1.   Includes IQ score of 70 or below
        2.   Difficulty in coping with age-appropriate tasks and life situations
        3.   Mainstreaming—children with mild retardation are placed in regular classrooms
        4.   Causes may be biological, environmental, or both
            a)   Biological causes include genetic or chromosomal disorders, brain damage and exposure to lead

b) Environmental cause is deprived family interaction – verbal and stimulating play activities

B. Intellectual giftedness
1. IQ of 130 or higher (98th percentile)
2. May benefit from enriched, faster-paced academic programs
3. Category also includes musical, artistic ability – skills not typically assessed by standard IQ

VI. Theories of Intelligence
A. Spearman's "g"—idea that there is a general underlying factor (ability in one area often correlated with ability in other areas) – good predictor of school performance in children but also job performance in adulthood
B. Thurstone's Primary Mental Abilities test to measure seven primary abilities: verbal comprehension, numerical ability, memory, inductive reasoning, perceptual speed, verbal fluency, and spatial relations
C. Gardner's model of multiple intelligences (8) – (now believes their maybe 9): linguistic, logical-mathematical, musical, spatial, bodily-kinesthetic, interpersonal, intrapersonal, and naturalist
1. Very influential model, especially in educational settings
2. Does not really explain how multiple intelligences interact with each other
D. Sternberg's triarchic theory of intelligence
1. Bringing together different aspects of our intelligence to address life challenges
2. Intelligence has three aspects: analytic, creative, and practical
a) Analytic—measured by traditional intelligence test
b) Creative—slows us to invent new ways of solving unfamiliar problems
c) Practical—ability to apply common sense or "street smarts" traditional tests fail to measure
3. More intelligent individuals integrate these aspects better
E. Overview
1. Clear that human intelligence involves multiple abilities, perhaps multiple intelligences (lack of data in support of latter)
2. Cultural context is always important (e.g., societies vary in what they value as intelligence and what they measure for)
3. Probably is a "general" intelligence; still, tests could be broadened to assure assessment of all abilities related to the notion of intelligence
4. Presently, we lack a consensus in the field to support the existence of separate types of intelligence

VII. Intelligence and the Nature-Nurture Question
A. Distinguishing between the influences of each
B. Closer genetic tie corresponds to closer intellectual similarity (MZ twins more similar than DZ twins)
C. MZ twins reared apart more alike in intelligence than DZ twins raised together, but environment also an influence (MZ twins raised together vs. apart)
D. IQ scores of adopted children closer to that of biological parents
E. Conclusion is environment and genetics influence together, in complex ways
F. Heritability of a trait—the degree to which genetic factor is a contributor
G. Racial differences in IQ
1. Racial disparity in scores even when income level accounted for
2. *The Bell Curve*—proposed a widening gap between high and low intelligence, corresponding to race (non-white other than Asian lag)

3.   Early intervention can make a difference (IQ is not fixed at birth) – Affluent families "can provide the mental stimulation needed for genes to build the brain circuitry for intelligence," says another researcher Erik Turkheimer (cited in Kirp, 2006, p 16)
4.   Individual potential always unique
5.   IQ scores have been rising in recent generations, especially among African Americans (relative to Euro-Americans)
6.   Conclusion—environment, not genetic factors, accounts for racial differences

SUMMARY

In this module, you learn about human intelligence and the attempts we have made to define it and measure it. It is difficult to measure something when you are not even sure what it is! Various theories regarding what intelligence is and how to measure it continue to emerge. However, unlike past views, researchers are moving away from the idea of one notion of intelligence and towards the belief that there may be many intelligences, or at least many abilities, which comprise the notion of intelligence.

The earliest specific work evaluating intelligence began in France, about 100 years ago. Alfred Binet was asked by Paris school officials to test children in the Paris system. The objective was to determine who might have difficulty with the existing school program and need special classrooms. Binet, along with assistance from Theodore Simon, developed an intelligence test based on the notion that brighter children would show abilities more typical of children older than they. Children of lesser ability would not be able to accomplish all the tasks that other children their age could. The intelligence test yielded, then, a mental age. This approach evolved into determining an intelligence quotient (IQ; the term is still used today, though it more often refers to Wechsler tests than the one developed by Binet). The intelligence quotient resulted from dividing a child's mental age (the score on the intelligence test) by that child's actual chronological age (how old he or she actually was, in years, at the time of taking the test), and multiplying by 100. Lewis Terman at Stanford University adapted Binet's test, and it became known as the Stanford-Binet Intelligence Scale (1916). More recently, David Wechsler created intelligence tests that include not only verbal tasks but also "performance" tasks, assessing abilities such as for picture arrangement, object assembly, and so forth. These have been created for different age groups. The IQ score derived from the test indicates how different the test-taker is from the typical score (the norm).

What makes a good intelligence test? First, the test must be standardized; that is, we must have results from testing large numbers of individuals with which we determine typical (average) scores and deviations. The mean (average) IQ score is set at 100, and approximately 2/3 of all people taking the intelligence test fall between the scores of 85 and 115. Secondly, a test must be reliable. That means that, each time it is given, it must yield a similar type of result. Lastly, a test must have validity. This is a very important criterion. Validity comes from the word "valid," meaning true. A valid test measures what it says it measures. One of our concerns with intelligence testing is that the tests are culture-fair. In other words, if someone taking the test is not familiar either with the words or the concepts used in the test, is it a test of that person's intelligence? Or is it a test of the ability to understand, let's say, a foreign language or objects (and concepts) common to a foreign culture.

Binet's intention when he developed the first intelligence test was that it would be helpful and allow for earlier identification of and intervention for children who needed special assistance in learning. We hope that that does occur with the intelligence tests in use today. However, such tests can be and are misused. A child scoring low on the test may be thought of as less capable, and thus less energy and enthusiasm are expended on such an individual. Children themselves may adopt a more helpless attitude and may approach their learning tasks with less confidence and few expectations. No intelligence test is a perfect predictor of a child's future achievements. Certainly that, and other assessment measures, must be considered.

Though we are not quite sure what intelligence is, results of intelligence tests do reveal that individuals who perform at scores of 70 and below are likely to show developmental delays (mental retardation) if they have difficulty with everyday life tasks as well. Mental retardation may be a result of biological or environmental factors. Intellectual giftedness (an IQ score at 130 or higher) is the other end of the spectrum. Giftedness now also means exceptional artistic or musical ability. Though intelligence is important, persistence and motivation are always crucial to one's overall success. IQ may predict long term health and longevity perhaps because people who tend to do well on IQ tests have the kinds of learning and problem-solving skills needed to acquire and practice healthier behavior.

Because we are not sure what intelligence is, there are a number of theories. The oldest is Charles Spearman's (1927), who thought that there is one general ("g") intelligence factor. Spearman noted that many people who show intelligence in one area show similar ability in other areas as well. Louis Thurstone, a bit later in the 20th century, had a different view and proposed seven basic mental abilities. These abilities (such as memory, verbal fluency and comprehension, spatial and numerical ability) are what we have traditionally thought of as indicating "intelligence." Howard Gardner expanded Thurstone's approach, suggesting that in fact there are multiple intelligences. These include not only the traditional intellectual abilities (e.g., verbal and mathematical skill) but also things like musical, kinesthetic, and interpersonal intelligence. Sternberg (1994) suggests intelligence is more how we pull our skills together to meet daily challenges. His theory is the triarchic theory of intelligence, and its three components are analytic, creative, and practical intelligence. More intelligent people, Sternberg says, are able to integrate these three skills better to manage everyday tasks.

Which contributes more to intelligence—nature (genes/heredity) or nurture (environment/how one is raised)? To help address this question, we look at kinship studies (studies on sets of relatives). Identical (monozygotic, or MZ) twins have a more similar intelligence than do fraternal (dizygotic, or DZ) twins. In fact, MZ twins raised apart are more similar in intelligence than DZ twins raised together. This finding suggests that genetics is an important factor. Yet, identical (MZ) twins raised together are more similar in their intelligence than identical twins raised apart. What would account for this latter difference? It must be environmental experience. The conclusion is that both genetic heritage and environmental experience are of great importance in determining intellectual ability. These two factors intimately interact, or influence each other, as a child grows and matures. Create a home that encourages verbal interaction, reading, and exploration.

Intelligence tests traditionally have shown a higher level of ability for Euro-American white test-takers than for African Americans. This holds true even when income level is taken into consideration. Some (see Herrnstein and Murray, *The Bell Curve,* 1994) have suggested this racial difference is genetic, and that social and educational intervention would not be productive. However, when existing research is considered as a whole, it does appear that the racial gap in intelligence is due to environment, not heredity. For example, African American and interracial children raised in upper-middle class white American families had IQ scores approximately 15 points higher than their counterparts in the African American community. Most likely, it is very important that children are exposed to a culture of books, communication, and learning in order to strengthen abilities and excel in these areas.

KEY TERMS

Intelligence

Mental age

Intelligence quotient (IQ)

Norms

Standardization

Reliability

Validity

Predictive validity

Dyslexia

Culture-fair tests

Mental retardation

Mainstreaming

Primary mental abilities

Multiple intelligences

Triarchic theory of intelligence

Heritability

SELF-TEST PRACTICE QUIZ

Match the following Key Terms and definitions (note: not every Key Term will be used):

1. _____ Standards used to compare one's test results with those of others

2. _____ A view on intelligence proposed by Robert Sternberg, suggesting that intelligence is the ability to successfully integrate analytical, creative, and practical skills

3. _____ Tests that eliminate potential bias due to lack of prior experience with the dominant culture

4. _____ The ability to think and reason clearly, and act purposefully in order to live effectively

5. _____ The degree to which genetic influence accounts for the manifestation of a trait within a population

a. Intelligence

b. Mental age

c. Intelligence quotient (IQ)

d. Norms

e. Standardization

f. Reliability

g. Validity

h. Predictive validity

i. Dyslexia

j. Culture-fair tests

k. Mental retardation

l. Mainstreaming

m. Primary mental abilities

n. Multiple intelligences

6. _____ Seven basic factors constituting intelligence, as proposed by Thurstone

7. _____ The result of a formula indicating degree of intelligence, based on score (mental age) derived from an intelligence test

8. _____ A desirable test feature wherein the test yields similar results when administered over time

9. _____ Experiencing developmental delays in both intellectual and social functioning

10. _____ An important feature of a test, wherein the test measures accurately the abilities it is designed to measure

11. _____ A concept, introduced by Howard Gardner, suggesting that there are a variety of intelligences (including social and kinesthetic skills) which give evidence of intelligent human behavior

12. _____ A score derived from an intelligence test, where ability is related to success at tasks typical for other individuals of a comparable age

13. _____ Placing children who have some intellectual deficit or impairment in a regular school classroom

14. _____ The extent to which a test accurately indicates the test-taker's future ability at the skill or area of knowledge being tested

15. _____ Establishing norms for a test, derived from administering the test to a large representative sample from the relevant population

16. _____ A learning disability characterized by impaired ability to read

o. Triarchic theory of intelligence

p. Heritability

17. Central to the definition of intelligence is the belief that it involves the ability to
    a. excel academically.
    b. adapt to the environment.
    c. survive on the streets.
    d. show exceptional social or analytical skills.

18. Binet and Simon developed the first intelligence test because they wanted to
    a. identify the most capable among French children.
    b. exclude children of low abilities from further education.
    c. conduct a longitudinal study on children who were classified as gifted.
    d. discover children with learning difficulties who would need extra help.

19. What method did Alfred Binet eventually adopt for use in calculating IQ?
    a. Subtracting chronological age from mental age
    b. Comparing the test-taker's performance to standardized norms
    c. Dividing mental age by chronological age, then multiplying by 100
    d. none of the above

20. Lewis Terman, in the United States, took Binet's intelligence test, added many items, and standardized the test by developing
    a. norms.
    b. Terman Evaluation Criteria.
    c. mental age chronology.
    d. test-retest reliability.

21. The most widely used intelligence test in the United States is the
    a. Stanford-Binet Intelligence Scale (SBIS).
    b. series of tests developed by Wechsler.
    c. Object Assembly Test.
    d. Primary Mental Abilities Test.

22. A teacher gives her psychology class a final exam that consists solely of impossibly difficult math problems. Thus, the entire class fails (and fails again when they take it a second time). This test is
    a. both reliable and valid.
    b. valid but not reliable.
    c. reliable but not valid.
    d. neither valid nor reliable.

23. How are IQ scores calculated on modern intelligence tests?
    a. Mental age is divided by chronological age, then multiplied by 100.
    b. Scores are compared to standardized norms for the test-taker's age group.
    c. The number of incorrect answers is subtracted from the number of correct answers.
    d. none of the above

24. What is one drawback of using intelligence tests to classify individuals in terms of mental ability?
    a. Individuals who do not perform well may be labeled and treated with lower expectations.
    b. Children who do not score highly may give up on themselves and simply not try to learn.
    c. Other criteria, besides scores on an intelligence test, are indicators of how likely a person is to achieve.
    d. all of the above

25. Cultural background is an important consideration when administering intelligence tests. An intelligence test is NOT an indicator of ability when it

    a. tests familiarity with a language rather than the concepts it was designed to evaluate.
    b. is given to individuals from a variety of different cultures.
    c. is given to children of just one age group.
    d. shows an unusually high level of predictive validity.

26. Which statement about Gardner's theory is correct?

    a. Gardner believes that there are multiple types of intelligence, each independent of the others.
    b. Gardner's theory has been criticized for putting too much emphasis on *g*.
    c. Gardner's theory has been proven to be more accurate than those of Sternberg or Spearman.
    d. none of the above

27. The practice of putting children with mild intellectual and social developmental difficulties into regular classrooms is known as

    a. integration.
    b. mainstreaming.
    c. pre-advancement.
    d. readiness training.

28. A problem with kinship studies, such as researching the factors involved in intelligence, is that

    a. nature and nurture are not the real issues with regard to intellectual functioning.
    b. it is difficult to get all members of a large family unit to participate.
    c. the closer the genetic link among family members, the closer (usually) are the environmental experiences as well.
    d. we cannot distinguish the heritability of traits between monozygotic (MZ) and dizygotic (DZ) twins.

29. Which statement best describes Spearman's theory of intelligence?

    a. Intelligence is almost entirely determined by genetics.
    b. There is one type of general intelligence that underlies performance on a wide variety of tasks.
    c. Intelligence is composed of seven primary mental abilities.
    d. Standard IQ tests are lacking because they do not measure creative or practical intelligence.

30. Studies that compare the intelligence of adopted children with the intelligence of both their biological and their adoptive parents find

    a. no differences between the intelligence of the adopted children and that of their adoptive parents.
    b. no differences between the intelligence of the adopted children and that of their biological parents.
    c. the intelligence of adopted children to be more like that of their biological parents.
    d. the intelligence of adopted children to be more like that of their adoptive parents.

31. Studies investigating the racial gap in intelligence scores provide evidence for

    a. a genetic explanation for intelligence.
    b. an environmental explanation for intelligence.
    c. quality of school system as the determinant of intelligence.
    d. age of parents at time of adoption as the determinant of intelligence.

32. One source of evidence that counters the notion proposed in Herrnstein and Murray's *The Bell Curve* that intellectual differences are racially based is the finding that

    a. IQ scores among African Americans have been rising slightly more quickly than those of Euro-Americans.
    b. African Americans score as high on intelligence tests as do Euro-Americans when socioeconomic factors are taken into account.
    c. IQ scores among African Americans have been declining more slowly than those of Euro-Americans.
    d. children adopted by African American parents score higher on intelligence tests than do children adopted by non-Hispanic white parents.

33. Between which two people would you expect to find the greatest similarity in IQ scores?

    a. Identical twins
    b. Fraternal twins
    c. Adopted children and their biological parents
    d. Adopted children and their adoptive parents

34. Which of the following is *not* a component of Sternberg's theory of intelligence?

    a. Creative intelligence
    b. Practical intelligence
    c. Linguistic intelligence
    d. Analytical intelligence

35. Regarding the notion of multiple intelligences,

    a. increasing amounts of evidence reveal support for this view.
    b. there are no more than 7 or 8 basic types of intelligence.
    c. evidence suggests that there are many factors contributing to intelligence, but support for multiple intelligences has not yet been widely found.
    d. there appears to be one pervasive underlying factor for cognitive ability.

ESSAY QUESTIONS

1. Explain how the first IQ (intelligence quotient) was computed. How is a deviation score different from an intelligence score computed this way?

2. Why is it difficult to develop a truly culture-free intelligence test?

3. How can kinship studies help us learn more about influences on intelligence? What are some findings we have from these studies?

ANSWER KEY

1. Norms
2. Triarchic theory of intelligence
3. Culture-fair tests
4. Intelligence
5. Heritability
6. Primary mental abilities
7. Intelligence quotient (IQ)
8. Reliability
9. Mental retardation
10. Validity
11. Multiple intelligences
12. Mental age
13. Mainstreaming
14. Predictive validity
15. Standardization
16. Dyslexia
17. b
18. d
19. c
20. a
21. b
22. c
23. b
24. d
25. a
26. a
27. b
28. c
29. b
30. c
31. b
32. a
33. a
34. c
35. c

SAMPLE ANSWERS TO ESSAY QUESTIONS

1. The first IQ score was, indeed, a quotient—the result of the mathematical process of division. A child was given an intelligence test. This test was composed of tasks that could be accomplished by typical children of various ages. The level of tasks the child taking the test was able to accomplish successfully yielded a mental age. For example, a child may be 10 years old (her chronological age). However, if she is able to accomplish all the tasks of the typical 9-year-old, 10-year-old, 11-year-old, and even some of those typical for a 12-year-old, she may have a mental age of, let's say, 11.7 years. In other words, she can accomplish tasks that normally a child would need to be 11.7 years old in order to carry out successfully. This mental age (MA) is then divided by her chronological or actual age in years (CA), and multiplied by 100 (to standardize so that scores have a mean or average of 100). This child's score would be 117. Since most intelligence test-takers (more than 2/3) score at or below an IQ of 115, this test-taker is above average. The traditional IQ (an example of which is computed here) is based on a ratio. More recent versions of intelligence tests use deviation scores. The deviation score just means it is an indication of how different the test-taker's score is from the norm, or arithmetic average.

2. Although it is important to have culture-free tests, they are difficult to develop. A culture-free test is one where a test-taker from any culture and environmental experience has equal familiarity with the concepts and objects used in the questions (and tasks) actually assessing intellectual ability. Thus, there is no bias against (no disadvantage for) a test-taker who may be unfamiliar, or less familiar, with the language in which the intelligence test is written, the tools (objects, concepts) by which intelligence is probed, or both. Note that if a test is given to someone less familiar or unfamiliar with these aspects, the test is not really a test of intelligence but rather a test of familiarity with the test items. The problem with creating culture-frees test is that they tend to predict future achievement less well. It may in fact be impossible to create a test of intelligence that is independent of the cultural source from which it was produced, since terminology and concepts of at least some kind must be utilized.

3. The two main accepted sources of influence on intelligence are nature (the genetic code that an individual inherits) and nurture (the experiences an individual has with his or her environment). Kinship studies should help distinguish between these two influences as there is a varying amount of genetic similarity among members of the same family unit. Indeed, kinship studies have shown that the more family members are alike in terms of genetic inheritance, the more alike they are in terms of exhibited intelligence. This finding then suggests a strong genetic source for intelligence. However, it should be remembered that nearly all closely-related family members also often share a similar, or in fact the same, environment. Thus, with kinship studies alone, we cannot completely distinguish between influences from nature vs. nurture.

    One kind of kinship study is with twins, and identical twins are of particular interest since they share exactly the same genetic code. Studies with identical twins are the most convincing with regard to a hereditary influence on intelligence; identical twins show the greatest intellectual similarity of all. However, our research with monozygotic (identical) twins has also revealed that MZ twins raised together are more similar than MZ twins raised apart. Why the difference in intelligence findings here? Clearly, it must be differing environmental experiences that account for the difference among twins where the genetic heritage is identical. In addition, African American children adopted by white parents scored far higher on intelligence tests than did their counterparts who remained within the African American community. This latter finding suggests that it is the exposure to what is valued as intelligent by the dominant culture in the USA that leads to higher levels of achievement on standard intelligence tests.

MODULE 7.4 APPLICATION: BECOMING A CREATIVE PROBLEM SOLVER

LEARNING OBJECTIVE

After you have mastered the information in this unit, you will be able to:

1. Discuss steps for becoming a creative problem solver.

OUTLINE

I. Keys to Becoming a Creative Problem Solver
   A. Adopt a questioning attitude—be aware of various alternatives and their potential
   B. Gather information—use the many information sources available
   C. Avoid getting stuck in mental sets
      1. Mental sets can impair problem-solving efforts (cannot see real problem)
      2. Examine what the real requirement is of a question or challenge
   D. Generate alternatives
      1. Best to come up with many possible solutions, not just grasp the first one
      2. Try personal brainstorming
         a) Write down as many solutions to problem as can be come up with
         b) Don't prejudge your list of solutions with a tendency to strike them off your list
         c) Seek all ideas, no matter how "off the wall" – today's strange idea maybe tomorrow's brilliant solution
      3. Let list sit a few days before contemplating
      4. Think of analogies—a prior problem related to what you are facing now
      5. Think "outside the box"
   E. Sleep on it—may enhance insight, creative thinking – many inspired ideas occurred shortly upon awakening
   F. Test it out
      1. Try out your possible solutions
      2. Let situation "incubate" if necessary
      3. Remember danger of mental set—the tendency to stick with traditional solution

SUMMARY

In this module, you learn about applying what we know about intelligence, thinking, and creativity with regard to problem solving. We all have problems to face. The key is in not avoiding the problem (this is an unhealthy approach!) but in finding an effective, practical, and relatively timely solution.

The most important thing to remember in solving problems is to avoid the allure of sticking with the same solutions just because they are the ones you have tried in the past. If you think of an analogous situation and the previous approach works fine. But that is not likely to be the case. If so, we need to be open-minded and allow ourselves to come up with a variety of other possible solutions, no matter how "wild" they may seem! As we know, finding fresh ways to view traditional (and perhaps previously unresolved) problems can lead to revolutionary breakthroughs, for ourselves and perhaps for others. These breakthroughs may even affect large numbers of the human population.

A good way to come up with creative solutions to problems is to allow yourself to brainstorm. In brainstorming, you let whatever solutions come to your mind enter the realm of consideration. Write them all down, and avoid making decisions at the time you are coming up with potential solutions. Ideally, let your list of possible solutions rest for a bit of time. You will come back to the list later, with perhaps a fresher and even more objective perspective. It always helps to get enough sleep. Remember that the key to creative solutions is not just a matter of problems and ideas, but also how you look at them. Try your solutions out, unless one is so wacky it may pose harm to someone. You never know where your innovative approach to problems in your life will lead you!

KEY TERM

Brainstorming

SELF-TEST PRACTICE QUIZ

1. Which of the following is NOT helpful, with respect to creative problem solving?
    a. Allow yourself to generate many possible solutions no matter how "weird" they may seem at the outset.
    b. Think of past experiences and consider what worked for you before in similar situations.
    c. Try out some of your potential solutions, assuming it is safe to do so.
    d. Try to come up with an answer or solution as quickly as possible.

ANSWER KEY

1. d

CHAPTER 7   APPLICATION EXERCISES

1. What do you think intelligence is? Write down three or four characteristics that you have found indicate intelligent thinking or behavior. How well do they correspond with the concepts presented in this chapter? Do you think intelligence can change? If not, why not? If so, how? Do you think your own intelligence is fixed, or can it change? Has it changed?

2. What kinds of problems have you had in your life recently? Have you solved them? How? What problem-solving strategies do you typically use? Which of the suggestions given in Module 7.4 might you add to your problem-solving techniques? In what way might they be helpful; that is, in what way would they be an improvement compared to the processes you use now? Choose one or two of the techniques listed—and try them out!

CHAPTER 8

Motivation and Emotion

In Chapter 8, you learn about the more subtle sources of energy that are the impetus behind what we do and why we do it. Motivation, of course, is related to our emotions, because much of what prompts us to do things is a function of that which we find to be personally meaningful or meaningful to the culture in which we were raised. Some sources of motivation are purely for survival. These are inborn biological needs, such as the need to obtain food. The experience of hunger seems to involve various parts of the brain, predominantly the hypothalamus. Eating, while of course physiologically based, has social and behavioral aspects as well. It is the social and behavioral aspects that have most led to current problems with various eating disorders. The best way to maintain ideal weight is through healthy eating and, most important of all, regular exercise. Obesity is increasing among children as well as adults. The emphasis on a very slender, trim body, especially for females, continues to grow, while at the same time the availability and promotion of appetizing (but high calorie/high fat) food is ever increasing. It is no wonder that eating disorders have emerged as a serious psychological and physiological problem. With anorexia nervosa, the individual feels very fat and avoids food, although in fact that person may be dangerously thin. In bulimia nervosa, the individual tends to appear at normal body weight, but binges at least periodically on large quantities of food and then eliminates the results of this gorging through various purging means (self-induced vomiting, laxatives). Untreated eating disorders can and do lead to death.

While nearly all inborn needs are for survival, we also have needs for exploration and activity. Though apparently not necessary to keep us alive, these stimulus motives seem to be programmed into human and animal functioning. Arousal theory proposes that there is an optimal level of stimulation, which can vary from individual to individual and from time to time. Moderate levels of arousal are best for performing most routine tasks. In addition to biological sources of motivation, there are psychological ones as well. Abraham Maslow proposed the hierarchy of needs, which incorporates both physiological and psychological needs as an individual strives towards self-actualization. Self-actualization is maximizing our unique potential—being all that we can be. Maslow later recognized that human behavior is motivated by higher pursuits as well as satisfaction of basic needs including cognitive needs (need to know), understand, and explore, aesthetic needs (needs for beauty, symmetry, and order), and self-transcendence (needs to connect to something beyond the self and help others realize their own potential) (Maslow, 1969, 1971, 1987).

Instincts have little, if any, role in human motivation. Rather, physiological needs (a physical lack) create drives (such as hunger), and drive theory is now the prevailing view in explaining motivation. The drive creates action to satisfy the need (resulting in drive reduction). A need may exist in the absences of a corresponding drive an example may be a vitamin deficiency that you may not know you have yet it is there. Drive theory is oriented around the notion of homeostasis. Homeostasis is a steady bodily state; it is thought that the body functions best at, and so seeks, an optimal level of fluid, sustenance, oxygen, and so forth. When the body is depleted of one or more of these biological necessities, the organism is motivated to act, obtain what is lacking, and restore homeostasis. Can everything be explained in terms of the disruption and subsequent restoration of homeostasis? No. In fact, humans sometimes deliberately upset homeostasis—in your latest rugby game or track and field match, for example. Psychological (interpersonal) motives include the need for affiliation and the need for achievement. People vary in their need to excel. For some, achievement is very important, and opportunities for it are sought. For others, presumably with a low need for achievement, there is little desire to find opportunities to excel, and the objective, rather, seems to be to avoid failure. Both of these components are factors in psychological sources of motivation. Factors that motivate behavior from outside an organism are incentives. Instead of motivation being a "push" from within ourselves, incentives (goals or rewards we want) pull us from outside of ourselves.

A powerful source of motivation comes from sexual desire and attraction. Our sexual orientation describes the type of individual(s) to whom we are romantically and physically drawn. There are some commonalities among males and females regarding their physical response to sexual arousal. A small percentage of men and women in the U.S. and Europe identify themselves as exclusively gay or lesbian. Research has not yet revealed a clear picture as to the source of sexual orientation. It is suspected that both biological and environmental sources are involved. Many of the typical stereotypes related to sexual orientation do not appear to stand up to objective scrutiny. It is not unusual to experience problems with regard to sexual response or activity. The term "sexual dysfunction" describes sexual difficulties that have become chronic and cause distress. Nearly all sexual problems can be treated with at least some degree of success through therapy.

We do not have the full or final picture on emotions, other than to say the experience of emotion is complex and appears to involve many parts of the brain. Emotions are considered to be feeling states, and to be comprised of physiological (activation of the nervous system), cognitive, and behavioral components. Emotions typically are expressed through our faces and how we act, though there are cultural norms (display rules) that direct more specifically how this is done within a given culture. There are six basic emotions that are universally recognized: happiness, sadness, anger, fear, surprise, and disgust. Other, more complex emotions are thought to be blends of these basic ones. The emotion of happiness, though somewhat neglected by psychologists in the past, is gaining attention via the field of positive psychology. We are beginning to understand how important the experiences of happiness and meaningfulness are, and we are learning how we might better incorporate these into our lives.

Debate continues as to how emotions are experienced, and how that experience is tied to situational factors. Must emotion always have a cognitive component? Must our cognitions about what is going on with us precede determining how we feel emotionally? Do we respond first, and then use our body's behavior as an indicator of the emotion we are feeling? All of these views regarding emotional experience have been proposed and are still being considered. Without doubt, emotions are vitally important in our everyday functioning. The gift of emotional intelligence helps us use the motivation and energy in emotions wisely. The polygraph is intended to detect the emotions associated with truth-telling vs. lying, but in fact at present is not scientifically reliable.

MODULE 8.1 MOTIVATION: THE "WHYS" OF BEHAVIOR

LEARNING OBJECTIVES

After you have mastered the information in this unit, you will be able to:

1. Define motivation.
2. Describe instinct theory.
3. Discuss drive theory.
4. Explain arousal theory.
5. Describe incentive theory, and explain how it differs from drive theory.
6. Discuss psychosocial needs.
7. Explain Maslow's hierarchy of needs.

OUTLINE

I.   Motivation
   A.   Involves factors that initiate, direct and sustain goal-directed behavior
   B.   Motives—what drives behavior and accounts for why we do what we do
      1.   We don't actually observe a motive; we infer that one exists based on the behavior observed

II.   Biological Sources of Motivation
   A.   Involves inborn needs (such as for food, water, oxygen)
   B.   Needs are predominantly those necessary for survival
   C.   Instincts
      1.   Behaviors programmed by nature (nest-building, salmon going upriver to spawn)
      2.   Instinctive behaviors
         a)   Fixed, inborn patterns of response
         b)   Specific to members of a particular species
      3.   Instinct theory—view that all behavior is motivated by instinct
      4.   Do humans have instincts?
         a)   Sigmund Freud (sexual and aggressive instincts), William James (37 different instincts; including curiosity, cleanliness)—proponents
         b)   Current view of motivation does not support notion of instincts (too many, not a useful approach) – merely a way to describe (a person lazy because of a laziness instinct attaches a label to it)
   D.   Needs and drives
      1.   Drive theory
         a)   Became model for human motivation beginning in 1950s – replacing instinct theory
         b)   Idea is biological needs demand satisfaction (Clark Hull) – food, water, and sleep
      2.   Need—state of deprivation or deficiency (usually biological)
      3.   Drive—bodily tension or unease arising from an unmet need (e.g., hunger, thirst)
      4.   Drive reduction—satisfaction of a drive
      5.   Homeostasis
         a)   Basis for drive theory
         b)   Idea is body tends to maintain a steady internal state
         c)   Disruption (e.g. drop in temperature, blood sugar) prompts behavior to restore homeostasis (biological equilibrium, balance)
      6.   Needs and drives related, but differ
         a)   Bodily need may exist but without corresponding drive – unaware of a vitamin deficiency the need may exist in the absence of a corresponding drive
         b)   Strength of need vs. drive may differ (e.g., when fasting, may feel less hungry on second day than on first)
      7.   Drive theory incorporates important role for learning
         a)   We learn responses that are reinforced by drive reduction
         b)   Primary drives are inborn – hunger, thirst, sexual; however, we may learn some drives as a result of experience (secondary drives) – money can be used to satisfy many primary and other secondary drives
   E.   Optimum level of arousal
      1.   Harry Harlow—not all drives are to satisfy basic survival needs
      2.   Humans (and other animals) may have innate needs for exploration, activity
      3.   Stimulus motives—needs to investigate environment, manipulate (especially novel stimuli, like trying the latest gizmos) – instigate behavior that leads to increased, not decreased arousal

      4. Arousal theory
- a) Notion that there is an optimal level of arousal – whenever the level of stimulation dips below an organism's optimal level, the organism seeks ways of increasing it
- b) This level can vary from individual to individual, and from time to time
- c) Sensation-seekers—high need for arousal, see life as an adventure
- d) Moderate level of arousal best for most tasks
- e) More difficult tasks—lower levels of arousal needed

III. Psychological Sources of Motivation
- A. We are not idle even when homeostasis level is perfect
  1. Also motivated by psychological needs – friendship or achievement – not satisfying any biological needs
- B. Incentive theory—attraction to particular goals or objects motivates much of our behavior (a drive is a "push," an incentive is a "pull")
  1. Incentives—rewards or other stimuli that motivate us to act
  2. Incentive value
     - a) The strength of the pull, or lure, a goal or object has
     - b) Culture, experiences are important determining factors
- C. Psychosocial needs (interpersonal needs)
  1. Need for affiliation—need for social contact with others – interpersonal needs
  2. Need for achievement
     - a) High need for achievement—strong desire to excel (and set realistic goals) – pride in accomplishing their goals
     - b) Low need for achievement—objective is to avoid failure; met with failure, they are more likely to quit than to persevere
  3. Sources of motivation
     - a) Extrinsic—desire is for external rewards (money, praise)
     - b) Intrinsic—effort is expended just for personal satisfaction or pleasure
  4. Goals regarding achievement may be in opposition
     - a) Achievement motivation—takes on challenges in order to gain success; do better in their courses and show higher levels of emotional well-being
     - b) Avoidance motivation—avoid challenges in order to avoid failure; may reduce the chance of failure, it also reduces the likelihood of success
  5. Achievement motivation strongly influenced by experience (parents and others; typically have parents who encourage independence and trying difficult tasks and reward for persistence

IV. Hierarchy of Needs
- A. Proposed by Abraham Maslow (1970)
- B. Incorporates both biological and psychological needs
- C. Basic needs
  1. Physiological, safety
  2. According to theory these must be met first
- D. Higher-order needs—love and belongingness, esteem, and self-actualization
- E. Self-actualization—all five levels of needs are met
  1. Knowing one's abilities, strengths, talents
  2. Putting one's unique potential to best use
- F. View has intuitive appeal
- G. Criticisms of Maslow's model:
  1. Needs may not always follow order as proposed in theory
  2. Same behavior may fit several of the levels (e.g., both nourishment and esteem)

3.   People may forgo seeking satisfaction need for intimate relationship, for status or prestige in their career

H.   Later in his career Maslow proposed other needs
1.   Cognitive needs – to know, understand and explore
2.   Aesthetic needs – beauty, symmetry and order
3.   Self-transcendence – connect to something beyond the self and help others realize their own potential (Maslow, 1969, 1971, 1987)

SUMMARY

In this module, you learn some of the basics regarding motivation. Most of motivation theory discussed in this unit has to do with human motivation. Motivation is incredibly important in that it is what gets us involved in a behavior and maintains our interest and effort at it. Nearly always our motivated behavior has some end objective—even if that final objective is simply the fun or learning gained from carrying out the actions. Motivation comprises the factors that activate, direct, and sustain goal-directed behavior. Motives, the objectives prompting us to do what we do, are the explanation—the answer to the question "Why?"—regarding our behavior.

A major motivating force, of course, has always been survival. Thus, we are motivated to meet certain needs—e.g., for food, water, oxygen—that are fundamentally biologically based. A question examined regarding human behavior is that of the role of instincts. Instincts are "wired-in" behavior patterns particular to a given species. Is human behavior, or any part of it, governed by instinctual reactions? The early view (especially as proposed by Sigmund Freud and William James) was that instincts are a substantial component in human motivation. The current thinking, however, does not attribute much, if any, human behavior to instincts. Rather, the view is that humans have needs. Most needs, as implied above, are biologically based. A need (for example, lack of sustenance in the body, low blood sugar levels) creates a drive (hunger). The drive is an uncomfortable or unsettled bodily state, which motivates us to seek its satisfaction or resolution (in other words, drive reduction). These views, together known as drive theory, are based on the concept of homeostasis. Homeostasis suggests that the body functions best when it is at a kind of physiological equilibrium. The body has sufficient fluid, nourishment, rest, and so forth. Disruption to the ideal levels of homeostasis motivates us to restore these optimal levels again. Thus, we eat until we are full, rest until we feel restored—and so forth.

Though much of motivation can be traced to these biological survival needs, not all behavior is driven by such survival factors. Harry Harlow, who did extensive research with monkeys, noted that animals will explore and manipulate the environment—whether or not reinforcers for doing so are present. Thus, there may be stimulus motives as well. Stimulus motives are also, it is believed, innate and biologically based, though apparently not necessary for survival. Arousal theory is related to the stimulation that we seek or experience, and it is thought that there is an optimal level of arousal for various tasks we need to perform. Simple and/or routine tasks can be performed well even at fairly high levels of arousal. The more difficult a task, however, the lower the level of arousal at which we will have the most success in completing the task effectively. Thus, a complicated or very unfamiliar task is made more difficult by becoming anxious (raising one's level of arousal) about it.

Notice that needs and drives are related (usually), but different. A need is something the body lacks—sustenance, oxygen, or even the opportunity to try out and explore, as with the stimulus motives. A need may exist, but it is not always translated into a drive—that uncomfortable or unsettled bodily state that heads us towards whatever objective will resolve that unsettled feeling. Our blood sugar level may have dropped, for example, but if we are so intensely involved in an activity that we are not aware of this need, we may not feel hungry and not act to bring sustenance our way. Physically or mentally we may really need some stimulation or a change of scene—but on the other hand, we just can't seem to get ourselves out of the chair, or out of the house. There is a need, but the drive is not accompanying it, or is not sufficiently strong.

Though most of the motivation factors we have discussed have been primary drives (innate, biologically based), there are psychological factors that motivate us as well. Our goals or objectives tempt us because they have incentive value. Thus, some behavior may not be based on a biological drive (a "push," from the drive) but rather we feel the "pull"—the lure, emanating from the objective or goal (incentive) that we seek. Some objectives, of course, can be very good things—getting that degree, earning the paycheck. But, for example, we may eat—even though we are not hungry, and even though in fact more food will make us feel uncomfortable—because that barbeque smells so good or the strawberry shortcake and chocolate torte look irresistible. Incentives can be powerful!

Psychosocial needs also motivate behavior. We have a need for affiliation, for example, which leads us to associate with others and seek social contact. We have, as well, a need for achievement. Motivation for achievement varies among individuals. Some people have a very high need to achieve. These individuals seek out numerous reasonable opportunities and challenges, ones that will allow them to apply themselves and excel. They also continue their efforts despite occasional setbacks. Others may be motivated more by a fear of failure, or simply have low achievement needs. In these latter cases, opportunities may be passed up, and goals that are set tend to be either very easy or nearly impossible to attain. These individuals are more likely to quit than persevere when faced with apparent failure. The desire to take on challenges and succeed is evident early in life, and rather closely related to parental interaction.

A theory proposed by Abraham Maslow helps incorporate both the biological and the psychological needs driving behavior. Maslow proposed the hierarchy of needs, where lower level needs (which first demand our attention) are biological in nature. If these (basic) needs are satisfied, we then can go on to higher-order needs; higher-order needs are more psychological in nature. These include needs for love and belongingness, esteem, and ultimately, self-actualization. Self-actualization involves knowing oneself and one's abilities, and putting these abilities to best use. Utilizing our potential fully leads to the state of self-actualization. Since everyone (according to Maslow's view) is unique, and has a different set of talents, becoming self-actualized is a different experience and process for every person. Later in is career Maslow proposed cognitive needs, aesthetic needs and self-transcendence. Criticisms of Maslow's hierarchy include that the order he suggested may not be fixed for all humans, and that one behavior on the part of an individual may fulfill a number of the needs Maslow proposed.

KEY TERMS

Motivation

Motives

Instinctive behaviors

Instinct theory

Drive theory

Need

Drive

Drive reduction

Primary drives

Secondary drives

Stimulus motives

Arousal theory

Incentive theory

Incentives

Incentive value

Psychosocial needs

Need for achievement

Extrinsic motivation

Intrinsic motivation

Achievement motivation

Avoidance motivation

Hierarchy of needs

Self-actualization

SELF-TEST PRACTICE QUIZ

Match the following Key Terms and definitions (note: not every Key Term will be used):

1. _____ The view that the body needs an optimal level of stimulation; if stimulation drops below this level the organism will act to restore it

2. _____ Motivation stemming from one's own interest in a goal, and the knowledge or pleasure gained from achieving it

3. _____ Relating to the factors that initiate, direct and sustain goal-directed behavior

4. _____ "Prewired," innate patterns of behavior that are particular to a given species

5. _____ The view that motivation stems from the pull, or lure, of a goal or objective

6. _____ A theory proposed by Abraham Maslow, which incorporates both biological (basic) and psychological (higher-order) needs, culminating in self-actualization

7. _____ Interpersonal needs that motivate us; they include a need for social contact and a need for achievement

8. _____ A state (usually physiological) where there is a deficiency or lack

a. Motivation

b. Motives

c. Instinctive behaviors

d. Instinct theory

e. Drive theory

f. Need

g. Drive

h. Drive reduction

i. Primary drives

j. Secondary drives

k. Stimulus motives

l. Arousal theory

m. Incentive theory

n. Incentives

o. Incentive value

p. Psychosocial needs

q. Need for achievement

r. Extrinsic motivation

s. Intrinsic motivation

t. Achievement motivation

u. Avoidance motivation

v. Hierarchy of needs

9. _____ Needs or wants that prompt behavior aimed at achieving them

10. _____ Innate, biologically based motives that lead an organism to explore and manipulate the environment; probably not necessary for survival

11. _____ Drives that are the result of experience

12. _____ Reflects a desire for external rewards, such as money or the respect of one's peers

13. _____ An unsettled or uncomfortable bodily condition, resulting from an unmet need

14. _____ The need to excel, experience success

15. _____ The view that behavior is motivated by a desire to satisfy unmet biological needs

16. _____ Connected to something beyond the self and help others realize their potential

17. _____ beauty, symmetry and order

18. _____ to now, understand and explore

w.   Self-actualization

x.   cognitive needs

y.   aesthetic needs

z.   self-transcendence

16. Fixed, inborn patterns that are unique to a particular species are known as
   a.   instincts.
   b.   incentives.
   c.   motives.
   d.   needs.

17. When our body is lacking in something biologically fundamental, such as appropriate sustenance or sufficient fluid, we experience a(n)
   a.   need.
   b.   drive.
   c.   instinct.
   d.   incentive.

21. William James and Sigmund Freud both believed that much of human behavior could be attributed to
   a.   needs.
   b.   drives.
   c.   instincts.
   d.   incentives.

22. The desire to _____ is an example of a primary drive.
    a. earn lots of money
    b. have sex
    c. earn a college degree
    d. none of the above
23. A need is different from a drive, in that a drive
    a. is based on a fundamental biological lack.
    b. prompts behavior, but a need may not.
    c. does not necessarily motivate behavior, but a need does.
    d. is closely related to incentive value.
24. Homeostasis means
    a. a balance between biological and psychological needs.
    b. that one or more primary drives have been triggered.
    c. that the body seeks, and functions best at, a state of biological equilibrium.
    d. a balance between arousal levels for both needs and drives.
25. Research shows that, for the best performance on fairly difficult tasks, we need a _____ level of arousal.
    a. high
    b. very high
    c. moderate
    d. low
26. Motives that seem to be inborn, but are not necessary for survival, are called _____ motives.
    a. arousal
    b. stimulus
    c. optimal
    d. incentive
27. Sensation-seekers
    a. have a high need for arousal.
    b. are more likely to fill their lives with many stimulating activities and thrills.
    c. may pose some risk to themselves, as they may have difficulty restraining impulsive behavior.
    d. exhibit all of the above characteristics.
28. Incentive theory suggests that
    a. we act because we have an unmet need.
    b. we act because we have an unmet drive.
    c. the "pull" or lure of a goal or objective motivates us.
    d. the desire for money motivates all of human behavior.
29. In his research with monkeys, Harry Harlow discovered that
    a. even animals are attracted to financial rewards.
    b. monkeys seem to grasp their own version of self-actualization.
    c. monkeys would play with a mechanical puzzle just because it was there.
    d. there is no real evidence for stimulus motivation.

30. The value of an incentive is affected by
    a. culture.
    b. the expectation that the incentive will prove rewarding.
    c. prior learning experience.
    d. all of the above

31. People with low levels of achievement motivation are likely to
    a. set goals that are either so low that anybody can achieve them, or so high that they are unattainable.
    b. set realistic goals.
    c. persevere in the face of failure.
    d. continually seek out new challenges.

32. Which is the highest level of needs in Maslow's hierarchy?
    a. Self-actualization
    b. Physiological
    c. Love and belongingness
    d. Safety and security

ESSAY QUESTIONS

1. What are instincts? What are some of the criticisms of instinct theory?

2. Explain Maslow's hierarchy of needs. In particular, discuss the concept of self-actualization. How does Maslow's theory explain motivation? What are some criticisms of his views?

ANSWER KEY

1. Arousal theory
2. Intrinsic motivation
3. Motivation
4. Instinctive behaviors
5. Incentive theory
6. Hierarchy of needs
7. Psychosocial needs
8. Need
9. Motives
10. Stimulus motives
11. Secondary drives
12. Extrinsic motivation
13. Drive
14. Need for achievement
15. Drive theory
16. z
17. y
18. x
169. a
20. a
21. c
17. b
183. b
194. c
205. d
216. b
227. d
238. c
249. c
30. d
31. a
32. a

SAMPLE ANSWERS TO ESSAY QUESTIONS

1. Instincts are reasons for behavior that are completely programmed into the functioning of a species. We do find instinctual behavior in animals. For example, spiders spin webs, birds build nests, salmon swim upriver to spawn—these occur in a species without prior training or even exposure to the behaviors. Thus, these behaviors are prompted by instincts.

    Since instincts so clearly exist in animals, it was assumed that human behavior was governed by instinct also. Sigmund Freud believed much of human behavior was motivated by sexual or aggressive instincts. William James listed many instincts which he proposed accounted for much of human behavior.

    Over time, support for instinct theory has all but disappeared. Attributing a behavior to an instinct does not really explain why the behavior occurs; in that sense, the notion of instincts is simply not very useful. Most important, human behavior tends to be quite complex and can vary greatly from situation to situation; behavior governed by instincts would be consistent across humans and across time. Instinct theory does not incorporate the important roles of culture and learning, major factors in human behavior. Though probably still applicable with regard to animals, it is unlikely that instincts have much to do with our unique and hugely variable human behavior.

2. Maslow's hierarchy of needs is an explanation of motivation that proposes we need to get our basic (physiological and safety) needs satisfied first, before we can meet what are called higher-order needs. Higher-order needs include the need for love and a sense of belonging, a need for esteem (regard for self and others) and, lastly, the need for self-actualization. Self-actualization is a very important feature in Maslow's theory. In Maslow's view, all human beings have unique talents and potential. The key to a fulfilling life is discovering these abilities and putting them to best use. Making full use of our abilities, consistently, is being self-actualized.

    The hierarchy explains motivation because our fundamental desire is to achieve self-actualization, and this motivation propels us, so to speak, through the lower levels in the hierarchy. We are not always aware of this desire, and certainly not everyone achieves it. Lack of satisfaction of a lower level need prohibits, according to Maslow's theory, movement up towards any of the higher needs. This view certainly makes sense, at least to a degree. Most of us, if starving or in danger for our lives, are not concerning ourselves with discovering our unique potential and putting it to best use. Maslow's ideas help explain why we are motivated to do things well beyond just maintaining physiological equilibrium (homeostasis), and why we sometimes in fact disrupt our homeostasis, intentionally—to achieve other goals.

    While Maslow's view is intuitively appealing, it has been criticized on several accounts. Among other things, there are too many examples where people are addressing a higher-order need, though lower (biological) levels have not been met. Sometimes great works and great deeds materialize under circumstances that may include severe deprivation. In addition, we may be motivated towards activities that fulfill two or more levels of needs (based on the hierarchy) at the same time. Most of us, when we work, are working to provide food, shelter, and clothing. But there may be little satisfaction in spending 8 or 10 hours a day just for these goals, important as they are. Simultaneously, our occupations may also provide us with companionship and a sense of belonging, with esteem for others and ourselves, with a sense of productivity or accomplishment, and, we hope, with a lasting sense of self-actualization as well.

MODULE 8.2 HUNGER AND EATING

LEARNING OBJECTIVES

After you have mastered the information in this unit, you will be able to:

1. Explain how hunger and appetite are regulated.

2. Discuss the causes of obesity.

3. Describe anorexia nervosa.

4. Describe bulimia nervosa.

5. Discuss the causes of eating disorders.

OUTLINE

I.   What Makes Us Hungry?
  A.   Stomach contractions
    1.   Stomach contractions correspond to hunger pangs and are cues
    2.   Individuals with stomach removed still experience hunger, eat regularly
    3.   Brain appears to be most important component with regard to hunger
  B.   Fat cells
    1.   Release fat for fuel when blood sugar level drops
    2.   Hypothalamus (in brain) detects these changes and responds
    3.   Physiological responses triggered include feelings of hunger
    4.   Hunger motivates eating—blood sugar levels and fat cells are restored
  C.   Parts in hypothalamus that regulate hunger
    1.   Lateral hypothalamus—initiates ("On" switch for) eating
    2.   Ventromedial hypothalamus—stops ("Off" switch for) eating
  D.   Brain chemicals involved in hunger and eating
    1.   Includes a number of chemicals—neurotransmitters and hormones
    2.   Neuropeptide Y stimulates hypothalamus to trigger appetite and eating
    3.   Other chemicals curb appetite and eating when body has had enough
II.   Obesity: A National Epidemic
  A.   Obesity—state of excess body fat
  B.   Two-thirds of US adults are overweight and one out of three are obese (was one in four in 1960s)
  C.   Number of overweight children has doubled during last 25 years
  D.   Serious concern because obesity a major health risk
  E.   Causes of obesity
    1.   Behavioral patterns
      a)   Too many calories consumed
      b)   Too little exercise
    2.   Genetics
      a)   Metabolism rate related to weight gain
      b)   Set point theory—brain regulates body weight around a genetically predetermined level (set point)
      c)   Number of fat cells (obese people have more) – we don't shed fat cells even when we lose weight

      3.   Environmental factors
         a)   Constant advertising of food, restaurants
         b)   Food served in large portions, often higher calorie and higher fat
         c)   Tempts food purchase and consumption, though not in hunger state
         d)   Shared among people in social networks, friends, neighbors, spouses and family members – what we eat, how much and judgments about acceptability of obesity (Christakis & Fowler, 2007)
      4.   Emotional states
         a)   Anger, fear, depression, and loneliness may lead to excess eating
         b)   Food is soothing, rewarding—at least for the time being

  F. Losing excess weight
      1.   Healthy eating, calorie awareness, and regular exercise are crucial
      2.   Exercise builds muscle, helps offset metabolic rate reduction
      3.   Diet drugs, "quickie" diets and the like not usually successful long term, may have serious side effects

III. Eating Disorders
  A. Anorexia nervosa
      1.   Self-starvation resulting in dangerously low body weight
      2.   Involves distorted body image (achieve the "perfect" body) and intense fear of being fat – unrealistic standard of thinness
      3.   Most cases teenage or young adult female
      4.   Physical risks: cardiovascular, gastrointestinal (constipation and abdominal pain), loss of menstruation, suicide – medical complication can result in death
  B. Bulimia nervosa
      1.   Characterized by binge eating (very large quantities; sweet, high fat) followed by purging (vomiting, laxatives) to rid body of food
      2.   May include excessive, compulsive exercise regimen
      3.   Unhappy with body like anorexics, but typically maintain normal weight
      4.   Physical complications: nutrient deficiencies, deterioration of tooth enamel, gastrointestinal problems (severe constipation from over use of laxatives)
  C. Causes of eating disorders
      1.   Cultural preoccupation with thinness; ultra thin the ideal
      2.   Majority of adolescent girls unhappy with weight, body image
      3.   Dieting, achieving slender figure the norm for American women
      4.   Some cases among males (young), especially those in sports (e.g., wrestling)
      5.   Eating disorders rare in non-Western cultures
      6.   May involve issues of control, perfectionism, more traumatic family background
      7.   Possibly disturbances in brain mechanisms (e.g., serotonin levels)
      8.   Unconscious wish in female adolescents to remain little girls

SUMMARY

In this module, you learn about a major motivator in our lives—hunger and eating! We are accustomed to thinking we eat because of stomach contractions (the stomach is "growling"), and indeed these two experiences are correlated. However, individuals who have had their stomachs removed still feel hunger (and eat regularly). Thus, other mechanisms must be involved. The brain seems to play a central role—including, most specifically, the structure in the forebrain known as the hypothalamus. The lateral hypothalamus seems to regulate "turning on" the act of eating; the ventromedial hypothalamus turns this action off again. Brain chemicals, including neurotransmitters (neuropeptide Y is one) and hormones, are related to the regulation of eating and to feelings of satiation when we have had enough.

Many people, especially in America, eat too much. Attractive, appetizing food, heavy in calories, seems ever present in the environment. Fast food menus usually consist of items that are high in calories and high in fat. Americans are leading more and more sedentary lives—the calories consumed are not being burned off by physical activity. We are figuratively tied to the computer, the T.V., and we rely on the car instead of our feet. Depleted fat cells trigger hunger, and obese individuals have more fat cells. Metabolism (how fast caloric intake is used up by the body) varies somewhat among individuals, and thus the genetic heritage involved in the regulation of metabolism can play a role. There are no "quick fixes" regarding having and maintaining an appropriate body weight. Long-term adherence to a healthy lifestyle—eating reasonable amounts of nutritious foods, engaging in regular exercise—is the only established way to promote good physical health and keep our weight within appropriate boundaries.

With a huge everyday emphasis on eating (the many ads we are exposed to that deal with food, cooking, eating, and restaurants), all the while accompanied by our society's desire for ever more slender levels of thinness (especially in women), it is no wonder that there are problems with eating that plague some members of our society. Obesity is just one of these problems. We also have serious eating disorders, such as anorexia nervosa (eating little or nothing out of a fear of being fat) and bulimia nervosa (eating huge amounts at one sitting, followed by episodes of purging to rid the body of the food consumed). These eating disorders are thought to be related to the unrealistic standards of thinness, combined with psychological factors such as control, perfectionism, and/or a history of abuse or family conflict. Eating disorders have medical complications and in severe cases can result in death.

KEY TERMS

Fat cells

Lateral hypothalamus

Ventromedial hypothalamus

Obesity

Set point theory

Anorexia nervosa

Bulimia nervosa

SELF-TEST PRACTICE QUIZ

Match the following Key Terms and definitions:

1. _____ The notion that the brain adjusts bodily processes to keep weight approximately at a level determined by genetics

2. _____ The "on" switch triggering the start of hunger and eating

3. _____ An eating disorder where large quantities of food are ingested, followed by self-induced vomiting or excessive use of laxatives (to rid body of the consumed food)

4. _____ Body cells that store fat

a. Fat cells

b. Lateral hypothalamus

c. Ventromedial hypothalamus

d. Obesity

e. Set point theory

f. Anorexia nervosa

g. Bulimia nervosa

5. _____ The "off" switch regulating
                   cessation of eating

6. _____ A state of excess body fat

7. _____ An eating disorder characterized
                   by self-starvation; serious medical
                   side effects

8. Approximately how many adult Americans are overweight?

    a. 25%
    b. 45%
    c. 55%
    d. 65%

9. According to set point theory,

    a. obesity is determined primarily by culture.
    b. the brain adjusts body metabolism in order to maintain a predetermined weight.
    c. genetic mutations are responsible for obesity.
    d. people tend to eat more food when it is served on larger plates.

10. When we are hungry, and blood sugar level has dropped, a substance is released from
_____, which we will utilize for energy until we again ingest food.

    a. the hypothalamus
    b. dopamine receptors
    c. fat cells
    d. neurotransmitter sites

11. The lateral hypothalamus acts as the

    a. "on" switch for eating.
    b. "off" switch for eating.
    c. regulator of fat cell content.
    d. regulator of feelings of satiety.

12. Neuropeptide Y

    a. is associated with feelings of satiation.
    b. stimulates activity of the brain's hypothalamus.
    c. decreases the body's production of basic neurotransmitters.
    d. can be detected by the stomach but not the brain for most individuals.

13. The rate at which the body burns available calories is known as

    a. set point rate.
    b. hyperthargic rate.
    c. metabolism.
    d. homeostasis.

14. Which statement about obesity is true?

    a. Obese individuals have the same number of fat cells as people of normal weight.
    b. Some people are genetically "doomed" to obesity.
    c. Childhood eating patterns have been linked to the odds of obesity in adulthood.
    d. none of the above

15. Which of the following has NOT been shown to be a potential cause of eating disorders such as
anorexia nervosa and bulimia nervosa?

    a. Societal preoccupation with being thin
    b. Damage to the frontal lobes of the brain
    c. Childhood history of physical or sexual abuse
    d. Neurotransmitter imbalances

16. The best way to take and keep excess weight off is to
   a.   follow new diets as soon as they are introduced.
   b.   rely on epinephrine and other weight loss drugs.
   c.   eat reasonable portions of healthy food and get regular exercise.
   d.   avoid worrying and fretting about excess weight.

ESSAY QUESTIONS

1. Why are so many Americans overweight, or even obese?

2. Discuss set point theory. According to this theory, how is the body's weight maintained? How might features suggested in this approach aid in human survival?

3. Discuss eating disorders and their causes. How are eating disorders treated?

ANSWER KEY

1.   Set point theory

2.   Lateral hypothalamus

3.   Bulimia nervosa

4.   Fat cells

5.   Ventromedial hypothalamus

6.   Obesity

7.   Anorexia nervosa

8.   d

9.   b

10.   c

11.   a

12.   b

13.   c

14.   c

15.   b

16.   c

SAMPLE ANSWERS TO ESSAY QUESTIONS

1.   A large and increasing number of Americans are overweight for many reasons. Genetic factors play a role, in that metabolic rates to burn consumed food vary among humans. Secondly, many foods of great variety are readily available, and we are assaulted with smells and attractive advertising in our environment. Since food has incentive value, particularly when it is presented to us in an appealing fashion, we can be drawn to it even when we are not hungry. Fast food and other restaurant food typically is high in calories and high in fat. Third, more Americans are leading sedentary lives. Many people have desk jobs and may sit in front of the television or computer for hours on end as well; our survival no longer mandates years of toiling in fields to produce crops. Lastly, food has comfort value. Eating brings pleasurable feelings, which we are especially likely to seek if we are feeling depressed, lonely, or bored. Since the number of overweight and obese children is increasing, too, this adds to the number of overweight adults.

2.   Set point theory proposes that the brain acts to maintain body weight at a level that is fairly consistent over time. That level, or appropriate weight, is known as the set point, and is believed to be genetically determined. A body's rate of metabolism, it is proposed, is a function of how close, or how distant, actual body weight is relative to this set point. If there is weight gain, then (according to set point theory) metabolism speeds up. Food will be burned more quickly since the body has more fat in storage than required by genetic guidelines. However, if an individual begins to consume less food than is burned in a typical day, and begins to lose weight—such as when on a diet—the process acts in reverse. Metabolism, according to the theory, will slow down, as part of the body's effort to conserve food. Thus, in times of food shortages, a body is protected, at least to an extent, since metabolic rates can be adjusted and energy can be conserved. However, if one wishes to lose weight, it's a different story! It may well take extra effort to get past the body's tendency to maintain the customary set point. Exercise can be particularly helpful here.

3. There are a number of eating disorders. The two major ones discussed in this module are anorexia nervosa and bulimia nervosa. Individuals with anorexia nervosa often look emaciated. They try to eat very little food or none at all. Though they are dangerously thin, in their eyes they are fat. Anorexics typically have a profound fear of gaining weight and of becoming or being fat. They tend to have a distorted body image; as mentioned previously, they see their bodies as overweight when in fact they are severely underweight. Anorexic individuals may have difficult family backgrounds, psychological issues relating to control or perfectionism. Since food intake is so greatly reduced, an anorexic is medically at risk. Disorders most typically a consequence of anorexia are irregular heartbeat, low blood pressure, gastrointestinal problems, and suicide.

Bulimics tend to gorge on food, then rid their body of it (by various means) shortly afterward. There are also often psychological factors in the backgrounds of individuals suffering from bulimia nervosa, including a history of abuse or family conflict. Both anorexics and bulimics tend to be teenage or young adult females and of white, non-Hispanic origin.

Causes for eating disorders center around societal standards for thinness, though biological and psychological factors (as mentioned above) also play a role. As the quantity and availability of food has increased, and excessive weight and obesity among Americans has increased, proportions for the "ideal" female body have decreased. The current standard for the female body is at an unrealistic level for thinness. It does not reflect the body proportions of a typical, healthy female. Yet, this ultra-thin image is what is projected as most desirable for the female body. Females are much more likely to be dissatisfied with their bodies than are males. There is pressure, then, to take even drastic measures (such as anorexic or bulimic behavior) to achieve and maintain these idealized levels of thinness.

Eating disorders are treated by both psychological and chemical means. An individual with an eating disorder likely will be placed in therapy, and antidepressant drugs may help. Recovery, however, is usually a lengthy process.

MODULE 8.3 SEXUAL MOTIVATION

LEARNING OBJECTIVES

After you have mastered the information in this unit, you will be able to:

1. Identify the phases of the sexual response cycle.

2. Discuss the conceptualization of sexual orientation.

3. Understand the causes and treatment of sexual dysfunctions.

OUTLINE

I. Sexual Orientation and Gender: two different aspects of our identity
   A. Gender identity—social sense of maleness or femaleness
   B. Sexual Orientation—direction of erotic attraction
   Note gender roles – behavior deemed appropriate for men and women (behave, dress, work and interact, including sexual practices)
II. The Sexual Response Cycle: How Your Body Gets Turned On
   A. Sexual response cycle (research from Masters and Johnson)—four phases:
      1. Excitement
      2. Plateau
      3. Orgasm
      4. Resolution

  B. Gender Differences in sexual response
    1. Males—penis erection
    2. Females—vaginal lubrication
    3. Both changes reflect biological process of vasocongestion
    4. Unlike females, males experience a refractory period following orgasm

III. Sexual Orientation
  A. Categories of erotic and romantic attraction
    1. Heterosexuals—attracted to members of opposite sex
    2. Gays and lesbians—attracted to members of own sex
    3. Bisexuals—attracted to both sexes
  B. Researchers conceptualize sexual orientation as a continuum

IV. Psychological Theories of Sexual Orientation
  A. Sigmund Freud
    1. Heterosexuality from "normal" identification process within family
    2. Homosexuality from overidentification with parent of opposite sex (and thus adoption of these characteristics)
    3. Freud's view not substantially supported by research findings
  B. Some cross-gender behavior recalled, feelings of being "different" at a very young age

V. Biological Theories of Sexual Orientation
  A. MZ twins higher concordance than DZ twins—even when MZ separated shortly after birth
  B. Genetic factors appear more of an influence for males than females
  C. Little difference in body circulating sex hormones
  D. Research on origins of sexual orientation remains unclear; likely a combination, including life/environmental experiences

VI. Sexual Dysfunctions
  A. Occasional problems with sexual interest or response are common
  B. Dysfunction involves problems that are persistent, cause distress
    1. Females—problems tend to involve lack of interest, lack of experiencing pleasure, inability to reach orgasm
    2. Males—performance-related anxiety; reaching orgasm too soon
  C. Biological Causes
    1. Neurological, circulatory—such as diabetes, result of prostate surgery
    2. Psychoactive drugs (including cocaine, alcohol, narcotics)
    3. Influence of testosterone—energizes responses in both men and women
    4. Usually sex hormone levels normal even where dysfunction is present
  D. Psychosocial Causes
    1. Negative attitudes toward sexuality—creates shame, inhibition
    2. Sexual routine or rut, and relationship problems
    3. Survivors of sexual trauma, other emotional problems
    4. Performance anxiety—creates a "failure" cycle
    5. Premature ejaculation—level of stimulation not controlled, exceeds threshold for ejaculation
  E. Sex Therapy
    1. Most sexual problems can be treated with success
    2. Biological, psychological, or combination of approaches
    3. Behavioral techniques in sex therapy
      a) Sensate-focus exercises—stimulation and communication, without demands
      b) Masturbation—for women, to learn more about sexual response
      c) Stop-start method—for male premature ejaculation

    4.   Biological therapies
        a)   Treatment with testosterone
        b)   Viagra—for erectile disorder; relaxes blood vessels in penis
        c)   Antidepressants—side effect is to delay sexual ejaculation (helps with premature ejaculation)

SUMMARY

In this module, you learn about sexual motivation, which most certainly is a powerful force and influence on behavior among human beings. Our gender identity (sense of being either a male or a female) and sexual orientation (the sex to whom we are attracted) not only impact our behavior but also are important components of our personality and self-identity.

There is wide variation in sexual practices. Much of what we know about sexual behavior comes from the research of William Masters and Virginia Johnson. The sexual response cycle consists of four phases: excitement, plateau, orgasm, and resolution. There are some similarities in male and female response, and the sex drive for both men and women involves the hormone testosterone (most typically thought of as the "male" sex hormone—though it is produced in females and involved in their response as well). Males experience a refractory period after orgasm, which, though it may be only a few minutes, prevents them from having another orgasm immediately. This is not true for women. Evidence from a survey of married couples showed the average couple engaged in intercourse at a frequency of slightly more than once a week (Deveny, 2003).

It is unclear as to what determines one's sexual orientation. It is thought that both biological and psychological factors play a role, and different factors may explain sexual expression for different people. It is suggested that one's sexual orientation is not fixed; that is, one may not be exclusively heterosexual or exclusively homosexual (and, of course, there are bisexual individuals). Freud's theory of overidentification with the opposite-sex parent does not seem to be supported by actual findings. Homosexual individuals do report more recollections of cross-gender behavior, and also report feelings of being "different." Perhaps this "difference" feeling expanded into same-sex attraction. Evidence does support the view that sexual orientation is not a conscious choice. Genetics is a factor, in that MZ (identical) twins have more commonality in their types of sexual orientation than do DZ (fraternal) twins. The sex hormone testosterone does not seem to be implicated, as levels of this hormone tend to be the same whether the individual has homosexual or heterosexual tendencies. However, there is some evidence suggesting that sexual orientation may be affected by prenatal levels of sex hormones.

It is not uncommon, over one's life, to have problems with sexual experiences. When problems are so substantial and chronic that they begin to create distress, these difficulties are known as sexual dysfunction. Sexual expression problems among females usually involve a lack of interest and/or lack of responsiveness with regard to sexual activity. Sexual dysfunction among males most typically involves either premature ejaculation or a failure to achieve and sustain erection. Very likely the causes of these problems are both physiological and psychological, and effective treatment of sexual dysfunction usually involves a combination of the two. Children's sexual interest may be shamed when they are young (most likely to influence women's sexual response), and males may feel much pressure to perform sexually (known as performance anxiety) to maintain their identity as a "real" man. Biological causes can include multiple sclerosis, spinal cord injuries, side effects of medication, and general circulatory problems. There are specific behavioral techniques (such as sensate focus exercises) and drugs (such as Viagra) to help remedy sexual dysfunction—nearly all problems can be treated with at least some degree of success.

KEY TERMS

Gender identity

Sexual orientation

Gender roles

Sexual response cycle

Vasocongestion

Sexual dysfunctions

Performance anxiety

Sensate-focus exercises

SELF-TEST PRACTICE QUIZ

Match the following Key Terms and definitions:

1. _____ Problems such as erectile disorder, lack of interest in or responsiveness to sexual activity

2. _____ Description which indicates the type of individual(s) one is erotically or romantically attracted to

3. _____ The pooling of blood in one's bodily tissues (leading to erection, vaginal lubrication)

4. _____ One's sense of being a male, or of being a female

5. _____ As proposed by Masters and Johnson; includes the phases excitement, plateau, orgasm, and resolution

6. _____ Term for psychological pressure (usually affecting a male) to engage in sexual activity frequently and with complete effectiveness

7. _____ One of the behavioral techniques used in the treatment of sexual dysfunctions

a. Gender identity

b. Sexual orientation

c. Gender roles

d. Sexual response cycle

e. Vasocongestion

f. Sexual dysfunctions

g. Performance anxiety

h. Sensate-focus exercises

8. When sexual partners practice mutual stimulation, but without the expectation of actual sexual intercourse, this is known as
   a. the start-stop method.
   b. sensate-focus exercises.
   c. vaginal lubrication.
   d. vasocongestion.
9. What is the correct order of the phases in the sexual response cycle?
   a. Excitement, resolution, plateau, orgasm
   b. Plateau, excitement, orgasm, resolution
   c. Excitement, orgasm, resolution, plateau
   d. Excitement, plateau, orgasm, resolution
10. Behaviors considered appropriate just because one is a male or is a female are termed
   a. gender roles.
   b. gender identities.
   c. sexual orientation.
   d. the sexual response cycle.
11. The percentage of people in the United States and Europe who report being exclusively homosexual is
   a. 3% or less.
   b. 8%.
   c. about 20%.
   d. unknown.
12. Freud thought heterosexuality developed from
   a. unconscious genetic influences leading to effeminate or masculine characteristics.
   b. learned behavior patterns modeled by opposite-sex individuals.
   c. typical identification processes with same-sex parent.
   d. overidentification processes with opposite-sex parent.
13. Evidence for a biological explanation for sexual orientation includes
   a. low or absent levels of testosterone in gay males.
   b. the finding that some gay males participate in traditionally very "masculine" sports.
   c. greater sexual expression similarities among MZ than DZ twins, even when reared apart.
   d. increased preference among gay males as children for female toys and clothes.
14. Which statement about sexual orientation is true?
   a. Anyone who has a same-sex sexual encounter is a homosexual.
   b. Sexual orientation seems to be due primarily to childhood sexual abuse.
   c. Most researchers conceive of sexual orientation as a continuum.
   d. People can choose whether to be gay or straight.
15. Some drugs, such as antidepressants, are identified as a cause for dysfunctions such as erectile disorder. However, coincidentally, we might use these drugs to treat
   a. performance anxiety.
   b. premature ejaculation.
   c. female sexual dysfunction.
   d. sexual trauma survivors.
16. Which of the following might be a cause of sexual dysfunction?
   a. Diabetes
   b. Anxiety
   c. Drug or alcohol use
   d. all of the above

ESSAY QUESTIONS

1. What are some causes of sexual dysfunction? What are effective ways of treating these disorders?

2. How is one's sexual identity determined? Explain our current understanding regarding sexual expression in humans.

ANSWER KEY

1. Sexual dysfunctions
2. Sexual orientation
3. Vasocongestion
4. Gender identity
5. Sexual response cycle
6. Performance anxiety
7. Sensate-focus exercises
8. b
9. d
10. a
11. a
12. c
13. c
14. c
15. b
16. d

SAMPLE ANSWERS TO ESSAY QUESTIONS

1. Sexual dysfunction appears to have both biological and psychological causes. Nearly all sexual dysfunction can be treated, at least to an extent. Biological causes of disorders include illnesses (e.g., diabetes, multiple sclerosis) and the result of accidents or surgery (such as for prostate cancer; spinal cord injuries). Biological causes also include chemicals introduced to the body, such as drugs and alcohol. Testosterone certainly plays a role in sexual desire for both males and females.

   Both behavioral and biological treatments are used to help with sexual dysfunctions. Women may need to explore their sexuality alone and more fully, and become comfortable both emotionally and physically with the experience of sexual arousal and orgasm. For males in particular it is important to alleviate the sense of pressure on performance. Sex therapy may include sexual stimulation and communication without the necessity for actual intercourse. Drugs may be useful; most commonly Viagra and the like can treat erectile dysfunction. A frequent side effect of antidepressants—impeding male erection and ejaculation—is helpful when there is a need to treat premature ejaculation. Fortunately, nearly all sexual dysfunctions are improved as a result of appropriate sex therapies.

2. The exact source or sources for sexual orientation continue to remain indeterminate despite continuing research. Very likely both biological and environmental factors influence orientation. The strongest evidence supporting a biological explanation involves the results of twin studies.

Individuals with an identical genetic heritage (monozygotic multiple births) are substantially more similar in sexual orientation than are fraternal twins, triplets and the like (with no greater genetic similarity than that of siblings in a family). Yet, not all identical twins will exhibit the same sexual orientation—suggesting that clearly environment and life experience must be factors as well. Though testosterone is the major sex hormone in sexual drive for men and women, there are no apparent differences in levels of this hormone among heterosexual individuals vs. their homosexual counterparts. Early experiences of children who become gay or lesbian do seem to involve a preference for more cross-gender toys and clothes. Yet, many homosexual individuals had childhoods which were very, very typical for individuals, most of whom grow up to be heterosexual. It has been established that sexual orientation is not a conscious choice. It is also suggested that many individuals are not exclusively one or the other (homosexual, heterosexual, or bisexual), but rather may exhibit different patterns of sexual expression at different times in their lives. Interestingly, although we think of sexual response as quite distinct in males vs. females, in fact there are a number of underlying similarities between the two.

MODULE 8.4 EMOTIONS

LEARNING OBJECTIVES

After you have mastered the information in this unit, you will be able to:

1. Describe three components of emotions.

2. Discuss whether facial expressions of emotions are universal.

3. Discuss factors influencing happiness.

4. Understand the role brain structures play in emotions.

5. Explain the major theories of emotions.

6. Define emotional intelligence.

7. Describe the polygraph, and discuss research on its effectiveness.

OUTLINE

I.   What Are Emotions? (complex feeling states that infuse our lives with color) Three states involved:
   A.   Bodily arousal—nervous system is activated
   B.   Cognition—subjective or conscious experience of the feeling as well as the thoughts or judgments we have about people or situations that evoke the feeling
   C.   Expressed behavior—what happens outwardly, on face or in actions
      1.   Situations involving pleasant emotions—we approach
      2.   Situations involving unpleasant emotions—we avoid, or challenge
II. Emotional Expression
   A.   Charles Darwin: emotions evolved because they are adaptive
      1.   Darwin was the first to link specific facial expressions to particular emotions
   B.   Universal facial expressions of emotion
      1.   Six basic emotional expressions universally identified (Ekman, 1989)
         a)   Anger, fear, disgust, sadness, happiness, surprise
         b)   Descriptions of experiences of basic emotions also very similar
         c)   Some expressions may be more widely recognized than others
      2.   Possibly more than six (e.g., Plutchik, 1980: add anticipation, acceptance)
      3.   Other emotions are complex; are combinations of the simpler basic emotions

       4.   More recent study suggests that facial expressions of emotions are hard-wired into the brain, rather than learned as the result of visual experiences (Matsumoto et al., 2009)

  C.   Cultural differences in emotions

      1.   Subtle cultural variations in appearance of facial expressions

      2.   Greater accuracy in identifying emotional expression within cultural group

      3.   Display rules—rules for displaying emotions do vary by culture (e.g., Asian cultures discourage displays of emotion in public)

      4.   Cultural differences involve gestures and bodily movements also

      5.   Rules for male vs. female expressiveness may differ

         a)   Women are given greater latitude in expressing joy, love, fear, and sadness

         b)   Men are permitted more direct displays of anger (Dittman 2003a)

         c)   The results of a recent study showed that women were better at recognizing happy or sad faces, but men held the advantage in discerning angry faces (Bakalar, 2006; Williams & Mattingley, 2006

         d)   Are men currently being allowed more freedom to express "sensitivity"

  D.   Happiness

      1.   Promoting happiness (positive psychology) important goal

      2.   What leads to happiness?

         a)   Not money; some slight influence from health, wealth

         b)   Married people are happier; but happiness might be cause and not effect

            1.   Bounce in happiness experienced by many newlyweds tended to be short-lived

         c)   Having close friends, family members and having religious faith seem to make a difference

         d)   Most important factor seems to be general disposition

         e)   Genetics important in overall happiness – "set point": level of happiness tends to settle (Wallis, 2005)

            1.   Our level of happiness is not genetically fixed – it can change over the course of a lifetime

         f)   Happiness involves pleasure at doing things (such as expressing gratitude), the gratification of great absorption in life's activities, and meaningfulness in what we do (Seligman, 2003)

         g)   Happiness is not so much a function of what you've got as what you make of it

  E.   Facial Feedback Hypothesis—Put on a Happy Face

      1.   Mimicking a facial expression induces corresponding emotional state

         a)   Practice smiling several times a day may lift your spirits

      2.   Duchenne smile—genuine smile (named for individual who discovered relevant facial muscles)

III. Brain Structures Involved in Emotions

  A.   There is no one emotional center in the brain. Rather, emotional responses are regulated by complex brain networks located primarily in the limbic system and cerebral cortex (Etkin el al., 2006)

  B.   Limbic system (in brain) important in emotions

      1.   Amygdala—evaluates whether stimulus is a threat; also processes stimuli relating to grief, despair

      2.   Hypothalamus—helps coordinate body's reaction

      3.   Hippocampus—processes related contextual memories

      4.   Role of cerebral cortex

         a)   Evaluates meaning of emotionally arousing stimuli

         b)   Plans/directs response to these stimuli

         c)   Processes subjective experience of emotion

        d)   Controls accompanying facial expression
        e)   Positive emotions—left prefrontal cortex
        f)   Negative emotions—right prefrontal cortex
        g)   No single specific location for experience of emotion

IV.   Theories of Emotion
   A.   Which comes first—cognitive awareness or emotional response?
   B.   James-Lange theory
      1.   Emotions follow bodily reactions (bear in the woods)
      2.   "I am afraid because I ran, my heart is pounding"
      3.   William James: distinct bodily changes are associated with each emotion
   C.   Cannon-Bard theory (1920s)
      1.   Challenges view of James-Lange theory
      2.   Notes same bodily changes (due to activation of sympathetic nervous system) regardless of emotion experienced
      3.   Proposes that physical reaction and subjective experience of emotion occur simultaneously
      4.   Emotions accompany bodily reaction, but are not caused by them
   D.   Two-factor model
      1.   Emotions depend on
         a)   General physiological arousal
         b)   Cognitive interpretation (labeling) of that arousal
      2.   Cues in environment explain why we feel aroused (allow us to label emotion)
      3.   Problems with Schachter and Singer's view:
         a)   Doesn't account for distinctive physiological patterns that accompany various emotions
         b)   Other research (Zajonc, 1980, 1984) demonstrates that feelings occur without cognitive awareness or labeling
   E.   Dual-pathway model of fear (LeDoux, 1994, 2000)
      1.   Proposes that brain processes incoming environmental information two ways (at same time), beginning with thalamus
      2.   "High road"—information then goes to cerebral cortex (processed carefully)
      3.   "Low road"—information goes directly to amygdala (quick emotional reaction; body is prepared to respond if necessary)
      4.   Allows quick response due to amygdala, in case there is danger; cortex can address with more cognitive analysis, which takes more time
      5.   May make difference between life and death
         a)   It is better to act quickly and to ask questions later
   F.   Conclusions and interpretation
      1.   General common physiological response (e.g., increased heart and breathing rate), but also differences among experienced emotions (e.g., blood flow, skin temperature)
      2.   Facial expression can lead to certain feeling states (thus partial support for James-Lange theory)
      3.   Though emotional reaction may precede cognition, cognitive appraisal still vitally important
      4.   Personal meaning (Lazarus, 1995) of experience also crucial
      5.   Still much to learn regarding emotion and brain's processing

V.   Emotional Intelligence (Goleman, 1995)
   A.   Ability to manage one's emotions
   B.   Probably five main characteristics:
      1.   Self-awareness; knowing true inner feelings

2. Can manage own emotions effectively—not usually overwhelmed, can bounce back reasonably well from disappointment (emotions are not out of control)
3. Can, utilize emotional energy to reach goals; delay gratification
4. Have empathy (perceive and feel emotions of others)
5. Can successfully manage meaningful emotional relationships – helping others handle their emotions

C. Essentially independent of IQ-type intelligence
D. Goleman believes more important to success in life than IQ-type intelligence

VI. The Polygraph (Lie Detector)
A. Based on notion that different physiological states accompany lying vs. telling the truth
B. Detects patterns of bodily arousal, not lying per se
C. Problem is cannot reliably detect liars/the innocent
1. Innocent people may become very nervous, aroused (appear guilty)
2. Cold, unfeeling liars show no physiological reaction (thus undetected by polygraph)
D. Currently not considered scientifically acceptable

SUMMARY

In this module, you learn about emotions—what we think they are, how they occur, and why. Emotions seem to involve many parts of the brain. The basic view of emotions (or feeling states) is that they have three components, consisting of (1) bodily arousal due to nervous system activation, (2) cognition, and (3) expressed behavior. Charles Darwin (1872) believed emotions evolved because they are adaptive—they help us function and survive in our environment.

The expression and interpretation of basic emotions seems to be universal. Research involving many unrelated cultures has indicated that six emotions (anger, happiness, fear, sadness, surprise, and disgust) are both facially manifested and interpreted as having the same meaning. When and how emotions are displayed, however, is more determined by culture and varies among cultures. For example, Americans are more likely to display emotions in public than are members of Asian cultures. Traditionally, females have been given more latitude in emotional range and display than have males.

Happiness is an important basic emotion, and promoting a positive outlook (e.g., positive psychology; Seligman, 2002) is a vital effort for our well-being. Happiness seems to be mostly a function of one's outlook, and genetic factors may be an important component in this outlook. Money, health, and marital status are only slightly involved with regard to the experience of happiness. Seligman (2003) suggests there are three kinds of happiness (pleasure at doing things, gratification from being absorbed in one's efforts, and meaning as a consequence of personal fulfillment). Seligman believes that a major part of the work of contemporary psychologists should be guiding individuals to these types of happiness.

There is a relationship between the expression displayed (on the face) and the emotion felt. Researchers have shown that moving facial muscles to result in a certain facial array (for example, a smile) elicits a corresponding emotion. The emotion stems from the facial array, not (in this case) the other way around. This finding is known as the facial-feedback hypothesis. It should be noted that an imposed expression may not be exactly the same thing as a genuine emotional experience.

The brain and nervous system are involved in emotional communication. When emotionally aroused, our nervous system directs the release of epinephrine and norepinephrine, and when the situation has passed the parasympathetic branch of the autonomic nervous system calms us down again. Brain structures comprising the limbic system (including the amygdala and hippocampus) are all involved in processing and responding to emotion. The cerebral cortex gives a cognitive evaluation of the process going on, as well as being responsible for the actual subjective feeling of emotion. Negative and positive emotions seem to activate different parts of the prefrontal cortex.

We are unsure as to the actual process involved in experiencing and responding to emotion; thus, a number of theories have been proposed. The first is the James-Lange theory, which states that we react first and then, based on our reaction, interpret how we must feel (I ran, I must be afraid). The Cannon-Bard theory (1920s) challenges this notion, and its proponents have pointed out that bodily reactions tend to be rather similar (increased heart and breathing rates, perspiration) regardless of the particular emotion experienced. Since there is this similarity, how then can different emotional interpretations result? The Cannon-Bard theory proposes instead that physical reaction and emotional experience occur independently, but simultaneously. Schachter and Singer (two-factor model, 1962) proposed that arousal occurs first, and then it is labeled (as a function of environmental features). The dual-pathway model of fear (proposed by LeDoux, 1994, 1996) suggests that the brain processes emotional information from the environment two ways at once, both beginning with the thalamus. The incoming information is then sent to the amygdala, which reacts in an emotional way immediately, including being prepared for a response (as to a threat). The incoming information also goes to the cerebral cortex, where it is processed more slowly, but more thoroughly. The cortex is responsible for a more cognitive evaluation of the events, plus the actual experience of the associated emotion. The immediate reaction (or readiness for) governed by the amygdala is for our preservation. The cognitive appraisal that follows later gives us the true state of affairs.

We are still researching emotion, so we have no final conclusions regarding the above theories. We do know that there are distinctive physiological patterns accompanying various emotions, and that we need not necessarily have a cognitive awareness of phenomena in order to experience it emotionally (Zajonc, 1980, 1984). We know that many different parts of the brain are involved. We also know that the personal meaningfulness of a given experience has much to do with our emotional response and interpretation of it.

Goleman (1995) has proposed that one kind of intelligence is emotional intelligence. Emotional intelligence constitutes the ability to understand emotions in oneself and others, and regulate and utilize them effectively. It is Goleman's view that this type of intelligence is more important to successful and fulfilling living than is the more traditional IQ-type of intelligence. There is little, if any, relationship between emotional intelligence and the traditional IQ-type of intelligence.

Lastly, information is presented in this module on the polygraph, also known as the lie detector. The objective of the polygraph is to detect emotional changes in test-takers, revealing who is telling the truth and who is lying. In fact, the polygraph simply assesses differences in physiological responses. The premise is the emotional arousal associated with feelings of guilt should reveal who is implicated in the case and who can be excluded. However, the polygraph cannot really detect truth vs. lying. Since the lie detector actually just measures level of arousal, someone anxious about taking the test or fearful that they will be wrongly convicted will likely show higher levels of arousal. This response may be misinterpreted as revealing guilt. Conversely, truly cold and calculating liars often can mask their feelings entirely, regardless of degree of guilt or involvement. Thus, polygraphs are currently not considered sufficiently scientifically reliable. The prohibiting feature of the lie detector test is that it may wrongly implicate the innocent while failing to detect the guilty.

KEY TERMS

Emotions

Display rules

Positive psychology

Facial-feedback hypothesis

Duchenne smile

James-Lange theory

Cannon-Bard theory

Two-factor model

Dual-pathway model of fear

Emotional intelligence

Polygraph

SELF-TEST PRACTICE QUIZ

Match the following Key Terms and definitions:

1. _____ A theory proposed by Schachter and Singer, that we experience general arousal first, then label it

2. _____ Equipment intended to test for individuals who are lying; measures physiological responses indicating arousal

3. _____ Norms and customs that vary from culture to culture regarding when, where, and to what extent emotions are expressed

4. _____ The view that emotional experience and physiological response occur simultaneously but independently

5. _____ Named after the physician who determined the facial muscles involved in a genuine smile

6. _____ Intelligence involving the ability to detect, regulate, and effectively utilize emotions

7. _____ A model of brain processing of emotion proposed by Joseph LeDoux, where two different parts of the brain process the same information in different ways

8. _____ Feeling states having physiological, cognitive, and behavioral components

9. _____ A focus, proposed by the psychologist Martin Seligman, on gaining meaning and happiness in life

a.   Emotions

b.   Display rules

c.   Facial-feedback hypothesis

d.   Duchenne smile

e.   James-Lange theory

f.   Cannon-Bard theory

g.   Two-factor model

h.   Dual-pathway model of fear

i.   Positive psychology

j.   Emotional intelligence

k.   Polygraph

10. _____ The perspective that we have a
bodily response to a situation first,
then emotions follow once we are
aware of this bodily response

11. _____ The view that arranging one's
facial features in an array
corresponding to what is typical for
a given emotional expression will
result in the experience of that
emotion

12. According to Charles Darwin, humans and animals convey emotional expression because it is

    a. adaptive.
    b. enjoyable.
    c. intellectually stimulating.
    d. genetically programmed behavior.

13. Which of the following is not one of the six basic emotional expressions as proposed by Ekman?

    a. Anger
    b. Surprise
    c. Disgust
    d. Anxiety

14. Which statement about emotions is NOT true?

    a. Different cultures have different rules for displaying emotions to others.
    b. Women tend to be more accurate than men in identifying angry faces.
    c. Men tend to experience both joy and sadness more often than women.
    d. People tend to be more accurate in identifying facial expressions among members of their
       own ethnic groups.

15. The part of the brain that appears to process positive emotions is the

    a. amygdala.
    b. hippocampus.
    c. left prefrontal cortex.
    d. right prefrontal cortex.

16. Which of the following tends to have large effects on happiness?

    a. Finding personal fulfillment
    b. Wealth
    c. Physical health
    d. none of the above

17. Research by Zajonc (1980, 1984) has revealed that

    a. emotion and cognition actually occur simultaneously.
    b. individuals receiving an injection of epinephrine labeled the accompanying emotion
       according to available environmental cues.
    c. an emotional reaction may not necessarily have a cognitive component.
    d. more thorough processing of emotional experiences is carried out by the cerebral cortex.

18. A problem with the two-factor model of emotional experience is

    a. we must cognitively identify our emotional state in order to experience it.
    b. different emotions have correspondingly different physiological characteristics.
    c. it is unethical to give study participants injections of epinephrine.
    d. we are more likely to feel frightened when in real danger than when in a movie theater.

19. Polygraph results are not considered scientifically reliable because
    a. the Supreme Court is currently debating the issue.
    b. individuals are considered innocent until they are proven guilty.
    c. the procedure has been replaced by facial thermal imaging techniques.
    d. the test detects arousal levels, not presence or absence of lying.

ESSAY QUESTIONS

1. What are the concepts and objectives behind positive psychology?

2. What is emotional intelligence? What are some characteristics of people who exhibit emotional intelligence?

ANSWER KEY

1. Two-factor model

2. Polygraph

3. Display rules

4. Cannon-Bard theory

5. Duchenne smile

6. Emotional intelligence

7. Dual-pathway model of fear

8. Emotions

9. Positive psychology

10. James-Lange theory

11. Facial-feedback hypothesis

12. a

13. d

14. b

15. c

16. a

17. c

18. b

19. d

SAMPLE ANSWERS TO ESSAY QUESTIONS

1. Positive psychology, as proposed by Seligman (2002, 2003), is a new emphasis within the field, recognizing the value of happiness and examining how to promote it within human experience. Seligman and associates believe that the work of psychologists should be more to focus on human strengths and good points, guiding us to the greatest state of personal happiness possible, rather than being confined to the study of negative emotions and addressing human fallibilities. Positive psychologists advocate the importance of being able to love and be loved, and finding meaning and purpose in our lives. Seligman suggests expressing gratitude, recognizing and appreciating good things that have happened in our lives, and sharing pleasant experiences with others do

much to promote our sense of happiness. Research indicates that happiness is, indeed, primarily a state of mind. It is less what we have, and more how we approach and utilize all that we have.

2. Emotional intelligence is the ability to perceive our own and others' emotions accurately, and to utilize this information wisely and well. Characteristics of emotional intelligence include the ability to (1) know ourselves well and fully and accurately grasp what we are feeling; (2) regulate and manage our emotions effectively—to not fly off the handle, to be able to weather difficult experiences and recover from them within a reasonable amount of time, to allow ourselves to express joy and happiness in appropriate ways and in appropriate settings, to be able to communicate our emotions successfully; (3) harness and use the energy from our emotions in appropriate ways in order to achieve meaningful goals; (4) accurately detect emotions in others, and be able to share in and understand what others are feeling (e.g., have empathy); and (5) apply what we know about our own and others' feelings to our relationships, so that these relationships are strengthened, enhanced, and fulfilling for all parties involved. Research indicates that there is little, if any, correlation between emotional intelligence and the traditional type of intelligence evidenced in standard IQ tests. It is food for thought that, between the two, emotional intelligence may be the more vital for happy and successful life experiences.

MODULE 8.5 APPLICATION: MANAGING ANGER

LEARNING OBJECTIVE

After you have mastered the information in this unit, you will be able to:

1. List suggestions for identifying and controlling anger.

OUTLINE

I.   Problems in controlling anger
   A.   Outbursts may occur that have undesirable and unproductive consequences
   B.   Frequent or chronic anger damages health – anger floods the body with stress hormones that may eventually damage your heart and arteries
II. Cognitive approach to anger
   A.   Anger and blame are responses to a situation, not the situation itself
      1.   It is NOT the "other guy"—people make themselves angry by thinking angering thoughts or making anger-inducing statements to themselves
   B.   Better to recognize influences on anger and take steps to manage effectively
III. Anger management strategies
   A.   Be aware of own emotional reactions
   B.   Review evidence objectively
   C.   Try adaptive approaches; think positively
   D.   Focus on soothing thoughts; relax – take a walk or practice self-relaxation
   E.   Try not to lose control
   F.   Try to understand other's perspective
   G.   Praise self for assertive (not aggressive) responses
   H.   Consider altering expectations of others
   I.   Stay calm; use moderate verbal responses
   J.   Try to express positive feelings

SUMMARY

In this module, you learn helpful anger-management strategies. Anger is not only harmful to our social relationships, if prolonged it can be harmful to our health. It is important to remember that our behavior may have consequences we don't really want when we speak or act in the heat of anger. We may further antagonize others, rather than promote solutions. Though we may have a tendency to blame others, whether or not we respond in anger is our choice. Even in anger-provoking situations, it is best if we remember what is really important in that situation, and act accordingly.

Effective anger management tips include being attuned to our emotional reaction, evaluating factors objectively, and trying to think of effective ways to work through a problem. It is important not to lose control of ourselves, though others may be doing so. We can think of things that help us stay calm, and keep our tone and our word choice within reasonable limits. Perhaps we are expecting too much of others. We need to consider the other person's point of view as well as our own. We can express positive feelings about others, which may help them calm down and think better of us. We need to try assertive, but not aggressive, approaches, and congratulate ourselves for using them. What is your emotional IQ?

CHAPTER 8   APPLICATION EXERCISE

What motivates you? Think of all the activities you are involved in at this stage of your life. They may be family- or work-related, they may involve academics (probably!) or sports, or they may be primarily social in nature. Some activities involve others; some are more often carried out alone such as artistic endeavors. Make a list of the major activities in which you are currently involved.

What is the source of motivation for each of these activities? Which meet primary or biological needs? Which seem to satisfy secondary or stimulus motives? How much of your behavior is motivated by a need for affiliation or achievement? Is some of your behavior prompted simply by the incentives presented to you? Does striving for self-actualization play a role in your activities?

Analyze your behavior and motives in light of what you have learned in this chapter.

CHAPTER 9

Human Development

Chapter 9 deals with human development from the moment of conception through the exhaling of our last breath. Much happens in between! Human development includes physical, social, emotional, and cognitive growth and change. We keep some questions in mind when studying human growth: Which is the greater influence, nature or nurture? What is development like? Is it a continuous, steady process, or is it characterized by stable periods interspersed with rapid, qualitative changes? Development begins with an ovum (mother's egg) fertilized by a sperm (father's reproductive cell), resulting in a zygote. The zygote is a single-celled organism, but cells begin to multiply and the organism grows rapidly. Fertilization is not the only component in the creation of a new offspring. Conception occurs in the Fallopian tubes but the organism must implant successfully in the uterus in order to grow further and to thrive. There are three stages of pregnancy, each with its own biological milestone. The mother's physical health and lifestyle choices, before and during pregnancy, are crucial to the baby's development before and after birth.

The newborn infant is quite small, but it is not at all incapable of dealing with its environment. A newborn has surprisingly good sensory capabilities, with hearing being the best-developed sense and vision the least well-developed. Infants are born with basic reflexes and can discriminate sounds, tastes, and other stimuli from birth. Babies show a preference for the human face and for the voice and smells associated with their mother. Development is rapid, and most evident is motor development. In the space of one year the little one goes from being basically immobile and rather physically helpless to mastering that great balancing act: standing, walking…and soon, running!

Children's emotional and social development is very much a function of the environment into which the child is born. Children do show some evidence of a temperament at birth; much of a child's emotional and social behavior, however, is related to how that child is treated. The more successful child is the one who is securely emotionally attached to a parent. The warm, consistent, authoritative parent is likely to have offspring who are successful, can relate more effectively with others, and who show higher levels of self-esteem. Authoritarian parents insist on their own rules, without explanation, and rarely if ever consider a child's point of view or feelings. Children suffer with this kind of parenting. Permissive parents may or may not show affection, but otherwise are not involved in establishing and maintaining guidelines for their children's appropriate behavior—also an unhealthy recipe for the child.

Cognitive development is also rapid during childhood. Most of what we know about cognitive development is from the work of Jean Piaget, who believed that children develop in qualitatively different stages. Piaget's stages correspond to the child's facility at what he called mental operations. The very young child interacts with the world primarily in a sensorimotor fashion. An older child develops through preoperational and then concrete operational thought. Piaget believed children were capable of entering the last stage, formal operational, by about the age of 12 years. He also proposed that children develop schemas for interacting with the world and these schemas are modified and expanded through experience. Vygotsky emphasized social and cultural influences on cognition.

Adolescence is a time of many changes and challenges. The task of adolescence is making the transition from being a rather dependent, immature child to becoming an independent, fully functioning and autonomous adult. This is a daunting undertaking. One of the most challenging features of being an adolescent is that one is thrust into the world of adulthood, with absolutely no prior experience! Teenagers seem to have the understanding that the family will not always be their reference group, and that in fact their peers will be. Thus, there is a gradual breaking away from the family, especially the parents, and the continued strengthening of ties with friends and other peers. This loosening of ties with the family may be traumatic for both parents and child, or a welcome relief! Often it is some of both.

For adolescents, sexual development and sexual relationships become a major focus. The body of the teenager is changing, and goes from physical immaturity to eventual full sexual maturity and the ability to reproduce the species. Cognitively, too, the adolescent is changing. According to Jean Piaget, the stage of cognitive development that is associated with adolescence and adulthood is formal operational thinking. Here, the teen potentially can contemplate not just real-life issues but those that involve abstract and hypothetical reasoning and concepts. Erik Erikson proposes that, psychosocially, the greatest task for adolescents is to form an identity—a sense of who they are, and where (at least, as it seems at the time) they are going. The teen continues to add and strengthen many cognitive skills, and considers moral issues as well. Adolescents do not show childhood egocentrism but still do tend to feel the world is watching them closely. As is true throughout human life, loving, supportive, close relationships (with both family and friends) help the transitions of adolescence go more smoothly.

Young and middle adulthood is also a time of great activity and many challenges. Most skills and abilities peak in young adulthood, including body strength and agility, and cognitive functions such as memory, mental quickness, and mental flexibility. Tasks of young adulthood include establishing a meaningful and lasting emotional relationship (Erikson termed the psychosocial challenge of young adulthood as intimacy vs. isolation), establishing one's career and one's place in the community, and often bringing children into the world and raising them. Middle adulthood may involve what is called a midlife crisis, but a true crisis at this time of life is the exception rather than the rule. The slight signs of decline (less muscle tissue, slipping from maximum cognitive functioning), can be offset at least in part by diet, regular exercise and an overall healthy lifestyle. Young adulthood is often more like an extension of adolescence; the middle-aged adult may feel (and appear) more like just an extension of the young adult years. Often, adults in their middle years find the new opportunities facing them refreshing and inviting. Children may be grown and out of the house, and many middle-aged individuals still experience very good physical health and sexual interest remains. Thus, the future still seems open-ended and full of promise. This may be a time to try new ideas, switch to a more satisfying career, return for more education, or just completely review one's philosophy and approach to life.

For the older adult, the recognition that life must be, sooner or later, coming to an end presents a great deal of challenge in and of itself. Physical and cognitive changes are evident; risk of illnesses such as cancer and Alzheimer's increases. However, older adults, too, often are remaining vital and active, and, as previously, a healthy lifestyle is crucial. It is projected that by 2050 one in five adult Americans will be over the age of 65. The overriding task is to continue to find life meaningful, rewarding, and to find a way to put one's talents to best use. A sense of optimism—a positive outlook on life—seems to be an important component in both living longer and living better. Even for the oldest adult, the best approach is to make the most of what one has and continue to find experiences that allow for social interaction and support, which make life meaningful. Most adults in their 70s report being happy and satisfied with their lives. Fortunately for older individuals, while they may not have quite the acuity of earlier years, they have gained immeasurably in experience. Knowledge increases over essentially all of the human life span. At any age, with a little thought and effort, we can live enriching, productive lives.

MODULE 9.1 PRENATAL DEVELOPMENT: A CASE OF NATURE AND NURTURE

LEARNING OBJECTIVES

After you have mastered the information in this unit, you will be able to:

1. Describe the major stages of prenatal development.

2. Discuss some of the threats to prenatal development.

3. Discuss nature, nurture or both.

OUTLINE

I. Developmental Psychology—changes that occur throughout the life span
   A. Explanations for patterns of development
      1. Nature and Nurture
         a) Nature—biological, hereditary (genetic) influences
         b) Nurture—derived from environment, experience
         c) Best opinion is development and developmental patterns a combination of both
            1) Some traits such as hair color, are determined by a single gene – intelligence and personality are influenced by multiple genes interacting with the environment (Diamond, 2009; Johnson et al., 2009; Gollesman & Hanson, 2005; Loehlin, 2010
      2. Maturation—biological unfolding; blueprint is genetically wired in
      3. Environmental/experiential factors—nutrition (even in the womb), emotional relationships also influence development
II. Stages of Prenatal Development
   A. Background factors in prenatal development
      1. Sexual reproduction began perhaps 300 million years ago
      2. Male organism: XY chromosome pair
      3. Female organism: XX chromosome pair
      4. Reproductive cells
         a) Egg (ovum; from mother) X chromosome—released from ovary, then travels through fallopian tube
         b) Sperm (from father)—two types: either X chromosome or Y chromosome
      5. Zygote: fertilized egg (from uniting of ovum and single sperm)
   B. Stages of Pregnancy- typical nine-month pregnancy is commonly divided into three trimesters
      1. Germinal
         a) Approximately the first two weeks after conception
         b) Spans from moment of fertilization to complete implantation within the uterine lining
      2. Embryonic (organism is an embryo)
         a) Period from two weeks to eight weeks after conception
         b) Basics of major organ systems develop
         c) Baby is cushioned by amniotic fluid in sac; nutrients, oxygen and wastes are exchanged via placenta
      3 Fetal—from 9th week of pregnancy until birth (organism is a fetus)
         a) All of the major organ system, as well as the fingers and toes are formed about the twelfth week

b) Middle of the fourth month typically marks the first fetal movements

c) End of the second trimester- fetus approaches the age of viability – capable of sustaining life on its own – less than 2 pounds would be a concern

III.   Threats to Prenatal Development

A.   Adequate nutrition important, including sufficient folic acid (reduces risk of neural tube defects if taken during and preferably before first trimester of pregnancy)

B.   Teratogens (cause harm to developing baby)

1.   Infectious diseases – most dangerous

a) Rubella (German measles)—can cause heart disease, deafness, or mental retardation

b) Sexually transmitted diseases (HIV, syphilis)

2.   Smoking—increases risk for miscarriage, premature birth, low birth weight, infant mortality, SIDS, respiratory problems, learning problems, and behavioral problems

3.   Alcohol (Fetal alcohol syndrome (FAS)) and drugs—increase risk of birth defects, infant mortality, mental retardation

SUMMARY

In this module, you learn about the earliest stages of life—prenatal development. Developmental psychology is the field that studies growth and changes in human organisms over the life span. A new life is created by the union of an egg cell (also called an ovum) produced by the mother and a sperm cell produced by the father. Egg cells carry the X chromosome only; sperm cells carry either an X or a Y chromosome. A baby with an XX combination is a female; a baby with the XY combination is male. The union of egg and sperm results in the creation of a one-celled organism called a zygote. Once a zygote is created, development occurs very rapidly. Pregnancy is divided into three biological stages: the germinal (first two weeks), embryonic (two weeks to eight weeks after conception), and fetal (eight weeks after conception up until birth). The first stage corresponds to the newly-formed organism completing the trip down the Fallopian tube and successfully implanting into the uterine environment. The second stage is marked by the preliminary development of the organism's basic body systems (respiratory, circulatory, and so forth). The last stage covers all final development leading up to birth.

Though nearly all births occur successfully, it is important that an expectant mother get adequate nutrition and avoid harmful substances (teratogens) which could permanently harm her baby. Alcohol, drugs, smoking, and infectious diseases all can lead to birth defects, premature birth, mental retardation, or even death for the fetus.

KEY TERMS

Developmental psychology

Maturation

Ovulation

Ovary

Fallopian tube

Zygote

Germinal stage

Fertilization

Uterus

Embryonic stage

Embryo

Neural tube

Amniotic sac

Placenta

Fetal stage

Fetus

Spina bifida

Teratogen

Rubella

Sudden infant death syndrome (SIDS)

Fetal alcohol syndrome (FAS)

SELF-TEST PRACTICE QUIZ

Match the following Key Terms and definitions (note: not every Key Term will be used):

1. _____ A disorder in newborns where the baby suffers physical deformities and mental retardation due to the mother's excessive drinking of alcoholic beverages during pregnancy

2. _____ A neural tube defect; appears to be related to insufficient levels of folic acid in the diet of the mother before and during pregnancy

3. _____ The first stage of development for the organism during pregnancy—covers the period of about the first two weeks (from conception to complete implantation within the uterus)

4. _____ Also called German measles; normally harmless if contracted during childhood, but can cause serious birth defects in baby if contracted by mother while she is pregnant

5. _____ Term describing the developing organism during the second through eighth weeks of prenatal development

a. Developmental psychology
b. Maturation
c. Ovulation
d. Ovary
e. Fallopian tube
f. Zygote
g. Germinal stage
h. Fertilization
i. Uterus
j. Embryonic stage
k. Embryo
l. Neural tube
m. Amniotic sac
n. Placenta
o. Fetal stage
p. Fetus
q. Spina bifida
r. Teratogen
s. Rubella

6. _____ A technique where high-pitched sound waves are "bounced off" the abdominal region of the mother, providing a picture of the developing organism

7. _____ A large membrane that develops within the uterus during pregnancy; allows the exchange of nutrients and oxygen from mother to baby, and carbon dioxide and wastes from baby to mother (which will be expelled by her system)

8. _____ The term given to the developing organism covering the span of prenatal development from the third month of pregnancy up until birth

9. _____ A fertilized egg

10. _____ The female reproductive organ (the womb) where the fertilized egg implants and develops until birth

11. _____ A chromosomal disorder characterized by mental retardation and physical abnormalities

12. _____ The removal of amniotic fluid to check for fetal abnormalities

13. _____ Also known as conception—the union of a mature egg and sperm

t. Sudden infant death syndrome (SIDS)

u. Fetal alcohol syndrome (FAS)

v. Amniocentesis

w. Chorionic villus sampling (CVS)

x. Chorion

y. Down syndrome

z. Ultrasound imaging

14. The newly developing organism, created by the union of one sperm cell from the father and one egg cell from the mother, is completely attached to the mother's body by about _____ after conception.

    a. one hour
    b. one day
    c. one week
    d. two weeks

15. The period of prenatal development covering the third month through the ninth month (or birth) is called the _____ stage.

    a. germinal
    b. embryonic
    c. fetal
    d. trimester

16. Which of the following is a teratogen?

    a. Alcohol
    b. Lead
    c. Rubella
    d. all of the above

17. When a person's development "unfolds" according to its genetic code, this is known as
    a. maturation.
    b. growth.
    c. evolution.
    d. germination.

ESSAY QUESTION

1. What are some problems a baby is more likely to have if the mother smokes or does not adhere to proper nutrition standards during pregnancy?

ANSWER KEY

1. Fetal alcohol syndrome (FAS)

2. Spina bifida

3. Germinal stage

4. Rubella

5. Embryo

6. Ultrasound imaging

7. Placenta

8. Fetus

9. Zygote

10. Uterus

11. Down syndrome

12. Amniocentesis

13. Fertilization

14. d

15. c

16. d

17. a

SAMPLE ANSWER TO ESSAY QUESTION

1. While not every woman who smokes (or uses drugs or alcohol) during her pregnancy causes lasting harm to her unborn baby, the likelihood for problems is greater. As smoking (or amount of alcohol/drug use) increases, the risk for subsequent harm increases. The mother who smokes during pregnancy increases the likelihood that her baby will be born pre-term, of lower birth weight, and with a greater risk for respiratory problems. There is a greater risk of miscarriage and a higher incidence of infant mortality and of sudden infant death syndrome (SIDS). Lastly, developmental problems such as hyperactivity and a lower IQ are more common among offspring of mothers who smoked during pregnancy. Poor nutrition on the part of a mother-to-be, whether due to scarcity or the mother's inappropriate eating habits, is associated with a higher incidence of premature birth, low birth weight, birth defects such as spina bifida, cognitive deficits, and other deficiencies. Some birth problems cannot be detected in advance or avoided. Those due to smoking, poor eating habits, and substance abuse are, in contrast, completely preventable.

MODULE 9.2 INFANT DEVELOPMENT

LEARNING OBJECTIVES

After you have mastered the information in this unit, you will be able to:

1. Identify and describe the reflexes that are present at birth.

2. Describe infants' sensory, perception, and learning abilities.

3. Explain how the infant's motor abilities develop during the first year of life.

OUTLINE

I. Reflexes—unlearned, automatic responses to stimuli (usually have survival value; most disappear within the first six months)
   - A. Rooting reflex—turn head in direction of stroke to cheek
   - B. Eyeblink reflex—protects from bright light, foreign objects
   - C. Sucking reflex—enables baby to get nourishment
   - D. Moro reflex (startle reflex)—response to being frightened (e.g., loud noise – or head falls backward)
   - E. Palmar grasp reflex—curling fingers tightly around an object
   - F. Babinski reflex—toes fan out and curl when sole of foot stroked

II. Sensory, Perceptual, and Learning Abilities in Infancy
   - A. Sensory ability
     1. Vision
        - a) Least well-developed sense at birth and the slowest of the senses to develop
        - b) Can recognize (and prefers) mother's face; tracks moving objects
        - c) Color vision by about 8 weeks
        - d) Depth perception—visual cliff research suggests develops by 6 months of age
     2. Hearing
        - a) Well developed at birth; know and prefer mother's voice
        - b) Babies especially responsive to sounds corresponding to range of human verbal expression
        - c) Several months of age can distinguish among various speech sounds - "ba" and "ma"
     3. Odors and tastes—newborns can differentiate among both, show preferences (especially toward the mother)
   - B. Perceptual ability
     1. Infants differentiate among meaningful stimuli shortly after birth
     2. Sensitive to voice qualities and how they are held
     3. Differentiate among facial expressions by four to six months of age
   - C. Learning ability
     1. Can learn and remember simple (e.g., operantly conditioned) responses
     2. Retain memories for faces and sounds of particular words
     3. Learning occurs prenatally; e.g., preference for sound of mother's voice and sounds reflecting their native language

III. Motor Development
   - A. Motor skills well beyond simple unlearned reflexes
   - B. Can imitate parents' facial expression; mimicking of expressions goes back and forth
   - C. Goal-directed behaviors evidenced early on (e.g., bringing fist to mouth in utero)
   - D. Early reflexive behavior slowly replaced by intentional, voluntary movements
   - E. Sitting alone, standing, and walking usually mastered by one year of age

SUMMARY

In this module, you learn about the incredible, and incredibly fast, early development in a human. Infants may seem to do little more than eat and sleep, but a closer look reveals they are both active learners and active perceivers of their environment. Babies are born with many reflexes (sucking, rooting, eye blink), which help them get their start and help them survive. Most reflexes are soon replaced with intentional, more complex behaviors. Babies usually triple their weight during the first year of life, and by adulthood the size of the brain has quadrupled. Although vision is the least well-developed sense at birth, hearing is quite well developed, and there is evidence for discriminations among stimuli for the remaining senses as well. The baby's rapid growth is perhaps most obvious with regard to motor development. Newborns typically have little mobility, but they soon can lift their heads, roll over, and by nine months of age sit without support. Balancing to stand and walk for a one-year-old is truly a daunting task. Amazingly, usually around one year of age, the little one can stand alone, walk, and may even run!

KEY TERMS

Rooting reflex

Eyeblink reflex

Sucking reflex

Moro reflex

Palmar grasp reflex

Babinski reflex

Maturation

SELF-TEST PRACTICE QUIZ

Match the following Key Terms and definitions:

1. _____ A reflex where the baby startles in response to a loud noise or loss of support

2. _____ An automatic turning of the head by a baby in response to her cheek being stroked

3. _____ An unlearned response by a baby, occurring when the bottom of the foot is stroked

4. _____ A pattern of growth and development in a human infant which is largely determined by heredity

5. _____ A reflex where the baby's fingers curl tightly around an object placed in his palm

a. Rooting reflex

b. Eyeblink reflex

c. Sucking reflex

d. Moro reflex

e. Palmar grasp reflex

f. Babinski reflex

g. Maturation

6. _____ A repeated response by the baby's lips when the tongue or mouth is stimulated

7. _____ A reflex that protects the baby from foreign objects and bright lights

8. Babies' weight at one year of age is approximately _____ times that of their birth weight.

   a. two
   b. three
   c. four
   d. five

9. Balancing to stand and walk for an infant is

   a. an easy matter and occurs just a few days before the first birthday.
   b. easier if the behaviors are modeled by older brothers and sisters.
   c. approximately the same experience as standing and walking for an adult.
   d. rather difficult because the infant is small and very prone to sway.

10. Which of the following statements about learning is accurate?

    a. Even young infants can retain memories for days or weeks.
    b. Learning can occur after birth, but not before.
    c. All babies can learn absolutely anything if only they are properly taught.
    d. Newborns are best taught through pictures because vision is their most well-developed sense.

11. Reflexes

    a. can be modified through proper teaching.
    b. are learned through imitation.
    c. mostly disappear within a few months because they are not really necessary for survival.
    d. tend to become strongest around one year of age.

12. Infants show a preference for visual stimuli that resemble

    a. colors.
    b. faces.
    c. toys.
    d. mobiles.

13. Research on depth perception uses an apparatus called a

    a. visual cliff.
    b. depth detection monitor.
    c. perceptive-reactive assessor.
    d. visual depth monitor.

14. By four or five months of age, infants seem to _____ before putting objects in their mouths.

    a. suck on their fingers
    b. roll onto their tummies
    c. vocalize to a parent or other caregiver
    d. first bring objects fully into view

15. Most babies are first able to stand without support by about _____ months of age.

    a. 3
    b. 6
    c. 12
    d. 18

ESSAY QUESTIONS

1.   Briefly trace the motor development of an infant from birth through one year of age.

2.   How does sensory, perceptual, and learning ability develop over the first year of life?

ANSWER KEY

1.   Moro reflex

2.   Rooting reflex

3.   Babinski reflex

4.   Maturation

5.   Palmar grasp reflex

6.   Sucking reflex

7.   Eyeblink reflex

8.   b

9.   d

10.   a

11.   c

12.   b

13.   a

14.   d

15.   c

SAMPLE ANSWERS TO ESSAY QUESTIONS

1.   Babies have little in the way of motor development when they are born, other than reflexes. Basic reflexes include those needed for survival (sucking for nourishment; rooting to find breast or bottle) and those that seem to have no current survival purpose (Babinski, Moro, Palmar grasp). Babies have very simple goal-directed behaviors, such as the ability to suck their thumbs (a behavior they exhibit even before birth). Newborns can respond to and imitate facial expressions, and early communication with babies consists in part of the exchange and mimicking of facial expressions. The reflexes babies exhibit initially are gradually replaced by more complex and more intentional motor behaviors. Babies can reach for things and eventually grasp them, and much ends up in the baby's mouth (intentionally). Muscles strengthen, and the baby can first lift the chin, the entire upper body, roll over, and eventually creep and sit up. By the baby's first birthday, standing alone has usually been mastered, followed not long thereafter by the ability to walk, and even run. Standing and balancing is quite difficult for babies because of their build and much smaller stature.

2.   We have recently learned that babies come into the world much more prepared to interact with and learn from it than has been previously thought. Most of a new baby's senses are well developed; the baby can hear even before birth, and shows early preferences for sounds within the range of human speech, the mother's voice in particular. Babies show taste and smell likes and dislikes at birth or shortly thereafter (the smell of bananas is popular!). Vision is least well developed at birth, but even so, babies look longer (and appear to prefer) human face-like stimuli, and again their mothers' face in particular. By two or three months of age, infants show they can discriminate among speech sounds, and by four to six months among various facial expressions.

Babies very early on are able to learn and remember simple responses—such as kicking to activate a crib mobile. Babies by six or seven months can remember various faces and also certain words they have recently heard. Clearly, the first year of life for the human infant is anything but a passive, stagnant time!

MODULE 9.3 YEARS OF DISCOVERY: EMOTIONAL, SOCIAL, AND COGNITIVE DEVELOPMENT IN CHILDHOOD

LEARNING OBJECTIVES

After you have mastered the information in this unit, you will be able to:

1. Identify and explain the three basic types of infant temperament.

2. Describe research on attachment.

3. Discuss the roles that peers, parents, and culture play in children's emotional and social development.

4. Understand the three major styles of parenting and how they differ.

5. Discuss the childhood stages of psychosocial development.

6. Explain the major features associated with Piaget's theory of cognitive development.

7. Describe Vygotsky's theory of cognitive development.

OUTLINE

I.   Temperament
    A.   The characteristic style of behavior or disposition
    B.   Types of temperament (based on New York Longitudinal Study [NYLS])
        1.   Easy children—40% of children in study; playful, adaptive with better peer relationships and self-esteem, and better adjusted as an adult
        2.   Difficult children—10% of children in study; negative, irritable that are likely to develop mental healthier problems in later childhood; however, may also have positive qualities (e.g., could become highly spirited and not become a "push over")
        3.   Slow-to-warm-up children—15% of children in study; "inhibited," need more time to adjust and are more likely to experience anxiety or depression in childhood
        4.   35% of children in study represented a mixed group, could not be classified
    C.   Temperament in childhood predicts adjustment as an adult
    D.   Both nature (genetics) and nurture (environment) are influences
    E.   Children can learn to adapt successfully to environment, regardless of temperament – whether it is possible to change basic temperament remains unanswered
II. Attachment—enduring emotional bond, develops over time
    A.   Attachment behaviors in other species – (do not confuse with bonding in which parents tie to infant)
        1.   Attachment found in many other species
        2.   Konrad Lorenz—studied ducks, geese, other fowl
        3.   Imprinting—following behavior; occurs in response to first moving object seen (shortly after birth)
        4.   Harry and Marguerite Harlow—rhesus monkeys
        5.   Baby monkeys prefer soft, cuddly surrogate "mother," even when other wire surrogate has food

B.   Attachment in human infants
1.   Mary Ainsworth and colleagues—developed methodology to assess attachment (Strange Situation) and identified three basic types
a)   Secure attachment (Type B)—65 to 70% of children show; rely on parent, warm reunion when mother returns
b)   Insecure-avoidant attachment (Type A)—about 20% of children show; child has little interest, little distress with regard to parent (may ignore her)
c)   Insecure-resistant attachment (Type C)—about 10% of children show; emotionally erratic, ambivalent or may rebuff mother
d)   Fourth type of attachment identified later—disorganized/disoriented (Type D)—child seems confused, unable to make effective use of available support, unable to approach parent directly even when they were very distressed
2.   Conclusions regarding Strange Situation research methodology
a)   Ainsworth's approach may be less well-suited to assess attachment in other cultures
b)   Infant attachment styles do show predictability for later child and adolescent characteristics
C.   Effects of daycare on attachment
1.   More preschoolers now in daycare centers than at home or in relative's home
2.   Apparently no differences in attachment patterns for children experiencing full-time daycare setting
3.   High-quality daycare centers may have positive influence on cognitive and emotional development
4.   Possibly long hours of daycare associated with more aggressiveness
5.   Likely that effects on child development related to *quality* of care, whether daycare setting or at home
III.   Child-Rearing Influences
A.   Raising children successfully
1.   Many factors influence child's emotional, intellectual, and social development
2.   Factors include genetics, peer groups, quality of parenting
3.   Peers important in development of social behaviors, competence—acceptance by peers pivotal in child's self-confidence, self-esteem
4.   Quality parenting
a)   Spending much time with children, modeling and reinforcing appropriate behaviors
b)   Setting and explaining clear rules, establishing limits
c)   Consistency in standards and interaction; sufficient praise for good behavior
d)   Providing warm, loving, secure environment
B.   Father's influence
1.   Involved fathers (sharing meals, spending leisure time and assisting with school work) have children who perform better academically
2.   Two-parent (mother, father) families have children with greater academic and social success
3.   Fathers (in western societies) engage in more active physical play with children, less basic caregiving, relative to mothers
C.   Lesbian and gay parents
1.   Do as well in school and have as good relationships with their peers as children of heterosexual parents (Paterson, 2009; Perrin, 2002; Wainwright et al., 2004)

D.   Cultural differences in parenting
1.   African American
a)   Strong kinship bonds; parenting is shared among family members
b)   Grandmother may assume most important role
2.   Hispanic
a)   Father is traditional provider, protector
b)   Mother usually assumes full childcare responsibility
c)   Fairly strict discipline standards; emphasis on demeanor, respect towards adults
d)   Currently changing as cultural characteristics change
3.   Asian cultures
a)   Emphasize respect for parental authority, particularly that of father
b)   Usually warm relationship with mother
4.   All cultures help children move from a state of complete dependence in infancy toward assuming more responsibility for their own behavior
E.   Parenting styles (Baumrind, 1971, 1991)
1.   Three basic types of parenting styles identified
a)   Authoritative
(1)   Reasonable expectations, consistent limits; loving; listen; explain – rely on reason not force
(2)   Child most likely to be successful, personable, competent, self-reliant
b)   Authoritarian
(1)   Rigid, demand unquestioning obedience; disregard for child's feelings or point of view
(2)   Child inhibited, moody, fearful—results in most negative outcome in adolescence for males
c)   Permissive
(1)   Little involvement on part of parent as far as establishing guidelines, rules; little follow-through
(2)   Child impulsive, lacks self-control; uncooperative and disrespectful of others – heightened risks of violence and drug abuse
2.   Critique
a)   Cultural influences may vary with regard to what are considered desirable parenting qualities
b)   Need to consider environment when evaluating effectiveness of parenting style (e.g., high-risk may necessitate different parenting tactics in comparison to low-risk environment)
c)   Some influence from child's personality
IV.   Erikson's Stages of Psychosocial Development
A.   Emphasized importance of social relationships (1963)
B.   Personalities shaped by psychosocial challenges
C.   First four stages—cover childhood development period
1.   Trust vs. mistrust
a)   First year of life—creates view of people, world in general
b)   Trust develops when infant treated with warmth, responsiveness
c)   Mistrust develops when child not attended to
2.   Autonomy vs. shame and doubt
a)   Second and third years of age
b)   Child's greater mobility, inquisitiveness, toilet training are major features – warmly encourage the child toward greater independence
c)   Shame and doubt if child criticized, given tasks beyond his abilities

3. Initiative vs. guilt
    a) Includes child's ages of three to six years
    b) Children come up with own ideas, not just adopting those of others – challenged to initiate actions and carry them out
    c) When praised, gain sense of confidence, competence
    d) When criticized, feel inept, incapable, and awkward
4. Industry vs. inferiority
    a) Includes elementary school ages (approximately six to twelve years)
    b) Not only initiate own tasks, interests, but much more likely to follow them through
    c) Very many skills and areas of knowledge gained (academic, social, physical/motor)
    d) Much comparison by children among themselves, in addition to feedback from parents, teachers
    e) "Failure" leads to sense of inadequacy, withdrawal and lack of motivation
D. Experiences later in life can alter impact of earlier stages

V. Cognitive Development
VI. Piaget's Theory of Cognitive Development
A. Basics of Piaget's theory
    1. Best way to learn about children is to observe them carefully – view children not as passive responders to stimuli but as natural scientist who seek to understand the world and operate on it
    2. Schema—organizational system of actions and a mental representation used by individuals to understand and interact with the world
        a) Social schemas make sense of their social environment
    3. Adaptation
        a) Changing in order to better meet challenges in the world
        b) Two complementary processes
            (1) Assimilation—adding a new item to an existing schema
            (2) Accommodation—modifying an existing schema (or creating a new one) to account for phenomena that do not fit in existing schemas
    4. Stage approach to cognitive development
        a) Assimilation and accommodation processes are life-long
        b) Cognitive development progresses through stages—universal ordered sequence for all children; each stage qualitatively different from others
B. Sensorimotor stage
    1. Birth to two years of age
    2. Gain object permanence (Piaget's traditional test) by about eight months of age – recognition that the objects continue to exist even if they have disappeared from sight
    3. Learn about world through motor actions; sensory system detects result
    4. According to Piaget, object permanence not complete till near end of stage, when child can form mental representations
C. Preoperational stage
    1. Two to seven years of age
    2. Still do not have logical cognitive ability
    3. Gain ability for symbolic representations (language, pretend play)
    4. Piaget's view—child egocentric until end of stage
        a) Not selfish; child *unable* to take others' points of view
        b) Animistic thinking—that inanimate objects have feelings same as child
    5. Do not yet understand principles of conservation (of number, area, volume)
        a) Other limitations
            1) Irreversibility – inability to reverse the direction of a sequence to starting point
            2) Centration – focus on only one aspect of a situation at a time at the exclusion of all others

    D.   Concrete operational stage
1. Seven to eleven years of age—no longer egocentric, according to Piaget
2. Gain understanding of conservation—when nothing added or subtracted, quantity does not change though form or appearance might; reversibility, decentration
3. Can perform simple logical operations provided they deal with real-world examples (e.g., do not involve abstract or hypothetical thinking)

    E.   Formal operational stage
1. Last stage—begins at about eleven or twelve years of age
2. Full cognitive maturity—but not everyone reaches this level even as adults
3. Can manage deductive, abstract, and hypothetical thinking

    F.   Evaluating Piaget's legacy
1. Tremendous influence, advancement regarding children's thinking, cognitive processes
2. Recognized children are active participants in their world
3. Continues to provide guiding framework for research
4. Critiques
    a) Stage model of development not really reflective of cognitive changes
    b) Cognitive development perhaps more steady, gradual, continuous
    c) Piaget underestimated abilities of young children
    d) Object permanence, for example, develops earlier than Piaget proposed
    e) Fails to account for cultural differences in timing (order is stable, ages for cognitive developmental milestones not)

VII.   Vygotsky's Sociocultural Theory of Cognitive Development
    A.   A Russian psychologist (1896-1934); social interactions are vehicle for learning
    B.   Zone of proximal development (ZPD)—what child can learn, with guidance, help
    C.   Parent acts like tutor; child, the student—child is able to master because adult provides boost

SUMMARY

In this module, you learn about emotional, social and cognitive development of the human during childhood. Leading figures in this research area, Jean Piaget and Erik Erikson, were inclined to believe that development occurred in stages. Functioning at each stage was rather dramatically different, and development consisted more of plateaus and rapid leaps than steady, "additive" kinds of changes. Not all developmental theorists share this stage-model approach.

Young children are obviously different beginning at birth. These differences have been termed temperament, and three basic kinds have been identified. Temperament has some carryover into adult personality characteristics. With proper, supportive environments, all children can grow up to be well-adjusted individuals, living effectively. Emotional attachment is crucial to a child's survival, in that babies and young children cannot fulfill their own needs and are dependent upon others to care enough to provide for them. We see examples of attachment in other species—Lorenz's research with geese and other fowl (for example, the phenomenon of imprinting, a following behavior) and the work of the Harlows with rhesus monkeys (baby monkeys prefer to be with a soft, cuddly surrogate mother rather than a wire surrogate equipped with a source of food). The formation of attachment in humans is most dependent upon characteristics exhibited by the parent. Parents who are warm, loving, consistent, responsive, and perceptive regarding their child's needs and cues will have the most securely attached children. A secure attachment in childhood is associated with higher self-esteem, better psychological adjustment, and better social and emotional relationships throughout life. The child's temperament is somewhat related to the quality of attachment with the caregiver.

Mary Ainsworth developed the Strange Situation, a laboratory method for assessing attachment in very young children. The quality of attachment is determined mostly by how the child responds when the mother returns after having left the little one for a brief period of time. Children who respond immediately to the parent's return, have a warm reunion, and show clear evidence of relying upon the mother for emotional support are classified as exhibiting secure attachment. Most children are in this category. Children who show no real reaction to the mother's return, and who seem little disturbed by her disappearance or absence, are classified as having an insecure-avoidant type of attachment. Children who seem excessively emotionally dependent upon the parent, and somewhat uncertain (perhaps even anxious or angry) about the nature of the relationship are classified as having an insecure-resistant type of attachment. These children have an erratic response to their mother's return— they may quickly seek her out, yet appear to fight her overtures once she reaches for the child. A fourth type of attachment, added by later researchers, is the disorganized/disoriented category. Children with this classification seem emotionally confused, and do not have an effective way for dealing with emotional difficulties. While attachment studies have been helpful in assessing the effectiveness of parent-child relationships, it is important to recognize that cultural practices may influence its manifestation. It does appear that attachment styles, too, have carryover into adult behavior patterns.

Three basic styles of parenting have been identified (Baumrind, 1971, 1991). These are (1) authoritative, (2) authoritarian, and (3) permissive. Parents who raise their children using the authoritative style tend to have the most successful and most well-adjusted offspring. The authoritative parent is consistent, has clear rules that are explained and modeled, and shows a great deal of love, caring, and respect for her child. Authoritative parents listen to their children, support and believe in their children, and show interest in their child's friends and activities. The authoritarian parent is rigid, demands unquestioning obedience, and relies on discipline and punishment to mold children's behavior. The child's point of view is not considered, nor, usually, are the child's feelings. Children raised in this manner may be withdrawn and somewhat inhibited in their behavior; they tend to have lower self-esteem. The permissive parent may show affection towards the child, but is not involved with regard to setting reasonable parameters for behavior, establishing and explaining rules, and following through to assure that desired behaviors and guidelines are met. Children raised in this latter fashion lack sociability, are uncooperative, and self-centered.

Though most American children are in some kind of daycare setting during the preschool years, children in daycare show little difference regarding attachment patterns when compared with children raised entirely at home. The quality of daycare (or home care) seems more important to a child's development than the setting in which this care occurs. There are cultural differences in parenting styles and parenting standards, and these variations need to be taken into consideration when evaluating parenting success. Hispanic cultures, for example, place a greater emphasis on respect and traditional discipline, so a parent who exhibits these characteristics may be reflecting cultural patterns and not necessarily an individual parenting style. Fathers interact differently with their children than mothers do, in that fathers tend to involve their children in more active and more physical play. Mothers' behaviors tend to involve the basic caregiving procedures—feeding, bathing, and so forth. Though most research on parenting, attachment, and child development has focused on the mother-child relationship, research does show that where fathers are present and are involved with their children, children show higher levels of academic and perhaps social abilities.

Erik Erikson has proposed stages for human psychosocial development, and four of these stages fall within the childhood years. Erikson's view is that an individual's development is heavily influenced by social experiences, from parents and also from others. At each stage, the individual is faced with a psychosocial challenge, and one outcome is preferred over the other (trust is preferred to mistrust, for example). During the first year of life, the psychosocial issue most crucial is whether the baby develops a sense of trust or a sense of mistrust. As indicated in the Ainsworth model for attachment, whether trust is established depends mostly upon how the child is treated, and this is predominantly in the hands of the parents. Caregivers who respond promptly and appropriately to the child's needs and signals help the child develop a sense of security and trust, and the belief that the world is a welcoming place. The second psychosocial stage is autonomy vs. shame and doubt; the third, initiative vs. guilt; and the fourth (spanning the elementary school years of about six to twelve years of age) the two pathways of industry vs. inferiority. A successful outcome in each case is related to the feedback a child receives. When the child is praised and supported for his attempts, the child tends to develop a sense of competence. By the fourth stage (industry vs. inferiority), feedback from peers also is crucial. Of course, this feedback is related to the child's already existing sense of self-worth, which is a function of previous stages.

Jean Piaget proposed the best-known model for cognitive development over the life span. Piaget's theory of cognitive development involves four stages, with the last stage beginning at about eleven or twelve years of age. Piaget believed that through their experience with the world individuals develop schemas, which are a sense of what a concept or notion is and how one would use it. You may have a schema for, let's say, "ball" or "mother" or "classroom." Why is a soccer ball a ball, but a grapefruit is not? You didn't always know this! But you have learned through your interactions and your experience with the environment. Much of this learning begins in the first stage Piaget proposes—the sensorimotor stage. In this stage, children act upon the world with even the simplest of motor skills. The world responds, and the child is aware of this reaction from the world via her sensory system. Gradually, the child learns what actions go with what consequences, and the child builds on this learning. We add to our knowledge either through assimilation (where a new item fits into an existing schema) or through accommodation (no current schema fits the new knowledge; either an existing schema is modified (why is a football still a ball?) or we create a new schema).

In Piaget's second stage (preoperational, covering ages two to seven years), much cognitive development occurs. Most importantly, the child acquires the ability for symbolic representations, and the number one symbol system we acquire is language. According to Piaget, the child during this stage is still egocentric; that is, he is unable to grasp anyone else's perspective but his own. Other symbolic representations are evident in children's play. Children still do not have full cognitive capabilities; for example, they lack conservation principles and do not recognize the reversibility of some procedures (such as pouring liquids back and forth).

The third stage of Piaget's theory is the concrete operational stage. It is only at this stage that children truly begin to think, said Piaget, because it is the first time youngsters can be truly logical and contemplate concepts (do mental "operations") in their heads. Concrete operational children gain the notion of reversibility and conservation—that the quantity of matter remains the same, even if the shape or other appearance of it changes. They are no longer egocentric, even by Piaget's standards. However, their logical thought must involve real-world (e.g., "concrete") objects and situations—the one thing concrete operational children still lack is the ability for abstract and hypothetical thinking. This last ability is the distinctive feature of Piaget's fourth and final stage of cognitive development, formal operational thought.

Some cognitive developmental researchers disagree with Piaget's view, beginning with the notion that development occurs in stages. Development, some experts say, does not occur in so neat and tidy a fashion, nor does progression from one phase in life to the next necessarily involve only qualitative differences. Development can be more steady, continuous, and can involve quantitative changes. Piaget's stage theory suggests a rather absolute, complete, and sudden shift from one stage to the next. In addition, though Piaget's approach seems to be correct across cultures regarding the order in which children go through stages, more recent research has shown there are cultural influences on the timing of these stages. Lastly, though Piaget's work provided rich information and advancements in our understanding of children's reasoning, evidence is growing that even Piaget underestimated the abilities of children. Piaget did point out that youngsters are not passive, but rather active participants in their environment and in their learning. Interestingly, though, even Piaget did not realize just how capable children are.

Lev Vygotsky presented another view of cognitive advancement. Vygotsky's emphasis is on the importance of social experiences and social exchange in the process of learning. Parents are parents, but they are also teachers, as are others with whom the child comes in contact. Vygotsky suggested the zone of proximal development (ZPD), that there is a certain realm of things that children have not yet mastered, but can learn—if they have a little help. Tasks or understandings that are far beyond the child's current level (that are beyond the zone of proximal development), but that the child shows a readiness for, can be acquired, provided an individual who already has the skill or knowledge helps with the acquisition.

KEY TERMS

Temperament

Attachment

Imprinting

Strange Situation

Schema

Adaptation

Assimilation

Accommodation

Object permanence

Symbolic representations

Egocentrism

Animistic thinking

Irreversibility

Centration

Conservation

Formal operations

Zone of proximal development

SELF-TEST PRACTICE QUIZ

Match the following Key Terms and definitions:

1. _____ An infant's understanding that objects or people still exist even though the person or object is not visible at the moment

2. _____ Attachment behavior exhibited by an animal (typically a gosling or other fowl) where it follows the first moving object it is exposed to after birth

a. Temperament

b. Attachment

c. Assimilation

d. Imprinting

e. Strange Situation

f. Schema

g. Adaptation

h. Accommodation

i. Object permanence

j. Symbolic representations

3. _____ A laboratory method developed by Mary Ainsworth to assess the quality of attachment between mother and child

4. _____ An enduring emotional bond between parent and child; forms over time and with extended contact

5. _____ Typical personality or disposition characteristics, thought to be inborn

6. _____ Piaget's fourth and final stage of cognitive development; the individual now exhibits abstract and hypothetical thinking

7. _____ The process of adjustment, according to Piaget, where people learn ways to function more effectively in their environment

8. _____ The ability to use something else (such as a word) to stand for something, allowing for easier mental operations

9. _____ A hypothetical area, described by Vygotsky, that includes what children have not yet learned but which they can learn with some assistance

10. _____ The tendency for children, according to Piaget, to contemplate and refer to inanimate things as if they had properties of living organisms

11. _____ The understanding, most likely gained during the concrete operational period, where children grasp that quantity of matter remains the same even if its shape or arrangement has been altered

12. _____ The tendency for younger children to focus on only one aspect of an object or situation

k.   Egocentrism

l.   Animistic thinking

m.   Irreversibility

n.   Centration

o.   Zone of proximal development

p.   Conservation

q.   Formal operations

13. _____ A framework we develop,
    according to Piaget, as we
    experience the world, where we
    come to understand what an object
    or concept is, and how to
    appropriately deal with it

14. _____ According to Piaget's theory, the
    inability to understand that doing
    the same process in reverse does
    not change the substance of that
    process

15. _____ Adding information to a schema
    where the schema must be
    modified, or a new schema created,
    in order to properly categorize the
    new information

16. _____ Adding a new item to an existing
    schema; the schema as it currently
    exists is adequate

17. _____ The tendency, according to Piaget,
    for a young child to be unable to
    grasp any point of view other than
    his own

18. Regarding the effects of temperament in later childhood,
    a. temperament and later behavior are largely uncorrelated.
    b. babies with easy temperaments never have behavior problems.
    c. difficult babies are most at risk for behavior problems, but this depends in part on their environment.
    d. babies with difficult temperaments usually prove to be the most well-behaved later on.

19. If basic temperament cannot be changed,
    a. difficult and slow-to-warm-up children have a poor prognosis for future relationships.
    b. caregivers can work with children and help them find more effective adaptive strategies.
    c. children with less desirable temperaments can be sent to special schools.
    d. genetic alteration may be one solution.

20. Using the Strange Situation for evaluation, children who are unresponsive when a mother returns after an absence, and who seem little concerned when she is not with them, are classified as having a(n) _____ type of attachment.
    a. secure (Type B)
    b. insecure-avoidant (Type A)
    c. insecure-resistant (Type C)
    d. disorganized/disoriented (Type D)

21. Studies regarding the formation of attachment for children who attend full-time daycare reveal that
    a. full-time daycare children are likely to be somewhat less securely attached to their mothers than are other same-age children.
    b. full-time daycare children are likely to be much less securely attached to their mothers than are other same-age children.

    c.   full-time daycare children are most likely to show a secure attachment to the daycare center regular attendant.

    d.   there are no appreciable differences in attachment between children enrolled in full-time daycare and other same-age children.

22. Ducks, geese, and other fowl that follow the first moving object to which they are exposed after birth are exhibiting a behavior known as

    a.   imprinting.
    b.   attachment.
    c.   bonding.
    d.   follow-the-leader.

23. Based on Harlow's work, when baby monkeys had both a terry cloth-covered surrogate mother and a wire surrogate mother in the cage with them, the baby monkeys tended to spend most of their time with

    a.   "wire mama," provided she had food.
    b.   "soft mama," whether or not she had food.
    c.   "soft mama," provided she had food.
    d.   "wire mama," whether or not she had food.

24. Children whose parents use a(n) _____ parenting style are at greatest risk for later behavioral problems.

    a.   authoritative
    b.   authoritarian
    c.   permissive
    d.   indulgent

25. Regardless of culture, all families

    a.   give a prominent role, and much authority, to the maternal grandmother.
    b.   cast fathers in the role of primary provider and protector.
    c.   place a high value on warm maternal relationships.
    d.   move children from a state of relative dependency to a state of relative independence.

26. Peer group relationships are important because

    a.   young children who are not accepted by peers tend to score lower on achievement tests and often do not look forward to going to school.
    b.   children with friendships learn prosocial behaviors and tend to have higher self-esteem.
    c.   older children who are not accepted by peers show more aggressive and antisocial behavior.
    d.   all of the above

27. According to Erikson (1963), the major goal of his second stage is for the toddler to

    a.   learn that the world is a safe place.
    b.   develop a sense of competence.
    c.   develop a sense of independence.
    d.   form lasting friendships.

28. What is the major accomplishment that marks the transition to Piaget's preoperational stage?

    a.   Learning to assimilate schemas
    b.   Developing symbolic representation
    c.   Developing a sense of object permanence
    d.   Acquiring the ability to conserve

29. Which of the following is NOT a criticism that has been directed toward Piaget's theory?

    a.   He underestimated children's actual abilities.
    b.   He didn't test his theories on actual children.
    c.   Development proceeds continually, not in stages.
    d.   He didn't pay enough attention to the role of culture in cognitive development.

30. Three-year-old Madison is on the phone with her grandma. When Grandma asks if Madison had a fun day Madison nods, not realizing that Grandma can't see her. This illustrates the concept of

    a. animistic thinking.
    b. conservation.
    c. centration.
    d. egocentrism.

31. Lily understands the concept of "table," and knows that's where she sits to eat dinner and to color in her coloring book. When she goes to school, she is given a desk. She comes to understand that "desk" does not fit with her previous schema for "table," and she develops a new schema for "desk." Lily is showing evidence of the process of

    a. animistic thinking.
    b. reversibility.
    c. assimilation.
    d. accommodation.

32. Which of the following statements best describes Vygotsky's theory?

    a. Learning is a process of continually refining schemas.
    b. Children progress through a series of stages in which they must resolve specific psychosocial issues.
    c. By interacting with older children and adults, children gradually acquire the skills, values, and behaviors valued by the culture in which they live.
    d. none of the above

33. When Piaget's ideas regarding cognitive developmental stages are tested cross-culturally, we find that

    a. Piaget's work has greater relevance for collectivist cultures.
    b. Piaget's work has universal application.
    c. The order of stages may vary, depending on culture, but the timing is consistent.
    d. The timing of the appearance of stages may vary, but the order of stages is consistent.

ESSAY QUESTIONS

1. Discuss how attachments are formed between parents and children. How is early experience with attachment related to interpersonal relationships for the individual as an older child and as an adult?

2. Briefly discuss the three basic parenting styles, as identified by Baumrind, and note the differences among them. What do children tend to be like when raised with the authoritative parenting style, and why is that parenting style the most preferred?

3. Trace the process of cognitive development in children, according to Jean Piaget.

4. How is Vygotsky's approach to cognitive development different from that of Piaget?

ANSWER KEY

1. Object permanence
2. Imprinting
3. Strange Situation
4. Attachment
5. Temperament
6. Formal operations
7. Adaptation
8. Symbolic representations
9. Zone of proximal development (ZPD)
10. Animistic thinking
11. Conservation
12. Centration
13. Schema
14. Irreversibility
15. Accommodation
16. Assimilation
17. Egocentrism
18. c
19. b
20. b
21. d
22. a
23. b
24. b
25. d
26. d
27. c
28. b
29. a
30. d
31. d
32. c
33. d

SAMPLE ANSWERS TO ESSAY QUESTIONS

1.   According to research by Ainsworth and others, attachment is a process that occurs over an extended period of time (from birth on) and is most linked to the behavior and responsiveness of the mother. Attachment is not the same as bonding; bonding is the parent-to-infant connection established in the hours shortly after birth. Attachment is the result of many, many hours, days, and months of contact between the baby and the parent. The parent who is consistently available to the infant, discerns the infant's needs and cues accurately, and responds promptly and appropriately encourages the establishment of a secure attachment with her baby.

     Based on Ainsworth's research utilizing the Strange Situation, about two-thirds of all children show signs of a secure attachment by the end of their first year. Securely attached children seek their parent's presence, feel comfortable leaving the parent for a brief period of time in order to explore or play, and clearly rely on the parent as an emotional base. A secure attachment not only provides a baby with emotional stability, which includes a sense of freedom and opportunity to explore and learn more about his environment, but it has consequences for later childhood and adulthood as well. Securely attached children show better psychological adjustment, higher self-esteem, and more effective social relationships. In adulthood, the type of childhood attachment is related to later emotional relationships. It appears that the emotional pattern established in childhood leads to behaviors and expectations regarding what adult relationships should be like.

2.   In the authoritative parenting style, parents are consistent, warm and loving; this is combined with clear rules and expectations that are carefully explained and modeled in the adults' behavior. Parents retain their authority in the home but treat their children with respect and regard. In the authoritarian parenting style, parents are rigid, inflexible, and emphasize obedience and punishment. The child's point of view (and usually the child's feelings) is not considered. The atmosphere is one of "might makes right." In the permissive parenting style, parents usually have abdicated their authority and their responsibility to parent, and do not get involved with regard to establishing and enforcing reasonable rules and boundaries. They may or may not show affection to the child, but the child is otherwise left free to determine whatever behaviors he or she will engage in. Offspring raised with the authoritative parenting style have the greatest likelihood for success in all avenues of their lives. They are emotionally secure enough to feel confident venturing into new things since they feel loved and accepted unconditionally. They are well-adjusted and have mastered effective prosocial skills. Because emotional relationships are stable and not draining, these individuals have the energy and confidence to apply the best of their abilities to the task at hand. Thus, the authoritative parenting style is the most preferred.

3.   Piaget believes that children's cognitive development begins with simple reflexes. His first stage of development is the sensorimotor stage, where children are basically nonverbal, and are involved in much physical interaction with their environment. Children utilize their motor abilities and experience the consequences of their actions by means of their sensory system. In this way, children begin to put together a picture of this world. Much of this picture, according to Piaget, involves the development of schemas. Our earliest schemas are quite simple. As we experience the world more, we add to our schemas (an understanding of what an object or concept is and how to interact with it), either through assimilation, where a new item fits well into an existing schema, or accommodation, where the new item really does not fit and the schema must be modified or a new schema must be created. Piaget's second stage for a child's cognitive development is the preoperational stage. This covers ages two to seven, and the most important advancement during this stage is the child's acquisition of symbol systems (language being preeminent). According to Piaget, the child is still egocentric; that is, he is still unable to perceive anyone else's view other than his own. A preoperational child also has not yet mastered conservation principles. The preoperational child believes that, if the appearance of something has changed (for example, a ball of clay is rolled out into a long, thin piece), then the quantity has changed also—even when in fact

it has not (in the example above, it is the same amount of clay, but a preoperational child will perceive the longer piece as "more"). During the concrete operational period (ages seven to eleven years), children do gain these concepts, and are able, according to Piaget, to think logically for the first time. It is not until Piaget's last stage of cognitive development, the formal operations stage, that he believes children can think deductively and grasp abstract and hypothetical notions. Piaget was a stage theorist; that is, he believed cognitive development occurred in distinct stages, and the child's abilities in one stage were qualitatively different from abilities in another stage.

4. Perhaps Piaget did not realize it, but he conceived of children's cognitive development more or less devoid of surrounding situational input. His theory of cognitive development presents the changes that occur in children's thinking as stages, rather regular and universal, regardless of social and cultural influences on the child. It is important to note that Piaget did recognize the child as an active participant in his or her environment, and he greatly advanced our understanding of children's cognitive growth. However, cross-cultural studies have indicated, for example, that there is variation as to when cognitive developmental stages occur, depending upon the cultural environment. Lev Vygotsky, in contrast to Piaget, heavily emphasized the social and cultural context in which a child's learning occurs. Vygotsky stressed the role of adults as teachers. Instead of children's learning unfolding automatically, Vygotsky noted that much of what a child learns is due to a parent's (or other skilled individuals) willingness to teach this information. Children could not learn this information on their own, but it is within their grasp if they have some assistance from an older individual who already has this knowledge. Thus, Vygotsky is pointing out a vital role for people around the child as he or she learns. This is a component Piaget did not really give recognition to.

MODULE 9.4 ADOLESCENCE

LEARNING OBJECTIVES

After you have mastered the information in this unit, you will be able to:

1. Define adolescence and describe puberty.

2. Explain the changes in cognitive development that occur during adolescence.

3. Describe Kohlberg's levels of moral reasoning.

4. Discuss criticisms of, and an alternative to, Kohlberg's theory.

5. Discuss psychosocial development during adolescence.

OUTLINE

I.   Background Factors in Adolescent Development – link between childhood and adulthood
    A.   Adolescent changing physically (children in adult bodies), intellectually
    B.   Conflicts arise with parents
    C.   Children still or kept dependent – financially and often emotionally upon parents
    D.   Adolescence—storm and stress?
II. Physical Development
    A.   Adolescent growth spurt
    B.   Puberty—reaching full sexual maturity
        1.   Secondary sex characteristics (include pubic hair, voice changes)
        2.   Primary sex characteristics—directly involved in reproduction
        3.   Menarche—onset of menstruation in females
        4.   Timing of puberty seems to have social consequences for both boys and girls
III. Cognitive Development

A.   Piaget's formal operational stage—abstract, hypothetical thinking possible
B.   Adolescent egocentrism
   1.   Imaginary audience—adolescents believe others are keenly interested in themselves and their concerns
   2.   Personal fable—exaggerated sense of own uniqueness and invulnerability (e.g., this could never happen to me or I am the only one with whom this happens)
C.   Cognitive developments change way adolescents see the world

IV.   Kohlberg's Theory of Moral Development
A.   Methodology—present participants with vignettes; ask why behavior seen as right or wrong
B.   Levels of moral reasoning (based on these responses)
   1.   Preconventional—only concerned with consequences
     a)   Stage 1: obedience and punishment
     b)   Stage 2: instrumental purpose – a behavior is judged good when it serves the person's needs or interests
   2.   Conventional—conformity with rules as they currently exist – a right or wrong
     a)   Stage 3: "good boy-good girl"
     b)   Stage 4: authority or law-and-order
   3.   Postconventional
     a)   Not everyone reaches
     b)   Applying one's own moral principles
     c)   Stage 5: social contract – laws based on mutual agreement of a society but no infallible
     d)   Stage 6: universal ethical principles – guided by own internal moral compass
C.   Note: moral reasoning not necessarily related to moral behavior – seems to have some degree of overlap
D.   Evaluation of Kohlberg's model
   1.   Children do tend to follow these stages, and there is evidence for universality of findings
   2.   May not reflect how people make moral decisions in everyday lives
   3.   Criticism: morality associated with western, and male, values
   4.   Carol Gilligan's research (some evidence for these views)
     a)   Females have a care orientation
     b)   Males have a justice orientation

V.   Psychosocial Development
A.   Adolescent-parent relationships
   1.   Children need to pull away somewhat in order to become independent
   2.   Close ties, secure emotional base with parents still crucial
   3.   Distance part of teen's effort to discover own individual identity
   4.   Adolescents tend to mimic parent's health-related behavior – such as smoking
B.   Erikson's view of adolescence
   1.   Answering "Who am I?"
   2.   Psychosocial challenge of adolescence (5th stage) is ego identity vs. role diffusion
   3.   Ego identity—clear, stable sense of self
   4.   Role diffusion—uncertainty regarding identity, lack of sense of direction; may be especially vulnerable to negative peer influences such as drugs
C.   Identity crisis—represents intense self-examination, need for knowing self
D.   Peer relationships
   1.   Become increasingly important
   2.   Parental closeness can ameliorate undesirable peer influences
   3.   Adolescent sexuality – more than just "hormones with feet"
     a)   Peer pressure can promote or restrain

      b)   Other factors related to sexual restraint
          (1)   Living in intact family, low levels of conflict
          (2)   Higher education levels for parents
          (3)   Importance placed on religion, attending services
          (4)   Less exposure to sexual content in music, movies, TV and magazines
      c)   Average age of first intercourse declined and attitudes toward premarital sex more lenient (Wells & Twenge, 2005)
      d)   Teen birth actually declined from its peak in early 1990's but beginning to edge upward (Hamilton, Martin & Ventura 2009; NCHS, 2008)
          (1)   Some mothers become pregnant to fill an emotional void or rebel against their families – most are the result from failure to use contraceptives
          (2)   Unwed mothers live below poverty level, quit school and depend on public assistance (Arnett, 2004) – fathers usually are absent or incapable of child's support
      e)   Several million teens contact sexually transmitted diseases or infections each year
      f)   Experimenting with other forms of sexual contact including oral and anal sex
      g)   Many gay adolescents face the challenge of coming to terms with their sexuality against social condemnation and discrimination in the broader culture (Meyer, 2003)

SUMMARY

In this module, you learn about the physical, cognitive, social, and emotional growth of the teenager. Adolescence has long been considered a time of turbulence and stress, and, although not every teen has this experience, there is probably good reason for that view. Very many changes face adolescents. They vacillate for various reasons between being a child and being an adult. The body of an adolescent undergoes many changes, preparing for adult reproductive capabilities. This transition stage leading to full sexual maturity is known as puberty. Females particularly are starting puberty earlier, and menarche (the onset of menstruation) is several years ahead of a century ago.

Cognitively, teenagers may be, but are not necessarily, in Piaget's last stage of cognitive development, formal operational. An adolescent at this level can reason abstractly and can speculate about things that do not and even cannot exist. Though teenagers have moved out of childhood egocentrism, they show signs of an adolescent egocentrism. David Elkind (1985) proposed the notion of the imaginary audience—the teen's idea that everyone is looking at her or him and is exceedingly interested in her or his concerns. Elkind has also proposed that during adolescence a teen develops a personal fable. This is an exaggerated sense of uniqueness on the part of the teen and a sense of invulnerability. The cognitive changes during adolescence, taken together, do lead a teen to consider world issues, intellectual controversies, personal relationships, and the like, differently than in the past.

Moral values also become a particular focus during the teenage years. How might we assess an individual for type of moral reasoning? A methodology was developed by Lawrence Kohlberg, in which brief stories are presented to the listener, who is then asked about behavior that occurred in the story. A classic story involves Heinz, his wife who is dying of cancer, and a drug store owner. The individual is asked whether the behavior was right or wrong, and then the question of greatest interest to Kohlberg—why? Why was the behavior seen as the right thing to do, or not? Responses to this last question are classified as indicating a level of moral reasoning. Individuals who are just concerned with the end result of the behavior (would Heinz get in trouble?) are classified as preconventional reasoners. People who are concerned with rules and regulations as they currently exist are said to be reasoning at the conventional level, and individuals who apply their own, personally developed set of principles (which may transcend existing law and order) are classified as postconventional reasoners. Carol Gilligan has challenged Kohlberg's interpretations, noting that differences in the classification of female respondents may well be due to women's care orientation, rather than the justice orientation that may be more typical of males. It should be noted that, though we have developed several ways of evaluating moral reasoning, the ability to reason about the moral components of an issue does not necessarily result in corresponding evidence of moral behavior.

As adolescents naturally move away from the dependency of childhood, they become more and more concerned with knowing who they are as a distinct individual. Peers become of increasing importance as the child grows older. Though not always evident, parents remain a very important influence and source of support for teenage offspring. A stable family life and wisely run home help teens make the transition to adulthood more smoothly. Erik Erikson proposed that the most overriding challenge of the teenage years is exploring and attempting to determine one's identity. The choice during adolescence, according to Erikson, is between ego identity and role diffusion. An identity crisis (stressful soul-searching) may well be a part of the psychosocial maturation process at this time. The teen needs to establish his or her identity in terms of morals and principles, career goals, as a social and community member, and the like. An individual with a firm identity, according to Erikson, knows who she or he is, where she is headed; that sense of self and direction does not waiver a great deal. The teen caught in role diffusion does not have a focus and may seem to drift. She or he does not have a plan and is confused about who she or he is. Though identities in various realms can be established, likely they will be revisited at later points during life. Our sense of who we are can change with increasing opportunities, experience, and life events.

KEY TERMS

Adolescence

Puberty

Secondary sex characteristics

Primary sex characteristics

Menarche

Imaginary audience

Personal fable

Ego identity

Identity crisis

Role diffusion

SELF-TEST PRACTICE QUIZ

Match the following Key Terms and definitions:

1. _____ Sexual characteristics emerging during adolescence that are not directly related to reproduction

2. _____ A term created by Erikson to describe the discomfort of not having a clear sense of identity and the stress involved in the effort to establish that identity

a.   Adolescence

b.   Puberty

c.   Secondary sex characteristics

d.   Primary sex characteristics

e.   Menarche

f.   Imaginary audience

g.   Personal fable

h.   Ego identity

3. _____ A belief among adolescents that their life and experiences are incredibly unique

i.   Identity crisis

j.   Role diffusion

4. _____ The period in life that spans moving out of childhood and into full adulthood

5. _____ The preferred outcome for the challenge facing adolescents, according to psychosocial theory

6. _____ Sexual characteristics developing during adolescence that are directly related to reproduction

7. _____ The less desired outcome of the adolescent psychosexual stage—a lack of clear understanding regarding oneself, and a lack of sense of direction

8. _____ A stage of physical, sexual development occurring during adolescence, when one reaches the level of becoming capable of reproduction

9. _____ The onset of the menstrual cycle

10. _____ The feeling adolescents have that everyone is watching them and is quite interested in their concerns

11. Although teenagers necessarily are moving away from the dependency of childhood and towards establishing their own identity, parents

   a.   remain an important influence on the child.
   b.   are likely to experience more conflicts with their teenage offspring.
   c.   can help adolescents resist unfavorable peer pressure by providing warmth and structure.
   d.   all of the above are correct.

12. Which of the following is a primary sex characteristic?

   a.   A boy beginning to produce sperm
   b.   A girl growing breasts
   c.   The development of pubic hair
   d.   A boy's voice deepening

13. Earlier physical development seems to be related to greater _____ in males, though this is not usually the case with females.

   a.   intelligence
   b.   self-esteem
   c.   emotional maturity
   d.   leadership qualities

14. According to Piaget, the ability to _____ differentiates the stage of formal operations from earlier stages.

    a. conserve
    b. make sophisticated moral judgments
    c. reproduce
    d. think logically and abstractly

15. Many sexually active teenagers do not use condoms because they are convinced that they are somehow immune to the risk of pregnancy or infection. This illustrates the concept of

    a. the imaginary audience.
    b. the personal fable.
    c. the zone of proximal development.
    d. postconventional reasoning.

16. When asked why it's wrong to hit his brother, Tyler answers "because I could get in trouble." Tyler would be classified as exhibiting a(n) _____ level of moral reasoning, according to Kohlberg.

    a. preconventional
    b. conventional
    c. postconventional
    d. unconstitutional

17. A criticism of Kohlberg's research on moral reasoning is that

    a. stages are portrayed that most individuals actually do not go through.
    b. cross-cultural studies do not support his conclusions.
    c. values associated with higher levels of moral reasoning reflect male, Western standards.
    d. the approach shows severe and systematic bias against women.

18. The psychosocial challenge facing teenagers, according to Erikson, is that of

    a. trust vs. mistrust.
    b. autonomy vs. shame and doubt.
    c. identity vs. role diffusion.
    d. intimacy vs. isolation.

ESSAY QUESTIONS

1. Discuss the concept of identity formation during adolescence. Why is this psychosocial issue not related only to adolescent development?

2. How is moral development studied, and what are some basic findings? Explain Gilligan's perspective relative to the research by Kohlberg.

ANSWER KEY

1. Secondary sex characteristics
2. Identity crisis
3. Personal fable
4. Adolescence
5. Ego identity
6. Primary sex characteristics
7. Role diffusion
8. Puberty
9. Menarche
10. Imaginary audience
11. d
12. a
13. b
14. d
15. b
16. a
17. c
18. c

SAMPLE ANSWERS TO ESSAY QUESTIONS

1. The major issue for adolescents, according to the psychosocial theorist Erik Erikson, is ego identity, as opposed to role confusion (no established identity). Most experts on adolescence believe that the teenage years may be particularly stressful. Teens are moving into their own sense of self, and perhaps realize they cannot depend upon their parents for everything the way they may have done as younger children. Teens may experience an identity crisis—a rather difficult time when one is searching hard for that sense of identity. Erikson believed identity needed to be established in various arenas in life (occupation, sexual identity, social identity, and the like). The task usually is not easy, and parental love and support remains very important. If an identity is not eventually established, however, the teenager drifts in role confusion. This is with no sense of self and no sense of direction. The establishment of an identity is not limited just to adolescence, however, as these same issues of determining who we are arise at later times periodically through life.

2. Moral development was studied at length by the researcher Lawrence Kohlberg; he told vignettes to children and then asked the children about the behaviors of various characters in the story. Kohlberg's theory incorporates six stages, divided into three levels of reasoning. The preconventional reasoner is mostly just concerned with himself or herself—looking good or avoiding punishment. The conventional reasoner goes along with the crowd, adhering to rules and laws as they currently exist—whether or not these rules are truly fair are not a topic of consideration. Only the post conventional reasoner steps back and evaluates existing regulations. This individual guides his or her life by a thoughtfully created personal set of moral beliefs and

values. Gilligan objected to Kohlberg's research findings, which put males in a more favorable light as exhibiting more moral behavior. Gilligan made the point, which has been supported, that the questions in Kohlberg's research were not phrased in ways that assessed moral behavior as females see it. Gilligan has expanded upon moral investigation and helped include a female perspective (that moral behavior is related to behaviors of care).

MODULE 9.5 EARLY AND MIDDLE ADULTHOOD

LEARNING OBJECTIVES

After you have mastered the information in this unit, you will be able to:

1. Describe the physical and cognitive changes that take place as people age.

2. Discuss social and personality development during early and middle adulthood.

OUTLINE

I. Early and Middle Adulthood
    A. Human development is a lifelong process
    B. Early adulthood encompasses age range of twenties and thirties
    C. Middle adulthood encompasses age range of forty to sixty-five
II. Cognitive and Physical Development
    A. Both peak in early adulthood
    B. In twenties best learning, memory, muscle strength, sensory acuteness, reaction time, cardiovascular fitness, intelligence test scores
    C. Declines occur in fluid intelligence (mental flexibility) – solve problems quickly, remember newly acquired information
    D. Crystallized intelligence (accumulated knowledge and experiences) is stable or may improve
    E. Some memory loss but not appreciable; may be offset by overall knowledge gains
    F. Physical issues
        1. Start of loss of muscle tissue, muscle strength
        2. Exercise helps retain strength, avoid weight gain
        3. Menopause—cessation of menstruation, reproductive capability in women
            a) Sex drive fueled by androgens, not estrogen
            b) Woman's psychological attitude is most important determinant to adjustment
        4. Males—retain fertility, gradual decline in testosterone
III. Psychosocial Development
    A. Emerging adulthood—twenties almost like extended adolescence
    B. Erikson's stage for early adulthood: intimacy vs. isolation
        1. Intimacy—forming very close emotional relationships (e.g., with agemates)
        2. Isolation—fear, lack of personal stability precludes intimacy, results in loneliness
        3. Ability to establish intimate relationships related to earlier formation of identity
    C. Erikson's stage for middle adulthood: generativity vs. stagnation
        1. Generativity—fostering the well-being of next generation
        2. Stagnation—continued self-absorption; inability to move ahead with psychosocial issues and development
    D. Midlife crisis
        1. Concern that options in life are disappearing and life is starting to slip away
        2. True crisis more the exception than the rule
        3. Many believe middle adulthood is time of new opportunities, perspectives
        4. May be period of greatest productivity – decades or promise rather than decline

SUMMARY

In this module, you learn about changes and issues facing young and middle-age adults. Human development is life long, and there still are many opportunities for growth and productivity across the life span. Physical and cognitive abilities tend to peak in the young adult years. Young adults typically experience their greatest levels of strength, agility, and cardiovascular health. Young adults tend to perform best on IQ-type tests, and show the greatest ability for memory, learning new skills, and sensory acuteness. Middle-age adults usually show the beginnings of some memory loss. By the middle adult years, both men and women begin to lose muscle tissue, and experience an accompanying loss of muscle strength. More lean tissue turns to fat, although substantial weight gain is not at all necessarily a part of growing older. Women experience a more dramatic physical change, and that is menopause, the cessation of the menstrual cycle and loss of ability to bear children. Menopause is more psychologically than physically related to sexual desire, however. A healthy diet and regular exercise can help adults retain muscle strength and avoid weight gain.

There are psychosocial issues that relate to the young and middle adult years of development as well. Erikson believed the most important challenge for the young adult was the establishment of intimate relationships. Erikson believed that the more effective the preceding psychosocial stage (where the formation of a stable identity is paramount), the greater the likelihood for a successful emotional relationship in young adulthood. Isolation is the consequence when a young adult is unable or unwilling to establish an intimate relationship. For the middle-age adult, the psychosocial issue is generativity vs. stagnation. Generativity refers to promoting the well-being of the next generation—bringing children into the world and raising them effectively, and/or helping with the development and environment of children elsewhere. The individual trapped in the outcome of stagnation remains concerned with his or her own issues only.

Erikson proposed that each stage of life offers us more opportunities for growth and development. It is true that at midlife there tends to be an assessing of achievement and an overall evaluation of one's life. The true midlife crisis may be an exception rather than the rule; many middle-aged adults see the rest of their lives as a time of promise.

KEY TERMS

Fluid intelligence

Crystallized intelligence

Menopause

Emerging adulthood

Midlife crisis

SELF-TEST PRACTICE QUIZ

Match the following Key Terms and definitions:

1. _____ The term, as coined by Arnett, characterizing the time of transition from about the ages of 18 to 25 years

2. _____ Concerns that tend to occur during the middle adulthood years, regarding potential loss of abilities and recognition that life and the future have a finite end point

a. Fluid intelligence

b. Crystallized intelligence

c. Menopause

d. Emerging adulthood

e. Midlife crisis

3. _____ A form of intelligence that tends to remain stable, or even improve, during the middle adulthood years

4. _____ The cessation of the menstrual cycle in a female

5. _____ Mental flexibility, including the ability to retain new information and detect patterns, solve problems quickly

6. Which statement about middle adulthood is most accurate?

   a. Most adults experience an emotional crisis during this stage of life.
   b. It is always accompanied by muscle loss and weight gain.
   c. According to Erikson, this is the stage of intimacy vs. isolation.
   d. According to Levinson, adults in this stage experience a transition as they compare their accomplishments to their earlier dreams and goals.

7. The type of intelligence involving accumulated knowledge and the ability to apply it

   a. deteriorates after peaking in young adulthood.
   b. is known as crystallized, rather than fluid, intelligence.
   c. is not involved in social or occupational functioning.
   d. all of the above.

8. The experience of menopause

   a. results in the cessation of estrogen production.
   b. is mostly related to how a woman thinks about it.
   c. involves the loss of the female sexual drive.
   d. tends to cause lasting emotional and psychological difficulties.

9. According to Erikson, the psychosocial challenge facing individuals in the young adult years is

   a. leaving a legacy for future generations.
   b. forming a sense of personal identity.
   c. forming lasting intimate relationships.
   d. all of the above.

10. According to Erikson, the successful mastering of adulthood issues is related to

   a. outcomes of preceding stages of development.
   b. levels of academic achievement obtained by the individual.
   c. early childhood attachment patterns.
   d. levels of career success obtained by the individual or his life partner.

11. As men age, they

   a. lose reproductive ability and sex drive similar to that experienced by women.
   b. experience a gradual decrease in testosterone, while retaining ability to reproduce.
   c. are more likely than women to experience a midlife crisis.
   d. become more and more despondent regarding future life choices.

12. Which statement best describes the typical pattern of cognitive changes in young and middle adulthood?

   a. Both crystallized and fluid intelligence increase.
   b. Both crystallized and fluid intelligence decrease.
   c. Fluid intelligence tends to decline, while crystallized intelligence stays the same or increases.
   d. Crystallized intelligence tends to decline, while fluid intelligence stays the same or increases.

13. Muscle loss and weight gain in middle adulthood
     a.   is inevitable.
     b.   is common, but can be prevented through healthy diet and weight-bearing exercise.
     c.   is common in men, but not women.
     d.   is common in women, but not men.

ESSAY QUESTIONS

1.   Are physical and cognitive losses inevitable as one ages? Discuss and cite examples to support your response.

2.   Discuss Erikson's concept regarding psychosocial development in middle adulthood.

ANSWER KEY

1.   Emerging adulthood

2.   Midlife crisis

3.   Crystallized intelligence

4.   Menopause

5.   Fluid intelligence

6.   d

7.   b

8.   b

9.   c

10. a

11. b

12. c

13. b

SAMPLE ANSWERS TO ESSAY QUESTIONS

1.   Physical and cognitive losses are not inevitable as one gets older. The key to maintaining physical and cognitive strengths is adhering to a healthy diet and participating in physical (and mental!) exercise. Physical and cognitive prowess peaks in the young adulthood years, after which there is a tendency for these attributes to decline. Muscle tissue tends to diminish, and the body can develop an increasing store of fat tissue. Though cumulative intelligence, such as vocabulary and knowledge gained from experience with the world, may remain at young-adult levels or even improve, mental agility overall tends to decline. There is a greater difficulty with tasks involving memory and with the learning of new and unfamiliar skills.

Physical ability can be maintained and enhanced, however, by engaging in strength-training exercises, such as appropriate lifting of weights. Other regular exercise is helpful as well. Gaining weight or becoming overweight are not automatic consequences of aging. While menopause in women is unavoidable, how a woman thinks about the experience seems to have the greatest impact as to what extent she is affected. Cognitive activity helps maintain mental agility, and even unavoidable losses in mental quickness may be offset by greater life experience and accumulated knowledge. Also, cognitive changes in the middle-adult years do not necessarily intrude on one's ability to function effectively in social and occupational realms. It is entirely possible that one's middle years are the most productive and satisfying yet.

2. The psychosocial issue facing adults in their middle years, according to Erikson, is whether an individual experiences the quality of generativity or the individual is caught up in stagnation. As with all of Erikson's stages, the outcome of the previous stage is a factor in the path of life that results in the subsequent stage. Thus, a good sense of identity (from adolescence and beyond) and the establishment of solid and supportive intimate relationships help prepare the adult in middle years for a life of generativity. Generativity is the desire to help the next generation, whether they are our children or others of younger generations with whom we come in contact. This psychological "giving," so to speak, is generally its own reward. Middle-aged adults who still do not have a sense of themselves, of who they are and where they are going, and who do not experience the psychological support of a loving, intimate relationship tend to have nothing to "give" (the generativity experience) and remain instead still trapped in stagnation. Development does not really go further because the individual does not have a firm psychological foundation and remains predominately absorbed with himself or herself.

MODULE 9.6 LATE ADULTHOOD

LEARNING OBJECTIVES

After you have mastered the information in this unit, you will be able to:

1. Describe the physical and cognitive changes that occur in late adulthood.

2. Explain psychosocial challenges of late adulthood.

3. Describe the qualities associated with successful aging.

4. Discuss the stages of dying as identified by Kübler-Ross.

OUTLINE

I.   Over 65—the Fastest Growing Segment of the Population
     A. Life expectancy is continuing to increase
     B. About one in eight American (12.5%) is age 65 or older, a percentage that is expected to climb to 20% by the year 2030 (Viteriello, 2009)
     C. Psychological adjustment and well-being most related to physical health
     D. For healthy older adults, age 65 mostly an extension of middle age
II. Physical and Cognitive Development
     A. Physical Abilities
         1. Continuing gradual decline in general sensory and motor abilities
         2. Losses in bone density, muscle mass, skin elasticity
         3. Night vision less acute, reaction time slower
         4. Immune system not quite as effective as younger years; increases susceptibility to minor and major illnesses
     B. Cognitive Development
         1. Performance on tasks requiring fluid intelligence tends to decline
             a) Age-related declines in memory are generally not at a level significant enough to impair daily functioning
             b) Our fund of information and knowledge actually increases across much of life span and only begins to decline around the advance age of 90 (Park et al., 2002; Singer et al., 2003)

       c) Preserved intellectual ability in later life is associated with such factors as general physical health, engagement in stimulating activities and openness to new experiences (Schaie, 1996)

   2. Older individuals need more time to solve problems, grasp new information

   3. Increasing difficulty with memory tasks, pattern recognition, reaction time

   4. Bulk of mental abilities are usually retained throughout life

   5. Crystallized intelligence (a store of knowledge gained from experience)

       a) Tends to remain intact till very old ages

       b) Overall knowledge store increases across most of the lifespan

       c) Preserving cognitive ability correlated with physical health, stimulating activities, and openness to new experiences

C. Dementia

   1. Not a normal consequence of aging

   2. Damages, destroys brain tissue involved in memory, other high-function mental tasks

D. Alzheimer's disease

   1. Irreversible brain disease leading to inevitable mental functioning deterioration

   2. Genetic factors may be implicated in this progressive death of brain cells

   3. Individuals lose memory, ability to care for selves, coherent speech

   4. No cure, but drugs may help boost memory functioning

   5. One in 10 over age 65; one in two over age 85 suffer from Alzheimer's

III. Psychosocial Development

  A. Psychosocial theories of late adulthood

   1. Erikson's stage for older adulthood: ego integrity versus despair

       a) Important issue is maintaining a sense of meaning

       b) Possible to remain satisfied and fulfilled throughout life

   2. Views of Daniel Levinson

       a) Recognized need is to accept physical and psychological realities

       b) Older adult can rediscover self, engage in meaningful activities that maintain connections with family, friends, and new friendships

   3. Most adults in 70s satisfied with lives

   4. Keys associated with more successful aging

       a) Maximize use of one's time and resources

       b) Maintain optimistic outlook

       c) Seek new challenges; do more of what matters

IV. Death and Dying

  A. Death in fact can occur at any age

  B. Though young, we may be severely affected by death of others (e.g., loved ones)

  C. Kübler-Ross's stages of dying

   1. Denial—refuse to believe

   2. Anger—resentment towards physician, others not in same predicament

   3. Bargaining—attempting to make a deal with God

   4. Depression—hopelessness in face of reality of situation

   5. Final acceptance—end result is inevitable, retain dignity and peace

  D. Many people pass through these stages, but not all, and not always in this order

SUMMARY

In this module, you learn of the many changes and challenges facing the older adult. Aging adults usually are aware of their decreasing ability with regard to their physical and cognitive attributes. These physical and cognitive challenges mean psychological issues come to the fore as well. The older adult must find a way to accept the physical and cognitive changes, while maintaining an optimistic outlook and continuing to find meaning in life. As individuals get older, too, they tend to experience the death and loss of loved ones. The loss of close friends and family members not only reminds the aging adult of his or her advancing years, but also removes sources of social and emotional support which would help the older adult cope with the many life changes that have to be faced. Still, exercise and healthy eating help older adults retain their abilities. One may be getting older, but there are lots more people one can get older with! The over-65 population is the fastest growing segment in the United States.

The older adult faces very many physical and cognitive changes, including increasing loss of muscle tissue, sensory capabilities, and cognitive agility. Still, older people often can function well as far as managing their own daily lives. Many tasks still can be accomplished, especially if the older adult has a bit more time to grasp the situation, to process information, or to react. Most of the challenges faced by the older individual involve crystallized intelligence, dealing with matters with which the individual is already familiar and experienced. As mentioned previously, accumulated knowledge and expertise may actually improve intellectual functioning in these areas as an individual grows older. Keys to retaining abilities are optimism, making use of what one has, and continuing to seek new experiences.

Some memory difficulty and loss are expected in older adults, but basic mental functioning normally remains intact throughout life. The exception is the development of dementia, the leading cause of which is Alzheimer's disease. This disease is characterized by increasing losses in the most basic mental processes, where the victim may no longer recognize family members or be able to care effectively for himself or herself. Because the numbers of older Americans are increasing, the incidence of Alzheimer's is increasing as well.

Psychosocial researchers agree that the issue for individuals in late adulthood is managing the physical and cognitive limitations while continuing to find meaning and purpose in life. Erikson characterized the challenge as one of ego integrity vs. despair. Despite the many challenges faced by the older adult, most individuals in their seventies report being satisfied with their lives. Successful aging involves maintaining a positive outlook, making the most of opportunities where one can compensate for possible deficiencies, and seeking challenges where one can continue to be fulfilled and grow. It is probably best, however, if death is recognized as inevitable and plans possibly made for it. Elisabeth Kübler-Ross (1969) delineated five stages that individuals facing death are likely to go through, beginning with denial and ending with a final resignation and acceptance.

KEY TERMS

Dementia

Alzheimer's Disease

SELF-TEST PRACTICE QUIZ

Match the following Key Terms and definitions:

1. _____ An irreversible brain disease with a gradual onset and a slow but progressive course toward inevitable deterioration of mental functioning

2. _____ A brain disorder where there are substantial losses in mental functioning due to injury or disease; may be accompanied by personality changes

a.   Dementia

b.   Alzheimer's Disease

3. By the year 2050, the expected proportion of Americans in the 65 and older bracket is
    a. 10%.
    b. 15%.
    c. 20%.
    d. 25%.

4. Which of the following is NOT a typical cognitive loss as an adult ages?
    a. Memory for new information
    b. Pattern recognition
    c. Vocabulary skills
    d. Processing speed

5. One area of cognitive functioning that remains stable or even improves in older adult years is
    a. problem solving.
    b. tracking the current topic of conversation.
    c. knowledge related to our career or specialization.
    d. reaction time.

6. Our store of knowledge and information from life experience _____ as we age.
    a. declines substantially
    b. declines modestly
    c. remains essentially the same
    d. increases

7. Factors associated with preserving mental abilities include
    a. overall physical health.
    b. openness to new experiences.
    c. remaining engaged in life and in meaningful, stimulating activities.
    d. all of the above.

8. The leading cause of dementia is
    a. losses due to the normal aging process.
    b. Alzheimer's disease.
    c. lack of appropriate nutrition and mental stimulation.
    d. delay in obtaining corrective surgery as soon as cognitive problems begin.

9. The psychosocial challenge for individuals in late adulthood, according to Erikson, is
    a. industry vs. inferiority.
    b. intimacy vs. isolation.
    c. ego integrity vs. despair.
    d. ego identity vs. role diffusion.

10. The psychosocial focus for older adults, according to Levinson, involves
    a. rediscovering oneself, and continuing with meaningful activities and emotional contacts.
    b. becoming involved in activities that increase the well-being of future generations.
    c. accomplishing tasks of aging, such as managing retirement, and adjusting to physical changes.
    d. recognizing that death is inevitable, and planning accordingly.

11. Which of the following is NOT a factor that has been found to be associated with more successful aging?
    a. Increasing income level
    b. Extent of contact with friends and family members
    c. Learning compensating strategies to retain maximum enjoyment in life
    d. Becoming involved with new goals or projects

12. In the stages of dying, as proposed by Elisabeth Kübler-Ross, the first stage is
    a. bargaining.
    b. depression.
    c. anger.
    d. denial.
13. Alzheimer's disease involves
    a. the development of multiple genetic mutations.
    b. the death of brain cells.
    c. the loss of the frontal lobe of the brain.
    d. all of the above.
14. Which of the following is a potential cause of dementia?
    a. Brain damage
    b. Stroke
    c. Alcoholism
    d. All of the above

ESSAY QUESTIONS

1. Discuss how Erikson and Levinson characterize the psychosocial tasks of the older adult.

2. What, based on the research we have so far, are some ways an older adult can maintain and preserve cognitive functioning?

ANSWER KEY

1. Alzheimer's Disease

2. Dementia

3. c

4. c

5. c

6. d

7. d

8. b

9. c

10. a

11. a

12. d

13. b

14. d

SAMPLE ANSWERS TO ESSAY QUESTIONS

1. As in previous stages of human development, Erikson and Levinson recognize there are challenges and changes that face the aging adult. The important task is to preserve one's abilities to the best extent one can and continue to find meaning and purpose in life, even though physical and cognitive losses are undeniable. Erikson characterizes the psychosocial challenge at this stage as a course of ego integrity versus despair. Despair results if we do not feel we have accomplished

what we wanted to in life; time now grows short and our physical and cognitive abilities grow relatively less and less. However, the individual who has lived life fully and feels satisfied with experiences and choices is likely to develop a sense of ego integrity. That person is comfortable with who he or she is, and has taken healthy advantage of all life has to offer. An optimistic attitude is very helpful and is correlated with greater health and longer life. Healthy older individuals do not view later years as simply a time of loss and decline. For many, it remains a time of opportunity, with yet more things to learn and new ways to grow. Levinson does point out that the older adult needs to recognize and accept increasing physical and cognitive limitations. However, he suggests that older adulthood (as at any other time in our lives) is an opportunity to rediscover who we are. Always, we need to find ways to make life meaningful, stay mentally and physically involved with life, and do those things that matter most to us.

2.   Some loss of cognitive functioning as we age cannot be avoided. Skills related to fluid intelligence are the ones most likely to be affected by aging. Older adults can take steps to help maintain and preserve cognitive functioning, however. For tasks involving fluid intelligence, it is not that older adults cannot do these tasks; rather, they simply need a bit more time—to be exposed to information (it may take an extra repetition or two), to grasp and process information, and to carry out their response. Thus, older adults can expect satisfactory cognitive functioning if they try to stick to matters that involve crystallized intelligence and seek opportunities where they will be provided with extra time if they need to call upon fluid intelligence skills in order to successfully complete a task.

Higher levels of cognitive functioning in later years have been associated with general physical health, involvement in stimulating activities, and openness to new experiences. General physical health is somewhat in response to what we do with our lives, and the latter two factors are completely under our control. General physical health, as has been mentioned previously, is related to diet, exercise, and lifestyle choices. Older adults can help keep the mind active by staying involved with mentally stimulating activities. This course of action is much more promising than choosing to withdraw from social contacts and live in relative isolation. An older adult need not be afraid to consider taking on new challenges and experiences, regardless of how advanced in age the individual may be. The wisest choice would be activities that match well with the older adult's abilities. Most older Americans report they are happy and satisfied with their lives. Social exchange and support, new learnings, and new experiences are the best avenue to help maintain physical and emotional health, and mental sharpness.

MODULE 9.7 APPLICATION: LIVING LONGER, HEALTHIER LIVES

LEARNING OBJECTIVE

After you have mastered the information in this unit, you will be able to:

1.   Discuss ways people can increase the likelihood of longer and healthier lives.

OUTLINE

I.   Living Longer, Healthier Lives
    A.   Genetic heritage one factor in longer life
    B.   Another, more important, factor is under our control—lifestyle choices, habits and behaviors
II.   Steps We Can Take to Increase the Likelihood of a Longer and Healthier Life
    A.   Osteoporosis—loss of bone density makes bones more porous, brittle, prone to fracture
    B.   Developing healthy exercise and nutrition habits
        1.   Physical exercise slows effects of aging, reduces risk for some diseases, aids in mental acuity
        2.   A nutritious, balanced diet helps reduce risk of disease

   C.   Staying involved
      1.   Keeps mind sharp
      2.   Reduces risk of depression
      3.   Associated with longevity
   D.   Avoiding harmful substances—tobacco, illicit drugs, excessive alcohol all related to health problems
   E.   Maintaining a healthy weight
      1.   Obesity is a major health risk
      2.   Adjust diet and exercise to compensate for slight slowing of metabolism rate
   F.   Managing stress—stress impairs physical and psychological well-being
   G.   Exercising the mind—intellectually stimulating activities help preserve cognitive functioning
   H.   Getting adequate sleep
   I.   Giving support to others was associated with a higher survival rate and was more strongly linked to extending longevity than receiving support (Brown et.al., 2003)
   J.   Study in U.K. showed that adopting four healthy behaviors (nonsmoking, regular exercise, moderate alhohol consumption, eating five servings of fruits and begetables daily) lived an average of 14 years longer (Khaw et.al., 2008)

SUMMARY

In this module, you learn of diet and exercise habits that, at any age, can help promote health and longevity. Things we can do to help extend the quantity and the quality of our years include being involved in regular exercise and eating healthy foods, such as those that are low fat. A diet that includes many whole grains, fruits, and vegetables also has been shown to reduce the risk for some diseases. Exercise and sufficient calcium in our diet help reduce the risk of osteoporosis. It is important to stay mentally and physically involved with life, which helps us maintain our cognitive abilities, helps guard against depression, and helps us continue to find meaning in what we do. As is true at any time in our lives, tobacco, illicit drugs, and excessive consumption of alcohol are all associated with a greater risk for health problems.

Though metabolism tends to slow somewhat as individuals get older, that does not mean that weight gain is unavoidable, and, certainly, excessive weight gain is not healthy for individuals of any age. A healthy diet will help us manage our weight and keep it within reasonable limits. Also, exercise, which has other benefits as mentioned above, helps in keeping our weight at an appropriate level. Excessive amounts of stress, of course, are not healthy for us at any age, and this remains true for older adults as well. Stress reduces the functioning of our immune system and makes us less resistant to many kinds of diseases. Again, a healthy lifestyle, including exercise, can help us reduce stress and reduce its impact.

There is no guarantee that following these suggestions will lead to a longer life, and perhaps we do not really want to live forever. However, people who have adopted these habits, and maintain them, live not only longer, but healthier (and probably happier) lives.

KEY TERMS

Osteoporosis—a bone disease characterized by a loss of bone density in which the bones become porous, brittle, and more prone to fracture.

CHAPTER 9   APPLICATION EXERCISE

Do you know an older individual? Think of an elderly family member or an older person as portrayed in a television program or a movie.

How is that person characterized? If it is a real person, what are his or her personality characteristics? How do others react to the elderly person? What do others seem to think of this older individual?

How does this older person live in terms of exercise, healthy habits, and mental outlook? Do you see a relationship between lifestyle choices and functioning as an older adult?

Lastly, list what you think are keys to healthy and happy living at any age.

CHAPTER 10

Psychology and Health

In Chapter 10, you learn about the field of health psychology and about the very close tie between psychological aspects of our lives and our physical health. The mind and body do not interact at any one point; they are inextricably connected in many ways. We need to be aware of the many psychological factors in our lives and recognize that they impact our physical state. To a great extent, our physical health is under our own control because the psychological factors that can affect it are under our own control.

Perhaps the most frequent psychological factor we deal with that impacts our physical health is stress. Stress is the pressure an organism experiences to adjust or adapt to its environment. Many people now consider life stresses, and even high levels of stress, unavoidable. True, to an extent stress is good for us, in that some stress keeps us alert and energized. With the many demands in our lives, however, it is easy for sources of stress to multiply in duration, number, and intensity, leading to psychological and physical problems. When stress levels become too high, we experience distress.

Potential sources of stress (called stressors) are many and varied. They include the many hassles we encounter daily—getting through traffic, meeting demands of school, work, family, and relationships. These are frequent or daily occurrences and usually are familiar and fairly predictable. Life events, especially if they are unexpected, can cause intense stress. Stressful events often involve change. Certainly, changes in our lives can be good! Going off to college, getting married, or starting a new job are events that we likely look forward to. Even desirable events, however, can and do cause stress. Other sources of stress are frustration (when our attempts at reaching a goal are blocked), conflict (when we must choose between opposing goals), and traumatic stressors. Experiencing traumatic stress can lead to the development of posttraumatic stress disorder (PTSD). Stress can be a function of one's personality type (such as the aggressive and hard-driving Type A personality) or result from the transition to a new culture and the necessity of fitting into that new culture.

Regardless of the type (or types) of stressors that are presented to us, our body tends to respond in the same kind of way. This underlying, fairly uniform pattern of reaction to stress is known as the general adaptation syndrome (GAS), proposed by Hans Selye. The general adaptation syndrome consists of three phases as a body attempts to respond to stress: the alarm stage, the resistance stage, and the exhaustion stage. If stressors are so intense and prolonged that the body's stored resources are fully depleted, death can actually result. Unfortunately, stress today is often unlike the experience of stress as our ancestors knew it. In earlier times, a stressor appeared, it was dealt with (in one way or another!), and then it was gone. Stressors today may be more subtle, but they also can be more prolonged. The body's way of meeting the demands of stressful situations is heightened arousal, and the mustering of physical resources with which to meet a threat. Bodily functioning is kicked into overdrive, so to speak, due mostly to the secretion of stress hormones that cause bodily changes. Stress hormones (epinephrine and norepinephrine are important stress hormones) increase heart and breathing rate to move nutrients and oxygen to muscles more quickly. This reaction to stress is important for our survival, but the prolonged presence of stress hormones in our system and the continued elevation of our physical functioning have consequences. Interestingly, people vary in their thresholds for stress and in their ability to resist the negative effects of stress. A sense of optimism, confidence in our abilities and our ability to control what happens to us, and interpreting stressful situations as challenges all help us live effectively and moderate the negative impact of stress.

Psychological factors are also important in the experience of physical illness, and many physical disorders can be minimized or eliminated if healthy psychological and behavioral steps are taken. Smoking, diet, high blood pressure, amount of physical exercise, diabetes, and cholesterol levels are all implicated in our nation's leading killers, heart disease and cancer. Negative emotional states (e.g., anger and anxiety) are also implicated in physical illness, along with excessive alcohol consumption. Some influences on our health we cannot currently control, such as age and genetic factors. However, a healthy diet, regular exercise, confidence and a positive outlook and the like all can do much to help us live longer and healthier lives.

Sexual behavior and choices also are under our own control and are closely related to the experience of sexually transmitted diseases (STDs). All STDs can be prevented if the proper steps are taken. Although some STDs can be treated successfully (those that are bacterial in origin), the viral STDs cannot be cured by means of antibiotics, and some (HIV/AIDS, for example) potentially will end in death. Thus, careful attention to one's sexual behavior is important to our overall well-being. The only way to assure that one does not contract an STD is to avoid intimate sexual contact altogether. Risk is greatly reduced if you are involved only with an uninfected monogamous partner and you yourself are monogamous and not infected as well. Barring that, risk for STDs can be reduced. Practicing safer sex includes knowing the sexual history of your partner, avoiding any sexual setting that has obvious risks (such as evident genital sores) or less obvious risk (a partner who engages in sex with multiple partners), and maintaining regular contact with your health professionals. Safer sex certainly includes the use of proper barriers such as condoms, which will prevent any infected bodily fluids from being transmitted. If any risk or uncertainty seems apparent, avoid sexual contact in that instance.

MODULE 10.1 STRESS: WHAT IT IS AND WHAT IT DOES TO THE BODY

LEARNING OBJECTIVES

After you have mastered the information in this unit, you will be able to:

1. Describe health psychology and define stress.

2. Describe the major sources of stress.

3. Explain the general adaptation syndrome (how the body responds to stress).

4. Explain how stress affects the immune system.

5. Discuss the psychological factors that buffer the effects of stress.

OUTLINE

I.   The Interrelationships between Psychology and Physical Health
   A.   Study of these relationships is called health psychology
       1.   Body affects the mind; mind affects the body
       2.   Understanding connection can help with healthy living
   B.   A particular concern of health psychologists is stress
       1.   Stress involves pressure, demands placed on an organism to adjust to its environment
       2.   Stress is inevitable, and moderate amounts keep us alert and energized
       3.   Distress occurs when stress level too high to manage comfortably
           a)   May result in psychological problems especially anxiety, depression, anger, and irritability
           b)   May result in physical health problems such as headaches, fatigue, upset stomach and more serious results, like cardiovascular disorders

        4.   Excessive stress leads to physical and psychological problems

        5.   Many Americans say stress is on the rise. According to a recent survey by the American Psychological Association, one-third of Americans say they are facing extreme levels of stress in their liver, and nearly (43 percent) report adverse health effects from stress (American Psychological Association 2006, 2007)

II.   Sources of Stress (Stressors) – can be positive as well as negative experiences

   A.   Hassles

        1.   Common, everyday annoyances

            a)   Traffic jams, weather, balancing various personal and professional demands

            b)   See Table 10.2 for typical hassles facing college students

        2.   Chronic stress—result of collective effect of daily hassles

            a)   Chronic stress is a state of persistent tension or pressure

            b)   Leads to feelings of exhaustion, irritability, depression

            c)   Include hassles, financial problems, job-related problems, relationships problems, persistent pain or other medical problems

   B.   Life events (major changes in life circumstances – that disrupt people's lives)

        1.   Even good changes (marriage, promotion, birth of a baby) can result in stress

        2.   Stress from life events occurs irregularly, sometimes unexpectedly

        3.   Greater number of life events associated with higher incidence of physical health problems (note relationship is correlational, not causal)

        4.   Stress threshold, coping abilities (have the skills needed to adjust), optimism related to vulnerability (for stress impact)

        5.   Evaluation, interpretation of life event related to the level of stress it presents

        6.   Questions of cause and effect remain open to debate

   C.   Frustration

        1.   Negative emotion when goals are blocked – the frustration needs to be perceived as "just" another challenge

        2.   May result if goals set unrealistically high

   D.   Conflict

        1.   State of tension when two or more goals compete and demand resolution

        2.   Approach-approach conflict

            a)   Simultaneously drawn towards two positive goals

            b)   Goals are mutually exclusive—choosing one eliminates possibility of choosing the other

            c)   Initially may vacillate between the two alternatives

            d)   Eventually choose one course of action or the other

            e)   Considered the least stressful type of conflict

        3.   Avoidance-avoidance conflict

            a)   Must choose between two opposing goals, both of which are unpleasant

            b)   Avoiding one unpleasant goal necessitates approaching the other

            c)   If no obvious resolution, decision may be put on hold

            d)   When conflict is very stressful, one may become immobilized

        4.   Approach-avoidance conflict

            a)   Goal has both positive and negative qualities

            b)   Resolution seems possible by adding up pluses and minuses

            c)   However, decision may flip-flop as various aspects considered

            d)   An example you may want to ask someone for a date, but feel panic-stricken by fears of rejection

        5.   Multiple approach-avoidance conflict

            a)   Involves the most complex type of conflict

            b)   Two or more goals are involved

        c)   Each goal has compelling positive and negative attributes

        d)   Resolution sometimes possible by combining both goals (an example getting started at a new job while taking night courses)

        e)   In other cases selection of one still results in concern over lost possibilities of the other

E.   Traumatic stressors

    1.   Potentially life-threatening events can have profound enduring effects on our psychology adjustment

    2.   Natural or technological disasters, combat, accidents, and attacks

    3.   Posttraumatic stress disorder (PTSD) may result

    4.   Characteristics of PTSD (maladaptive response to trauma)

        a)   Avoidance of cues associated with the trauma

        b)   Flashbacks, dreams, intrusive memories and images occur

        c)   Depression, anxiety impairs ability to function

        d)   May be chronically on guard, tense, on edge

        e)   Current emotional experience may be numbed

        f)   Can develop months or years after traumatic experience

    5.   PTSD found in many cultures; culture may influence vulnerability to effects of stress

F.   Type A behavior pattern (TABP)

    1.   Hard-driving, competitive, impatient, and ambitious

    2.   In a rush, aggressive, and intense

    3.   Unlike Type B behavior pattern, which is more relaxed and mellow

    4.   Type A individual at greater risk for heart disease (most likely it is the anger and negativity aspect of personality that contributes the risk)

G.   Acculturative stress—demands of adjusting to a new or different culture

    1.   Acculturation is process of adopting characteristics of the new culture

    2.   Economics, social support, and language proficiency related to adjustment

        a)   The host country may lead to anxiety and depression, perceptions of discrimination and erosion of traditional family net works and values

    3.   Relationship between acculturation and psychological adjustment is complex—acculturation is sometimes helpful, sometimes harmful

    4.   Withdrawal from the larger culture may prevent the individual from making the necessary adjustments

    5.   Adjusting to the demands of the larger culture while maintaining one's own ethnic identity is associated with better psychology adjustment (LaFromboise, Albright, & Harris, 2010; Oyserman, 2008; Smith et al., 2009; Rodriguez et al., 2009)

III.   The Body's Response to Stress

A.   The general adaptation syndrome (stress response)—GAS

    1.   Much of what we know is due to research from Hans Selye ("Dr. Stress")

    2.   Body responds in similar ways to various kinds of stress

    3.   Alarm stage (response is prewired into nervous system)

        a)   Body's first reaction to a stressor; defenses prepare for action

        b)   Fight-or-flight response (physical – heart pounds, breath quickens, sweat and emotional terror, fright, anxiety, rage or anger characteristics)

           1)   Characterized by biological changes that prepare the body to deal with a treat by either fighting it off or fleeing from it

        c)   May be physical or psychological source of stress

        d)   Death will occur within hours if stressor extremely damaging (such as extreme cold)

    4.   Resistance stage (adaptation stage)

        a)   Occurs if organism lives beyond alarm stage

        b)   Stressor continues; body attempts to adapt

        c)   Attempt is made to return to normal biological state

        d)   Arousal remains high; may be negative emotional reactions

    5.   Exhaustion stage

        a)   Final stage if stressor continues

        b)   Heart rate and respiration decrease to conserve bodily resources

        c)   Continued exposure to stress still depletes body

        d)   "Diseases of adaptation" may occur (kidney or heart disease, digestive disorders, allergies, depression)

    6.   Original threatening stressor was designed not to last very long

    7.   Stresses of today are more persistent, may overtax the body's resources, making us more susceptible to stress-related disorders

    8.   Gender differences in response to stress

        a)   Women engage in more nurturing behaviors during stress

        b)   Males more likely to exhibit aggressive or hostile responses

            1)   Hormone testosterone may play a pivotal role

B.   Stress and the endocrine system

    1.   Endocrine system is a series of ductless glands throughout body

    2.   Glands release secretions (known as hormones) into bloodstream

    3.   Hypothalamus in brain controls responses of endocrine system

    4.   Stress regulatory response involves coordination action within the hypothalamus pituitary adrenal (HPA) axis

    5.   Biological steps in stress response

        a)   Hypothalamus secretes corticotrophin-releasing hormone (CRH)

        b)   CRH stimulates pituitary gland to secrete adrenocorticotrophic hormone (ACTH)

        c)   ACTH travels through bloodstream to adrenal glands (located just above kidneys)

        d)   ACTH stimulates adrenal glands to secrete corticosteroids (stress hormones)

        e)   Corticosteroids help body resist stress; make stored nutrients more available

        f)   Adrenal medulla (inner layer in adrenal glands) secretes stress hormones epinephrine and norepinephrine

        g)   Epinephrine and norepinephrine increase heart rate; blood sends more oxygen and nutrients more quickly to muscles

        h)   Muscles then more capable of fight or flight response

IV. Stress and the Immune System

    A.   Immune system is body's primary defense against disease

    B.   Diseases fought by means of lymphocytes (specialized white blood cells)

    C.   Lymphocytes constantly circulate, alert for antigens

    D.   Antigens activate immune system to produce antibodies

    E.   Antigen is a recognizable foreign substance in the body

    F.   Antibodies are specialized protein molecules that fit precisely into invading antigen (like key fitting into a lock)

    G.   Antigen marked for destruction by "killer" lymphocytes

    H.   "Memory" of an antigen possible due to prior exposure

    I.   Immunity or resistance occurs due to this prior exposure (body is fully ready to respond, and quickly, to known antigen)

    J.   Vaccination (immunization) also provides immunity

    K.   Chronic stress weakens immune system; individual more susceptible to disease

    L.   Stress increases interleukin-6, lowers production of immunoglobulin A

    M.   Corticosteroids inhibit immune system's ability to respond to microbes

    N.   Can be impaired by the use of synthetic steroids

    O.   Psychological treatments can help lower stress and thus its effects

V.   Psychological Moderators of Stress
    A.   Social support—friends, wide social network help buffer stress
    B.   Writing about traumatic or stressful experiences
    C.   Self-efficacy
        1.   Belief that we are capable of doing what we set out to do
        2.   High self-efficacy individuals view stressful situation as a challenge
        3.   Confidence in abilities strengthens will to persevere
    D.   Perceptions of control and predictability
        1.   Greater sense of control and predictability—less experience of stress
        2.   Locus of control
            a)   Internal locus of control—belief that one has considerable influence over events and outcomes (sense of ability to control may result in less experience of stress)
            b)   External locus of control—belief that fate is out of one's hands (likely to be more susceptible to experiencing stress)
    E.   Psychological hardiness (research by Kobasa, 1979)
        1.   Cluster of personality traits related to resilience to stress
        2.   Characteristics of individuals with psychological hardiness
            a)   Commitment to one's work and belief that it is important
            b)   Openness to challenge—stressors and addressing them a regular part of life
            c)   Internal locus of control—belief that outcome predominantly in their hands
        3.   Stress is accepted as normal challenge of life, may be interesting
        4.   Seek to solve problems not avoid them
    F.   Optimism
        1.   People with more optimism also more resilient with regard to effects of stress
        2.   Optimism associated with better health outcomes, fewer negative health issues
        3.   True that relationship is correlational, not causal—but optimistic attitude would suggest giving it a try!

SUMMARY

In this module, you learn about the many aspects of stress and how the experience of stress can affect us. Life is impossible without some stress, and indeed a moderate level of stress helps keep us active, alert, and involved with life. Excessive stress, however, does take its toll in terms of both physical and psychological problems. Interestingly, stress cannot be precisely quantified. What is beyond the level of manageable stress to one person may be invigorating, engrossing, and challenging to another. Still, conflicts and demands can be so great that everyone may experience undesirable stress at some time. When levels of stress become too great, we experience distress. Distress means we have reached the point of physical and psychological suffering. The field of health psychology investigates the relationship between psychology and physical health.

Stress is the demand put on an organism to adapt to features of the environment. Sources of stress are termed stressors. Stressors often involve change, whether for bad or for good! Certainly holidays, marriage, job promotions or transfers, and the arrival of a new baby are positive experiences, yet much stress accompanies each one of these events. Typical sources of stress include hassles (everyday annoying experiences); life events that are not expected or do not typically occur; and frustration, which is most likely to occur when we are blocked in our attempt to reach a goal. Conflict also leads to much stress. There are four basic kinds of conflict. Approach-approach conflict is one, but it is not too stressful since both alternatives are desirable and resolution is simply a matter of choosing one over the other. Avoidance-avoidance conflict is more difficult (and therefore probably more stressful) because both possibilities are unpleasant outcomes. Avoidance-avoidance conflict means when we move away from choosing one alternative, we must move towards selecting the other. Conflict tends to leave an individual vacillating between the choices. Avoidance-avoidance conflict can be so stressful that an individual literally cannot decide and becomes in essence immobilized. In approach-avoidance conflict, the same goal has both negative and positive aspects. This situation, too, can cause some difficulties! The positive features draw us to the goal, but then the negative features may well push us away again. Multiple approach-avoidance conflict is the most complex type of conflict. Two or more goals are involved, and each goal has both powerful positive and powerful negative aspects. Faced with choices where there is no one clear course of action can leave us feeling confused and stressed. Stress may come from traumatic experiences (which may result in posttraumatic stress disorder), from pressures to adjust to an unfamiliar culture, or as a function of personality (the Type A personality, for example).

How does our body respond to stress? Research by Hans Selye has revealed that although there are specific variations the body responds to many different types of stressors in the same general pattern. This pattern he termed the general adaptation syndrome (GAS). It should be noted that, historically, the experience of stress was probably a briefer event. Centuries ago a stressor would emerge, the organism would respond (and hopefully live through it), and then the threat passed. At that point, the body's systems could return to normal. As most of us well know, that is not so with today's stress. Facing fairly intense stressors from a variety of sources on a daily basis can lead to chronic stress.

The first stage in the general adaptation syndrome is the alarm stage. This is the body's first reaction, and it prepares us to face the stress through means of the fight-or-flight response. Have you noticed that your heartbeat speeds up and your breathing rate quickens when you are faced with something frightening? Among other things, these physiological changes get needed oxygen and nutrients to the body's tissues faster. The muscles may well be called upon to deal with the stress.

The second stage in the general adaptation syndrome is the resistance stage. Here, the body's energies have been elevated for sometime and the body attempts to return to normal. However, if the stress is still present, arousal levels will still remain fairly high. If the stressor continues and the organism is still alive, the third stage, called the exhaustion stage, kicks in. Heart rate and respiration decrease in order to preserve what is possible among the body's energy stores. If the stressor continues beyond this point, the organism is at risk for developing stress-related diseases. Women are likely to show nurturing behaviors when intensely stressed; men are more likely to show aggressive behaviors.

When the body is faced with stress, the endocrine system becomes more active. The hypothalamus in the brain secretes a hormone that stimulates the pituitary gland to secrete ACTH (adrenocorticotrophic hormone). ACTH (transmitted by the bloodstream) stimulates the adrenal cortex of the adrenal glands (above the kidneys) to produce stress hormones known as corticosteroids. Corticosteroids aid in the body's reaction to stress by making stored nutrients more available. At the same time, the adrenal medulla (in the center of each adrenal gland) secretes norepinephrine and epinephrine, stress hormones that increase heart rate and thus move blood more quickly through the body, bringing needed resources to the body tissues.

Stress, as you may have believed, does impair the functioning of our immune system and makes us more susceptible to contracting illnesses. Normally, the immune system is primed to fight off disease by attacking antigens (substances in the body identified by the immune system as foreign) with specialized lymphocytes (white blood cells). During intensive stress, the ability to produce certain antibodies (which fight antigens) is lowered. Corticosteroids produced during the stress response do help the body meet an external threat, but their continuing presence within the body makes it more difficult to fight off invading microbes. Psychological interventions can help lower the incidence and impact of stress.

Not everyone experiences debilitating stress on a regular basis, and some people are just more able to manage fairly high levels of stress compared to others. What psychological attributes contribute to an individual's ability to manage stress? Five major categories have been identified. The first attribute is having strong social and emotional support. Close relationships with others help us manage stress. People with many friends actually have better immune system functioning and greater resistance to infection than do less social individuals. The second attribute is a sense of self-efficacy. Self-efficacy means believing in oneself, and that one has the ability to see an endeavor through successfully. Individuals high in self-efficacy see stress-producing situations more as a challenge than a problem. The third attribute is having a sense of control—over the stressful event and over our lives in general. Individuals with an internal locus of control (a sense that their actions are closely tied to the course of events and that they can influence those events) are less susceptible to feeling overwhelmed because of that sense of control. The fourth attribute is psychological hardiness—the psychological characteristics making one more resistant to stress. Psychologically hardy folk believe in and are committed to their work, appreciate an occasional challenge and perceive it as normal, and have that inner sense of influence over life events. The last attribute is optimism (a positive outlook). Individuals who show more optimism are more resilient when it comes to stress. They also are less likely to suffer from some physical or psychological disorders, and have better outcomes with regard to various health procedures and events. It should be noted, at least at present, that the relationship between optimism and health is correlational only (that is, it is not established that one causes the other).

KEY TERMS

Health psychology

Stress

Distress

Stressors

Hassles

Chronic stress

Life events

Frustration

Conflict

Posttraumatic stress disorder (PTSD)

Type A behavior pattern (TABP)

Acculturative stress

General adaptation syndrome (GAS)

Alarm stage

Fight-or-flight response

Resistance stage

Exhaustion stage

Hypothalamus pituitary adrenal (HPA) axis

Corticotrophin-releasing hormone (CRH)

Adrenocorticotrophic hormone (ACTH)

Adrenal glands

Adrenal cortex

Corticosteroids

Adrenal medulla

Immune system

Lymphocytes

Antigens

Antibodies

Vaccination

Psychological hardiness

SELF-TEST PRACTICE QUIZ

Match the following Key Terms and definitions (note: not every Key Term will be used):

1. _____ Specialized white blood cells that attack antigens

2. _____ The outer layer of the adrenal glands; secrete corticosteroids in response to stress

3. _____ The typical pattern of human response to stress, proposed by Hans Selye

4. _____ A state of tension where one must make a choice regarding goals that have positive and negative attributes

5. _____ A set of psychological characteristics that help an individual resist the impact of stress

6. _____ The field within psychology which investigates the relationship between psychological factors and physical health

7. _____ A particular behavior pattern, involving impatience, competitiveness, and possibly aggression which may be associated with higher levels of experienced stress

8. _____ A feeling of pressure or tension due to the organism's need to adapt to certain environmental demands

9. _____ Our physical defense system which, under normal conditions, fights off disease and helps keep us healthy

a. Health psychology

b. Stress

c. Distress

d. Stressors

e. Hassles

f. Chronic stress

g. Life events

h. Frustration

i. Conflict

j. Posttraumatic stress disorder (PTSD)

k. Type A behavior pattern (TABP)

l. Acculturative stress

m. General adaptation syndrome (GAS)

n. Alarm stage

o. Fight-or-flight response

p. Resistance stage

q. Exhaustion stage

r. Hypothalamus pituitary adrenal (HPA) axis

s. Corticotrophin-releasing hormone (CRH)

t. Adrenocorticotrophic hormone (ACTH)

u. Adrenal glands

v. Adrenal cortex

w. Corticosteroids

10. _____ Substances produced by the immune system that fit precisely into an antigen and mark it for destruction

11. _____ When stress has reached the level that it causes physical or emotional suffering and pain

12. _____ The second stage of response by the body to stress, as characterized by the general adaptation syndrome (GAS) model

13. _____ The feeling typically experienced when one's path towards a goal is blocked

14. _____ When the experience of fairly intense stressful events is persistent

15. _____ The inner part of the adrenal glands; secretes stress hormones epinephrine and norepinephrine which increase heart and breathing rates

x. Adrenal medulla
y. Immune system
z. Lymphocytes
aa. Antigens
bb. Antibodies
cc. Vaccination
dd. Psychological hardiness

16. Demands put on you, such as school or employment, traffic, chores, relationship issues, and the like, are
    a. stressors.
    b. problems.
    c. negative events.
    d. frustrations.

17. When there seems to be no let up to the stress you experience, and eventually you are beginning to feel tired, irritable, and depressed, you are suffering from
    a. physical illness.
    b. psychosomatic illness.
    c. chronic stress.
    d. final exam week.

18. When our efforts to achieve an objective are thwarted, we are likely to experience
    a. stress.
    b. frustration.
    c. conflict.
    d. depression.

19. Jackie has a dilemma: She wants to go to the beach with some friends, which will be fun, but doing so would also entail missing class and therefore losing some points on her class grade. Jackie is facing a(n) _____ conflict.
    a. approach-approach
    b. avoidance-avoidance
    c. approach-avoidance
    d. multiple approach-avoidance

20. Which of the following is NOT a characteristic of posttraumatic stress disorder?
    a. Difficulty in feeling love or other strong emotions
    b. Flashbacks, intrusive memories or dreams regarding the event
    c. Unwillingness to talk about the trauma that has been experienced
    d. Avoidance of situations that serve as reminders of the experience

21. Demands placed on an individual that involve learning a new language, new values, and social customs which are different from one's own are known as
    a. culture shock.
    b. accumulated stress.
    c. multicultural perspective taking.
    d. acculturative stress.

22. The degree of stress associated with adjusting to a new culture will depend in large part on
    a. whether or not the adjustment involves economic hardship.
    b. the degree to which the individual experiences conflict of values.
    c. the individual's proficiency in the new culture's language.
    d. all of the above

23. The fight-or-flight response is part of the _____ stage of the general adaptation syndrome.
    a. alarm
    b. resistance
    c. exhaustion
    d. resolution

24. Events including natural disasters, accidents, and physical or sexual assault are known as
    a. avoidance-avoidance conflicts.
    b. traumatic stressors.
    c. frustrations.
    d. debilitating factors.

25. Which statement about stress is correct?
    a. Stress can be caused by both pleasant and unpleasant experiences.
    b. Life events can affect both physical and mental health, while hassles only affect mental health.
    c. Stress is always bad.
    d. none of the above

26. The research contributed by Hans Selye revealed that
    a. the body's response to extremes of temperature differs from the body's response to other stressors.
    b. the body's response to infectious agents differs from the body's response to other stressors.
    c. the body's response to psychological pressures differs from the body's response to other stressors.
    d. despite some stressor-specific reactions, in general the body responds to most kinds of stress in the same way.

27. Based on our body's response to stress, it appears that our physiology was designed to best accommodate
    a. lifestyles that really involve no stress.
    b. stressful experiences that are over rather quickly.
    c. stressful experiences no matter how long they may last.
    d. high stress or no stress—whatever life presents to us.

28. Heart rate and breathing rate decrease during the _____ stage of the general adaptation syndrome.

    a. alarm
    b. resistance
    c. exhaustion
    d. resolution

29. During stress, females are more likely to exhibit comforting and friendship behaviors and men are more likely to exhibit aggressive behaviors. These stress behaviors are most likely due to

    a. sexual and reproductive hormones.
    b. the general adaptation syndrome.
    c. cultural variation.
    d. observational learning.

30. Which element of the Type A behavior pattern is most strongly related to the risk of coronary heart disease?

    a. Competitiveness
    b. Hostility
    c. Impatience
    d. Ambitiousness

31. The stress hormones epinephrine and norepinephrine are secreted by the

    a. hypothalamus.
    b. adrenal medulla.
    c. adrenal cortex.
    d. pituitary gland.

32. Foreign bodies (such as bacteria and viruses) are known as

    a. antibodies.
    b. lymphocytes.
    c. antigens.
    d. corticosteroids.

33. People with _____ levels of self-efficacy tend to be better able to withstand stress.

    a. high
    b. medium
    c. low
    d. none of the above

34. Which of the following statements would indicate that the speaker has an internal locus of control?

    a. "I crashed my car because the road was icy."
    b. "I have remained in good health due to exercise and a well-balanced diet."
    c. "I got that job because I was in the right place at the right time."
    d. "I got an A on the test because I am lucky."

35. Which of the following is NOT a characteristic of individuals who exhibit psychological hardiness?

    a. Commitment
    b. Recognition that what one is doing is not really going to change the world
    c. Viewing stressful situations as challenges, not problems
    d. Having an internal locus of control

ESSAY QUESTIONS

1. Describe and discuss some of the ways that stress can make us more vulnerable to physical illnesses or other health problems.

2. What are some of the factors that seem to moderate the extent to which people experience stress or suffer from its effects?

ANSWER KEY

1. Lymphocytes
2. Adrenal cortex
3. General adaptation syndrome (GAS)
4. Conflict
5. Psychological hardiness
6. Health psychology
7. Type A behavior pattern (TABP)
8. Stress
9. Immune system
10. Antibodies
11. Distress
12. Resistance stage
13. Frustration
14. Chronic stress
15. Adrenal medulla
16. a
17. c
18. b
19. c
20. c
21. d
22. d
23. a
24. b
25. a
26. d
27. b
28. c
29. a

30. b

31. b

32. c

33. a

34. b

35. b

SAMPLE ANSWERS TO ESSAY QUESTIONS

1. There is a distinct connection between the level of stress we experience and our ability to ward off disease. Stressors most likely to affect our physical health include loss of loved ones, exposure to traumatic events, divorce, prolonged unemployment, and chronic sleep problems. One clear way that stress impacts our physical health is that, when an individual is under a great amount of stress, the individual's body produces less of the antibody immunoglobulin A. This antibody helps keep us from contracting cold viruses. Also, during stress, the human body is less able to fend off attacks by the Epstein-Barr virus.

    Another way that the physical state of the body is affected by stress is the damage done by corticosteroids when they linger within the physiological system. Corticosteroids are secreted by the adrenal glands during stress in order to help manage the stress better. Thus, of course, they are helpful in boosting the body's immediate ability to respond effectively to threats or trauma. However, continued stress leads to the continued secretion of these hormones. The continued presence of cortical steroids in the body reduces the immune system's ability to function optimally. Corticosteroids make the immune system less able to fight off invading microbes.

    Lastly, as pointed out in Hans Selye's research, when the physiological resources of the human body are severely depleted, as in the exhaustion stage of the general adaptation syndrome, the body becomes prone to "diseases of adaptation." These diseases include kidney and heart disease, psychological disorders such as depression, and digestive disorders. Thus, prolonged exposure or severe stressors leave the human body more vulnerable to health problems.

2. Not everyone experiences debilitating levels of stress, and not everyone interprets a stressful situation as an unpleasant experience. It appears that there are psychological factors that are related to how one perceives stress and how one deals with it. These psychological moderators of stress include the following: our sources of social and emotional support; our confidence in our abilities and our ability to control what happens to us; the interpretation of stressful situations as opportunities or challenges (not problems); and an outlook of optimism.

    Research indicates that having good friends and other sources of social support is associated with more resistance to physical disease. Self-efficacy means a person believes that he or she is competent and has the skills and abilities to meet and resolve a problem effectively. High self-efficacy is associated with the perception of stressful situations as challenges rather than as obstacles. How much we believe we can control what happens to us, and how predictable events are in our lives, are both related to how stressful these events are. Unpredictable and uncontrollable events are, of course, more stressful than those over which we have some influence or which we know may occur. The perception of the controllability of events is somewhat of a subjective matter. People vary in their locus of control; that is, people usually either take the perspective that they have substantial impact on events and on outcomes of events that happen to them (an internal locus of control) or they believe that they are rather helpless and that whatever happens lies more or less in the hands of fate. Individuals with an internal locus of control manage stress more effectively and exhibit a greater resilience to its effects.

Another factor that buffers the impact of stress is what is called psychological hardiness. The concept of psychological hardiness is derived from the research of Suzanne Kobasa (1979), who studied business executives who were in high-stress positions but still remained physically healthy. The components of psychological hardiness are commitment to one's work, recognizing change as a normal part of life, and having an internal locus of control.

A last and important buffer regarding the impact of stress is one's outlook. Individuals who approach life with a basic attitude of optimism are generally more resilient to the effects of stress. This resilience relates to both physical and psychological health matters.

MODULE 10.2 PSYCHOLOGICAL FACTORS IN PHYSICAL ILLNESS

LEARNING OBJECTIVES

After you have mastered the information in this unit, you will be able to:

1. Explain how psychological factors are linked to the heart and circulatory system health.

2. Discuss the role of psychological factors in the development of cancer.

3. Describe from the nature, prevalence, and treatment, and prevention of sexually transmitted diseases.

OUTLINE

I. Background Factors in Physical Health
   A. Physical health is a function of many influences
   B. Physical health clearly related to behavior, lifestyle choices
   C. Unhealthy behavior accounts for an estimated 40% of premature deaths in the United States (Schroeder, 2007)
II. Coronary Heart Disease
   A. Background factors related to coronary heart disease
      1. The heart is muscle tissue, which needs oxygen and nutrients
      2. Oxygen and nutrients are carried to heart by means of arteries (a type of blood vessel)
      3. Coronary heart disease (CHD) results when flow of blood to heart is insufficient
      4. Usual underlying cause for CHD is atherosclerosis
      5. Atherosclerosis results from buildup of plaque along artery walls
      6. Atherosclerosis is the major form of arteriosclerosis (hardening of the arteries)
      7. Narrowed arteries (due to atherosclerosis) more likely to be location of blood clots
      8. A blood clot in a coronary artery causes a heart attack (myocardial infarction, or MI), because flow of blood to heart is blocked
      9. Severity of heart attack related to tissue damage from loss of oxygen
      10. More men and women in the U.S. die of CHD than from any other cause
   B. Risk factors for CHD
      1. Overall personal risk is related to individual risk factors
      2. Prominent risk factors
         a) Age—risk increases after age forty
         b) Gender—men more likely to be affected
         c) Family history
         d) Hypertension (high blood pressure)
         e) Factors related to lifestyle (smoking, obesity, lack of exercise)
      3. CHD factors that can be controlled through behavior or medical treatment
         a) Hypertension—can be controlled through medication
         b) Smoking—doubles risk of heart attack

        c)   Obesity

        d)   Diabetes

        e)   Cholesterol levels

        f)   Sedentary lifestyle—lack of exercise doubles risk of heart disease

   4.   Adopting healthier lifestyle associated with reduced risks for individuals who have had heart disease in addition to those who have not

   5.   Currently non-Hispanic black Americans at greater risk

  C.   Emotions and your heart

     1.   Emotions implicated in greater risk for heart disease

        a)   Hostility (one component in Type A personality)

        b)   Persistent anxiety

     2.   How emotions affect cardiovascular system

        a)   Persistent emotional arousal related to cardiovascular damage

        b)   Anger, anxiety result in release of epinephrine and norepinephrine (stress hormones)

        c)   Stress hormones increase heart rate, blood pressure, and strength of heart contractions—all add to burden on heart

        d)   Stress hormones (especially epinephrine) increase stickiness of blood clotting factors to protect against possible injury—may increase risk of dangerous blood clots within arteries

        e)   Individuals who anger easily may also develop higher levels of cholesterol, blood pressure

        f)   Other emotional distress also related to cardiovascular risk (such as depression, marital stress)

        g)   Therapies available to aid in managing chronic anger, anxiety

III.   Cancer

  A.   Cancer kills almost as many Americans as heart disease

  B.   Disease occurs because body cells reproduce uncontrollably

  C.   Ability to regulate cell multiplication is lost

  D.   Malignant tumors are these masses of excess tissue

  E.   Tumors can originate in any body tissue or organ; can spread to other parts of body

  F.   Tumors damage vital body organs and systems, may result in death

  G.   Possible causes of cancer

     1.   Heredity

     2.   Exposure to cancer-causing chemicals

     3.   Exposure to some viruses

     4.   Two out of three cancer deaths in U.S. attributable to smoking and diet

     5.   Alcohol and excess sun exposure are also related

  H.   Risk factors in the development of cancer

     1.   Family history, age (older ages at greater risk)

     2.   Smoking

        a)   90% of lung cancer deaths directly attributable to smoking

        b)   Smoking related to other cancers, causes perhaps one-third of cancer deaths

        c)   Use of tobacco in other forms also harmful, can cause cancer

     3.   Diet and alcohol consumption

        a)   High levels of consumption of saturated fats—linked to prostate and colon cancers

        b)   Dietary patterns may account for 30% of cancer deaths

        c)   Obesity also associated with increased risk for some types of cancer

        d)   Heavy alcohol consumption raises risk of several cancers (including cancers of mouth, pharynx, and esophagus)

4. Sun exposure
   a) Prolonged sun exposure may lead to basal cell carcinoma (most common, least dangerous type of skin cancer)
   b) Basal cell carcinoma accounts for 75% of skin cancers
   c) Curable as long as detected early, surgically removed
   d) Severe sunburn early in life related to occurrence of melanoma
   e) Melanoma least common, most deadly skin cancer
   f) Melanoma accounts for about 5% of skin cancers
5. Stress
   a) The role of stress with regard to cancer not yet fully established
   b) Persistent stress may affect immune system's ability to rid body of cancerous cells
   c) Health professionals provide counseling, other services to assist those with cancer; also promote cancer preventative behaviors
G. Behaviors That Can Help Prevent Cancer
   1. Avoid tobacco use
   2. If you use alcohol, limit consumption
   3. Maintain physical activities
   4. Healthy diet and limit intake of saturated fat
   5. Maintain a healthy weight
   6. Avoid unprotected exposure to sun
   7. Get regular medical examination and follow recommended cancer screening procedures
IV. Sexual Behavior and STDs: Are You at Risk?
   A. Background factors in STDs
      1. AIDS: one of history's worst epidemics (caused by HIV)
      2. Three million deaths from AIDS occur annually
      3. 70% of HIV transmission worldwide from heterosexual contact
      4. HIV transmission is via contact with infected bodily fluids
      5. Body's immune system attacked and disabled—leaves individual vulnerable to other infections
   B. Other STDs (sexually transmitted diseases)
      1. 20 million Americans suffer from HPVs (cause body warts, including in genital regions)
      2. Chlamydia—most common bacterial type of STD
      3. STDs can cause cancer, infertility, damage to heart and brain, death
      4. Genital herpes can cause serious complications, especially in women, including increased risks of miscarriage and cervical cancer (Nevid, 1998)
   C. Treatment
      1. Vaccine now available which can protect against many strains of HPV
      2. Antibiotics can cure bacterial forms of STD
      3. HIV/AIDS and genital herpes—viral STDS (antibiotics cannot eliminate infectious organisms)
      4. Possible new antiviral drugs may increase manageability of HIV infection
      5. HIV shows ability to mutate to drug-resistant strains
   D. Prevention
      1. Abstinence—avoid any sexual relationships or sexual contact
      2. Monogamous relationship with a monogamous uninfected partner
      3. Reducing risk via safer sexual practices
         a) Know your partner's sexual background

b) Avoid multiple partners (especially partners who themselves have multiple partners)
c) Be sure to communicate health safety concerns with your partner
d) Avoid sexual contact if your partner appears to have sores or blisters on genitals
e) Avoid unprotected sexual behavior
f) Get medical attention promptly if you may have been exposed to an STD
g) Have periodic medical check-ups to assure you are treated for any diseases you may not realize you have contracted
h) When in doubt regarding your health or safety risk, avoid sexual contact

SUMMARY

In this module, you learn about the psychological factors that may play a very large role in whether or not we contract a physical illness and how severe or prolonged our experience with that illness is. Some influences on our physical health we cannot completely control, especially those relating to our genetic heritage. Yet much regarding our overall health and longevity is affected by our behaviors and lifestyle choices. These behaviors and lifestyle patterns are entirely under our control.

The first major disease discussed in this module—listed first because currently it is the leading cause of death in the United States—is heart disease. Coronary heart disease (CHD) occurs when blood vessels carrying nutrients and, even more importantly, oxygen to the heart become obstructed. Typically the blood vessels (arteries) have become narrowed (a condition known as atherosclerosis) because of the buildup of plaque (fatty deposits) along the inner artery walls. Because of the plaque buildup, the obstructions (blood clots) are much more likely to become lodged in an artery and block it. If the artery is completely blocked, and oxygen is cut off to the heart, the heart tissue not supplied with sufficient oxygen is damaged or dies. The more heart tissue that is cut off from sources of oxygen, and the longer this deprived condition lasts, the worse the heart attack. Though age and family history relate to whether or not you are at risk for heart disease, many other psychological factors are implicated as well.

Smoking, obesity, cholesterol level, hypertension (high blood pressure), diabetes, and lack of physical activity are all implicated in the risk of heart attacks. All of these factors can be minimized through healthy diet, medications, and physical exercise. In one study of 84,000 nurses (Stampfer et al., 2000), those who followed a low fat diet, did not smoke, and participated in regular exercise had a much lower risk of coronary heart disease compared to nurses in the study who did not adhere to these practices. Emotional equilibrium is also a factor in whether or not an individual develops heart disease. People who are chronically angry are at a higher risk for developing heart disease than people who are calmer and have a lower incidence of anger. Individuals who experience chronic anxiety, too, are at great risk for heart disease. How do our emotions affect us? Persistent anger or anxiety parallels the experience of stress, and triggers the release of stress hormones. Stress hormones (such as epinephrine and norepinephrine) influence our body to prepare to react to a threat or stressor, and this preparedness includes an increase in heart rate, blood pressure, and strength of heart contractions. All of these physiological reactions to stress put greater demands on the heart. Factors in the blood that help it to clot are increased during stress (since the possibility of injury due to a threat is greater), and the increased ability to clot may be related to the formation of blood clots, which cause heart attacks. People who are frequently angry also are at greater risk for high blood pressure and high cholesterol levels. Both of these physical conditions are factors related to the incidence of heart disease.

Cancer kills almost as many Americans as heart disease. Cancer occurs when the normal reproduction of body cells becomes out of control, and body cells replicate in excessive numbers. This abnormal body tissue comprises malignant tumors, which can spread to any part of the body and which can result in death. Controllable factors in the occurrence of cancer are smoking, diet (especially a high fat diet), high levels of alcohol consumption, excessive exposure to the sun, and stress. Most of the cancer deaths in the United States can be traced to smoking or poor dietary habits. Although the relationship of stress to the incidence of cancer is not clearly established, it is proposed that stress impedes the immune system's ability to rid the body of cancerous cells, just as it fights off other harmful invaders such as antigens.

Another source of disease and potential death that is entirely the result of lifestyle choices are STDs (sexually transmitted diseases). These diseases, as the name implies, typically are transmitted through intimate sexual contact where no barriers are provided to prevent passage of infection from one participating individual to another. STDs range from the very common genital herpes and chlamydia to the very serious HIV, the virus that causes AIDS. There are approximately three million deaths worldwide each year from AIDS, and as yet there is no cure. Antibiotic drugs can treat bacterial infections such as syphilis, but, at best, antiviral treatments can only help control viral STDs, not eliminate them altogether. Obviously, the best "treatment" for these diseases is prevention. You should always know the sexual history and current health condition of your sexual partner. Avoid high-risk partners, and, finally, use proper barriers to avoid transmission of infected fluids (this is also important, of course, if you want to reduce the risk of pregnancy). Get medical attention promptly if there is a chance you have been exposed to an STD, and regular medical check-ups will help detect diseases that you do not realize you have contracted.

KEY TERMS

Arteries

Coronary heart disease (CHD)

Atherosclerosis

Plaque

Arteriosclerosis

Heart attack

Malignant tumors

Basal cell carcinoma

Melanoma

Sexually transmitted disease (STD)

SELF-TEST PRACTICE QUIZ

Match the following Key Terms and definitions:

1. _____ The most lethal form of skin cancer

2. _____ Diseases caused by contamination from infected bodily fluids, usually transferred from an intimate partner via sexual contact

3. _____ The most common form of heart disease, where coronary arteries become obstructed

4. _____ Blood vessels that carry oxygenated blood away from the heart and through the body

a. Arteries

b. Coronary heart disease (CHD)

c. Atherosclerosis

d. Plaque

e. Arteriosclerosis

f. Heart attack

g. Malignant tumors

h. Basal cell carcinoma

5. _____ Fatty deposits that can build up and narrow the inner walls of arteries

6. _____ The condition more commonly known as hardening of the arteries

7. _____ A common form of skin cancer that is treatable if discovered and removed promptly

8. _____ Also termed myocardial infarction; a life-threatening condition where the supply of oxygenated blood to the heart is cut off due to an arterial blood clot

9. _____ What is formed in the body when the orderly reproduction of cells is disrupted and cell growth is out of control; can cause destruction of other body organs or systems

10. _____ The condition that occurs when artery walls narrow due to buildup of plaque

i. Melanoma

j. Sexually transmitted disease (STD)

11. Psychological factors are related to the occurrence of a heart attack because _____ increase the risk of heart disease.

    a. smoking and poor dietary habits
    b. chronic anger or anxiety
    c. a sedentary lifestyle and failure to control blood pressure
    d. all of the above

12. The buildup of plaque, which causes arteries to become narrower, is known as

    a. arteriosclerosis.
    b. atherosclerosis.
    c. melanoma.
    d. coronary heart disease (CHD).

13. Which of the following is a risk factor for coronary heart disease?

    a. Obesity
    b. Hypertension
    c. Lack of exercise
    d. all of the above

14. Tumors are formed when

    a. cholesterol levels get too high.
    b. levels of the neurotransmitter dopamine get too low.
    c. cells multiply uncontrollably.
    d. arteries become narrow and hardened.

15. How many lung cancer deaths are directly attributable to smoking?

    a. 20%
    b. 30%
    c. 60%
    d. 90%

16. The dietary ingredient most related to the incidence of prostate and colorectal cancers is
    a. dietary fiber.
    b. saturated fat.
    c. sugar and other sweeteners.
    d. alcohol.

17. The vast majority of HIV transmission occurs through
    a. intravenous drug use.
    b. contact with infected blood.
    c. homosexual sex.
    d. heterosexual sex.

18. Which type of skin cancer is most common?
    a. Basal cell carcinoma
    b. Prostate cancer
    c. Melanoma
    d. Ulcerative cancer

19. Antibiotics currently can cure the _____ type(s) of STDs.
    a. genital herpes
    b. bacterial
    c. HIV/AIDS
    d. infectious

20. The best "treatment" for STDs is prevention. Which of the following is an effective prevention method?
    a. Avoiding high-risk individuals, multiple partners
    b. Assuring one has and uses proven barriers such as condoms
    c. Being alert to health risks, and knowing the sexual history of a potential intimate partner
    d. all of the above

ESSAY QUESTIONS

1. What are the leading causes of death in the United States? Of factors relating to these deaths, which involve aspects of our lives that we cannot control? Which involve factors that we can control? How are emotions related to the state of our physical health?

2. What can be done to help avoid being exposed to or contracting an STD?

ANSWER KEY

1.   Melanoma

2.   Sexually transmitted disease (STD)

3.   Coronary heart disease (CHD)

4.   Arteries

5.   Plaque

6.   Arteriosclerosis

7.   Basal cell carcinoma

8.   Heart attack

9.   Malignant tumors

10. Atherosclerosis

11. d

12. b

13. d

14. c

15. d

16. b

17. d

18. a

19. b

20. d

SAMPLE ANSWERS TO ESSAY QUESTIONS

1.   The leading causes of death in the United States are heart disease, followed closely by cancer. Currently, heart disease is the leading cause of death for both men and women. Factors related to heart disease that we cannot control are our genetic heritage, age, and to an extent gender. Presently we cannot change our genetic heritage nor stop the process of aging. Men are somewhat more prone to heart disease than women up until the age of 65. Black non-Hispanic Americans currently are at greater risk for heart disease than are other ethnic groups.

Factors implicated in both heart disease and cancer that we can control include, most importantly, diet, exercise, and smoking. Smoking is implicated in very many illnesses, and nearly all deaths from lung cancer are attributable to smoking. It is possible to stop smoking, and there are programs available to help with this effort. Our risk for disease is lowered if we follow a healthy diet and particularly avoid foods high in saturated fats. A healthy diet will help keep weight under control; obesity is one of the factors related to heart disease. Even moderate exercise (such as a brisk walk) helps reduce the likelihood of heart disease. Other factors related to the leading causes of death are high blood pressure, diabetes, and cholesterol level. All of these can be controlled to an extent through diet and maintaining an appropriate weight; however, there are medications available that will provide further help in managing all of these physiological conditions. Emotions are related to physical health in that chronic anger, chronic anxiety, and perhaps other characteristics related to the Type A personality all are implicated in a higher risk for heart disease. Chronic anger and chronic anxiety trigger the stress response in the human body. Stress hormones such as epinephrine and norepinephrine are secreted: the normal reaction when the body is faced with stress. Chronic emotional arousal means these hormones are always present in the system. They tend to make the heart beat faster, increase blood pressure, increase potential for blood clotting and increase the number of heart contractions. Cholesterol levels may be affected. Persistently agitated emotional states, then, are clearly related to our physical health. It is remarkable to think that so very many major factors relating to our longevity, physical health, and quality of life are simple things that we just need to practice every day.

2. STDs are nearly always contracted through intimate sexual contact, and it should be noted that 70% of AIDS cases worldwide were contracted through heterosexual contact. A far less frequent secondary source for STD infection is shared needles or accidental exposure in a medical setting. The best way to assure that one is not infected with any of the STDs is to prevent any exposure to the diseases in the first place. One can abstain from any intimate sexual contact, or at least until one has established a monogamous relationship with a partner who is also monogamous and not infected in any way. As an alternative, one can practice "safer" sex (there are no certainties regarding prevention when one is involved in a sexual relationship). Safer sex tips include knowing your partner and his or her sexual history; avoiding multiple partners, especially high-risk partners; being alert to obvious and less obvious health risks; using proper barriers; having regular medical care; and avoiding intimate contact with an individual if there are any concerns whatsoever. Since some STDs are life-threatening and currently incurable, thoughtfulness, planning, care, and caution are very important in sexual relationships.

MODULE 10.3 APPLICATION: TAKING THE DISTRESS OUT OF STRESS

LEARNING OBJECTIVE

After you have mastered the information in this unit, you will be able to:

1. Discuss basic skills for effective stress management.

OUTLINE

I. Some Stress is Unavoidable
    A. Life always presents stress of some kind, in some aspect
    B. Some stress seen as helpful in that it keeps us alert, involved in life
    C. Some stress presents challenges which we can effectively meet—enriches life and our sense of accomplishment
    D. Excessive stress unhealthful, need to keep at manageable levels
II. Steps to Take the Distress Out of Stress
    A. Maintain stress at a tolerable level
        1. Reduce daily hassles
        2. Know own limits
        3. Adopt a reasonable schedule
        4. Take frequent breaks
        5. Develop more effective time-management skills
        6. Learn to prioritize
    B. Develop relaxation skills
        1. Perhaps listen to music
        2. Biofeedback, meditation, deep-breathing exercises may be helpful

        3.   Consider a stress-management course

C.   Take care of your body
1.   Get enough sleep
2.   Follow a nutritious, balanced diet
3.   Participate in regular exercise
4.   Get regular medical check-ups
5.   Avoid harmful substances, such as drugs

D.   Gather information—whatever particular issue or illness you are facing, learn more about it

E.   Expand your social network—social support is an important buffer against stress

F.   Humor – laugh a lot

G.   Prevent burnout (physical and emotional exhaustion)
1.   Set reasonable limits and goals
2.   Learn to say "no"
3.   Delegate responsibilities

H.   Replace stress-inducing thoughts with stress-busting thoughts
1.   What is your reaction to disappointing or stressful events?
2.   Are things blown out of proportion?
3.   Review thought pattern in reaction to stress
4.   Keep things in perspective
5.   Remember advantage of self-efficacy (belief in one's capabilities)
6.   Choose achievable goals
7.   Respond to disappointments as opportunities to learn from your mistakes, not as signs of inevitable failure

I.   Don't keep upsetting feelings bottled up
1.   Expressing feelings helps minimize demands on autonomic nervous system
2.   Share with a trusted friend, or consider writing in a journal

J.   Control Type A behavior
1.   Take things slower
2.   Read books for enjoyment (not a textbook)
3.   Leave your computer at home
4.   Avoid rushing through your meals
5.   Engage in enjoyable activities
6.   Develop relaxing interests that you enjoy not simply those preferred by others
7.   Set realistic daily goals
8.   Recognize that hostility is not helpful

K.   Stress may be a fact of life, but it is a fact you can learns to live with

SUMMARY

In this Applications module, you learn about ways to reduce unhealthy stress in your life. There are many things you can do you make the stress in your life manageable and make your life more satisfying and productive. First, review your typical daily pattern. How can you reduce the regular hassles you face? Try not to take on too much. Schedule tasks so you have a reasonable amount of time to get things completed. It is O.K. to take a break once in a while! Prioritize and delegate responsibility as needed. Recognize that problems and obstacles will happen—it is a normal part of life.

Develop relaxation skills. Find what works for you as far as activities or surroundings that you find calming. Take good care of your body. This means that, in general, you get adequate sleep, eat reasonably healthy foods, and exercise regularly. Avoid harmful substances.

Whatever issue (illness-wise, or other) you are facing, learn more about it. Being informed is usually less stressful than being mystified. There may be things you can do, too, to help with the necessary adjustments. Remember how important friends are. We can improve our own social skills and strengthen emotional ties with our families and with other individuals emotionally important to us. There are clubs and organizations at schools and through the community where social activities are arranged, and guests or new members are welcome. Burnout can be prevented through keeping work-related responsibilities within reasonable limits. Allow time for other activities, and participate in these activities. If work demands exceed appropriate levels, learn to say "no," and to delegate responsibilities.

Remember the importance of positive thinking. Attend to your mindset when you respond to life events. Avoid exaggerating the impact of something disappointing that happens to you. Believe in yourself and your ability to handle the events and situations that come your way. If you need to, sharpen your skills and take advantage of opportunities where you can practice and improve your skills with a good likelihood of success. When you are emotionally upset, find a way to share it, either with a trusted friend or family member, or through writing about your experiences and feelings in a journal. Reflect on whether you have the characteristics associated with the Type A personality. If so, recognize that this personality style can take a toll on your health. Find ways to relax and to reduce the sense of pressure and time constraints. Come up with a schedule that allows you sufficient time to get your work done, and avoid taking on more obligations than what you can comfortably meet. Slow down, and take time to relax and enjoy your food and the company of others during meals. All of these steps will help make our lives both physically and psychologically healthier.

CHAPTER 10   APPLICATION EXERCISE

Think of the last time you were sick. What other things were going on in your life? Was it a period of extra stress, or not? How did you become ill? How long did it take for the illness to run its course?

Do you think you are more prone to getting sick during periods of high stress? If so, what can you do to reduce the stress in your life?

CHAPTER 11

Personality

In Chapter 11, you learn about the many different explanations we have for personality. Personality is a relatively stable set of psychological characteristics and behavior patterns that make individuals unique and account for the consistency of their behavior over time. Personality is a composite of the ways in which individuals relate to others and adapt to the demands placed on them by the environment. Personality is such a fascinating feature of ourselves—no wonder there are a myriad of ways to describe and explain it! There is debate as to what personality is, and, in fact, if it even exists. We tend to think of everyone as having a fairly consistent set of traits, which we can expect to encounter most every time we run into someone we know. But is that uniformity and consistency in personality really there? Or do we rely on classifications we have given friends and acquaintances (and even ourselves) because it makes our world more orderly and manageable? Most perspectives on personality presented in this chapter stem from the assumption that personality is fairly stable across time and situations. However, we want to remember that we may be underestimating situational factors and variations.

The earliest modern-day approach to personality was contributed by Sigmund Freud, who felt that all real motivation behind our behaviors lay out of our awareness, deep within the unconscious. He came to this view in part because he was influenced by Charles Darwin, who emphasized the need for a species to ensure its survival. Freud believed that activities necessary for survival (a crucial one being reproduction) had to be pleasurable, otherwise an organism would not do them. Freud proposed a three-part personality structure, which he likened to an iceberg. He felt that the hidden motivation driving all behavior was not in our conscious awareness—it was a hidden, primitive desire for sexual gratification. Freud believed that the inner psyche of the human was dynamic, not static, as the organism was always attempting to strike a balance among its various needs. Freud's developmental stages were characterized by a shift in the locus for that sexual gratification as a child grows older.

Trait theorists take a wholly different view regarding personality. We know innumerable words to describe personality and character. Do we need thousands of different descriptors? Or can personality traits be distilled to fundamental or underlying factors? Trait theorists believe that the latter can be done. They believe human beings have a set of characteristics (traits) that by and large are stable over time and in a variety of situations. The 16PF, the five-factor model, and other tests have been derived to measure these underlying factors. What is still debated among trait theorists is how we acquire our personality traits. The two main explanations, which are well supported, are from genetic influence and sociocultural experiences. How genetic input and environmental experience impact each other continues to be a major focus of study. Personality trait theorists may have attempted to reduce personality to fewer, broader characteristics than really is reflective of human individuality.

The social-cognitive perspective reminds us that much of our personality is probably the cumulative result of learned behavior, with the added component of our reflecting upon various experiences, behaviors, and consequences. Each one of us has a long history of interaction with the world, and our experiences usually result in pleasant or unpleasant outcomes (to a behaviorist, these are reinforcers and punishments). Certainly, we generally keep characteristics that result in desirable outcomes, and we do not exhibit those that have led to unpleasant outcomes. Thus, learning (the behavioral perspective) is a major influence on personality. This view is expanded upon by social cognition theorists to include the notion that personality is influenced by experiences other than just those where we are directly reinforced. Observational (vicarious) learning and our imitation of the behaviors of others also shapes personality. Expectations, past successes or failures, how we think about and interpret our behavior, and our beliefs about consequences clearly influence why humans act as they do.

Lastly, the humanistic perspective turns inward again for an explanation of behavior. The humanistic perspective proposes that all of us are motivated from within to aspire towards self-actualization. Self-actualization involves discovering all of our unique abilities and putting them to best use. As we strive to do this, our efforts are revealed through our external behavior—e.g., our personality. Humanists emphasize the importance of the self and subjective reality in personality. How one interprets a situation is as important as objective features of the situation itself. An important tenet of humanism is the need to treat all people with unconditional positive regard. This means accepting and valuing others (and ourselves!) simply for what we are, allowing everyone space for self-actualization. As Elisabeth Kubler-Ross once shared, we need a t-shirt that says "I am not OK, you are not OK, but that's OK."

How can we measure personality? Currently, both objective (e.g., the MMPI-2) and subjective (e.g., the inkblot test) measures are used. The MMPI-2 is accepted as a valid personality measure. Always, though, it should be remembered that results of a personality test are just one source of information based on interpretation.

MODULE 11.1 THE PSYCHODYNAMIC PERSPECTIVE

LEARNING OBJECTIVES

After you have mastered the information in this unit, you will be able to:

1.   Understand the nature of personality.

2.   Describe the three levels of consciousness that Freud believed comprise the human mind.

3.   Explain the structures of personality in Freud's theory.

4.   Identify psychological defense mechanisms.

5.   Discuss the five stages of psychosexual development in Freud's theory.

6.   Explain the contributions of other psychodynamic theorists, and discuss criticisms of psychodynamic theory.

OUTLINE

I.   Sigmund Freud: the architect of the first major theory of personality called psychoanalytic theory
   A.   Basics of psychoanalytic theory
      1.   A dynamic struggle within the psyche
      2.   Human has sexual (and aggressive) instincts—for survival
      3.   These inborn forces must be balanced with needs of society in socially appropriate ways
         a)   They need to learn that aggression or sexual touching is unacceptable except in socially-acceptable contexts, such as the football field (aggressive impulses) and the marital bed (sexual impulses)
      4.   Psychoanalytic theory created to explain how this balance is achieved
      5.   Represented in terms of four major concepts: levels of consciousness, structure of personality, defense mechanisms, and stages of psychosexual development
   B.   Levels of consciousness
      1.   Mind is like an iceberg; most of mass lies out of range of visible detection
      2.   Contains three parts
         a)   Conscious—present awareness; what we are thinking or feeling at any given moment in time (tip of iceberg we can see)

      b)   Preconscious—stores past experiences or prior learning (easy to access)

      c)   Unconscious—primitive impulses, unacceptable desires, disturbing past experiences (the iceberg mass under the water that we cannot see); not easy to access

C.   The structure of personality—consists of three (hypothetical) mental entities

   1.   Id ("it")

      a)   Operates only in unconscious

      b)   Only psychic structure present at birth

      c)   Contains animal drives, instinctive impulses

      d)   Basic energy that fuels our behavior – stirs us to action to ensure that our basic biological needs are met

      e)   Functions according to pleasure principle—instant gratification, no regard for social rules or customs

   2.   Ego

      a)   Formed during first year of life – represents "reason and good sense" (Freud 1964, p.76)

      b)   Realizes not all instinctual desires will be immediately satisfied

      c)   Learns how to cope with frustration, delay of gratification

      d)   Operates according to reality principle – what is practical and acceptable — satisfy demands in way that is acceptable to society

   3.   Superego

      a)   Internal moral guardian, conscience

      b)   Develops about ages three through five years

      c)   Internalizes norms, moral teachings to which we are exposed

      d)   Most of superego also unconscious

      e)   Judges, evaluates our actions – can impose self-punishment in the form of guilt or shame

   4.   Ego negotiates – great compromiser (balances) between superego and id

   5.   Freud perceived these conflicts (among personality facets) as ongoing

      a)   Behavior a product of ongoing struggles

      b)   Take place outside of conscious awareness

D.   Defense mechanisms

   1.   Prevent anxiety that would occur if unconscious contents were in awareness

   2.   Repression—motivated forgetting involves the banishment of the unconscious of unacceptable wishes, fantasies, urges, and impulses (Boag, 2006), sometimes revealed by slips of the tongue

      a)   Repression permits people to remain outwardly calm and controlled even though they harbor hateful or lustful urges under the surface of awareness – may become revealed in disguised forms, such as in dream symbols and in slips of the tongue (Freud, 1938)

   3.   Other defense mechanisms: regression, displacement, denial, reaction formation, rationalization, projection, and sublimation

   4.   Defense mechanisms can lead to, or be an attempt to hide, abnormal behavior

E.   Stages of personality development

   1.   Psychosexual stages—each related to how individual seeks physical pleasure

   2.   Erogenous zones—sexually sensitive parts of the body

   3.   All bodily processes sexual—because pleasurable, necessary for survival

   4.   Conflicts at any stage can lead to fixations (too much or too little) (being "stuck" in a stage)

5. Freud's five psychosexual stages:
   a) Oral stage—0 to 18 months; mouth, sucking fixation (smoking, nail biting alcohol abuse, overeating)
   b) Anal stage—18 months to 3 years; fixation may make one either excessively fastidious or messy, or cause lack of self-discipline and carelessness
   c) Phallic stage—3 to 6 years; conflicts with parents over masturbation; core conflict is Oedipal, Electra complexes or the desire for parents of the opposite sex leading to rivalry with parents of the same sex; much influence on personality
   d) Latency stage—6 to 12 years; sexual impulses dormant (says Freud!)
   e) Genital stage—puberty; return of sexual interests expressed in mature sexual relationships

II. Other Psychodynamic Approaches
  A. Common characteristic is emphasis on unconscious conflict
  B. Less sexual, aggressive emphasis; more focus on social relationships, tasks of the ego
    1. Erik Erikson posited stages of psychosocial development
  C. Leading neo-Freudians:
    1. Carl Jung—analytical psychology
      a) Broke close ties with Freud
      b) More emphasis on present experiences (vs. early childhood)
      c) Greater emphasis on conscious (vs. unconscious) processes
      d) Have both a personal (repressed memories and impulses) and a collective unconscious (collective unconscious contains accumulated knowledge of the species—explains cross-cultural similarities)
        1. Collective unconscious contains primitive images called archetypes that reflect ancestral or universal human experiences – Jung believed that while these images remain unconscious, they influence our dreams and waking thoughts and emotions
    2. Alfred Adler—individual psychology
      a) Also broke close ties with Freud
      b) Emphasis on individual's unique potential
      c) Important role for consciousness—creative, self-aware of itself and organizes goal-seeking behavior
      d) Proposed concept of inferiority complex – leads to a desire to compensate, since children start out small, with limited abilities; desire to overcome obstacles that lie in the path of pursuing our potentials; drive for superiority
    3. Karen Horney—early feminine perspective
      a) German physician and early psychoanalyst
      b) Agreed that unconscious conflicts shape personality
      c) Less emphasis on sex, aggression; more on social, cultural forces
      d) Emphasized importance of parent-child relationships
      e) Parental impact may lead to basic anxiety or basic hostility in children
      f) Opposed Freud's view of penis envy; females' inferiority more due to lower social status (and women admirable because of ability to reproduce)

III. Evaluating the Psychodynamic Perspective
  A. Most detailed and comprehensive theory on personality to date
  B. Many terms have become part of everyday vocabulary
  C. Possible greatest contribution—suggesting unconscious forces motivate behavior
  D. Criticisms
    1. Too much emphasis on sexual and aggressive drives
    2. Lack of evidence to support many components (e.g., Oedipal complex)
    3. Notions of castration anxiety, penis envy frequently challenged

4. Limited evidence for all of psychosexual theory
5. Much of phenomena cannot be tested (or substantiated) scientifically
6. Is some support for repression, other defense mechanisms (functioning outside of conscious awareness)

SUMMARY

In this module, you learn about the first modern view on personality. Our personality consists of those characteristics that make each of us unique. Early personality theory and a large body of other work relating to human psychology were contributed by one of the most major figures in the field, Sigmund Freud. Freud was influenced by the views of Charles Darwin, and thought that all behaviors necessary for survival were pleasurable, in that an organism must desire to do them and enjoy the experience, otherwise that organism would die. Since most crucial to human survival is that we reproduce ourselves, he came to see human sexuality as the primary motivator in all of existence. He felt that the human was born with this drive for sexual behavior, and that initially our sexual desires override any other consideration. This is the action of the id, the only personality structure Freud said was complete and functioning at birth. The id is driven to satisfy its desires, regardless of the needs or conditions of the rest of the social world (Freud pointed to the typical behaviors of a newborn baby). Freud's theory, known as psychodynamic theory, was an explanation of how humans balance these inborn, powerful, and not always admirable inner drives with the need of the larger society for order and restraint. The inner nature was characterized as "dynamic" because it was always an active struggle between various life forces. Freud believed that most of what substantially influenced us and our behavior was out of our awareness; rather, he believed it was kept within our unconscious.

Freud's view of the personality was that there were three tiers, and the structure of personality resembled the features of an iceberg—most of what is truly powerful lies below the surface and out of our immediate sensory awareness (in the unconscious). The innermost structure, the source of our energy, is the id, as mentioned above (the id is the massive part of the iceberg lying beneath the surface). The id operates by means of the pleasure principle—in other words, "give me what I want, everything that I want, and right now!" Obviously, this extremely selfish point of view will not make it far in the world, and Freud proposed that, after the first year of life, the child begins to develop an ego, which is more sensible (so to speak) and operates under the reality principle.

The ego, according to Freud, is a negotiator and compromiser. It is aware of the needs and boundaries established by society, and attempts to find ways for the id to satisfy its desires yet stay within the confines of what is considered acceptable. This is an ongoing challenge. Freud did not see the aspects of personality as particularly harmonious. Eventually, for most people, according to Freud, we develop the superego.

The superego parallels the notion of a conscience; we have internalized the moral values and beliefs espoused by the individuals and society surrounding us. The conscious part of the superego is our grasp of right and wrong. The powerful, unconscious part of our superego (according to Freud), notes all that we do and sits in judgment of our actions. Obviously, then, the superego can be the source of many feelings of guilt, shame, and self-condemnation. Part of our unconscious involves the use of defense mechanisms, another concept proposed by Freud. Defense mechanisms (such as denial, repression, sublimation, projection) help alleviate anxiety that arises when we fear that the aspects of our personality, in the id, may become visible or apparent to others. The "Freudian slip" is when a hidden part of ourselves accidentally appears; our misspeaking reveals, in fact, what we truly do feel (according to Freud).

Freud believed that our personality developed in stages, keeping in mind that the driving force in human existence, according to Freud, was sexual energy. Thus, Freud's stages of development were known as psychosexual stages. The emphasis is on sexuality (and, he added later, aggressive urges), and each stage represents a different body zone (an erogenous zone), which is the focus of that sexual pleasure for a given stage. Movement through the stages is due to shifts in the site of the reigning erogenous zone.

The earliest stage of psychosexual development is the oral stage. This involves the mouth region, and Freud believed sucking and other stimulation of the mouth was the greatest source of sexual gratification for the infant. One of the features of psychosexual development is the notion of fixation—one can be "stuck" in a stage and retain characteristics of that stage forever if the experience during that period involved too much or too little in the way of appropriate gratification.

The anal stage is the second stage in psychosexual development, covering approximately the ages of one to three years. As the title suggests, the erogenous zone has now shifted to the anal region, and matters relating to urination, defecation, and control of these bodily processes become paramount. Again, aspects of personality are, according to Freud, heavily related to how a child is toilet-trained during this stage.

The third stage of psychosexual development is the phallic stage, covering the ages in childhood of three to six years. This is the stage of development proposed by Freud that is perhaps most controversial of all. Freud said the locus of sexual pleasure is the phallus (the penis in males, clitoris in females). Little girls become aware that they are not "equipped" in the same way as boys, and as a consequence feel inferior. In fact, said Freud, this feeling of inferiority never goes away until, eventually, girls substitute a desire for babies to compensate for their "missing" parts and corresponding inadequacy! According to Freud, female children experience penis envy, and resent their mothers for allowing them to be created without this equipment. Also during this stage, said Freud, boys go through the Oedipal phase, where they sexually desire their mother and plot to destroy their father because he stands in the way of sexual gratification. Boys soon realize, though, that their father may detect this hatred and the boys experience castration anxiety—their fathers would castrate the sons to avoid a potential problem. This fear of castration is eventually resolved (according to Freud) by an identification with the same-sex parent; this is predominantly a means of survival for the young boy. It has been suggested that young girls go through the same type of experience, incestuously desiring their fathers and wishing to destroy their mothers (who are competition).

Ages six to twelve years in psychosexual development is known as a latency period, and in Freud's view sexual matters lay dormant while the child mastered many other skills and activities necessary to life. The final stage of psychosexual development was the genital stage, where the focus is on the genitalia of both sexes, and more appropriate (as opposed to desiring one's parents) sexual partners are chosen.

While Freud's views remain controversial, during his lifetime he attracted a number of followers (who became known as neo-Freudians), many of whom became well known in their own right. They tended to place less emphasis than Freud on sexual and aggressive components, but did share with him a belief in the influence of unconscious conflicts.

The greatest difficulty with the psychosexual perspective was that Freud was unwilling to consider any other substantially important influence on the human besides sexuality. His well-known protégés (Carl Jung, Alfred Adler, and Karen Horney, among others) all concurred regarding the existence and impact of the unconscious, but all suggested other influences (predominantly social and emotional) that were important as well. They emphasized that experiences after childhood were influential too. Many of these neo-Freudians eventually broke their formerly close ties with Freud because he grew increasingly obstinate regarding his own point of view. Carl Jung suggested the interesting notion of a collective unconscious (a common repository shared by all humans consisting of our common history, experiences, and understandings) in addition to the personal unconscious. Alfred Adler created the concept of the inferiority complex, suggesting that this feeling develops naturally in children because they begin their lives smaller and weaker than others. Some of our motivation for behavior, according to Adler, is the drive to overcome these childhood feelings of inferiority. Karen Horney emphasized the powerful influence resulting from parent-child relationships. She was most critical of Freud regarding his views on women, and his relegating of women to a second-class status. She pointed out that the male dominance in society was much more a reason for a sense of inferiority in women than any difference in physiological design. Horney argued that there was no more reason for women to be "jealous" regarding the male's penis than for men to regret that they were not born with a womb and the marvelous physical capacity to reproduce the human species. She suggested that, in fact, males might well be envious of females ("womb envy"!) for having this incredible reproductive ability.

Without question Freud had substantial impact on the field of psychology. He certainly got us talking more about sex! Many noteworthy individuals came into the field because of his work and views. He suggested unconscious sources for human behavior—desires and drives we may truly not be aware of. He provided encompassing, detailed explanations for personality, and how the structure of personality might be derived. However, it is difficult to scientifically prove much, if any, of Freud's theories. In part this is due to components of his theory not easily lending themselves to study—the unconscious or the preconscious, for example. Many of his findings were based on case studies, which may well not be representative of human society at large. We do not find evidence for the Oedipal complex, one of the primary tenets in Freud's thinking. There is support for his notion of defense mechanisms, and the more general idea that influences, perhaps important influences, may be outside of our conscious awareness.

KEY TERMS

Personality

Psychoanalytic theory

Conscious

Preconscious

Unconscious

Id

Ego

Superego

Pleasure principle

Reality principle

Defense mechanisms

Repression

Denial

Reaction formation

Rationalization

Projection

Sublimation

Erogenous zones

Fixations

Oral stage

Anal stage

Anal-retentive personality

Anal-expulsive personality

Phallic stage

Oedipus complex

Electra complex

Castration anxiety

Penis envy

Latency stage

Genital stage

Personal unconscious

Collective unconscious

Archetypes

Individual psychology

Creative self

Inferiority complex

Drive for superiority

Basic anxiety

Basic hostility

SELF-TEST PRACTICE QUIZ

Match the following Key Terms and definitions (note: not every Key Term will be used):

1. _____ The part of the human mind, according to Jung, that contains elements of the history of all humanity

2. _____ A defense mechanism where humans criticize others for faults that they themselves actually have

3. _____ According to Freud, the component of personality that is completely within the unconscious and is the seat of our sexual energy

4. _____ The behaviors and characteristics of the human that remain relatively consistent over time and across situations

5. _____ The standard by which the ego operates—finding socially acceptable ways to satisfy the id's primitive desires

6. _____ A tenet of psychoanalytic theory; it states that young males sexually desire their opposite-sex parent and wish to destroy the same-sex parent who is a rival

7. _____ The view of personality advocated by Freud

8. _____ A defense mechanism where plausible and acceptable (but inaccurate) explanations are provided to justify behavior

9. _____ The defense mechanism where painful or unacceptable thoughts and desires are kept out of conscious awareness

10. _____ A defense mechanism where the individual unconsciously refuses to recognize that a given phenomenon exists

a. Personality
b. Psychoanalytic theory
c. Conscious
d. Preconscious
e. Unconscious
f. Id
g. Ego
h. Superego
i. Pleasure principle
j. Reality principle
k. Defense mechanisms
l. Repression
m. Denial
n. Reaction formation
o. Rationalization
p. Projection
q. Sublimation
r. Erogenous zones
s. Fixations
t. Oral stage
u. Anal stage
v. Anal-retentive personality
w. Anal-expulsive personality
x. Phallic stage
y. Oedipus complex
z. Electra complex
aa. Castration anxiety
bb. Penis envy
cc. Latency stage
dd. Genital stage
ee. Personal unconscious
ff. Collective unconscious

11. _____ According to psychoanalytic theory, the problems and behaviors that result when an individual does not successfully move through a psychosexual developmental stage

12. _____ The fifth and last stage of psychosexual development, according to Freud

13. _____ The portion of the human mind that is completely out of conscious awareness

14. _____ The portion of the personality that, according to Freud, attempts to balance between the desires of the id and the demands and constraints of society

15. _____ The defense mechanism that involves redirecting unacceptable impulses and desires into more socially-acceptable avenues

16. _____ According to Freud, unconscious attempts to protect oneself from anxiety

17. _____ Personality characteristics that manifest a psychosexual fixation resulting from toilet training experiences that were too harsh and demanding

gg. Archetypes

hh. Individual psychology

ii. Creative self

jj. Inferiority complex

kk. Drive for superiority

ll. Basic anxiety

mm. Basic hostility

18. Freud characterized personality structure as consisting of three basic components, which
   a. are the oral, anal, and phallic components.
   b. coexisted harmoniously, leading to the overall productivity of the organism.
   c. were predominantly in our conscious awareness.
   d. had conflicting and sometimes unacceptable objectives.

19. The level of consciousness that involves our awareness of our current state and of everyday events is the
   a. preconscious.
   b. conscious.
   c. unconscious.
   d. reality consciousness.

20. Which component of personality, according to Freud, acts as an internal moral compass?
   a. Superego
   b. Ego
   c. Id
   d. Unconscious

21. What is the correct order of Freud's psychosexual stages?

    a.   Anal, oral, genital, latency, phallic
    b.   Anal, oral, phallic, latency, genital
    c.   Oral, anal, phallic, latency, genital
    d.   Oral, anal, genital, latency, phallic

22. The task of the ego is

    a.   balancing between desires of the id and moral boundaries prescribed by the superego.
    b.   operating under the reality principle.
    c.   finding acceptable avenues to satisfy the organism's desires for gratification.
    d.   all of the above

23. Which of the following is a function of defense mechanisms?

    a.   To prepare an organism to fend off threatening physical attacks
    b.   To provide an excuse for what would otherwise be morally offensive behavior (such as sexual assault)
    c.   To resolve underlying conflicts such as the experience of childhood sexual abuse
    d.   To keep more unpleasant aspects of ourselves out of conscious awareness

24. Freud viewed basic bodily processes such as eating and elimination as sexual because

    a.   they provide feelings of intense sexual pleasure.
    b.   they are vital and necessary for an organism's survival.
    c.   this perspective was part of the theory advocated by Jean Martin Charcot.
    d.   his childhood experiences associated these activities with sexual behavior.

25. If an individual receives either too much or too little gratification at a psychosexual stage, that individual experiences

    a.   repression.
    b.   sublimation.
    c.   fixation.
    d.   reaction formation.

26. Max has unconscious wishes that are inappropriately violent. So he channels them into more acceptable outlets by becoming a boxer. This illustrates the defense mechanism of

    a.   reaction formation.
    b.   sublimation.
    c.   rationalization.
    d.   projection.

27. According to Freud, the Oedipal and Electra experiences occur during the _____ stage.

    a.   phallic
    b.   anal
    c.   latency
    d.   oral

28. According to Freud, boys resolve Oedipus complex by

    a.   developing castration anxiety.
    b.   identifying with their fathers.
    c.   developing a superego.
    d.   identifying with their mothers.

29. Adler felt that feelings of inferiority could lead to

    a.   a drive for superiority.
    b.   a collective unconscious.
    c.   basic hostility.
    d.   basic anxiety.

30. Karen Horney believed that if children's parents are harsh or neglecting
    a. children will repress their feelings of hostility.
    b. the pain of this experience remains in conscious awareness.
    c. children will commit aggressive acts that manifest their anger.
    d. long-term consequences will usually be resolved in adulthood.

ESSAY QUESTION

1. What would you say are important contributions from Freud? What are some aspects of the theories he proposed that you do not see as helpful in promoting our understanding or healthy psychological adjustment?

ANSWER KEY

1. Collective unconscious

2. Projection

3. Id

4. Personality

5. Reality principle

6. Oedipus complex

7. Psychoanalytic theory

8. Rationalization

9. Repression

10. Denial

11. Fixations

12. Genital stage

13. Unconscious

14. Ego

15. Sublimation

16. Defense mechanisms

17. Anal-retentive personality

18. d

19. b

20. a

21. c

22. d

23. d

24. b

25. c

26. b

27.   a

28.   b

29.   a

30.   a

SAMPLE ANSWER TO ESSAY QUESTION

1.   There is no doubt Sigmund Freud has been a tremendously influential figure in the history of psychology. Not all of that influence has, in fact, been good. Freud provided what remains the most comprehensive and detailed picture we have of personality—though it may not be truly accurate. He proposed the useful and substantiated notion of the unconscious, suggesting that there may be reasons or drives outside of our awareness that help explain why we do what we do. Freud brought the topic of sexuality to the forefront as part of psychological development, and this aspect truly had been suppressed and ignored by the society of his time. Freud's theories inadvertently helped trigger the examination of women's roles in society, and reflected the societal notion according females a lower status—a view that was then vigorously challenged. Although perhaps off base, psychosexual stages of development highlight the experiences of early childhood as crucial, and this is an understanding that is now widely advocated. Freud believed all stages of psychosexual development, and movement through them, were driven by desires for sexual gratification. Freud's psychodynamic theories spawned work by a number of neo-Freudians who themselves made substantial contributions to the field.

The greatest drawback to Freud's views and theories is that, no matter how provocative, far-reaching and detailed they may be, they still may be wrong. It is next to impossible to test or to substantiate nearly all of the components that are fundamental to psychoanalytic thinking. How can we research the unconscious? How can we identify or verify the "negotiations" of the ego? Did you or your adorable young son or daughter really hate the same-sex parent as a four-year-old, and desire sexual relations and gratification involving the opposite-sex parent? Does sexuality truly motivate everything we do? Another, perhaps more subtle, drawback to Freud's theorizing is that he characterized the human as fundamentally selfish, dominated by sexual impulses and consumed (no matter how graciously the ego attempts to channel it) solely with obtaining one's own wants. Freud not only assumed that interpersonal conflict is unavoidable (competition for desired sexual targets, for example), but that the inner nature of the human, too, seethes with hostility and unrest, no matter how well this seething conflict is masked by outward behavior. He does not propose that the human is inherently a creature of peace, regarding dealings both within and without the boundaries of the organism; rather, we must all adopt a façade in order to coexist socially, and there is always inner struggle. Interestingly, the latency phase in psychosexual development covers the childhood ages of six to twelve years. During this time, according to Freud, the child's sexuality is dormant because psychological energies are directed elsewhere. It is a less dramatic criticism of Freud's views, but the ages of six to twelve years (pre-puberty) are one time we can be sure sexual interest and activity are a focal point for the developing child!

MODULE 11.2 THE TRAIT PERSPECTIVE

LEARNING OBJECTIVES

After you have mastered the information in this unit, you will be able to:

1.   Define trait and explain the three types of traits in Allport's model.

2.   Describe Cattell's view on the organization of traits.

3.   Identify the three traits represented in Eysenck's model.

4.   Explain the "Big Five" trait model of personality.

5.   Discuss the role of genes in personality.

OUTLINE

I.   The Approach of Trait Theorists
  A.   Look within personality to explain behavior
  B.   Relatively stable, enduring characteristics are traits
  C.   Traits help explain behavior across situations
  D.   Traits suggest why people differ with regard to personality
  E.   Considerations: How are traits organized, measured? Learned or innate?

II.   Gordon Allport: A Hierarchy of Traits
  A.   Traits inherited, but influenced by experience
  B.   Traits occur in a hierarchy with regard to degree of influence
    1.   Cardinal traits—highest level; are pervasive characteristics that influence a person's behavior in most situations- few people possess such dominant traits
    2.   Central traits (basic building blocks)—most common though less far-reaching; influence behavior in many situations – example competitiveness, generosity, independence, arrogance and fearfulness (the kinds of traits you would generally use when describing the general characteristics of other people's behavior)
    3.   Secondary traits—more superficial (e.g., preferences in clothing, music) – which affect behavior in fewer situations

III.   Raymond Cattell: Mapping the Personality – organized personality traits into a complex hierarchy
  A.   Two basic levels of traits
    1.   Surface traits—rather obvious – correspond to ordinary descriptions of personality
      a)   We can infer from observations of behavior
      b)   Examples are friendliness, helpfulness, and emotionality
      c)   Surface traits often occur together
      d)   These linkages suggest more general, underlying traits
    2.   Source traits
      a)   Describe more general aspects of personality at a deeper level that give rise to surface traits
      b)   Derived from factor analysis
      c)   Basis for 16 Personality Factor Questionnaire (16PF)

IV.   Hans Eysenck: A Simpler Trait Model
  A.   Constructed a simpler model with three major traits
  B.   Eysenck's traits:
    1.   Introversion (solitary, reserved and unsociable) - extraversion (outgoing friendly and people –oriented)
    2.   Neuroticism – tense, anxious, worrisome, restless and moody
    3.   Psychoticism – cold, antisocial, hostile and insensitive
  C.   Combinations yield four basic personality types: extraverted-neurotic, extraverted-stable, introverted-stable, and introverted-neurotic (Eysenck, 1982)
  D.   Variations in personality are due to biological (neurological) differences

V.   The Five-Factor Model of Personality ("Big Five")
  A.   The most widely adopted trait model of personality
  B.   Five broad personality factors consistently found in personality research
    1.   Neuroticism
    2.   Extraversion
    3.   Openness – imaginative, curious, intellectual, and open to nontraditional values

4. Agreeableness – sensitive, warm, tolerant, easy to get along with, concerned with other's feelings and needs

5. Conscientiousness – tends to increase in early and middle adulthood, which is a time of life when people tend to take on more career and family responsibilities (Caspi, Roberts, & Shiner, 2005; Donnellan & Lucas, 2008)
   a) Conscientiousness is also linked to living longer and healthier lives, perhaps because it is associated with lower rates of reckless behavior, such as unsafe driving, and with healthier eating patterns, lower body weight, and less use of alcohol and drugs (Brummett et al., 2006 Deary et al., 2008; Kern & Friedman, 2008; Roberts et al., 2009)

C. A consolidation and integration of factors previously identified

D. Good support from many cross-cultural studies

E. Still not the final word regarding basic factors in personality

F. Consists of few, broad categories—may not capture richness, variety in human personality

VI. The Genetic Basis of Traits
   A. Heredity has an important role in shaping personality
   B. Genes are linked to neuroticism, shyness, and aggressiveness
   C. Greatest focus is how environment, biology interact (mutually influential)

VII. Evaluating the Trait Perspective
   A. Trait perspective has intuitive appeal
   B. Trait terms are commonly used, convenient
   C. Trait theories are basis of many personality tests
   D. Traits tend to be relatively—but not completely—stable over time
   E. Criticisms:
      1. Traits label but do not explain behavior, may overlook individuality
      2. Behavior not at all necessarily stable over time or across situations
      3. Do we need to consider situational factors?
      4. Personality probably an interaction between traits, environment

SUMMARY

In this module, you look at a second way of characterizing personality (Freud's psychodynamic model proposed inborn, unconscious motives). This way of looking at personality is the trait perspective. Personality theorists who adhere to the trait perspective believe that personality is relatively stable over time, but rather than emanating from the unconscious, as in Freud's model, trait theorists see personality as a function of where each human being falls relative to basic human characteristics. What these basic human characteristics are has remained something of a debate.

Gordon Allport (1897–1967) believed traits had a hereditary component, but were also influenced by environmental experience. In this sense, he was ahead of his time because that is the conclusion personality theorists have arrived at as of the current thinking. Allport divided traits into categories that fit a hierarchy. Cardinal traits were those overreaching characteristics that were consistent with an individual, and present (though perhaps not clearly overt) in most behavioral situations. Central traits were the middle ground, and he felt these were what typically characterized most people. The most transient, rather superficial traits were categorized as secondary traits. Raymond Cattell (1905–1998) also looked at traits as an explanation for behavior, and began with many, which he then distilled down to a few (by means of the statistical procedure known as factor analysis—finding the central, underlying characteristic that was the common factor representing a cluster of related traits). He felt that there were surface traits (the obvious ones that we see in our daily interactions with others) and the deeper-level source traits; these source traits were the result of his factor analysis procedure. He could measure the degree of source traits by means of the personality test he invented, the 16 Personality Factor Questionnaire (16 PF). Each trait was not a single concept but a continuum, and the test-taker could score anywhere along that continuum as to the degree of one pole or another that individual exhibited. Hans Eysenck (1916–1997) narrowed personality down to just three traits (or trait dimensions): introversion-extraversion, neuroticism, and psychoticism. He concluded that there were four basic personality types that were simply combinations of his personality dimensions. He felt that personality was biological in nature, in that qualities of the human nervous system vary. These neurological differences, Eysenck believed, led to the different manifestations known as personality. The "Big Five" approach to personality is the modern-day distillation of previous personality theories and identified traits. This five-factor model (FFM) suggests the basic traits are: neuroticism, extraversion, openness, agreeableness, and conscientiousness. It is an interesting concept if everything about you reduces to these five trait dimensions! However, cross-cultural studies to date do provide extensive solid support for this model.

Why would there be such universal findings of basic personality trait dimensions? Increasingly, especially as we gain a better ability to study genetic coding, we are turning to biology to provide the answer. Indeed, already we know there are genes that are related to the manifestation of neuroticism, aggression, shyness, and novelty-seeking. Our focus in personality, in fact, has become a study of how "nature" and "nurture" influence each other. Much of the behavior exhibited by humans undoubtedly is a combination and interplay of genetic heritage and cultural-environmental experience.

The trait approach to personality is extremely useful, and fits the perspectives and assumptions of most individuals. It is helpful for classification purposes. However, one objection to the trait approach is that it, like "instinct" used elsewhere to explain human behavior, does not really explain behavior after all. Rather, it simply describes, or labels, certain personality features. A substantial argument against the trait theory approach is that perhaps we want personality in others, and ourselves, to be stable—but is it really? Have we, perhaps by choice, overlooked the influence of situations, and the unavoidable ensuing variability? Other people and ourselves are surely more manageable and less threatening if we can think of humans as exhibiting fairly consistent personality and behavioral traits. However, with personality and other aspects of human behavior, we should not underestimate the power and influence of unique individuality and situational factors.

KEY TERMS

Traits

Cardinal traits

Central traits

Secondary traits

Surface traits

Source traits

Introversion-extraversion

Neuroticism

Psychoticism

Five-factor model (FFM)

SELT-TEST PRACTICE QUIZ

Match the following Key Terms and definitions:

1. _____ One of Eysenck's three personality dimensions, describing an individual who is characterized by emotional instability, anxiousness

2. _____ Allport's term for the most superficial and transient category of traits included in his personality trait hierarchy

3. _____ The most overriding and stable characteristics of personality, according to Allport

4. _____ One of Eysenck's three personality dimensions, describing an individual who is characterized as being distant, unfeeling, antisocial, and hostile

5. _____ Underlying traits, according to Cattell, that represent a distillation of more apparent surface traits

6. _____ The general term for personality characteristics exhibited by an individual that are relatively consistent over time and across situations

7. _____ A term from Cattell's research on personality describing numerous characteristics that are obvious to an observer

8. _____ Fairly common personality characteristics that, according to Allport, are the basic building blocks influencing behavior in many situations (like generosity, independence)

9. _____ The current most widely advocated trait model of personality, where all of personality is revealed by means of five basic dimensions

a. Traits

b. Cardinal traits

c. Central traits

d. Secondary traits

e. Surface traits

f. Source traits

g. Introversion-extraversion

h. Neuroticism

i. Psychoticism

j. Five-factor model (FFM)

10. _____ One of Eysenck's three personality dimensions, representing a continuum with regard to how sociable and outgoing, or how reserved, an individual is

11. The trait perspective adheres to the approach that personality is

    a. a set of characteristics describing an individual that are fairly stable across time and situations.
    b. a function of unconscious conflicts and desires that are out of our awareness and often out of our control.
    c. a consequence of one's thinking and the development of behavioral schemas.
    d. dictated predominantly by whatever environment we happen to be in.

12. With respect to the genetic basis of personality,

    a. most traits have been shown to be largely determined by single genes.
    b. there is no way to study the effects of genetics on personality
    c. genetics may influence personality, but life experiences may also affect biology in turn.
    d. there does not seem to be evidence for a biological basis for personality.

13. Cattell created a personality test that was called the

    a. Cattell Personality Hierarchy of Traits (CPHT).
    b. 16 Personality Factor Questionnaire (16 PF).
    c. Cattell Personality Trait Inventory (CPTI).
    d. Five-Factor Model of Personality (FFM).

14. Which of the following is a criticism of the trait approach to personality?

    a. It lacks intuitive appeal.
    b. It labels behavior, but does not explain that behavior.
    c. It focuses too much on the role of the unconscious.
    d. It has not proven useful in the development of personality tests.

15. Which of the following is NOT one of the "Big Five" personality traits?

    a. Conscientiousness
    b. Extraversion
    c. Openness to experience
    d. Psychoticism

ESSAY QUESTIONS

1. Discuss how the "Big Five" (or five-factor model) approach to personality is in large part a combination and integration of previous trait theorists' work.

2. How is the trait model approach to personality an effective tool in understanding human behavior? What are some limitations or criticisms of trait theory?

ANSWER KEY

1. Neuroticism
2. Secondary traits
3. Cardinal traits
4. Psychoticism
5. Source traits
6. Traits
7. Surface traits
8. Central traits
9. Five-factor model (FFM)
10. Introversion-extraversion
11. a
12. c
13. b
14. b
15. d

SAMPLE ANSWERS TO ESSAY QUESTIONS

1. The work of all trait theorists has been to determine the set of true personality characteristics or dimensions, which then provide the means to represent all personality variations in the human. Although the trait approach seems intuitive, and inherently useful, this is a task that is easier said than done. Gordon Allport was the first contemporary personality theorist to adopt a trait perspective. There were many different personality traits in his model, and these traits were classified according to how extensive their influence on an individual was. Cardinal traits were the broadest, and according to Allport few people really had characteristics of this nature. Mother Teresa, for example, who devoted her life to serving and helping the poor in India, or Joan of Arc, might be viewed as having this cardinal trait of spiritual commitment. Allport's category of central traits again included many characteristics—these are the terms we use every day (helpful, friendly, competitive, a loner). Allport's central traits and Cattell's surface traits both covered the same kinds of concepts. Cattell took these many traditional trait labels and distilled them, he believed, into the truly accurate underlying dimensions of personality. Thus, the many different traits identified by Allport and later Cattell (as surface traits) were reduced to a smaller (and eventually much smaller) set of personality dimensions. The "Big Five" approach has built upon the many and extensive trait investigations carried out by earlier personality trait researchers.

2. The trait approach to human personality has been very useful, in part because the concepts seem so apparent, and they are commonly expressed within the whole of our society. In addition, extensive cross-cultural studies and other research variations based on the model have resulted in consistent support for a trait approach to personality. Characterizing other individuals (whether they are our friends or not) on the basis of traits seems almost intuitive, and is a needed and handy way to organize, categorize, and thus better manage our social world. As with any widespread psychological phenomena, however, there are some relevant criticisms or short-comings to this model. A major criticism is that "traits" may in fact be far less stable, or far less consistent, than we would like to believe. The trait approach does not account for situational factors, which surely

must be a powerful source of influence upon how we act at any given time. In addition, people described with the same "trait" may still have differences in personality; that is, even with regard to this particular trait, it may be manifested at different times and in different ways, depending upon the individual. Traits may appear to explain, when in fact they really just label. Lastly, the major trait approaches discussed here tend to limit personality characteristics to a few basic dimensions. Again, this may be convenient, but personality is very rich, very unique, and with endless variety. We can focus not just on commonalities, but upon individual variation as well.

MODULE 11.3 THE SOCIAL-COGNITIVE PERSPECTIVE

LEARNING OBJECTIVES

After you have mastered the information in this unit, you will be able to:

1. Discuss locus of control and understand the role of expectancies and subjective values.

2. Explain the model of reciprocal determinism.

3. Discuss the role of situation and personal variables.

OUTLINE

I. Personality as Resulting from Learned Behaviors
    A. Another view besides Freud's and that of trait theorists
    B. Personality is learned, like all of behavior
    C. Total experience is history of reinforcements, punishments
    D. Exhibited personality characteristics are those strengthened by family, culture

II. Contemporary Version: Social-Cognitive Theory
    A. Broader view regarding learned behavior
    B. Consider cognitive, social aspects of behavior
    C. Includes expectancies, values, and role of imitation
    D. Humans think about and act on world, not just react to it
    E. Psychologist Julian Rotter, Albert Bandura, and Walter Mischell

III. Julian Rotter: The Locus of Control
    A. To understand personality, know history of reinforcements—and some cognitive aspects
    B. Expectancies—beliefs regarding end result of behavior
    C. Subjective value—personal importance placed on various outcomes
    D. Locus of control—belief regarding source of forces that ultimately determine outcomes
        1. Internal locus of control
            a) Individual believes outcomes are primarily in his or her own hands
            b) "Internals" more likely to succeed in school, cope with pain, recover more quickly from minor surgery
        2. External locus of control—individual believes outcomes are due to forces out of one's control that one cannot influence

IV. Albert Bandura: Reciprocal Determinism and the Role of Expectancies
    A. Reciprocal determinism—cognitions, behaviors, and environmental factors influence each other; interaction between what we do (our behavior) and what we think (our cognition) – mutually influence each other
    B. Importance of observational learning
    C. Two types of expectancies
        1. Outcome expectations—what we predict about a given behavior
        2. Efficacy expectations—beliefs in one's ability to perform a behavior; success also boosts efficacy expectations

V.   Walter Mischel: Situation versus Person Variables
  A.   Theoretical model has overlap with Rotter, Bandura
  B.   Behavior influenced both by situation and internal personal factors
  C.   Person variables
    1.   Expectancies, subjective values (same as Rotter's model)
    2.   Competencies—knowledge and skills we possess
    3.   Encoding strategies—personal way of interpreting an event
    4.   Self-regulatory systems and plans—the ability to plan courses of action to achieve our goals and to reward ourselves for accomplishing them
  D.   Environment and personal factors interact to produce behavior
  E.   Interactions of emotions with personal factors also important
    1.   Emotional state influences how we encode experiences, form expectations
    2.   Way that events are interpreted and processed (how we encode experiences) is related to subsequent emotional state
VI. Evaluating the Social-Cognitive Model
  A.   Continues long history of impact from learning theorists
  B.   Ongoing reminder of importance of environmental factors
  C.   Learning approach enhanced by adding cognitive factors
  D.   Behavioral and social-cognitive perspectives in therapeutic treatments
  E.   Important to see humans as inquisitive, active, initiating agents (not just passive respondents)
  F.   Criticisms from other personality perspectives (Freudian, trait, humanistic) – critics claim that it doesn't account for unconscious processes and genetic factors in personality
  G.   Today many behavior therapists subscribe to a broader treatment model called cognitive-behavioral therapy which incorporates cognitive as well as behavioral approaches to therapy

SUMMARY

In this module, you learn about a third perspective regarding the source of personality—that proposed by the social-cognitive theorists. Social cognition is primarily an outgrowth of the behavioral perspective. Thus, its history is that of the behavioral school, with influence from Pavlov, Watson, and Skinner. According to behaviorists, we exhibit certain personality characteristics now because we have been reinforced (received a pleasant or desirable outcome) when we exhibited the same behaviors in the past. We refrain from manifesting other behaviors because when we acted in that fashion in the past, the behaviors either were ignored or met with an undesirable outcome. Note that whether or not a behavior is reinforced is unrelated, actually, to how "good" or "bad" that behavior is. A "good" behavioral characteristic such as trust may not be supported by environmental experience. Counter-productive behaviors may be reinforced, perhaps inadvertently or by a subgroup that holds a more aberrant set of values. The behavioral perspective in personality teaches us that personality traits that seem bizarre may be manifested because somewhere in a person's history that type of behavior was reinforced. "Good" personality characteristics may have gone without notice.

The more recent version of behaviorism (social cognition) recognizes that humans don't just react to their environment, being passively shaped by environmental experiences, but they also think about experiences, develop expectations, and initiate activity. This expansion to the traditional behavioral approach is considered by nearly all as an improvement, a better representation of how humans actually are influenced by, and interact with, the environment.

Central to the social-cognitive perspective on personality is the notion that humans develop expectations regarding the results of a behavior they may contemplate doing. We can predict, with some accuracy, what outcomes to our behavior will be, and that understanding impacts, of course, whether we will actually do that behavior we are contemplating. Another feature helping to determine whether or not we will exhibit a behavior is the value, or worth, we place on a potential outcome. If the outcome is something that we very much want, it is far more likely we will exhibit the actions necessary to achieve it. Expectancies and subjective value are personality concepts introduced by Julian Rotter. In addition, those of us who feel more helpless (an external locus of control) regarding what happens in our lives will likely exhibit less effortful personality characteristics than those of us who believe that we are masters of our fate (an internal locus of control).

Albert Bandura proposed a personality model involving reciprocal determinism; that is, behavior, environment, and cognitions all influence each other. Bandura is well known for establishing the impact of observational learning on human behavior. Bandura pointed out that an individual does not have to experience direct reinforcement (the view held by the behaviorists) in order to learn a behavior. We can and do learn much vicariously—through watching what others do, and the consequences they experience. Thus, certainly, part of personality attributes are the result of watching those to whom we are exposed. Bandura concurred with Rotter's view that our personality is affected by expectations; however, Bandura advocated that expectancies are of two different kinds. We have expectations about (1) what the outcome of a given behavior will be, and (2) whether our abilities are sufficient to carry out that behavior. Both of these expectations come into play with regard to whether we show certain personality characteristics or not. Predictions about whether or not we have the ability for a given behavior are known as efficacy expectations. It should be noted that the determination of self-efficacy is somewhat subjective. Whether or not we believe we have certain abilities, and our degree of confidence in those abilities, is closely related to prior successes that involved these abilities. How successful we are has very much to do with whether we believe we will be successful.

Walter Mischel is best known for advocating the important role of situational factors in behavior and personality. His views also by and large parallel those of Rotter and Bandura. He endorses the position that both environment (situation variables) and characteristics of the individual (person variables) influence behavior and thus personality. Mischel notes a total of five relevant person variables: expectancies, subjective values (both of these as in Rotter's model), competencies, encoding strategies, and self-regulatory systems and plans. Recently, Mischel has emphasized the impact of emotions on person variables. Our emotional state may influence how we think, how we evaluate ourselves, and how we perceive the environment. The social-cognitive approach to personality certainly advances our understanding in this field. Criticisms of the social-cognitive perspective arise from those who hold other theoretical positions regarding personality, such as the perspectives discussed elsewhere in this chapter.

KEY TERMS

Social-cognitive theory

Expectancies

Subjective value

Locus of control

Reciprocal determinism

Outcome expectations

Efficacy expectations

Situation variables

Person variables

SELF-TEST PRACTICE QUIZ

Match the following Key Terms and definitions:

1. _____ According to Mischel, an influence on our behavior derived from our history of experience with the environment

2. _____ A factor in personality advocated both by Rotter and Mischel, relating to the consequence one anticipates as the result of a certain action or behavior

3. _____ The notion proposed by Bandura where behavior, cognitions, and environmental experience all interact and influence each other

4. _____ A concept proposed by Rotter, relating to where we think the major force determining the outcome of events in our lives emanates from

5. _____ A term proposed by Bandura that conceptualizes how likely we think it is that we can accomplish certain behaviors

6. _____ A component in the personality approach advocated by Mischel, emphasizing the attributes and capabilities an individual brings to a behavioral setting

7. _____ A factor in personality advocated both by Rotter and Mischel, relating to how meaningful or what worth is placed on achieving a possible outcome

8. _____ A term proposed by Bandura that conceptualizes how likely we believe it to be that a certain end result will occur

a. Social-cognitive theory

b. Expectancies

c. Subjective value

d. Locus of control

e. Reciprocal determinism

f. Outcome expectations

g. Efficacy expectations

h. Situation variables

i. Person variables

9. How would a behaviorist explain why Sharona consistently is polite to others?

   a. Sharona has previously been reinforced for such behavior.
   b. Sharona's politeness is the result of unresolved unconscious conflicts.
   c. Sharona is genetically predisposed to get along with others.
   d. Sharona has an external locus of control.

10. Social-cognitive theory builds on our understanding that a powerful influence on behavior and personality

    a. is derived from our deep-seated fears and anxieties.
    b. involves actions and attributes we have manifested in the past, and whether the end result of these was a positive or unpleasant experience.
    c. is derived from unconscious influences we are not really aware of.
    d. results from our striving to be the best person we can be.

11. Individuals who have confidence in their abilities and who believe they have much impact on the course of events occurring during their lives are categorized as having

    a. unrealistic dreams and expectations.
    b. an egocentric personality.
    c. an internal locus of control.
    d. an external locus of control.

12. Which theorist placed the greatest emphasis on the role of emotions in determining how we evaluate ourselves and our environments?

    a. Julian Rotter
    b. Sigmund Freud
    c. Albert Bandura
    d. Walter Mischel

13. If a teachers offers her students candy bars for high grades, not every student will find them equally attractive. Perhaps one student loves chocolate, another doesn't care for it, and the third is allergic. This illustrates the principle of

    a. efficacy expectation.
    b. outcome expectation.
    c. subjective value.
    d. personal value.

14. Which of the following is NOT one of the person variables proposed in Mischel's model of personality?

    a. Expectancies
    b. Competencies
    c. Encoding strategies
    d. Objective value

15. You decide you will greet whomever you encounter with a positive attitude. You smile and nod politely at the woman in line ahead of you at the grocery store. She smiles back and moves her cart in order to give you more room. This experience exemplifies Bandura's notion of

    a. self-efficacy.
    b. reciprocal determinism.
    c. outcome expectations.
    d. self-regulatory systems.

ESSAY QUESTION

1. What influence has social-cognitive theory had on psychological therapy approaches?

ANSWER KEY

1. Situation variables
2. Expectancies
3. Reciprocal determinism
4. Locus of control
5. Efficacy expectations
6. Person variables
7. Subjective value
8. Outcome expectations
9. a
10. b
11. c
12. d
13. c
14. d
15. b

SAMPLE ANSWER TO ESSAY QUESTION

1. Behavioral therapy, upon which social-cognitive approaches are based, emphasizes the importance of environment, experience, and learning on behavior and personality. If a behavior is exhibited, it is likely that behavior was reinforced (the individual received a pleasant or desirable outcome previously as a consequence of the behavior). If a behavior is not manifested, then perhaps prior experience with the behavior resulted in an unpleasant consequence ("punishment," to a behaviorist). This consequence diminished the frequency with which the preceding behavior occurred, or eliminated it altogether. The knowledge provided from the behavioral perspective is extremely helpful in that we can often pinpoint the cause(s) of a behavior and, presumably, change that behavior by changing the circumstances. If consequences are changed, then associated behaviors likely are altered. Infrequent desirable behaviors can be encouraged.

   Social-cognitive theory and cognitive-behavioral therapy (the term for the treatment approaches based upon social-cognitive theory) have taken psychotherapy a step further beyond the pure behaviorist methodology. Cognitive-behavioral therapy incorporates the realization that the individual is not usually a passive recipient of life experience (of reinforcing and punishing consequences) but rather an active participant and influence upon outcomes. One can learn much just by watching the behavior of, and corresponding consequences for, others. With time and experience, an individual comes to develop certain expectations about a given behavior. Individuals have beliefs as to whether they are capable of certain behaviors, and what likely outcomes are should they do them. Some outcomes in life have more value to us than others.

   As a therapeutic method, cognitive-behavioral treatment gives us the added opportunity to treat not just reinforcers and other consequences present in one's environment, but the thoughts and expectations an individual has about the environment as well. An individual who does not feel successful likely will not attempt new challenges and opportunities and thus will perpetuate a chain of failure. Confidence in our abilities increases the likelihood of a successful outcome. We can objectively evaluate the features of a situation, independent of our own role. Behaviors can still be addressed by means of conventional behavioral therapy. The social-cognitivist approach, however, incorporates the opportunity to examine (and, if need be, suggest appropriate change to), one's thinking, confidence, valuing, and expectations about those behaviors as well.

MODULE 11.4 THE HUMANISTIC PERSPECTIVE

LEARNING OBJECTIVES

After you have mastered the information in this unit, you will be able to:

1. Explain self-theory and self-actualization.

2. Discuss how collectivistic and individualistic cultures view the concept of self.

OUTLINE

I.   Humanistic Perspective
    A.   Conscious choice and personal freedom are crucial
    B.   Our ability to know ourselves, make choices, gives life meaning and personal direction

II. Carl Rogers: The Importance of Self
    A.   Self-theory—Rogers's theory of personality
        1.   The self is the source that directs how we experience the world
        2.   Inner drive leads us towards self-actualization (realizing our own unique potentials)
    B.   Unconditional positive regard—acceptance of any person's basic worth – regardless of whether their behavior pleases or suits us. (This does not mean turn a blind eye toward undesirable behavior - the behavior is undesirable not the person)
    C.   Conditional positive regard—valuing granted only when certain standards met
    D.   Self-ideals—sense of who we should be (sense of self-esteem is closely related), a process of self-discovery and self-awareness; tapping into our true feelings and needs, accepting them as our own
    E.   Client-centered therapy helps people get in touch with their true feelings and come to value and prize themselves

III. Abraham Maslow: Self-Actualization –few of us become fully self-actualized – more a road to be followed than a final destination
    A.   Personality is manifest as we strive towards our unique goals, fulfill potential
    B.   Psychological health involves recognizing, developing our abilities – the path to psychological health is paved with awareness and acceptance of all parts of ourselves, warts and all (we all have our warts)

IV. Culture and Self-Identity—culture influences sense of self
    A.   Collectivistic culture—self is defined as member of a group
    B.   Individualistic culture—self is defined in terms of unique, distinctive characteristics
    C.   Excessive collectivism may stifle creativity, innovation, and personal initiative, whereas excessive individualism may lead to unmitigated greed and exploitation

V.   Evaluating the Humanistic Perspective
    A.   Tremendous impact—focus on inner identity, self-direction, meaning in life
    B.   Emphasis on subjective, conscious experiences (e.g., our interpretation of them)
    C.   Criticisms: perhaps self-indulgent (so absorbed with themselves that they develop a lack of concern for others), cannot study scientifically

SUMMARY

This module discusses yet a fourth, and equally worthwhile, approach to personality, and that is based on our sense of who we are. Humanists believe individuals are striving towards self-actualization, which is the maximum fulfillment of our potential. Since, to a humanist, everyone is unique, only you yourself can truly know who you are and where you want to be headed. A core aspect of the humanistic view is unconditional positive regard. This means we treat all others, and ourselves, with respect and acceptance. This acceptance is appropriate whether or not we like or agree with characteristics exhibited by another. They are permitted their place in the world, as we are permitted and need ours. It is important to honor other people's views, even though they are not our own, because we know we need to be true to our own sense of self in order to progress. We need to discover who we are, like ourselves, and allow ourselves to follow the path that seems right for us. Respect and regard for ourselves, and respect and regard for others, should be approximately equally valued and practiced. We have a sense of ourselves (self-concept) and a sense of who we want to be (self-ideal). Self-esteem is a function of how closely these two match. We need to have regard for ourselves (self-esteem) in order to function well. The drive towards self-actualization is an inner need, so inasmuch as our striving towards self-actualization impacts our personality, personality characteristics are determined from within. The humanistic view emphasizes the importance of having meaning and direction in our lives; thus, the subjective experience of events and relationships is important. How the self interacts with the world, and views the world, determines how an individual will behave in the world.

Culture is a major influence on our sense of self; thus, culture is a strong determinant of personality. A basic difference between cultures is whether they are collectivistic (emphasis is on the group and community values) or individualistic (emphasis is on the individual and autonomy, self-worth).

KEY TERMS

Self-theory

Unconditional positive regard

Conditional positive regard

Self-ideals

Collectivistic culture

Individualistic culture

SELF-TEST PRACTICE QUIZ

Match the following Key Terms and definitions:

1. _____ A cultural view more typical of Asia and South America, where the greater emphasis is placed on needs and roles within the communal group

2. _____ A theory of personality proposed by Carl Rogers, emphasizing that the self is the force that interprets and acts upon the world

a. Self-theory

b. Unconditional positive regard

c. Conditional positive regard

d. Self-ideals

e. Collectivistic culture

f. Individualistic culture

3. _____ Value and acceptance are accorded only when an individual meets our standards or does what we specifically direct

4. _____ A cultural view more typical of the United States and other western countries, where the greater emphasis is placed on the individual and his or her distinctive achievements

5. _____ A component in the theory proposed by Carl Rogers, which suggests the person we would like to be or think we ought to be

6. _____ Treating all individuals with respect and valuing, whether or not they mirror the behaviors and principles we hold as our own standards

7. Knowing our true selves, and trying to make full use of who we are, is known as

   a.   achievement orientation.
   b.   unconditional positive regard.
   c.   self-actualization.
   d.   achievement motivation.

8. When a parent lets children know that Mom or Dad will be unhappy if they don't try out for baseball or the school play, that parent is conveying a message of

   a.   unconditional positive regard.
   b.   action-oriented motivation.
   c.   energizing momentum.
   d.   conditional positive regard.

9. According to humanist theory, our sense of who we want to be (our self-ideal) should come from

   a.   our sense of inner guidance.
   b.   parental and family guidelines.
   c.   teachers and school counselors.
   d.   self-help manuals.

10. Which statement is most likely to be uttered by a member of a collectivist culture?

   a.   "I hope my son gets the highest grades in his class."
   b.   "It is important for me to respect my elders."
   c.   "I like to do things my way."
   d.   "It is good for children to each have their own bedrooms."

11. Which statement about the humanistic perspective is most accurate?

   a.   It suggests that people look within for a sense of direction.
   b.   It can lead to a focus on self that becomes excessive.
   c.   It emphasizes the importance of meaningfulness and purpose in life, despite the demands of one's employment obligations.
   d.   all of the above

12. What is Rogers' term for the impressions that we have of ourselves?
    a. Creative self
    b. Sense of self
    c. Self-concept
    d. Self-esteem

ESSAY QUESTION

1. What are some basic tenets to the personality theory proposed by Rogers and Maslow? How are these approaches different from those of other personality theorists?

ANSWER KEY

1. Collectivistic culture

2. Self-theory

3. Conditional positive regard

4. Individualistic culture

5. Self-ideals

6. Unconditional positive regard

7. c

8. d

9. a

10. b

11. d

12. c

SAMPLE ANSWER TO ESSAY QUESTION

1. Rogers and Maslow differ from other personality theorists discussed in this chapter because they put the greatest emphasis for personality on an inner sense of self, with that self directing an inner sense of guidance which then determines our personality. The humanists point out that how a human experiences the world is subjective—that is, the view is very unique, depending upon the individual. In order to live effectively, the best path for us to take, according to humanists, is to get in touch with our inner person, come to know it and know it well, then put the unique talents and abilities we all have to best use; this leads to a sense of personal fulfillment, known as self-actualization. In this manner, too, we are most effective for others. Because we need our space to be ourselves and live as we feel directed to, humanists propose that we give the same "space" to others, accept them with unconditional positive regard, so that these other individuals may be free to live as they most need to as well. True, not everyone achieves self-actualization, and sometimes following this course means remaining loyal to ourselves and our inner sense of direction despite perhaps contrary demands from others. Although not a component in humanist theory as proposed by Rogers and Maslow, to some the humanistic approach may lead one to be self-indulgent, focused solely on what is occurring with that one individual and excluding concern for the significance or well-being of others. The humanist theory of personality puts the greatest emphasis of all on inner experience and the self. Unlike other theories presented in this chapter, it does not particularly address the influence of situational factors, of experience or learning per se, or of any influences that may emanate from unconscious sources.

MODULE 11.5 PERSONALITY TESTS

LEARNING OBJECTIVES

After you have mastered the information in this unit, you will be able to:

1. Describe self-report personality inventories.

2. Explain projective tests of personality.

OUTLINE

I. History of Attempts to Measure Personality
    A. Early attempts utilized external physical characteristics
    B. Phrenology—judging mental and personal attributes based on bumps on the head
II. Self-Report Personality Inventories (also called objective tests)
    A. Tests can be scored objectively; "yes/no" or "agree/disagree" format rely on people's judgments as to whether they agrees or disagree with particular statements
    B. Minnesota Multiphasic Personality Inventory (MMPI)
        1. MMPI-2 has 567 true-false questions; yields scores on ten clinical scales
        2. Originally constructed to help diagnose psychological disorders
    C. Evaluation of self-report personality tests
        1. Informative, inexpensive, validity supported by research
        2. Answers may not be honest (tendencies to respond in a socially desirable directions); use other sources as well for diagnosis
III. Projective Tests
    A. General features
        1. Use unstructured, ambiguous, open-ended stimuli
        2. Test-takers "project" their unconscious needs, desires onto these vague stimuli
    B. Rorschach test
        1. As a child, Rorschach found inkblots interpreted differently
        2. Scoring is complex; results must be interpreted by test administrator
    C. Thematic Apperception Test (TAT)—stories about TAT's ambiguous scenes may reveal aspects of personality, psychological issues
    D. Evaluation of projective tests—drawbacks include subjective nature of scoring (largely based on the examiner's subjective impressions), possible "pull" in features of ambiguous stimuli

SUMMARY

In this module, you learn about the avenues we have for measuring someone's personality. There are more objective approaches, such as the MMPI-2 (Minnesota Multiphasic Personality Inventory) and more subjective personality tests such as the Rorschach (inkblot) and TAT (Thematic Apperception Test). The MMPI consists of a great number of questions, to each of which the respondent indicates "true" (it applies to the respondent) or "false" (it does not apply). The MMPI was originally designed to detect mental disorders, but is now a very widely used personality test. We cannot completely assure that a test-taker has responded to MMPI questions truthfully. The Rorschach test and TAT are useful indicators of personality, since they are more open-ended and reveal themes in a test-taker's responses. A problem with subjective tests, however, is that much rests on how they are scored. Interpretation is mostly in the hands of the test administrator. Self-report inventories (such as the MMPI) do show consistent evidence of validity. The objective tests indicate scores on mental and clinical scales, and also can reveal much about the test-taker's personality and interests.

KEY TERMS

Phrenology

Personality tests

Self-report personality inventories

Objective tests

Standard scores

Projective tests

SELF-TEST PRACTICE QUIZ

Match the following Key Terms and definitions:

1. _____ A type of personality test where the test-taker is free to choose among test responses

2. _____ Scores that have been converted to interpretable differences relative to the average score

3. _____ Determining personality based on the pattern of bumps on the head

4. _____ Tests that have a consistent and standardized method for scoring (such as the MMPI)

5. _____ Tests such as the Rorschach and TAT, where scoring is more a matter of interpretation

6. _____ Tests to evaluate fairly enduring behavioral features that characterize an individual

a. Phrenology

b. Personality tests

c. Self-report personality inventories

d. Objective tests

e. Standard scores

f. Projective tests

7. What does it mean to describe a personality test as "objective"?
   a. It is always accurate.
   b. It is based on psychoanalytic theory.
   c. Test-takers may only choose from a small number of answer options.
   d. none of the above

8. Scores on the MMPI are obtained by comparing the test-taker's responses to
   a. scores of other individuals taking the personality test at the same time.
   b. the mean and standard deviations of test-takers from the current year.
   c. patterns of responses reported by diagnostic groups and normal controls.
   d. subjective interpretations provided by the test administrator.

9. If you were asked to tell stories about some ambiguous scenes, you just took the
   a. MMPI.
   b. Rorschach test.
   c. phrenology test.
   d. TAT.

10. What is the common characteristic of all projective tests?
    a. They involve multiple-choice questions.
    b. They ask the test-taker to interpret ambiguous stimuli.
    c. They are based on humanistic theory.
    d. They are widely considered to be the most accurate type of personality test.
11. Which of the following is NOT a common criticism of projective tests?
    a. They involve too many multiple-choice questions.
    b. There are concerns about the reliability of such tests.
    c. They may "pull" for certain types of responses.
    d. Scoring is dependent largely on the examiner's subjective impressions.

ESSAY QUESTION

1. Why must we be careful about the results of any personality test?

ANSWER KEY

1. Self-report personality inventories

2. Standard scores

3. Phrenology

4. Objective tests

5. Projective tests

6. Personality tests

7. c

8. c

9. d

10. b

11. a

SAMPLE ANSWER TO ESSAY QUESTION

1. We always need to be careful about the results of any personality test. Self-report tests can be scored objectively and allow the respondent to reply however he or she wishes, but the responses may not always be forthright. Projective tests are very subjective, with the interpretation resting very much in the hands of the administrator. Personality tests are just one source of information about an individual; a variety of indicators regarding psychological assessment should be used.

MODULE 11.6 APPLICATION: BUILDING SELF-ESTEEM

LEARNING OBJECTIVES

After you have mastered the information in this unit, you will be able to:

1. Describe some ways of building self-esteem.

OUTLINE

I.   Ways We Can Strengthen Our Self-Esteem (self-esteem is not a fixed quality; it goes through ups and downs throughout the course of life (Robins et al., 2002)
   A.   Acquire competencies—self-esteem is related to ability for accomplishments
   B.   Set reasonable goals
   C.   Have confidence in your abilities and likelihood of success
   D.   Create a sense of meaningfulness—think of what is really important to you
   E.   Be willing to accept level less than perfectionist
   F.   Moderate need for approval from others – psychologist Albert Ellis believed that an excessive need for social approval is a sure-fire recipe for low self-esteem (Ellis, 1977; Ellis & Dryden, 1987); we all encounter the disapproval of people who are important to us, and we also run into people who fail to appreciate our finer points
      1)   Evidence links higher self-esteem in adolescence to better emotional and physical health, lower levels of criminal behavior, and greater financial success in adulthood (Trzesniewski et al., 2006)

SUMMARY

The humanistic school in particular emphasizes how important it is that we have a good sense of self-esteem. Self-esteem is our confidence in ourselves and our belief that we are capable and effective individuals. Self-esteem is closely related to the successes we have achieved over the course of our lives. Of course, part of being successful is believing in our self-efficacy, and choosing tasks that are at a level appropriate for us.

We can increase our sense of self-esteem by making sure we have skills and abilities that we want to have. It is important to be good at something, and everyone can be good at something. It may take a little effort to develop skills leading to proficiency. We want to set reasonable goals—our achievements should be geared to a level that we can realistically achieve. It is important to choose tasks at our level and believe that we will succeed. Meaningfulness in our lives and in our work is related to our sense of self-esteem. If we believe in ourselves, have developed some skills and proficiencies that we find useful, and find life meaningful, we will achieve enough of a sense of confidence that we will be less dependent upon the approval of others. We can set our own reasonable standards for achievement.

CHAPTER 11   APPLICATION EXERCISE

What do you think shapes our personality? Why are you the way you are? Take a few minutes to jot down a brief description of your characteristics. Ask a friend to add his or her list regarding your personality.

Now—analyze your personality. Review the different approaches to personality discussed in this chapter. Which has influenced you the most? Unconscious drives? A cluster of fairly stable traits you may have inherited? Habits and actions you imitate from seeing behavior in others? Situational factors? Characteristics that manifest themselves as you move towards self-actualization? Come up with your own explanation for personality, and what best explains the characteristics you exhibit. You may contemplate, too, whether your theory of personality fits only you and your characteristics, or whether it is applicable to others you know as well.

CHAPTER 12

Psychological Disorders

In Chapter 12, you learn about some of the many psychological disorders that are considered to constitute abnormal behavior. In the United States and many other countries, the *Diagnostic and Statistical Manual of Mental Disorders (DSM)* is used to help make the determination of psychological disorder. Diagnosing someone as mentally ill is not easy. To help in the diagnosis, we look for a set of characteristics regarding psychological problems, but psychologically healthy people can show these characteristics at times also. Specifically, mental health professionals look for unusualness, degree of social deviance, evidence of emotional distress, maladaptive behavior, dangerousness, and, key to the severe psychotic disorders, distortions of reality.

Psychological disorders are grouped into categories, and disorders common to a classification share a pool of psychological symptoms. Abnormal behaviors presented in this chapter include anxiety disorders, dissociative disorders, somatoform disorders, mood disorders, schizophrenia, and personality disorders. When evaluating a person for psychological disturbance, we must always consider cultural factors. It is true that some behaviors may be accepted or even expected in some cultures but not in others. Also, the way in which symptoms are manifested may vary by culture.

Only recently have people with mental illnesses been treated somewhat benignly. For most of the history of humanity, people with psychological disorders were viewed as being possessed. They were thought to be controlled by supernatural forces, or to be inhabited, literally, by demons. The standard treatment for "possession" was exorcism. Beginning sometime in the 18th century, society took a more accurate and compassionate look at psychological disorders as we began to learn more about the functioning of the human body in general. Due to medical advances, researchers began to regard psychological disorders as having some similarities to physical disorders and illnesses.

Probably the most widespread disorders relating to westernized societies are anxiety (in the classification of anxiety disorders) and depression (classified among the mood disorders). Women are nearly twice as likely as men to develop major depression. Psychological disorders affect just about everyone in one way or another – either directly or we may know someone. People suffering anxiety disorders tend to be agitated, cannot find peace, and often are consumed with perpetual worry. Phobias, panic attacks, and obsessive-compulsive disorder (OCD) are also included in the anxiety disorders classification. Dissociative disorders include dissociative amnesia and dissociative identity disorder (formerly classified as multiple personality disorder). Somatoform disorders involve individuals who experience physical problems, but there is no obvious underlying physical cause (hypochondriasis is one example). The category of mood disorders includes depression and also bipolar disorder, which in the past was referred to as manic-depression. Mood disorders affect our emotional state to the extent that we cannot function effectively. The most serious psychological disorder is schizophrenia, in that it is classified as a psychotic disorder (the individual has truly lost touch with reality); it tends to affect individuals over the course of their entire lives, and its treatment consumes the bulk of our mental health expenditures. Personality disorders are the last classification of disorders presented, and the most-researched personality disorder is the antisocial personality. Individuals with this disorder were previously known as psychopaths or sociopaths.

What are the causes of psychological disorders? The nature and manifestation of psychological disorders is complex, and as such we expect that a variety of factors contribute, probably in combination, to the emergence of the problem. Genetic (If you have an identical twin with schizophrenia, your chances of developing the disorder yourself are less than 50 percent.), biological, cognitive, environmental, and unconscious influences all appear to be implicated in the experience of psychological disorder. With ongoing research, we are continuing to learn more about these troubling, yet fascinating, disorders. The descriptions in this chapter are not intended to make you a diagnostician. Discuss any concerns you may have with a qualified professional.

MODULE 12.1 WHAT IS ABNORMAL BEHAVIOR?

LEARNING OBJECTIVES

After you have mastered the information in this unit, you will be able to:

1.   Describe the criteria generally used to determine whether behavior is abnormal.

2.   Identify the major models of abnormal behavior.

3.   Explain the nature, prevalence, and classification of psychological disorders.

OUTLINE

I.   Charting the Boundaries between Normal and Abnormal Behavior
  A.   Criteria for abnormal behavior (psychological determination of disorder is complex)
    1.   Unusualness—experienced by only a few
    2.   Social deviance—not considered acceptable given social context
    3.   Emotional distress—anxiety or depression, are considered abnormal when inappropriate, excessive, or prolonged relative to the person's situation
    4.   Maladaptive behavior—causes distress, self-defeating, self-destructive - associated with significant health, social, or occupational problems
    5.   Dangerousness—harmful, violent behavior; again, consider social context – may be an act of bravery in times of war or in a sports event
    6.   Faulty perceptions or interpretations of reality—hallucinations, delusions, and distortions of reality
  B.   Cultural bases of abnormal behavior
    1.   Always must consider social, cultural context when making evaluation
    2.   Disorders may take different forms in different cultures
    3.   Behaviors may be considered disordered or not, depending on era in history (e.g., evaluation of homosexuality)
  C.   Applying the criteria—apply several criteria in order to accurately evaluate
II.   Models of Abnormal Behavior
  A.   Early beliefs
    1.   Ancient times through Middle Ages—disturbed people thought possessed by demons or controlled by supernatural forces
    2.   Treatment was exorcism, or more severe
  B.   The medical model
    1.   18th and 19th centuries—medical discoveries and advances
    2.   Shift to ideal that mental disturbance is an illness – having a biological or psychological not a demonic basis
  C.   Psychological models
    1.   Psychodynamic (Freud)—disturbance due to unresolved unconscious conflict, stemming from childhood
    2.   Behavioral—disturbed, maladaptive behaviors learned or acquired through experience the same way normal behaviors learned
    3.   Humanistic

a) Disturbance due to encountering roadblocks on path to self-actualization

b) Individuals have lost touch with inner self , over-concern with standards of others, distorted self-image

4. Cognitive

a) Disturbances due to irrational, distorted thinking

b) Interpreting negatively, exaggerating negative consequences

D. The sociocultural model

1. Must evaluate in terms of broader social, cultural context

2. Problem may lie with social ills, failures of society

3. Poverty, ethnic background, discrimination included in study

4. Labeling sufferers results in social prejudices; compounds problem – denied job or housing opportunities and become stigmatized

E. The biopsychosocial model

1. Many useful models to explain abnormal behavior

2. Disturbance is the result of combination, interaction of factors (including psychological, biological, or sociocultural)

3. Diathesis-stress model

a) Diathesis is a predisposition –(increases the risk of developing a particular disorder), vulnerability (genetic or psychological)

b) The stronger the diathesis, the less stress is typically needed to produce the disorder

III. What Are Psychological Disorders?

A. Basic characteristics of psychological disorders

1. Also known as mental disorders, mental illnesses

2. Patterns of disturbed behavior, mood, thinking, or perception that cause personal distress or impaired functioning

B. How many are affected?

1. Approximately half (46 percent) of Americans have a diagnosable disorder at some point

2. Essentially everyone is affected by psychological disorders

C. How are psychological disorders classified?

1. *Diagnostic and Statistical Manual of Mental Disorders (DSM)*

2. Features of DSM

a) Descriptions and diagnostic criteria for every recognized mental disorder

b) Classification system based on distinctive features or symptoms – the DSM goes beyond merely classifying it is used to assess multiple dimensions, five in total: (1) major clinical syndromes; (2) personality disorders and mental retardation; (3) general medical conditions affecting a person's mental health; (4) psychosocial and environmental problems impairing the person's ability to functions, and (5) overall level of functioning in meeting life responsibilities

c) Multiaxial system; dimensions result in categories of disorders

3. Widely used; some concern that reliability, validity not fully established; may rely too much on medical model in which abnormal behaviors are assumed to be symptoms of underlying disorders or mental illnesses

SUMMARY

In this module, you are introduced to psychological disorders. Making the diagnosis of abnormal behavior is not easy because there are no human behaviors that are exclusive to the "disturbed" category. Psychologists look at a variety of criteria and use a combination of these criteria in their attempt to determine psychological status. Patterns of behavior for an individual are evaluated in terms of how unusual, how deviant, and how emotionally stressful they are. Psychologists also consider whether the behavior patterns are maladaptive (do they impede the individual's ability to function effectively?), dangerous to self or others, or involve distortions of reality. All of these factors are considered together, and a mental health professional almost always relies on the DSM *(Diagnostic and Statistical Manual of Mental Disorders)* as well to help make a final diagnosis. The DSM lists every recognized psychological disorder, a description of that disorder, and standards for diagnosing whether or not that disorder is present in an individual. The DSM categorizes disorders by major groupings (e.g., whether the disorder affects mainly personality, or mood, or anxiousness, and the like). Increasingly we recognize that an awareness of the impact of culture is crucial in evaluating mental illness. Some mental illnesses are acceptable in some societies (hearing voices, for example) and considered disorders in others. Some psychological problems take differing forms, depending on the society. For example, among the Chinese, depression is manifested via headaches or other physical symptoms, rather than by feelings of sadness as we would find in the United States.

The approach to and treatment of psychological disorders continues to improve, but disturbed behaviors were not always viewed as benignly as they are today. The belief during most of human history was that mental illness was due to an individual being possessed—either controlled by unknown spirits or literally inhabited by demons. The accepted treatment was exorcism, to rid the body of these forces. Finally, beginning in the 18th century, substantial medical advances helped us understand much more about human functioning. Psychological disorder eventually was approached in a manner similar to that of physical illnesses; and in fact this approach is termed the medical model, which also has its limitations.

There are a variety of explanations regarding the cause of psychological disorder. These explanations parallel the various philosophical perspectives that comprise different approaches within psychology. The psychodynamic model, based on the views of Sigmund Freud, interprets psychological disorder as stemming from early childhood problems and inner conflicts. These difficulties are buried deep within the unconscious. The behavioral model, not surprisingly, points to maladaptive learning as the source of psychological problems. Poor behaviors are learned in the same way that more effective behaviors are learned. To humanists, psychological difficulties arise when we lose contact with our inner selves. Only our inner self knows the way to the self-actualization we seek, so when we lose clear contact with our inner self we have lost our sense of guidance and meaningfulness in the world. Cognitivists find psychological problems to be the result of distorted and self-destructive thinking. Change the thinking, and you change the maladaptive behavior. The sociocultural model suggests that the problem lies less with the individual himself or herself and more within the society of which that individual is a member. The most widespread contemporary approach to mental disorders is the biopsychosocial model. This model, as its name implies, looks at the combination of influences (genetic, biological, social, emotional, cultural, psychological) and how they interact to produce behavior.

KEY TERMS

Hallucinations

Delusions

Medical model

Biopsychosocial model

Diathesis-stress model

Diathesis

Psychological disorders

SELF-TEST PRACTICE QUIZ

Match the following Key Terms and definitions:

1. _____ An explanation for psychological disorder proposing that an individual may have a predisposition (usually genetic) to a disorder, but environmental experiences determine if the disorder becomes manifested

2. _____ An approach to psychological disturbance that interprets it as a physical disorder

3. _____ Distortions of reality that are manifested as false beliefs

4. _____ The general term for mental illnesses; distinctive patterns of abnormal behavior that impair functioning or cause distress

5. _____ A contemporary explanation for psychological disorder involving an integrated combination of known factors (emotional, genetic, environmental, and so forth)

6. _____ A predisposition or vulnerability

7. _____ Distortions of reality that involve perceiving stimuli that do not really exist

a. Hallucinations

b. Delusions

c. Medical model

d. Biopsychosocial model

e. Diathesis-stress model

f. Diathesis

g. Psychological disorders

8. Diagnosing psychological disorders is difficult because
   a. behaviors that are considered disturbed in one culture may not be viewed as abnormal in another.
   b. there are no human behaviors that are exhibited exclusively by psychologically disturbed individuals.
   c. some criteria used for diagnosis (for example, unusualness) may describe highly desirable behaviors as well.
   d. all of the above

9. Which of the following is NOT a criterion used to determine whether behavior is abnormal?
   a. Emotional distress
   b. Social deviance
   c. Maladaptive behavior
   d. Legality

10. Whereas depression is manifested among western cultures as the experience of sadness and lethargy, for Asian cultures such as the Chinese it is likely to appear in the form of
    a. stomach aches and ulcers.
    b. headaches and fatigue.
    c. muscle aches or tension.
    d. sleep difficulties.

11. Considering psychological disorder as an illness somewhat along the lines of physical sickness first appeared during the
    a. Middle Ages.
    b. 16th and 17th centuries.
    c. 18th and 19th centuries.
    d. 20th and 21st centuries.

12. Which model attributes the cause of psychological disorder to poor or destructive behaviors learned as a consequence of reinforcements and punishments?
    a. Cognitive
    b. Psychodynamic
    c. Humanistic
    d. Behavioral

13. The psychodynamic model attributes most abnormal behavior to
    a. genetic causes.
    b. barriers to self-actualization.
    c. irrational or distorted thinking.
    d. unresolved sexual conflicts.

14. A vulnerability or predisposition to a disorder that increases the likelihood that this disorder will develop in an individual is known as a(n) _____.
    a. anxiety disorder
    b. diathesis
    c. immunological deficiency
    d. psychological propensity

15. The DSM uses a multiaxial system, which means that it
    a. takes into account the cultural context of behavior.
    b. is based on the medical model.
    c. requires the examiner to evaluate the patient's behavior on many dimensions.
    d. groups disorders into categories based on common symptoms.

ESSAY QUESTION

1. We have a number of different models, or explanations, for abnormal behavior, such as the medical, psychological, and biopsychosocial models. What are the various psychological models, and how do they differ from each other?

ANSWER KEY

1.   Diathesis-stress model

2.   Medical model

3.   Delusions

4.   Psychological disorders

5.   Biopsychosocial model

6.   Diathesis

7.   Hallucinations

8.   d

9.   d

10.   b

11.   c

12.   d

13.   d

14.   b

15.   c

SAMPLE ANSWER TO ESSAY QUESTION

1.   We have a number of explanations regarding what mental illnesses are and why they occur. There are five different psychological explanations, reflecting the major perspectives within the field of psychology. The historically earliest perspective was that advocated by Sigmund Freud (the psychodynamic model). His view was that the source of motivation and most of one's personality lay deep in the unconscious, out of our awareness. Personality was comprised of often-conflicting components, according to Freud. Thus, the psychodynamic model explains psychological disorders as caused by deep-seated, unconscious conflicts, often emanating from early childhood. Behaviorists, believing that everything about us is the result of learning through environmental experience, see disturbed behaviors as acquired the same way normal behaviors are acquired— through being reinforced, or not, for characteristics that we exhibit. Humanistic psychologists propose that disturbed behaviors arise from having lost one's way, so to speak, on the path towards self-actualization. Disorders can also result from a great disparity between what we think of ourselves and what we want to be. Cognitive psychologists trace psychological disturbances to errors in thinking and interpretation. Negative and irrational thoughts can lead us to misconstrue facts or a situation, and then act inappropriately or ineffectively. Sociocultural theorists propose that problems are caused more by ills (poverty, violence, and the like) within society than by disordered, maladaptive characteristics within the individual. Since all of these psychological models of abnormal behavior highlight important influences on human functioning, it is no wonder that a combined approach (the biopsychosocial model) is now taking center stage.

MODULE 12.2 ANXIETY DISORDERS

LEARNING OBJECTIVES

After you have mastered the information in this unit, you will be able to:

1. Describe the major anxiety disorders.

2. Describe causal factors implicated in anxiety disorders

OUTLINE

I. Types of Anxiety Disorders
   A. Basic characteristics of anxiety disorders
      1. Among the most commonly experienced psychological disorders
      2. Formerly classified as neuroses
      3. A general emotional state of uneasiness or distress associated with worry or apprehension about future uncertainties
      4. Anxiety can be an adaptive response in some situation – motivating us to study before an exam and to seek regular medical checkups
   B. Phobias
      1. Irrational or excessive fear of object or situation
      2. Types of phobic disorders
         a) Social phobia—fear of being with others, speaking in public
         b) Specific phobia—such as acrophobia (fear of heights), claustrophobia (fear of enclosed spaces), or agoraphobia (fear of open spaces, going out in public)
      3. People with phobias usually recognize that their fears are irrational or excessive, but they still avoid the objects or situations they fear
   C. Panic disorder
      1. Sudden episodes of sheer terror (panic attacks) – lasting from a few minutes to more than an hour
      2. Many physiological symptoms; feeling as if one is dying or having a heart attack or "going crazy" or losing control
      3. Seem to come "out of the blue," yet later become connected with particular situations
   D. Generalized anxiety disorder (GAD)
      1. Pervasive, persistent fear, not related to specific object or location
      2. Unrest, excessive worry, include shakiness, inability to relax, fidgeting, and feelings of dread and foreboding
   E. Obsessive-compulsive disorder (OCD)
      1. Behaviors or thoughts repeated over and over again
      2. Obsessions are persistent thoughts; compulsions are rituals or repetitive behaviors – person feels unable to control
   F. Posttraumatic stress disorder
      1. Exposure to any event that results in psychological trauma (example 9/11) – it can occur immediately after the exposure or months later
II. Causes of Anxiety Disorders
   A. Biological factors
      1. Twin/adoptee studies helpful—do reveal hereditary link
      2. Biochemical changes in brain may trigger a type of mental alarm
         a) Recent evidence indicates that the amygdale, the fear-generating part of the limbic system in the brain, may be overactive in people with anxiety disorders, making

　　　　them especially anxious or jumpy in response to threatening cures (Beesdo et al.,
　　　　2009; Nitschke it al., 2009; Stein & Stein, 2008)
　　3.　OCD—increase in brain activity in region associated with responding to danger
B.　Psychological factors
　　1.　Classical conditioning—neutral stimulus paired with one that is frightening
　　2.　Operant conditioning—negative reinforcement through relief of avoiding situation,
　　　　engaging in compulsive behaviors offering short term relief from anxiety but it does
　　　　not help people overcome their fear
C.　Cognitive factors
　　1.　Misinterpretation of relatively minor changes in bodily cues which leads to even
　　　　greater anxiety—a spiral effect that may escalate into a full-blown panic attack
　　2.　Internal or external cues may act as conditioned stimuli
　　3.　Social phobias—excessive, unrealistic concerns about others' social judgments

SUMMARY

In this module, you learn about a very large class of psychological disorders, the anxiety disorders. Anxiety is a state of upset, unrest, worry, and the inability to relax. Anxiety may be chronic, as in generalized anxiety disorder, or short-term, such as the experience of a panic attack. Anxiety that is in response to a specific object or setting is known as a phobia. Phobias are unfounded, irrational, excessive fears. Obsessive-compulsive disorder is also classified as an anxiety disorder because the repetitive thoughts or behaviors are believed to be triggered by states of anxiety. Engaging in compulsive behaviors is thought to relieve anxiety, at least temporarily.

There appear to be both biological and psychological causes leading to anxiety disorders. Suggested biological causes include the inappropriate signaling of danger by brain chemicals and/or from brain structures. Twin and adoptee studies have indicated a genetic factor in anxiety disorders. Psychological factors include learning maladaptive (usually fear) responses to harmless situations because we have had an unpleasant experience in that kind of situation earlier. Avoiding anxiety-producing situations inadvertently reinforces the continuance of the avoidance behavior because the reduction in anxiety is a desirable outcome: for example, why go out in public when it is so stressful? Staying at home and watching television is much less anxiety-producing. A cognitive explanation for anxiety disorders is also a possibility. Some individuals may cognitively misinterpret signals from their bodies. A minor reaction or low level of arousal may be misinterpreted as signaling a serious threat or cause for alarm.

KEY TERMS

Anxiety disorders

Phobic disorders

Phobia

Social phobia

Specific phobia

Acrophobia

Claustrophobia

Agoraphobia

Panic disorder

Generalized anxiety disorder (GAD)

Obsessive-compulsive disorder (OCD)

SELF-TEST PRACTICE QUIZ

Match the following Key Terms and definitions:

1. _____ An anxiety disorder where the individual repeatedly engages in unproductive thoughts or ineffective behaviors

2. _____ An anxiety disorder involving excessive, irrational fear of enclosed spaces

3. _____ The experience of episodes of intense terror, overwhelming physical distress (but no underlying medical cause)

4. _____ A class of psychological disorders involving the episodic or chronic experience of agitation, worry, or unrest

5. _____ Feelings of unfounded, intense fear when faced with meeting or speaking with others

6. _____ An anxiety disorder where one is irrationally and excessively afraid of heights

7. _____ Intense, irrational fear in response to a particular object or situation

8. _____ Excessive, unfounded fear in response to objects or situations

9. _____ An anxiety disorder characterized by excessive fear of entering the public domain

10. _____ A persistent state of anxiousness and worry not connected to any single cause or situation

11. _____ A class of psychological disorders involving excessive fears

a. Anxiety disorders

b. Phobic disorders

c. Phobia

d. Social phobia

e. Specific phobia

f. Acrophobia

g. Claustrophobia

h. Agoraphobia

i. Panic disorder

j. Generalized anxiety disorder (GAD)

k. Obsessive-compulsive disorder (OCD)

12. Someone who is afraid to enter open spaces where there are people, and who eventually often becomes afraid simply to leave the home is suffering from
    a.   social phobia.
    b.   panic attack.
    c.   agoraphobia.
    d.   generalized anxiety disorder.

13. What is the difference between an obsession and a compulsion?

    a. An obsession is an unwanted intrusive thought; a compulsion is a repetitive behavior or ritual.
    b. An obsession reduces anxiety; a compulsion increases anxiety.
    c. An obsession is normal, but a compulsion is not.
    d. There is no difference between obsessions and compulsions—they are two names for the same thing.

14. How does generalized anxiety disorder (GAD) differ from a phobia?

    a. GAD involves rational anxiety; phobias are irrational.
    b. GAD has biological causes, but phobias do not.
    c. In GAD, the anxiety is free-floating; in a phobia, it is tied to a specific object or situation.
    d. GAD interferes with normal functioning; phobias may not affect a person's life at all.

15. A suspected biological cause for abnormal behavior is aberrations in the functioning of _____ in the brain.

    a. the genetic code
    b. biochemicals
    c. glial cells
    d. neurilemma

16. Phobias may be caused by classical conditioning. In such cases, the anxiety caused by the phobia is a(n)

    a. unconditioned response.
    b. conditioned response.
    c. unconditioned stimulus.
    d. conditioned stimulus.

17. A cognitive explanation for panic attacks proposes that individuals with the disorder _____ neurological signals they receive about the state of their body.

    a. misinterpret
    b. ignore
    c. respond appropriately to
    d. think rationally about

ESSAY QUESTIONS

1. Phobias, panic attacks, generalized anxiety disorder, and obsessive-compulsive disorder all belong to the broader psychological category of disturbed behaviors known as anxiety disorders. What manifestations of symptoms do this class of disorders share?

2. Compare and contrast biological, psychological and cognitive explanations for anxiety disorders. How is the behavioral concept of negative reinforcement a potential explanation for obsessive-compulsive disorder?

ANSWER KEY

1. Obsessive-compulsive disorder (OCD)

2. Claustrophobia

3. Panic disorder

4. Anxiety disorders

5. Social phobia

6. Acrophobia

7. Specific phobia

8. Phobia

9. Agoraphobia

10. Generalized anxiety disorder (GAD)

11. Phobic disorders

12. c

13. a

14. c

15. b

16. b

17. a

SAMPLE ANSWERS TO ESSAY QUESTIONS

1. Phobias, panic disorder, generalized anxiety disorder, and obsessive-compulsive disorder are all included in the anxiety disorders category because all are characterized by a state of excessive worry, agitation, or unrest. Phobias and panic attacks tend to be in response to a specific object or setting, and both are short-lived in that when one leaves the threatening situation, or when the panic attack subsides, the psychological problem one was experiencing is no longer apparent. Phobias are irrational fears in response to objects or situations; panic attacks may be triggered by certain situations more than others but the precipitating factor is not as obvious as with phobias. Generalized anxiety disorder and obsessive-compulsive disorder tend to be more chronic. With generalized anxiety disorder, there is no precipitating object or condition, and the individual is more or less always in a state of upset, worry, or concern. With obsessive-compulsive disorder, the worry or upset is not so obvious; in a sense, it is masked by the repetitive thoughts and repeated behaviors. These obsessions (repeated thoughts) and compulsions (repeated behaviors or rituals) may in fact be an attempt to relieve or deal with anxiety.

2. The biological explanation for anxiety disorders approaches psychological problems in the same way as any physical illness. It is proposed that irregularities in brain structure and/or problems with brain chemicals (neurotransmitters) lead to the experience of various anxiety disorders. The psychological approach for anxiety disorders suggests that phobias, avoidance behavior, and so forth are learned in the same way that any other behaviors are learned—through reinforcement (a desirable outcome to behaviors; this increases the likelihood that a behavior will occur again) and punishment (an unpleasant consequence to a behavior which serves to decrease the likelihood of it occurring again). Cognitive explanations for anxiety disorders include that a person may misinterpret bodily cues, thinking that his or her physiological reactions (sweating, increase in

heart rate) are indicating a greater threat than there actually is. Or, people may be affected by their concern that they are being evaluated, judged by others (usually negatively) which leads to a sense of fear and embarrassment. The individual eventually may avoid the public eye altogether. Negative reinforcement, specifically (a component in the behavioral perspective) may play a role in OCD. Negative reinforcement increases the likelihood that a behavior will occur again by following that behavior with a reduction or removal of something unpleasant. It is suggested that repetitive behaviors (a characteristic of OCD) may function to temporarily remove the distress created due to repetitive thoughts. Note that this alleviation of discomfort is temporary at best.

MODULE 12.3 DISSOCIATIVE AND SOMATOFORM DISORDERS

LEARNING OBJECTIVES

After you have mastered the information in the unit, you will be able to:

1.   Describe dissociative disorders and their causes.

2.   Describe somatoform disorders and their causes.

OUTLINE

I.   Dissociative Disorders—interfere with cohesive sense of self, unity of personality
    A.   Dissociative identity disorder (DID)
        1.   Also known as multiple personality or split personality
        2.   Two or more distinct personalities exist within same individual (also called alter personalities – sometimes the alter personalities compete for control) and even assume a completely new self-identity
        3.   May be a core personality and hidden alternative personalities
        4.   Women with the disorder tend to have fifteen or more identities, whereas men average about eight (American Psychiatric Association, 2000)
    B.   Dissociative amnesia
        1.   Loss of parts of memory about self or life experiences (no physical cause)
        2.   Usually a traumatic or stressful event involved that the person may be motivated to forget
        3.   Much less common is generalized amnesia in which people forget their entire lives
II.   Causes of Dissociative Disorders
    A.   May be an attempt to distance self from psychological pain, conflict – also a means of expressing the deep-seated hatred and anger they are unable to integrate within their primary personalities
    B.   DID—frequently a background of severe, repetitive physical and/or sexual abuse
    C.   Many people were highly imaginative as children
    D.   DID diagnosis still in question – there is controversy among professional as to whether multiple personality (now called dissociative identity disorder) even exists
III.   Somatoform Disorders—physical problem, no underlying physical cause
    A.   Conversion disorder
        1.   Called hysteria during time of Sigmund Freud
        2.   Loss of physical function, loss of feeling in a limb—that defies any medical explanation
            a)   Some people with conversion symptoms appear indifferent to their situations – a phenomenon called al belle indifference ("beautiful indifference") (Stone et al., 2006)

          b)   Sometimes incorrectly diagnosed in people who turn out to have bona fide medical conditions (Stone et al., 2006)

    B.   Hypochondriasis—preoccupation with belief that one has a terrible illness

IV.   Causes of Somatoform Disorders

    A.   Freud's explanation—manifestation of unconscious conflict

    B.   Secondary gain—"problem" may help individual avoid anxiety-producing situations

    C.   Cognitive explanation—misinterpretation of minor bodily sensations as severe, unhealthy

SUMMARY

In this module, you learn about two other classes of psychological disorders, the dissociative and the somatoform disorders. These categories are sometimes grouped together because they both may involve defenses against anxiety. Dissociative identity disorder (DID) was formerly called multiple personality disorder. Here the individual seems to have two or more complete personalities residing together (but apparently unknown to each other) within himself or herself. Dissociative amnesia is the forgetting of events, or even one's own identity and life experiences. DID is a controversial diagnosis. There was severe and prolonged abuse in the childhood backgrounds of well-known dissociative identity disorder cases. Dissociation seems to occur when people, knowingly or not, distance themselves from experiences or other aspects of their lives, probably because those aspects were painful or traumatic. Somatoform disorder occurs when there is something wrong with the body, or a part of the body, with no underlying physical cause. These disorders include conversion disorder (where a body part may appear paralyzed, lose feeling, or simply not function), and hypochondriasis, a well-known disorder where the individual continues to report symptoms of illnesses, but there is nothing medically wrong. Somatoform disorders may occur to help avoid difficult situations, or even enable the sufferer to enjoy the concern and attempts at comfort from others. It is possible that there really is a physical problem underlying somatoform disorder, or sufferers may in fact be misinterpreting ordinary or minor signals from the body as indicating trauma or ill health.

KEY TERMS

Dissociative disorders

Somatoform disorders

Dissociative identity disorder (DID)

Conversion disorder

Hypochondriasis

Secondary gain

SELF-TEST PRACTICE QUIZ

Match the following Key Terms and definitions:

1.   _____ One of the categories of psychological disorders where the individual experiences or reports physical problems but there is no evidence of a true medical condition

    a.   Dissociative disorders

    b.   Somatoform disorders

    c.   Dissociative identity disorder (DID)

    d.   Conversion disorder

    e.   Hypochondriasis

    f.   Secondary gain

2. _____ A disorder in the classification of somatoform disorders where a person has lost the use of, or feeling in, a limb or other body part, but there is no underlying physical cause

3. _____ Formerly known as multiple personality disorder, a dissociative disorder where the individual exhibits two or more distinct personalities

4. _____ A class of psychological disorders involving disruptions in the unified sense of self, such as loss of memory (for a traumatic event) or the creation of additional identities

5. _____ "Problem" actually helps sufferer avoid anxiety-producing situations, attract attention and caring

6. _____ Great concern that one has a serious illness (yet no apparent medical foundation)

7. A controversial psychological disorder, where an individual exhibits several personalities and which may involve a background of severe, prolonged physical abuse is

    a. hypochondriasis.
    b. dissociative identity disorder (DID).
    c. conversion disorder.
    d. dissociative amnesia.

8. An interesting phenomenon regarding individuals who suffer from conversion disorder is that

    a. there seems to be a genetic link to such disorders.
    b. paralysis in one arm is soon followed by paralysis in the other arm.
    c. the sufferer sometimes seems unconcerned or indifferent about the loss of functioning.
    d. there is never a true underlying physical cause.

9. Which statement about dissociative identity disorder (DID) is correct?

    a. Most people with DID were very imaginative as children.
    b. Most people with DID are faking their symptoms.
    c. Men with DID usually have more personalities than women with DID.
    d. none of the above

10. Individuals who suffer from hypochondriasis

    a. are convinced they are ill despite having no physical symptoms whatsoever.
    b. may make their physical symptoms worse because of the extreme anxiety they feel.
    c. interpret minor symptoms as signs of serious illness.
    d. both B and C are correct

11.   Which type of dissociative disorder is most common?

    a.   Amnesia for a traumatic or stressful event

    b.   Generalized amnesia

    c.   Dissociative identity disorder

    d.   all of the above

ESSAY QUESTION

1.   How might dissociative and somatoform disorders actually serve to aid the existence of the sufferer?

ANSWER KEY

1.   Somatoform disorders

2.   Conversion disorder

3.   Dissociative identity disorder (DID)

4.   Dissociative disorders

5.   Secondary gain

6.   Hypochondriasis

7.   b

8.   c

9.   a

10.   d

11.   a

SAMPLE ANSWER TO ESSAY QUESTION

1.   Both somatoform and dissociative disorders may end up being something positive in an individual's life if the disorder allows the individual to either gain desired attention or avoid situations that he or she finds unpleasant. People (especially children) usually get more attention when they are ill or injured. Thus, it may be tempting to someone, especially if that person feels lacking in sufficient appreciation or recognition from others, to have some serious or remarkable disorder that is not readily diagnosed or easily cured (thus prolonging the opportunity for attention). A conversion disorder may allow an individual to avoid a situation he or she would otherwise have to face. Dissociative identity disorder has been a long-standing controversial diagnosis. While it does appear that individuals with this disorder are not pretending and often have a history of abuse in childhood, it has been suggested that a DID sufferer is simply role-playing or, again, trying to gain greater attention from others.

MODULE 12.4 MOOD DISORDERS

LEARNING OBJECTIVES

After you have mastered the information in this unit, you will be able to:

1.   Describe the major mood disorders.

2.   Identify causal factors implicated in mood disorders.

3.   Describe who is at risk for suicide and the causal factors implicated in suicide.

OUTLINE

I.   Basic Characteristics of Mood Disorders
    A.   Severe, persistent disturbances of mood – not the normal ups and downs that most people have
    B.   Impair ability to function, will to live – often feel down when things are going right

II. Types of Mood Disorders
    A.   Major depression (major depressive disorder)
        1.   Feelings of worthlessness, changes in sleep or appetite, lethargy, and loss of interest in pleasurable activities or attempt suicide
        2.   Can last months, years or more; has a high rate of recurrence – especially when untreated
        3.   Experienced twice as often by women as men – men are more likely to distract themselves from their emotional concerns; underlying hormonal or other biological differences between men and women may play a role in explaining the gender gap
        4.   Women may encounter more life stress such as physical and sexual abuse, poverty, single parenthood and sexism, and women tend to handle stress differently
        5.   Many people suffer depression in silence out of ignorance or shame; they think it's just all in their heads or they may feel that asking for help is an admission of weakness and that they should bear it on their own
        6.   We should also note that stress contributes to depression
    B.   Bipolar disorder – formerly called manic-depression
        1.   Alternating, fairly extreme moods of elation (manic), depression
        2.   Manic episodes—euphoria, boundless energy, talking too rapidly, inflated sense of self-worth, possibly reckless, delusional (hold false beliefs)
        3.   Depression—sinking into hopelessness, despair; possibly suicidal
        4.   They may have intervening periods of normal moods

III. Causes of Mood Disorders
    A.   Psychological factors
        1.   Psychodynamic explanation—anger turned inward against self
        2.   Behavior model—too little reinforcement, especially social reinforcement (lacking attention, approval and emotional support)
        3.   Cognitive approach
            a)   Aaron Beck (developed cognitive therapy)
            b)   How people interpret events is related to depression; a minor disappointment is blown out of proportion experienced more as a crushing blow than as a mild setback
            c)   Negative mindset, cognitive distortions are the problem
        4.   Learned helplessness model (Martin Seligman)
            a)   Depression resulting from sense of inability to control reinforcement in life events
            b)   Stop making effort when faced with seemingly uncontrollable situations
            c)   Concept also includes attributional style—the characteristic ways in which individuals explain the causes of events that happen to them
            d)   The reformulated helplessness model proposes that attributions vary along three dimensions: internal vs. external, global vs. specific, and stable vs. unstable; depressive attributional style people tend to explain disappointments and failures by attributing them to internal, global, and stable causes

    B.   Biological factors
1. Chemical imbalances in the brain (involving neurotransmitters)
2. Antidepressants (e.g., Prozac, Zoloft) increase levels of norepinephrine and serotonin; may also affect number of receptors or their sensitivity
3. Depression not just a lack of certain neurotransmitters
4. Possible oversensitivity or overabundance of related neural receptors
5. Genetic link likely, especially with regard to bipolar disorder

IV. Suicide
    A.   Rate of occurrence
1. 500,000 Americans each year make a serious attempt
2. A leading cause of death among older teens, young adults

    B.   Who is most at risk?
1. Age—greatest among older adults – especially white males aged 75 and above (Joe et al., 2006; Szanto et al., 2003)
2. Gender
    a) More women attempt suicide
    b) More males complete the act—use more lethal, violent methods
3. Race/ethnicity—higher rate among white European Americans, Native Americans

    C.   Factors in suicide
1. Closely related to mood disorders, especially depression, bipolar disorder
2. Suicide, like depression, may be linked to biochemical factors
3. Disinhibition effect
    a) Possible result of low levels of serotonin
    b) Removes natural tendency to curb impulsive activity (including attempt to commit suicide)
4. Alcohol and drug abuse are often preludes to depression and suicide
5. Alcohol dependence—again may lead to impulsivity
6. Lack of coping responses among those who attempt, commit suicide
7. Exit events—losing people who are sources of emotional support
8. Copycat suicides among adolescents
9. Most people who attempt suicide may feel hopeless, but they are not insane (i.e, out of touch with reality)

SUMMARY

In this module, you learn about the class of psychological disorders known as mood disorders. Mood disorders impact our emotional, or affective, state—how we feel. Individuals suffering from mood disorders usually are feeling sad and lethargic, although some mood disorders involve a highly aroused or agitated state referred to as mania. One of the most common mood disorders is depression. Because of the misery one is experiencing when depressed, depression is closely linked to attempts at suicide.

The category of mood disorders includes major depression and what is known as bipolar disorder. Bipolar is the term we now use for what was once called manic-depression. Major depressive disorder is the experience of extreme unhappiness, despondency, feelings of unworthiness, lasting months or even years if left untreated. About twice as many women as men suffer from depression. This may be linked to how women handle problems in their lives, but may also be a result of the many kinds of stress women are prone to experience. Individuals suffering from bipolar disorders exhibit alternating extremes of mood. Bipolar disorder is characterized by states of severe depression, alternating with highly energized, perhaps abrasive states known as manic episodes. There may be normal states of mood between the extreme periods, but the bipolar individual is characterized as mostly "highs" and "lows." There is much less in the way of stable, moderate experience in comparison to individuals without the disorder. The "lows" in bipolar disorder are also associated with increased suicide risk.

It is thought that both psychological and biological factors cause mood disorders. Low levels of brain chemicals (especially norepinephrine and serotonin) are associated with an individual's experience of depression, and antidepressants that improve neurotransmitter functioning are used successfully to treat depression. Ongoing research suggests a genetic factor in mood disorders, especially for bipolar disorder. Psychological causes include cognitive factors, a lack of positive reinforcement, and learned helplessness. Freud's explanation of anger turned within is also a possible cause for mood disorders. Cognitive factors related to mood disorders involve how we think about our life experiences. If someone adopts a consistently negative pattern of interpreting events, misconstruing minor events as major catastrophes with consequences far-reaching and profound, life will be perceived as dismal and depression will result. These are called cognitive distortions. Learning theorists point out that desirable consequences to our actions (reinforcement) is related to motivation, and, if reinforcers diminish, motivation dwindles and one may feel depressed. Social reinforcers (emotional support, positive feedback from others) are particularly important. Martin Seligman introduced the notion of learned helplessness—that if we have experienced what we believe is a chronic lack of control over our lives, we may feel unable to influence outcomes with regard to personal events. This sense of lack of control triggers depression. Seligman proposed that depression and learned helplessness are related to how one makes attributions about life situations. This is somewhat related to the concept of cognitive distortions discussed above. If we make internal, global, and lasting attributions regarding an unsuccessful life event (known as a depressive attributional style), we are far more likely to experience depression.

There is a high risk for suicide among those who are clinically depressed or who are experiencing bipolar disorder. Though suicide is a leading cause of death among adolescents, young adults, and college students, the highest rate of suicide still occurs among the elderly. More women than men attempt suicide, but far more men actually complete the act of suicide because men tend to use more violent, immediate means. There is a higher risk of suicide among white European Americans and Native Americans than among African Americans or Hispanic Americans. Alcohol use and low levels of important mood neurotransmitters may have a disinhibiting effect—that is, they lower the constraints we normally have on impulsive, destructive behavior. There is a higher incidence of suicide attempts among teenagers where a friend has just attempted suicide, and the use of drugs (as well as alcohol) is correlated with the incidence of suicide. Lastly, individuals who attempt suicide may be less capable with regard to devising other, more effective ways of coping with problems. If such individuals lose or also feel a lack of social and emotional support, the risk for attempting suicide is greater.

KEY TERMS

Mood disorders

Major depressive disorder

Manic episodes

Learned helplessness model

Attributional style

Depressive attributional style

Disinhibition effect

SELF-TEST PRACTICE QUIZ

Match the following Key Terms and definitions:

1. _____ One kind of bipolar disorder, characterized by excessive, highly-charged levels of activity; may include extreme talkativeness and grandiose ideas or plans

2. _____ One feature of alcohol use and low levels of some neurotransmitters; normal constraints on impulsive, perhaps harmful activities are diminished

3. _____ The pattern one tends to exhibit regarding explanations for life events

4. _____ A very common type of depressive disorder, where extreme feelings of sadness, lack of interest, unworthiness persist for an extended period of time

5. _____ A model, proposed by Martin Seligman, where prior experiences with events we could not control stifles future effort, even when opportunities we could impact occur

6. _____ A class of psychological disorders where one's feelings, or affective states, are impaired

7. _____ An attributional style that involves explaining events in a negative way; related to the incidence of depression

a. Mood disorders

b. Major depressive disorder

c. Manic episodes

d. Learned helplessness model

e. Attributional style

f. Depressive attributional style

g. Disinhibition effect

8. A person who feels very sad or low, has no energy, and has experienced sleeping problems for some months or more is probably suffering from
   a. major depression.
   b. bipolar disorder.
   c. manic-depression.
   d. manic disorder.

9. Why might women experience depression more frequently than men?
   a. Nervous system functioning in female organisms is less able to adapt to traumatic events.
   b. Women have fewer physical and psychological demands placed upon them, leaving more time for dwelling on problems, and for worry and anxiety.
   c. Because women are more emotional, they experience more intense levels of all emotions.
   d. Women may differ from men in how much stress they experience and how they handle it.

10. The individual who has been feeling depressed and lethargic for some time then suddenly feels full of energy, is quite agitated, and rarely sleeps is probably experiencing
    a. a recovery from major depression.
    b. caffeine jolt impact.
    c. bipolar disorder.
    d. learned helplessness.

11. Which of the following has NOT been shown to be a potential cause of depression?
    a. Neurotransmitter imbalances
    b. Low intelligence
    c. Distorted patterns of thinking
    d. Low levels of reinforcement compared to the amount of effort expended

12. In Martin Seligman's research with animals, when laboratory animals were repeatedly exposed to shock they could not escape, they
    a. eventually showed physical and neurological damage and died before the completion of the study.
    b. found ways to shock other animals when given the opportunity.
    c. did not attempt to escape when later they were free to do so.
    d. were able, with time, to find ways to turn off the shocking mechanism.

13. How do cognitive theorists explain the origins of depression?
    a. They focus on the ways in which people engage in negative thinking.
    b. They focus on the genetic risk factors involved in depression.
    c. Depression involves anger that has been turned inward onto the self.
    d. Depression results when effort expended yields little or no reinforcement.

14. According to Seligman, individuals with depression are more likely to attribute failures to causes that are
    a. external, specific, and stable.
    b. internal, global, and stable.
    c. internal, specific, and stable.
    d. external, global, and unstable.

15. Which of the following is NOT a factor associated with a greater risk for suicide?
    a. Age
    b. Gender
    c. Divorce
    d. Alcohol and drug use

ESSAY QUESTION

1. How are individuals with mood disorders unlike people who do not suffer from this psychological problem? What does the usefulness of antidepressants tell us about the cause of mood disorders?

ANSWER KEY

1.   Manic episodes

2.   Disinhibition effect

3.   Attributional style

4.   Major depressive disorder

5.   Learned helplessness model

6.   Mood disorders

7.   Depressive attributional style

8.   a

9.   d

10. c

11. b

12. c

13. a

14. b

15. c

SAMPLE ANSWER TO ESSAY QUESTION

1.   Individuals with mood disorders are more likely to experience extremes of mood (or emotional state) with fewer and shorter periods of normal functioning between these extremes. The most common mood disorder is major depression; thus, many people with mood disorders exhibit chronic characteristics of sorrow, misery, lethargy, disruptions in sleeping and eating behaviors, and a loss of interest in life. Individuals with bipolar disorder show periods of abnormally elevated activity and agitation as well. These experiences of mood extremes are sufficient to substantially hamper one's psychological well-being and ability to function. Antidepressants are helpful in treating mood disorders. Because antidepressants influence the levels and functioning of neurotransmitters (brain chemicals), especially norepinephrine and serotonin, this knowledge helps us understand that brain chemicals are important to regulating emotional states.

MODULE 12.5 SCHIZOPHRENIA

LEARNING OBJECTIVES

After you have mastered the information in this unit, you will be able to:

1.   Describe schizophrenia and its symptoms.

2.   Identify three types of schizophrenia.

3.   Discuss causal factors implicated in schizophrenia.

4.   Explain the diathesis-stress model of schizophrenia.

OUTLINE

I.   Background Factors in Schizophrenia
    A.   Disorder most closely related to typical concept of madness, lunacy
    B.   Involves bizarre, irrational behavior; roughly one percent of population is affected
    C.   Slightly more common, more severe, and with earlier onset in men
    D.   Tends to occur at uniform rates in all cultures, though symptoms vary
    E.   Onset corresponds to transition from adolescence to adulthood

II. Symptoms of Schizophrenia
    A.   A psychotic disorder—inability to distinguish reality from fantasy
    B.   Experience things that in actuality do not exist
        1.   Hallucinations—perceptions not based on actual stimuli (e.g., hearing voices)
        2.   Delusions—adhering to beliefs that are clearly, completely false
    C.   Exhibit bizarre behavior, incoherent speech, illogical thinking
    D.   Thought disorder—ideas not really connected, organized, or meaningful (loose association between expressed ideas)
    E.   Not all symptoms necessary for diagnosis of schizophrenia
    F.   Disorder also includes negative symptoms - extreme withdrawal, isolation, apathy, blunted emotions

III. Types of Schizophrenia
    A.   Disorganized
        1.   Confused behavior, hallucinations, disorganized delusions
        2.   May neglect personal hygiene, fail to control bodily functions
        3.   Inappropriate emotions, difficulty in relating to others
    B.   Catatonic
        1.   Bizarre movements, postures, and grimaces
        2.   May adopt a motionless stupor, unresponsive for hours
        3.   Waxy flexibility—body can be molded without difficulty by others into unusual even uncomfortable positions that they can hold for hours at a time
        4.   A rare form of schizophrenia
    C.   Paranoid
        1.   Most common form of schizophrenia
        2.   Delusions of grandeur, persecution, or jealousy
        3.   Accompanied by frequent auditory hallucinations

IV. Causes of Schizophrenia—remain a mystery
    A.   Genetic factors
        1.   Heredity plays an important role
        2.   Higher concordance rate among monozygotic than dizygotic twins
        3.   Higher incidence in adopted children whose biological parents afflicted
        4.   Likely that multiple genes are responsible for disorder
    B.   Biochemical imbalances
        1.   Dopamine pathways and dopamine receptors are implicated
        2.   Helpful antipsychotic drugs (e.g., Thorazine) reduce dopamine activity
    C.   Brain abnormalities
        1.   MRIs, CTs reveal abnormal brain development
        2.   Most affected areas are prefrontal cortex, limbic system
            a)   Prefrontal cortex helps organize thoughts, carry out plans
            b)   Limbic system involved in memories, emotional experiences

D.   Psychosocial influences
1.   Life experiences a factor; may interact with genetic vulnerability
2.   Diathesis-stress model
a)   Diathesis—genetic predisposition, biological susceptibility to disorder
b)   Stress (brain trauma, difficult childhood) triggers onset of schizophrenia

SUMMARY

In this module, you learn about the leading serious psychological disorder, schizophrenia. Schizophrenia is a psychotic disorder, meaning the individual has truly experienced a break from reality. Delusions (false beliefs) and hallucinations (faulty perceptions) are common. The occurrence of schizophrenia coincides with our transition from adolescence to adulthood. More men than women experience schizophrenia, with earlier onset; patterns of occurrence of the disorder are similar worldwide.

Schizophrenics exhibit behavior that is irrational and bizarre. They show severe social impairments, and, if they speak, their speech may well be incoherent. Thought patterns appear to be disorganized, and there is no logical connection in the arrangement and expression of ideas. Verbal utterances may seem random, singsong, and often meaningless. Types of schizophrenia include disorganized, catatonic, and the most common, paranoid. Paranoid schizophrenics exhibit psychotic behavior and experience delusions, usually that they are being persecuted. Disorganized schizophrenics show confused behavior, blunted or inappropriate emotion, and do not attend to personal hygiene or bodily functions.

What causes schizophrenia? As with other abnormal behavioral disorders, we suspect a combination of biological, environmental, and psychological influences. There is clearly a genetic component to schizophrenia, in that the incidence is higher among family members (including twins) sharing close or identical gene codes. It is expected that not just one gene, but multiple genes are a factor. However, even sharing an identical genetic heritage (as do monozygotic twins) results in only about a 50% concordance rate. The brain pathways and receptors for the neurotransmitter dopamine seem implicated, and drugs that reduce dopamine activity reduce the frequency and severity of psychotic symptoms. Brain imaging data provide evidence that the prefrontal and limbic portions of the schizophrenic brain have developed abnormally. The functions of these brain regions correspond to the decrements found in the behavior of schizophrenics. Life stressors are also considered to be a factor, and these may include an abusive family environment or other traumatic experiences. The diathesis-stress model proposes that a human may have a genetic predisposition (a diathesis) to a disorder, creating greater vulnerability. The disorder will not manifest in the individual, however, unless sufficient stresses and difficulties in life trigger its onset.

KEY TERMS

Schizophrenia

Psychotic disorder

Thought disorder

Positive symptoms

Negative symptoms

Disorganized type

Catatonic type

Waxy flexibility

Paranoid type

SELF-TEST PRACTICE QUIZ

Match the following Key Terms and definitions:

1. _____ Symptoms present in excess which suggest the diagnosis of schizophrenia, such as irrational behavior and utterances, hallucinations, and delusions

2. _____ A severe psychological disorder, where an individual experiences a break with reality

3. _____ A psychotic disorder where an individual experiences hallucinations, delusions, disturbed thought patterns, extreme social impairment, and absent or inappropriate emotions

4. _____ One component in the behavior of catatonic schizophrenics, where the body may be arranged to take any shape, even one that is probably very uncomfortable

5. _____ The most common type of schizophrenia, where the disorder is accompanied by delusions (usually of grandeur or persecution)

6. _____ One of the sub-types of schizophrenia, where the individual exhibits confused behavior, inattention to bodily processes and personal hygiene, and inappropriate emotions

7. _____ One characteristic of schizophrenia, where the organization and connection of expressed ideas is not apparent

8. _____ Behaviors whose lack suggests the diagnosis of schizophrenia, such as the inability to establish and maintain social and emotional relationships

a. Schizophrenia

b. Psychotic disorder

c. Thought disorder

d. Positive symptoms

e. Negative symptoms

f. Disorganized type

g. Catatonic type

h. Waxy flexibility

i. Paranoid type

9. _____ A rare type of schizophrenia, where the individual may assume and hold rigid body postures for many hours on end

10. The term schizophrenia, or "split brain," means
    a. the normal ties among thoughts, emotions, and perceptions are lacking.
    b. the corpus callosum joining the two hemispheres in the brain has been severed.
    c. an individual has experienced a severe brain injury.
    d. an individual will vacillate between rational and irrational behaviors.

11. The age at which the onset of schizophrenia is most likely to occur is
    a. early childhood (especially just prior to the start of school years).
    b. adolescence through young adulthood.
    c. the middle years of adult development.
    d. in late adulthood, when other mental faculties begin to fail.

12. The schizophrenic disorder that is accompanied by delusions and may be accompanied by auditory hallucinations is the _____ type of schizophrenia.
    a. disorganized
    b. catatonic
    c. paranoid
    d. psychotic-release

13. If an individual has a genetically identical twin with schizophrenia, the likelihood that that individual will develop schizophrenia is
    a. 13%.
    b. 30%.
    c. 50%.
    d. 65%.

14. Which of the following has NOT been shown to be a potential cause of schizophrenia?
    a. Genetics
    b. Dopamine imbalance
    c. Childhood brain trauma
    d. Alcoholism

15. The psychological disorder that we have termed schizophrenia appears worldwide, and at about the same level of frequency. _____ determines what symptoms will be manifested.
    a. The DSM-IV
    b. Education
    c. Culture
    d. Genetic variation

ESSAY QUESTION

1. Characterize the behavior of a typical individual who suffers from schizophrenia. What are the suspected causes of this psychotic disorder?

ANSWER KEY

1. Positive symptoms
2. Psychotic disorder
3. Schizophrenia
4. Waxy flexibility
5. Paranoid type
6. Disorganized type
7. Thought disorder
8. Negative symptoms
9. Catatonic type
10. a
11. b
12. c
13. a
14. d
15. c

SAMPLE ANSWER TO ESSAY QUESTION

1. An individual with schizophrenia seems to no longer have contact with, or at least a grasp of, reality. Schizophrenics experience perceptual disturbances (hallucinations) and false beliefs (delusions). Their behavior does not fit, or is unrelated to, the environment surrounding them. Often, a schizophrenic shows no emotional response to others, and does not establish or maintain social contacts. Thought patterns appear to be disturbed, and this is most evident in the schizophrenic's speech. Ordinary words may be strung together, but their collective arrangement conveys no meaning. A schizophrenic is likely to neglect the most basic hygiene functions. Schizophrenia is a severe, pervasive disorder, and thus it probably is caused by a combination of factors. The diathesis-stress model is a good example of potential causal sources. Genetics alone is not a perfect predictor of schizophrenia. The diathesis-stress model suggests we may have a genetic predisposition, or vulnerability, for a disorder such as schizophrenia. Psychological and environmental factors then, if stressful, ultimately trigger the disorder's onset.

MODULE 12.6 PERSONALITY DISORDERS

LEARNING OBJECTIVES

After you have mastered the information in this unit, you will be able to:

1. Describe the major types of personality disorders.
2. Understand the characteristics associated with antisocial personality disorder.
3. Identify causal factors implicated in antisocial personality disorder.

OUTLINE

I.   Background Characteristics of Personality Disorders
    A.   Excessively rigid patterns of behavior
    B.   Maladaptive—limits adjustment to environment; difficult for the person to adjust to external demands and to form long-term, satisfying relationships with others
    C.   Belief is problem lies with others, not themselves (and others should change)

II.   Types of Personality Disorders
    A.   Narcissistic personality disorder—inflated sense of self
    B.   Paranoid personality disorder—extreme suspiciousness, distrust of others
    C.   Schizoid personality disorder
        1.   Little or no interest in social relationships
        2.   Limited range of emotional expression
        3.   Appear distant and aloof
    D.   Borderline personality disorder
        1.   Stormy relationships with others
        2.   Unstable self-image and lack of a clear identity or direction in life, dramatic mood swings (range from anger and irritability to depression and anxiety)
    E.   Total of ten personality disorders identified by DSM
    F.   Antisocial personality disorder (APD)—the most widely studied

III. Symptoms of Antisocial Personality Disorder
    A.   People with this disorder have also been labeled psychopaths, or sociopaths
    B.   Flagrant disregard for rules of society
    C.   Complete lack of regard for well-being of others
    D.   Not a psychotic disorder; APD individual is in touch with reality
    E.   Impulsive, irresponsible, take advantage of others
    F.   Lack remorse for misdeeds, mistreatment of others
    G.   Not concerned or threatened by punishment or possibility of punishment
    H.   Most are law-abiding; some engage in criminal behavior
    I.   May be unusually intelligent, exhibit superficial charm
    J.   Most often found in males

IV.   Causes of Antisocial Personality Disorder
    A.   Abnormalities in parts of brain that help with regulating emotion, controlling aggressive impulses, weighing consequences
    B.   Lower levels of activity in frontal lobes of cerebral cortex
    C.   Possible structural damage to prefrontal cortex
    D.   APD, craving for stimulation to maintain an optimum level of arousal – (quickly bored with routine activities –possibly more dangerous activities like alcohol and drug use, racing cars, risky sexual encounter) may have genetic influence
    E.   Environmental factors
        1.   Characteristics of homes, families where APD individuals raised
            a)   Lack of parental warmth
            b)   Parental neglect, rejection
            c)   Use of harsh punishment
            d)   Emotional, physical abuse
        2.   History of abuse may lead to lack of empathy, lack of genuine emotional ties
        3.   Failure to develop concern for others, moral compass, conscience
        4.   APD individuals treat others with callous disregard

SUMMARY

In this module, you learn about the class of psychological disorders known as personality disorders, and most particularly about the widely studied disorder known as the antisocial personality. Narcissistic personalities are self-focused and have an inflated self-image. The paranoid personality is suspicious and mistrustful. Individuals with schizoid personalities have no real social interest in others, and do not exhibit emotional warmth or empathy. Individuals who are diagnosed with borderline personality disorder have an unstable personality, show dramatic mood swings, and demonstrate an inability to form stable and peaceful relationships. All individuals with personality disorders show rigid patterns of behavior and an inability (or unwillingness) to adjust to the environment and needs of others.

Individuals with antisocial personality disorder (APD) have also been referred to as psychopaths or sociopaths. The antisocial personality is characterized by a lack of empathy and emotional response to others, combined with a disregard for others' well-being and a tendency to take advantage. An individual with APD may draw others to him via superficial charm, but no meaningful emotional relationships are established. The individual with APD generally exhibits impulsive behavior and has no regard for socially accepted ethical standards. No regret for suffering brought to others is apparent. Characteristics in families where APD individuals are raised reveal a lack of warmth and caring, instances of harsh punishment, and emotional and physical abuse. There is some evidence that the APD individual may have brain functioning and structure differing from that of normal individuals. Brain abnormalities occur in the brain region responsible for the control of impulsive behavior. Mechanisms inhibiting destructive behaviors of these individuals are thus diminished. Most cases of APD are male. The threat of punishment or even actual punishment has little or no impact on individuals with APD.

KEY TERMS

Personality disorders

Narcissistic personality disorder

Paranoid personality disorder

Schizoid personality disorder

Borderline personality disorder

Antisocial personality disorder

SELF-TEST PRACTICE QUIZ

Match the following Key Terms and definitions:

1. _____ Emotional aloofness, lack of interest in social relationships

2. _____ Exaggerated image of and focus on oneself

3. _____ Impulsive, dispassionate behavior towards others, lack of regret for this disregard, inflicted harm

4. _____ Erratic emotional behavior, unstable self-image, unstable personal relationships

a. Personality disorders

b. Narcissistic personality disorder

c. Paranoid personality disorder

d. Schizoid personality disorder

e. Borderline personality disorder

f. Antisocial personality disorder

5. _____ A category of psychological disorders involving rigid, maladaptive personality traits

6. _____ Exhibiting pervasive suspicion and mistrust of others (but in touch with reality)

7. Tom is convinced that he is one of the smartest people in the world. He also has an excessive need for admiration, and does not feel empathy for others. Tom most likely would be diagnosed with_____ personality disorder.

    a. narcissistic
    b. paranoid
    c. schizoid
    d. borderline

8. Individuals with antisocial personality disorder exhibit the need for _____ levels of stimulation relative to other individuals without the disorder.

    a. varying
    b. lower
    c. higher
    d. about the same

9. Lower levels of activity in the brains of males with APD are found in the _____ lobes, the brain region responsible for inhibiting impulsive behavior.

    a. frontal
    b. parietal
    c. occipital
    d. temporal

10. Which statement about antisocial personality disorder (APD) is true?

    a. It is more common in women than in men.
    b. Most are law-abiding.
    c. They almost always suffer from hallucinations.
    d. none of the above

11. Which of these has been identified as a potential contributor to the development of APD?

    a. Genetic predisposition
    b. Brain abnormalities
    c. Childhood history of abuse
    d. all of the above

ESSAY QUESTION

1. What are some background factors we find in individuals who exhibit antisocial personality disorder?

ANSWER KEY

1. Schizoid personality
2. Narcissistic personality disorder
3. Antisocial personality disorder
4. Borderline personality disorder
5. Personality disorders
6. Paranoid personality disorder
7. a
8. c
9. a
10. b
11. d

SAMPLE ANSWER TO ESSAY QUESTION

1. People who show evidence of antisocial personality disorder appear to have brain abnormalities, particularly in the region of the frontal cortex. Lower levels of activity in the frontal lobes are present with APD individuals, and there is also greater evidence of structural damage to this region. The frontal cortex is particularly involved in the inhibition of impulsive and aggressive behaviors. The damage and low levels of frontal lobe activity suggest that these inhibitory mechanisms are impaired. There seems to be a genetic component to APD, and APD individuals have a higher-than-normal need for stimulation. People with APD tend to be raised in homes where there was not a great deal of parental warmth and caring. The child may have experienced outright neglect, emotional abuse, physical abuse, and harsh punishments. It appears that the early environmental experience of at least some people who develop antisocial personality disorder involved being raised in a cold, unfeeling, and unresponsive emotional climate. Perhaps it is no wonder, then, that individuals with APD exhibit a cold and uncaring attitude towards others. People with antisocial personalities have no empathy or regard for the welfare of those around them, and exhibit no feelings of remorse or regret. They exhibit no respect for the ethical rules of society, and are unaffected by punishment or the threat of punishment. Very likely both genetic and environmental factors are involved in the occurrence of antisocial personality disorder.

MODULE 12.7 APPLICATION: SUICIDE PREVENTION

LEARNING OBJECTIVE

After you have mastered the information in this unit, you will be able to:

1. Discuss general guidelines for helping someone who is threatening suicide.

OUTLINE

I. Background Factors in the Occurrence of Suicide
   A. Difficult to detect, even by professionals - we tend to respond to the news of a suicide of a friend or family member with shock or with guilt that we failed to pick up any warning signs
   B. Important to take action when signs evident; there are steps one can take to help prevent

II.   Facing the Threat—General Guidelines
  A.   Recognize that threatened suicide is serious
  B.   Also consider seriously indicators that are implied though not overt
  C.   Show warmth, compassion, and understanding
  D.   Suggest alternatives
  E.   Evaluate immediacy of the event
  F.   Encourage the individual to agree regarding getting help (help is available by calling 1-800 - SUICIDE or a local crisis center or health center)
  G.   Accompany the person to seek help

SUMMARY

In this module, you learn about steps you can take should someone you know indicate that he or she is considering suicide. Potential suicide is a life and death event and its mention, whether indirect or direct, should always be taken for the serious matter that it is. Detecting, understanding, and preventing suicidal behaviors are difficult even for professionals. Since you may well be in the company of someone who at some time may attempt suicide, keep the following steps in mind. Recognize that threatened suicide is always serious. Try to determine how immediate the risk of a suicide attempt is. Even if your companion hints at considering suicide but does not say this outright, consider that a warning sign of a suicide attempt as well. Respond to the talk of suicide with warmth, compassion, and understanding. Gently suggest other ways that a problem might be solved. Take steps promptly to get the individual at risk to enlist the assistance of a professional, and accompany him or her if necessary.

CHAPTER 12   APPLICATION EXERCISE

Do you know someone with a psychological disorder? Reflect on that person's behavior. Do you think it is abnormal? If so, what makes you think so? List specific characteristics that lead you to believe the behavior is, or is not, disturbed. How serious does the disorder appear to be?

Can you think of causes that might contribute to the psychological difficulties? Do other members of the family show similar characteristics? Are there environmental factors that seem to keep the abnormal behavior going, despite its maladaptiveness? How long has the individual had the disorder, and when did it begin? Does it fit any of the categories we have discussed in this chapter?

CHAPTER 13

Methods of Therapy

In Chapter 13, you learn about the various treatment methods that are available for individuals suffering from psychological disorders. These treatments include psychological interventions and biomedical therapies, which usually involve prescribing one or more of the available psychiatric drugs. In the last 50 years, treatment of the severely psychologically disturbed has moved from these individuals being institutionalized (perhaps indefinitely) in state mental hospitals to the more humane, more visible, and hopefully more effective community mental health centers. Community-based mental health centers offer a variety of services, but, frequently, demand exceeds the resources, programs, and staff available.

In many cases, the most effective approach to the treatment of abnormal behavior over the long run is a combination of biomedical and psychological interventions. Often, drug therapy is used to stabilize a patient and get symptoms of the psychological disorder under control. The development of drug therapies has been a tremendous breakthrough in the treatment of mental illness. However, drugs can only treat symptoms. Drugs alone do not provide a cure for psychological disorder, although they may contribute a great deal towards helping a patient manage debilitating symptoms and thus be able to live more effectively and productively. Be aware of the side effects that drugs may have on some people. Once psychotropic drugs have helped moderate emotional extremes experienced by an individual, or brought other maladaptive symptoms under control, then therapists can proceed with psychological intervention with a greater likelihood of success or long-term improvement.

As mentioned above, a combination of psychotherapy and biomedical treatment provides the greatest promise for improvement among those suffering from psychological disorders. A variety of psychotherapy approaches are available, and research confirms that individuals who receive some kind of psychological treatment intervention fare better than those who do not. The major approaches to psychotherapy parallel the philosophical approaches found within the field of psychology. In other words, the psychodynamic perspective considers psychological problems to emanate from conflicts buried deep in the unconscious, and thus therapy is based on uncovering those conflicts and finding a better resolution. The humanistic perspective traces psychological disorder to losing touch with one's inner guidance and sense of self. Humanistic therapy is aimed at restoring that inner connectedness. Cognitive psychologists see disorder as resulting from erroneous thinking. Thus, cognitive therapy addresses reasoning and interpretation patterns, with a view towards making thoughts more rational and realistic. Some Gestalt therapists have their clients talk to an empty chair. The behavioral perspective proposes that maladaptive behaviors are learned or observed, and can be replaced when the client learns more effective living patterns. Psychiatric drugs can help manage aberrant psychological symptoms. Antianxiety drugs, antidepressants, and antipsychotics are among the drugs found useful in treating psychological disorders.

MODULE 13.1 TYPES OF PSYCHOTHERAPY

LEARNING OBJECTIVES:

After you have mastered the information in this unit, you will be able to:

1. Understand the nature of psychotherapy.

2. Identify the major types of psychotherapy.

3. Describe psychodynamic therapy.

4. Describe humanistic therapy.

5. Describe behavior therapy.

6. Discuss cognitive therapy.

7. Explain eclectic therapy.

8. Compare and contrast group, family, and couple therapy.

9. Discuss whether psychotherapy is effective.

10. Explain the cultural factors that therapists need to consider when working with members of diverse groups.

OUTLINE

I. Background Factors in Psychotherapy
   A. Psychologically based form of treatment to help with emotional, behavioral problems and attempts to resolve them
   B. Involves exchange of communication between client and therapist ("talk therapy")
   C. Numerous therapy methods; major ones based on psychological perspectives regarding human behavior
II. Various Mental Health Professionals Provide Treatment (see Table 12.1 in text for review)
    Note the differences in their training, backgrounds and areas of expertise
III. Psychodynamic Therapy
   A. Traditional psychoanalysis (Freud)
      1. Root of problem is unconscious conflict, stemming from childhood and an assumption that working through them are key steps toward restoring psychological health
      2. Free association—patient speaks whatever comes to mind
      3. Dream analysis—examine latent content of dreams for real meaning
      4. Interpretation
         a) Insight—understanding regarding inner conflict and unconscious source
         b) Resistance—client blocks when topic very sensitive
         c) Transference relationship—clients reenact troubled, conflicted relationships with others in the context of the relationship they develop with the analyst; a female client may respond to the analyst as a "father figure"
         d) Countertransference—therapist experiences impact from own past relationships
   B. Modern psychodynamic approaches
      1. Traditional psychoanalysis lengthy, intensive, dwells on past
      2. Modern focus more on present, adaptive functioning, current relationships
      3. Concern less with sexual issues, more on work of ego
      4. More direct approach by therapist, briefer therapy format – one or two times a week
      5. Greater mutual dialogue, format usually face to face

IV. Humanistic Therapy
    A. Basic factors in humanistic therapy
        1. Humans have free will and can make conscious, enriching choices
        2. Focus is on the present, client's perception of issues and events; changes must occur in the here-and-now
    B. Client-centered therapy (Rogers)
        1. Client has lost own unique pathway, awareness of personal needs and values
        2. Therapy is to restore individual's ability to know own inner self
        3. Emphasis is on warmth, empathy, genuineness, unconditional positive regard
        4. Therapist reflects back client's statements and apparent feelings, encourages clarity – nondirective approach allowing client to take the lead and set the tone
        5. Atmosphere is emotionally safe, allows client self-exploration
        6. Therapist models expressing true feelings, acceptance
    C. Gestalt therapy (Perls)
        1. Important to blend conflicting parts of personality into a unified whole – becoming aware of opposing parts (take a chance vs. play it safe)
        2. Approach is direct, even confrontational; clearly identify and express feelings at each moment in time – in the here and now
           a) Not letting them slide into discussing events from their past or to ramble in general
        3. Empty chair conversations, role-playing integrate inner self with conscious experience
V. Behavior Therapy (Behavior Modification)
    A. Principles of learning are applied to make changes – the therapy is relatively brief, usually lasting weeks or months rather than years
    B. Learning principles to weaken undesirable behaviors and strengthen adaptive behaviors
    C. Focus is on present, and on problem behaviors rather than on exploring the client's feelings
    D. Methods of fear reduction
        1. Systematic desensitization—create fear hierarchy; work through, maintain relaxed state
        2. Gradual exposure—real-life objects or experiences used; self-relaxation, work through
        3. Modeling—(pioneered by Albert Bandura) imitate others exhibiting adaptive behavior
        4. Virtual therapy—creates simulated real-life environment
    E. Aversive conditioning—pair undesirable stimulus with unwanted (example – electric shock or nausea) learned response – often temporary
    F. Operant conditioning methods (to strengthen desirable behavior and weaken or eliminate undesirable behavior)—principles of reinforcement, punishment, and token economy
    G. Cognitive-behavioral therapy (CBT)—combines behavioral methods with changing thinking
VI. Cognitive Therapies
    A. Basic cognitive therapy approach
        1. Root of problem is distorted interpretation of events, not events themselves
        2. Therapy is brief – (involving months rather than years); focus is on present, helping clients recognize and correct beliefs and ways of thinking
    B. Rational-emotive behavior therapy (REBT)
        1. "ABC" approach developed by Albert Ellis—Activating event, Beliefs, Consequences
           a) Ellis later added a "D" (dispute to the ABC helping clients challenge or dispute their irrational beliefs)
        2. Recognize irrationality of beliefs ("should", "must"); adopt more effective strategies
        3. Ellis notes that while the desire for approval is understandable, it is irrational to believe that one will always receive approval or that one couldn't possible survive without it.
        4. To Ellis, negative emotional reactions, such as anxiety and depression, are not produced directly by life experiences, they stem from irrational beliefs we hold about our experiences

C.   Aaron Beck's cognitive therapy approach
1.   Dysfunctional emotional reactions result from errors in thinking
2.   Reality testing (expectations of danger had no basis in reality), develop rational alternatives to cognitive distortions
3.   He believes that depressed people tend to magnify or exaggerate the consequences of negative events and to blame themselves for disappointments in life while ignoring the role of external circumstance
D.   Cognitive-behavioral therapy
1.   Focuses on changing maladaptive thoughts and beliefs as well as problem behaviors and replace them with more adaptive ways of thinking

VII. Eclectic Therapy
A.   Use combination of therapeutic approaches; integrate techniques
B.   Most widely endorsed theoretical orientation among practicing clinicians
C.   Many believe that the differences between schools of therapy are so compelling that therapeutic integration is neither desirable nor achievable

VIII. Group, Family, and Couples Therapy
A.   Group therapy
1.   Therapy conducted among small number of participants – learn how others in the group have coped
2.   Less expensive; particularly helpful for social, interpersonal problems
3.   May not provide sufficient confidentiality, individual attention – may also be reluctant to disclose their personal problems to other members of a group
B.   Family therapy—the family, not the individual is the unit of treatment; learn to communicate better and resolve their differences
1.   Change how family members interact and relate to one another so that members can become more accepting and supportive of each other's needs and differneces
C.   Couples therapy (marital therapy if applied to a married couple)
1.   Both members of couple considered unit of treatment
2.   Power struggles and lack of communication

IX. The Effectiveness of Psychotherapy
A.   Measuring effectiveness
1.   Meta-analyses (average the results across a large number of such studies): individuals who receive treatment vs. those who do not
2.   Greatest gains shown in first few months of therapy
3.   Not everyone benefits from therapy, and some people even deteriorate
B.   Which therapy is best?
1.   Overall, all therapies better than receiving no treatment at all
2.   Ongoing evaluation: type of therapy relative to particular problem
a)   Behavioral and cognitive-behavioral—help anxiety, eating disorders, personality disorders
b)   Psychodynamic—helps with depression, bulimia, borderline personality
c)   Humanistic best for connecting with inner self, finding direction
C.   Accounting for benefits of therapy – a movement toward evidence-based therapies called empirically supported treatments or ESTs
1.   Nonspecific factors
a)   Common characteristics shared by different therapies
b)   Include quality of client-therapist relationship; expectation for improvement
2.   Placebo effect or expectancy effects)—responses to positive expectancies

   X.   Multicultural Issues in Treatment
       A.   Background considerations in multicultural treatment
          1.   Clients, therapists from a multitude of ethnic, racial backgrounds
          2.   Cultural bias destructive in therapeutic relationship
       B.   African Americans
          1.   Experienced a long history of oppression, discrimination
          2.   Hesitation and reserve to be expected; not a result of paranoid thinking
       C.   Asian Americans
          1.   Asian culture discourages open display of emotion, feelings may conflict with the emphasis in psychotherapy on open expression of emotions
          2.   Matters relating to group valued over those relating to an individual
       D.   Hispanic Americans
          1.   Strong emphasis on family interdependence may clash with the emphasis on independence and self-reliance in mainstream U.S. culture
          2.   Therapist needs sensitivity regarding linguistic preferences
       E.   Native Americans
          1.   Remember customs, tribal culture (these may be source of comfort to client)
          2.   May be expectation that therapist will do most of talking

SUMMARY

In this module, you learn about the many different types of therapy that are available for individuals with psychological problems. Problems both big and small can be helped by means of psychotherapy. Although there are many different approaches regarding how it is carried out, research does indicate that an individual getting any kind of therapy is more likely to show improvement than an individual getting no therapy whatsoever. The different therapeutic approaches parallel the underlying view on the nature of the human being and general explanations regarding human functioning that pertain to each perspective within the field of psychology. Cognitive psychologists take an approach that looks at thinking patterns; behavioral psychologists examine environmental influences, and so forth.

The traditional psychoanalytic perspective, founded on Sigmund Freud's ideas, portrays the inner nature of the human as full of conflict, with primitive sexual desires motivating all of behavior. Traditional psychoanalytic therapy, then, is built around uncovering the repressed sources of conflict and bringing them to light. Once these deep-seated conflicts are in conscious awareness, the individual, with the aid of the therapist, can come up with better ways of working through and resolving these issues. Crucial to the process of psychoanalysis is free association. The patient is permitted and encouraged to free associate—to say whatever comes to mind, no matter how meaningless or relevant it may seem at the time. Freud also encouraged the recording and reporting of dreams, believing that dreams were "the royal road" to uncovering what was really going on in the unconscious. Psychoanalysts help the patient with dream interpretation. Psychological resistance means that the patient changes the subject or leaves the session whenever a certain topic emerges. This resistance is a signal that the topic is of great importance because of its obvious sensitivity. The process of transference in psychoanalysis means the patient starts to see the therapist in a role that was crucial in his or her past. Like resistance, interpreting transference too can be helpful, since both of these phenomena reveal the traumatic childhood experiences that have led to the current psychological abnormality. Freud's psychoanalysis takes many years. Most current versions of psychoanalysis focus less on sexual drives and the unconscious, and more on the here-and-now and finding adaptive solutions. Therapy today tends to occur over a much shorter period of time.

Humanists believe that all of us are on the road towards self-actualization—discovering our unique inner potential and putting it to best use. Obviously, knowing our inner selves is crucial to living a psychologically healthy life. Problems arise, according to the humanistic perspective, when an individual has lost touch with that inner self and source of guidance, or when our sense of ourselves is in conflict with what others have conveyed they think we should be or want us to be. The opinion of others may be conditionally, rather than unconditionally accepting as advocated by humanistic therapists. Thus, a humanistic therapist will try to help a client get back in touch with that inner self. Humanistic therapy is typically client-centered; that is, since every human is unique, only the client has the answer to his or her problems. The therapist acts mostly as a facilitator to help clients discover their own sense of self and their own aspirations. Since humanists think the source of psychological difficulty is others who were not supportive and accepting, humanistic therapists incorporate an approach of empathy, warmth, genuineness, and unconditional positive regard as they deal with their clients. The objective of humanistic therapy is to help clients reconnect with who they are, and realize that they are completely acceptable as they are. Gestalt therapy is a form of humanistic therapy where again the objective is to aid the client in getting back in touch with that inner self and integrate all aspects of the personality. However, gestalt therapists may be more confrontational in the hope that this directness will help clients also be direct in confronting their true feelings at the moment.

Behavioral psychologists believe everything about the human has been learned, directly through experience or indirectly through observation and imitation of others' behavior. Clearly, poor, offensive, ineffective or maladaptive behaviors can be learned just as more desirable behaviors are learned. According to behaviorists, we adopt behaviors because in the past these behaviors have led to a pleasant outcome. We avoid exhibiting behaviors that have led to unpleasant outcomes. We may have, perhaps inadvertently, gotten "desirable" results from behavior that really is not productive. Perhaps our prior acceptable behavior has gone unnoticed, leading to the decrease of its manifestation. Note that if a behavior has been learned, it can be changed—either by changing the consequences or by learning more effective behaviors. The treatment of fears (phobias and other anxiety disorders) may be approached behaviorally by means of systematic desensitization. With systematic desensitization, the client first reaches a state of relaxation, then slowly works his or her way up through a fear hierarchy. This is carried out over a period of therapy sessions. The objective is that the client will learn to replace a reaction of fear (such as to an object or situation) with a reaction of peace and calmness. This draws upon the behavioral phenomenon known as classical conditioning, and also incompatible responses (e.g., one cannot be simultaneously relaxed and afraid). The behavioral phenomenon of operant conditioning (behavior shaped by consequences) has therapeutic application in the form of behavior modification. This may be done in combination with the issuing of tokens (positive reinforcers) that can be exchanged for something the client wants. The objective of behavioral treatments is more preferable behaviors are reinforced, and undesirable ones are not maintained.

Cognitive therapists, such as Aaron Beck and Albert Ellis, believe that the source of psychological problems is less the situations or events themselves, and more how we construe those situations or events. Cognitive psychologists believe that a key to good psychological health is keeping one's perspective. Was that event really the ruination of your life, or was it a setback that you are fully able and willing to overcome? Cognitive therapy involves encouraging clients to contemplate their thoughts, and how they interpret events in their lives. Albert Ellis, as part of rational-emotive behavior therapy, encourages clients to recognize, for example, that expecting everyone's approval, all the time, is irrational. Ellis also advocates a positive attitude. Thoughts such as "I can manage this" help create a more positive response, and thus help prevent thinking that is self-defeating, which leads to self-defeating behaviors. Aaron Beck suggests that clients examine their negative emotional reactions. Beck points out that it is the negative emotional reaction that ultimately causes our problems. If we stay in touch with reality, and truly examine our thoughts and emotional reactions for accuracy, we may well see that our negative interpretation is unfounded. Rational-emotive behavior therapy may be more direct and confrontational than Beck's cognitive therapy.

A popular approach to psychological problems is eclectic therapy. With eclectic therapy, the therapist calls upon all the available treatment methodologies. They may be used in combination, or one approach may help with one aspect of a problem, while a different therapeutic approach is used for a different aspect of the problem. More clinical and counseling psychologists advocate an eclectic approach to psychotherapy than any other single methodology.

Therapy often is carried out in individual sessions, with just client and therapist, but it also may take the form of group therapy, family therapy, or couples therapy. These basically constitute what their names imply. Group therapy can be advantageous in that it is less expensive, and participants may explore aspects of their problems that are shared by other group members. The experience of sharing with other group members particularly helps with relationship and social problems. In family therapy, there is no one individual with the problem. The source of the psychological difficulty is thought to lie within the entire family system, and thus the therapeutic approach addresses the family as a unit. Couples therapy (or marital therapy if the pair are married) addresses relationship issues, which very often involve the inability to communicate effectively, and/or power and control issues.

Though the effectiveness of psychotherapy is still undergoing detailed research, in general we know that any kind of psychotherapy results in more improvement for individuals than if they do not receive therapy at all. Statistical procedures known as meta-analyses compare the functioning of individuals who have received therapy with those who have not, across hundreds of the individual studies that have been conducted. It does appear that some therapies may be more preferable for a given problem than others; these matters are still being explored. It is thought that much of the reason why psychotherapy is productive lies with factors common to many approaches, and these are known as nonspecific factors. These factors include the effectiveness and overall quality of the client-therapist relationship and the clients' hopes or expectations that the therapy will work and they will get better. Therapists need to remember that clients come from a wide range of ethnic and racial backgrounds. Therapy is most effective when practitioners are sensitive to the cultural factors pertaining to each of their clients.

KEY TERMS

Psychotherapy

Psychoanalysis

Psychoanalysts

Free association

Dream analysis

Interpretation

Insight

Resistance

Transference relationship

Countertransference

Behavior therapy

Systematic desensitization

Fear hierarchy

Gradual exposure

Modeling

Virtual therapy

Aversive conditioning

Cognitive-behavioral therapy (CBT)

Rational-emotive behavior therapy (REBT)

Cognitive therapy

Eclectic therapy

Group therapy

Family therapy

Couples therapy

Meta-analysis

Nonspecific factors

Placebo effects

SELF-TEST PRACTICE QUIZ

Match the following Key Terms and definitions (note: not every Key Term will be used):

1. _____ A helpful result of psychotherapy that occurs because the patient hopes and believes in the treatment and that the improvement will occur

2. _____ A type of therapy that involves utilizing aspects of any available therapeutic methodology in order to best treat the psychological disorder at hand

3. _____ One of the strategies involved in behavior therapy, where the client observes the real-life adaptive behavior of others and attempts to imitate it

4. _____ The psychotherapy approach first begun by Sigmund Freud, where the cause of psychological disorder is believed to be deep-seated, repressed, unresolved conflicts

5. _____ The objective of psychoanalysis as devised by Freud; the patient comes to understand the connection between the psychological disorder and repressed childhood experiences

a.   Psychotherapy

b.   Psychoanalysis

c.   Psychoanalysts

d.   Free association

e.   Dream analysis

f.   Interpretation

g.   Insight

h.   Resistance

i.   Transference relationship

j.   Countertransference

k.   Empathy

l.   Behavior therapy

m.   Systematic desensitization

n.   Fear hierarchy

o.   Gradual exposure

p.   Modeling

q.   Virtual therapy

r.   Aversive conditioning

s.   Cognitive-behavioral therapy (CBT)

6. _____ One component of psychoanalysis as developed by Sigmund Freud; the patient comes to regard the therapist as representing a key individual from an earlier difficult time, and manifests this conceptualization during therapy sessions

7. _____ One approach to psychotherapy, where the emphasis is on what the client has learned from experience, either through classical or operant conditioning

8. _____ A key component in client-centered therapy; the ability to detect and feel the emotions and perspective of the client

9. _____ An approach to psychological treatment developed by Albert Ellis, where the patient is challenged to evaluate the truth and rationality of beliefs underlying behaviors

10. _____ A type of psychotherapy developed by Aaron Beck, where clients are encouraged to evaluate the truth of cognitive distortions underlying unhealthy emotional reactions

11. _____ A behavioral approach to psychotherapy most specifically geared towards alleviating phobias and other fear-based disorders; involves gradually learning to replace response of fear with a response of calmness and relaxation

12. _____ A fundamental technique that is part of traditional psychoanalysis; the patient is completely free to say whatever comes to mind, whether or not apparently meaningful

13. _____ A form of treatment for psychological disorders constructed around a supportive relationship between client and therapist and involving extensive verbal exchange

t. Rational-emotive behavior therapy (REBT)

u. Cognitive therapy

v. Eclectic therapy

w. Group therapy

x. Family therapy

y. Couples therapy

z. Meta-analysis

aa. Nonspecific factors

bb. Placebo effects

14. _____ A type of therapy built upon the basic behavioral approach but adding an awareness of one's thoughts and interpretations as important to behavior and psychological functioning

15. _____ Qualities that seem to contribute to a positive psychotherapeutic experience, but do not appear to be exclusive to one approach to psychotherapy or another

16. _____ Treatment for psychological disorder involving approaching the entire family unit and its functioning as the presenting psychological problem

17. One difference between traditional psychoanalysis, as begun by Sigmund Freud, and modern psychodynamic approaches is that traditional psychoanalysis

    a.   discourages the use of free association.
    b.   is completed over a relatively brief span of time.
    c.   focuses primarily on the effects of primitive sexual instinct.
    d.   is conducted in a face-to-face manner.

18. In psychoanalysis, when a therapist's issues with others carry over onto the therapist-client relationship, this is known as

    a.   interpretation.
    b.   countertransference.
    c.   insight.
    d.   resistance.

19. In client-centered therapy, the role of the therapist is to _____ the statements and apparent feelings of the client.

    a.   rephrase, or reflect back
    b.   explain
    c.   interpret
    d.   critique

20. The source of psychological problems, according to the humanistic view, is

    a.   failing to adhere to behavioral standards established by close family members.
    b.   an excessive concern with one's own issues and inner feelings.
    c.   deep-seated sexual conflicts stemming from early childhood.
    d.   becoming out of touch with one's sense of direction towards self-actualization.

21. Which of the following is NOT a necessary component of humanistic therapy, according to Rogers?

    a.   The therapist must approve of everything that the client does.
    b.   The therapist should demonstrate empathy for the client.
    c.   The therapist should never hide his or her true feelings.
    d.   The therapist should accept the client unconditionally.

22. What is the underlying premise of behavioral therapy?

    a. In order to treat psychological problems, it is necessary to understand what unconscious conflicts are causing those problems.
    b. Therapists need to help clients integrate different parts of themselves into a whole, or Gestalt.
    c. Therapists can help clients learn adaptive behaviors through the application of classical or operant conditioning.
    d. none of the above

23. The difference between systematic desensitization and gradual exposure is that systematic desensitization

    a. does not make use of a fear hierarchy.
    b. puts the client in real-life experiences.
    c. is more effective for personality disorders than for anxiety disorders.
    d. involves extensive use of the client's imagination.

24. A component of humanistic therapy, where the therapist is able to understand, fully grasp, and essentially experience the feelings of his or her client is known as

    a. empathy.
    b. warmth.
    c. genuineness.
    d. unconditional positive regard.

25. In cognitive therapy, the source of psychological problems is believed to be not so much events or situations that occur, but rather

    a. genetic influences that lead to consistent behavioral patterns across situations.
    b. a lack of unification among various aspects of one's personality.
    c. maladaptive behaviors resulting from emotional reactions that occur as a consequence of the interpretation of events and situations.
    d. genetic influences that lead to consistent thinking patterns across situations.

26. What does the "ABC" stand for, in rational-emotive behavior therapy?

    a. Affect, beliefs, consequences
    b. Activating event, beliefs, consequences
    c. Activating event, behavior, consequences
    d. Affect, behavior, cognition

27. One erroneous assumption in families where there are psychological difficulties is that

    a. the therapist works miracles and holds all the answers for family problems.
    b. poverty, discrimination, and lack of education are always to blame.
    c. all other families within the culture share the same difficulties.
    d. a single family member is the source of all the problems.

28. Which statement about the effectiveness of different types of therapy is true?

    a. Psychoanalytic methods are generally acknowledged to be the most effective type.
    b. It is almost impossible to assess the effectiveness of any given method.
    c. Most effects are due to specific factors.
    d. The effectiveness of a particular psychotherapeutic method depends in part on the type of disorder being treated.

29. It is likely that _____ best explain why there are psychological improvements in clients after therapeutic treatment.
    a. the principles involved in cognitive therapy
    b. the techniques involved in behavioral therapy
    c. nonspecific factors
    d. genetic factors

30. What kinds of cultural issues must therapists be sensitive to when dealing with clients from varied backgrounds?
    a. Different cultures have different norms regarding expression of emotions.
    b. People may place different levels of importance on being independent.
    c. Clients may have had different experiences with prejudice and discrimination.
    d. all of the above

31. Someone who draws from a variety of available psychological treatment methodologies, depending on the nature of the client's problem or problems, is a(n) _____ therapist.
    a. cognitive
    b. cognitive-behavioral
    c. rational-emotive behavior
    d. eclectic

ESSAY QUESTIONS

1. Briefly explain the traditional approach to psychoanalytic therapy. How is modern psychoanalysis different?

2. What are empathy, genuineness, and unconditional positive regard? Why are they considered crucial to effective client-centered therapy?

3. Explain the relationship between events, beliefs, and consequences as presented in Albert Ellis's rational-emotive behavior model.

ANSWER KEY

1.   Placebo effects
2.   Eclectic therapy
3.   Modeling
4.   Psychoanalysis
5.   Insight
6.   Transference relationship
7.   Behavior therapy
8.   Empathy
9.   Rational-emotive behavioral therapy (REBT)
10. Cognitive therapy
11. Systematic desensitization
12. Free association
13. Psychotherapy
14. Cognitive-behavioral therapy (CBT)
15. Nonspecific factors
16. Family therapy
17. c
18. b
19. a
20. d
21. a
22. c
23. d
24. a
25. c
26. b
27. d
28. d
29. c
30. d
31. d

SAMPLE ANSWERS TO ESSAY QUESTIONS

1. The traditional approach to psychoanalysis was begun by Sigmund Freud. Freud believed the cause of psychological abnormality lay out of an individual's conscious awareness and involved conflicting factors that were often related to early childhood experiences. Thus, to get to the cause of the psychological disorder, the therapist needed to gain access to, and probe, the client's unconscious. The objective is to bring these hidden conflicts to light (into conscious awareness), gain insight as to how they have impacted the client's life, and find a resolution that will cure problems (such as hysterical paralysis) and allow the client to invest energy in more worthwhile pursuits. Psychoanalysts believe that gaining access to the unconscious is difficult to do, because the contents of the unconscious consist of selfish desires and unacceptable sexual and aggressive impulses. The patient does not want these unacceptable aspects to be seen by others, and it is concern about unintentional exposure of the unconscious that can lead to anxiety and other psychological disorders. The traditional psychoanalyst directs the patient to free associate—to say whatever comes to mind, without regard to meaningfulness or apparent cohesiveness of the statements. Psychoanalysts believe these free associations and how they are reported by the patient (e.g., what thoughts seem to occur together) eventually suggest the conflicts within the unconscious. During psychoanalysis, the patient may exhibit transference; that is, he or she may begin to act as if the therapist were a key member in the patient's past, one with whom the patient had psychologically troubling experiences. The patient may also exhibit resistance. Here, the patient consistently avoids or fails to respond to a certain line of questioning presented by the therapist. Both transference and resistance are considered helpful by the psychoanalyst because both aid in bringing hidden difficulties to light. The analyst's role through all of the therapy sessions is to interpret what is happening and help the patient gain insight as to what the underlying factors are and how they have influenced the patient's psychological state. Traditional psychodynamic therapy takes many months or, more often, years. Eventually the patient comes to a conscious understanding of the underlying conflicting forces and, with this insight, is able to live more effectively.

    Modern psychoanalysis has many of the features of traditional psychoanalysis, including the components of free association, transference, resistance, probing the unconscious, and interpreting dreams. It is still believed that the root of psychological problems lies in unresolved unconscious conflicts, usually traced to childhood and of a sexual or aggressive nature. However, modern psychotherapy focuses more on the present, and on the adaptive functioning of the ego in handling these difficulties and dealing with reality. Therapy does not take the years of sessions that it did in the past. Dialogue between client and therapist is usually increased, and the therapist likely takes a more direct and succinct approach.

2. Empathy, genuineness, and unconditional positive regard are all key components in effective psychotherapy, according to the humanistic viewpoint. Empathy means the therapist can perceive, and in fact can herself feel, the emotions and experiences of the client. Exhibiting empathy for the client's feelings and experiences helps confirm that the client's emotions and interpretations are valid and are important to the therapist. Genuineness means the therapist is always his true self and conveys his own feelings, reactions, and characteristics honestly to the client. When the therapist is completely genuine, and allows no falseness or façades in his own behavior, this sets the stage for the client to do the same. It suggests that the therapist values genuineness in others, thus encouraging clients to adopt an approach of genuinely detecting and reporting their own feelings. Unconditional positive regard means the therapist approaches the client as someone who is completely worthy and valuable exactly as he or she is at the moment. Everything about that client is completely acceptable and worthwhile, whether or not the client exhibits behaviors that parallel the therapist's behaviors and whether or not the client's behavior and personality characteristics are those that meet society's standards.

These approaches that are components of client-centered therapy are crucial because humanists believe psychological disorder stems from disliking oneself because one does not measure up to standards set by others. Or, psychological problems stem from losing touch with one's inner sense of guidance, again because others said the client "should" not feel or behave a certain way. The objective of client-centered therapy is to get the client back on track—back in touch with his or her feelings and that inner sense of guidance that leads the client to reaching self-actualization. Client-centered therapists let the client more or less direct what happens in therapy sessions; therapists act mostly as a facilitator, simply reflecting back what the client has conveyed. Thus, the client's connection with inner feelings and direction is restored, and the client develops confidence in and acceptance of his own sense of self-identity.

3. The rational-emotive behavior model, upon which rational-emotive behavior therapy is based, is the view that thoughts and interpretations that are irrational lead to emotional distress, and maladaptive behaviors then result from this distress. The debilitating aspects of the process are not so much the events that happen to an individual, but rather the individual's construal of events, and the emotional reactions that spring from this interpretation. Albert Ellis's treatment method is to help clients face the irrationality of their thinking. Ellis suggests an "ABC" model to represent the relationship between events in a person's life and that person's resulting behavior. "A" stands for the events that occur in someone's life. We all have challenging experiences in addition to more pleasant ones. Thus, some life events, although presenting difficulties, are unavoidable. "B" stands for an individual's set of beliefs, in light of which the individual makes an interpretation regarding the precipitating event. These interpretations are under our own control. Our beliefs impact how we construe a situation and lead to "C," the emotional consequence of that interpretation. If one's beliefs are not logical (e.g., believing one must always be perfect, or that one must always be completely acceptable to everyone else in every way possible), the emotional reaction will be maladaptive. No one can consistently reach unrealistically high standards, for example. Failure will inevitably result, and the sense of failure further diminishes one's ability to function effectively. Ellis challenged clients, sometimes in a confrontational manner, to recognize the irrationality of their beliefs. Rather than having events lead automatically to an emotional consequence, Ellis encouraged clients to be aware of the existing belief system through which the activating event is processed. With a more rational belief system, emotional reactions to events will not be so negative and debilitating. The client's response to an event will be more rational, and interpretations and resulting emotions will be kept in perspective. Rational-emotive behavior therapy also helps clients learn new, more adaptive behaviors and ways of dealing with others.

MODULE 13.2 BIOMEDICAL THERAPIES

LEARNING OBJECTIVES

After you have mastered the information in this unit, you will be able to:

1. Describe the major types of psychotropic drugs.

2. Discuss the advantages and disadvantages of psychiatric drugs.

3. Explain electroconvulsive therapy (ECT).

4. Describe psychosurgery.

5. Describe community-based mental health centers, and evaluate the success of deinstitutionalization.

OUTLINE

I.   Background Factors in Biomedical Therapies
   A.   Many gains in biomedical treatments for individuals with psychological disorders
   B.   Drugs have side effects; electroconvulsive shock, psychosurgery more controversial

II. Drug Therapy
   A.   Basic approach in drug therapy
      1.   Neurological transmission in the brain depends upon brain chemicals (neurotransmitters) to conduct messages from one neuron to another
      2.   Some psychological problems (e.g., anxiety, mood, and eating disorders; schizophrenia) related to irregularities in brain chemical action
      3.   Psychotropic drugs work on neurotransmitter systems in the brain to help regulate mood and thinking processes, do not cure problem
   B.   Antianxiety drugs (sometimes called minor tranquilizers)
      1.   Category includes diazepam (Valium), chlordiazepoxide (Librium), and alprazolam (Xanax)
      2.   Act on neurotransmitter gamma-aminobutyric acid (GABA)
      3.   Enhance GABA's ability to keep neural flow calm, in check
   C.   Antidepressants
      1.   Increase availability of norepinephrine and serotonin (neurotransmitters) in the brain
      2.   Tricyclics
         a)   Examples are imipramine (Tofranil), amitriptyline (Elavil), and doxepin (Sinequan)
         b)   Raise brain levels of norepinephrine and serotonin by interfering with reuptake process (reabsorption of these brain chemicals by transmitter cells)
      3.   Monoamine oxidase (MAO) inhibitors
         a)   Examples are phenelzine (Nardil) and tranylcypromine (Parnate)
         b)   Inhibit action of MAO, which normally breaks down norepinephrine and serotonin in synapse
      4.   Selective serotonin-reuptake inhibitors (SSRIs)
         a)   Examples are fluoxetine (Prozac) and sertraline (Zoloft)
         b)   Specifically raise levels of serotonin by limiting its reuptake
      5.   Evaluation of use of antidepressant drugs
         a)   Use of antidepressant medication has greatly increased in recent years
         b)   Complete symptom relief is found in 30% or fewer of the patients receiving antidepressant medication (Menza, 2006)
         c)   Improvement usually modest
         d)   SSRIs have less severe side effects, less dangerous regarding overdose
         e)   Antidepressants also helpful in treating other psychological disorders
   D.   Antipsychotics (major tranquilizers)
      1.   Used to treat schizophrenia and other psychotic disorders
      2.   First class of drugs (1950s): phenothiazines
         a)   Includes Thorazine, Mellaril, and Prolixin
         b)   Now possible to control most severe symptoms of schizophrenia
         c)   Phenothiazines and newer antipsychotic drugs work by blocking action of dopamine at dopamine receptor sites in the brain
      3.   Newer antipsychotics
         a)   Includes clozapine, risperidone, and olanzapine
         b)   Largely replaced phenothiazines due to fewer neurological side effects; however, may have their own dangerous side effects – substantial weight gain and serious metabolic problems (Morrato et al., 2010; Parsons et al., 2009)

E.   Other psychiatric drugs
   1.   Mood-stabilizing drugs (such as lithium)—help with bipolar disorder, mania
   2.   Anticonvulsant drugs help in treatment of epilepsy
   3.   Stimulant drugs
      a)   Methylphenidate (Ritalin) and pemoline (Cylert)
      b)   Improve attention spans, reduce disruptive behavior in hyperactive children
         1.   Currently the news related that many children have been misdiagnosed and have taken Ritalin that did not need it
      c)   Work by increasing activity of dopamine in frontal lobes
F.   Evaluating psychotropic drugs
   1.   Do reduce or control symptoms of many psychological disorders
   2.   Psychotropic drugs do not provide a cure; relapses are common
   3.   Drugs alone do not teach more effective life skills
   4.   Each has risk of adverse side effects
      a)   Drowsiness (from antianxiety drugs), dry mouth and problems with sexual response (from antidepressants)
      b)   Antidepressants may increase risk of suicide in children and adolescents
      c)   Muscular tremors, other motor problems from antipsychotic drugs
      d)   Lithium potentially toxic, may affect memory
      e)   Most serious side effect of antipsychotic drugs—tardive dyskinesia (TD; permanent neurological damage to motor system)
      f)   Possible that clozapine (Clozaril, for treatment of schizophrenia) may have fewer neurological side effects
      g)   Some drugs (e.g., Valium) lead to dependency, addiction, death from overdose or if mixed with alcohol or other drugs
      h)   Concern (e.g., with widespread reliance on Ritalin) is over eagerness for "quick fix" regarding psychological problems
      i)   Psychotherapy may be more work, but appears crucial for long-term drug-free improvement—drugs provide temporary relief, treat symptoms
      j)   Psychotherapy as effective or more effective than psychiatric drugs
      k)   Best approach is often combination of drug therapy and psychological intervention
      l)   We also know little about the long-term effects of Ritalin and other stimulant drugs on the developing brain (Geller, 2006, 2006; Lagacea et al., 2006)
III.   Electroconvulsive Therapy (ECT)
   A.   Jolt of electricity is passed through brain of patient, resulting in convulsions
   B.   May produce dramatic relief for individuals who are severely depressed
   C.   Anesthesia, muscle relaxants used to prevent experience of pain or injuries
   D.   Involves six to twelve treatments over period of several weeks
   E.   Most likely to be used when patient (severely depressed) does not respond to other therapies
   F.   Perhaps regulates levels of neurotransmitters related to mood
   G.   High rate of relapse; possible permanent memory loss—used as a last resort
IV.   Psychosurgery
   A.   Brain is surgically altered to control deviant or violent behavior
   B.   Prefrontal lobotomy
      1.   Previously most widely used psychosurgical technique
      2.   Nerve connections between frontal lobe and lower brain centers are severed
      3.   Eventually eliminated because of serious complications, death of patients
   C.   More sophisticated psychosurgery techniques introduced in recent years (e.g., for OCD)
   D.   Involve surgical alterations to smaller areas of the brain
   E.   Again used only as a last resort; many concerns regarding later complications

V.   Movement Toward Community-Based Care
    A.   Outcry for improvement in treatment of seriously mentally ill
        1.   Conditions in mental hospitals deplorable—1950s
        2.   1960s—community-based facilities created to provide alternative for care
        3.   Antipsychotic drugs available; would help control symptoms (e.g., of schizophrenia)
    B.   Deinstitutionalization
        1.   Redirection of patients with severe psychological disorders from mental hospitals to community centers
        2.   Many state mental hospitals closed, populations greatly reduced
        4.   A work in progress
    C.   Community-based mental health centers
        1.   Offer variety of services (outpatient, crisis intervention, supervised residential)
        2.   Hope is for transition to community life – but in far too many cases it remains a hope as yet unfulfilled
        3.   Many more alternatives available to help support patient in community
    D.   Evaluation of deinstitutionalization
        1.   Criticism is mental health center a revolving door—just temporarily stabilizes
        2.   Patients returned to community when really still unable to cope; community cannot absorb or manage
        3.   Effort is laudable, but really not fully effective—patient in fact may well end up among homeless left to fend for themselves
        4.   Severely mentally ill need extensive array of support services, regular basis
        5.   Effort continues to improve quality of life, provide sufficient intensive programs

SUMMARY

In this module, you learn about another approach to treating psychological disorders and about more recent improvements that have been made in the treatment of the severely mentally ill. The approach to treating mental illness discussed here, in addition to psychological therapies presented previously, involves the use of biomedical interventions. Biomedical therapies include the many currently available psychiatric drugs and other lesser-used biomedical interventions such as electroconvulsive shock therapy (ECT) and psychosurgery. Far and away the most widely used biomedical treatments are the psychotropic drugs, which are available to treat severe and less severe psychological disorders.

Psychotropic drugs are grouped into classes, the major classes being antianxiety drugs, antidepressants, and antipsychotics. All drug therapy is aimed at smoothing the workings of the brain's neurological pathways. Although neural messages are electrical in nature within the length of the neuron, they convert to chemical form when traveling from one neuron to the next. The neural messages are transmitted among many interconnecting neurons by means of neurotransmitters, which are chemical messengers. Note, then, that these neurotransmitters (such as norepinephrine, dopamine, and serotonin) are chemical in nature. It is here (at the junctures between neurons, which are called synapses) that the psychiatric drugs go to work. Because the drugs are chemicals, they are designed to affect the chemicals naturally present in the brain, the neurotransmitters. They also impact the neural sending and receiving sites (located on the ends of each neuron; not every neuron accommodates all brain chemicals) associated with these neurotransmitters. Although the underlying biological cause of abnormal behavior is not fully understood, irregularities in neural pathway functioning are associated with the presence of psychological disorder. Psychotropic drugs help to smooth the operations of these neural pathways by impacting the availability of relevant neurotransmitters and possibly by affecting the action at neural sending and receiving sites. The use of drugs helps, sometimes substantially, in the treatment of psychological disorder. When psychiatric drugs were first introduced in the 1950s, their use was a radical breakthrough in treating psychologically disturbed patients. It is important to recognize that the drugs do not provide a cure for the problem. However, in many cases, they control symptoms and make the psychological disorders more manageable.

Antianxiety drugs are minor tranquilizers, such as Valium and Xanax. All antianxiety drugs act upon the neurotransmitter gamma-aminobutyric acid (GABA), helping enhance its effects. Since GABA keeps neural impulses in check and flowing smoothly, individuals taking antianxiety drugs are expected to feel calmer and less prone to worry and agitation.

Antidepressants help keep the neurotransmitters norepinephrine and serotonin at sufficient levels within the brain. Both of these neurotransmitters are associated with mood or emotional states. The three major types of antidepressants are (1) tricyclics, (2) monoamine oxidase (MAO) inhibitors, and (3) selective serotonin-reuptake inhibitors (SSRIs). All of these antidepressants affect the levels of the neuro-transmitters mentioned. Serotonin and norepinephrine levels are impacted because normally these brain chemicals are reabsorbed by transmitting (sending) neurons once the neural message has been passed to the next (receiving) neuron. Antidepressants either limit the amount of the neurotransmitters that are reabsorbed from the synaptic gap or stop the enzyme (MAO) that causes the neurotransmitters to be broken down once they have been released from the neural sending sites. Antidepressants have become very widely used. They are successful in a majority of cases in treating depression. They also help in the treatment of nearly all well-known anxiety disorders and in some eating disorders. Common antidepressants include Prozac and Zoloft (both SSRIs) and the tricyclic Elavil. It is important to remember that all drugs have side effects, sometimes serious. There is risk that the drugs may become addictive, are potentially toxic, and may be seen as a substitute for more personal effort geared toward desired improvement from purely psychological interventions.

Antipsychotics are major tranquilizers and are used to treat schizophrenia (and other psychotic disorders). Antipsychotic drugs include Thorazine, Mellaril, and Prolixin. Again, while they control symptoms, antipsychotics do not provide a cure. However, being able to reduce and manage some of the most difficult aspects of schizophrenia (hallucinations, for example) is a tremendous step forward. Antipsychotics are effective because they appear to block receptor sites associated with the neurotransmitter dopamine. Though antipsychotics have been extremely helpful in treating serious psychological disorder, they also are the drugs with the most serious side effects. Long-term use of antipsychotic drugs damages the neurological systems of psychological patients, most particularly the motor nervous system. Tardive dyskinesia (TD) is the most serious side effect of antipsychotic drugs, and the patient eventually will experience permanent impairment of motor functioning. Advanced tardive dyskinesia is characterized by various uncontrollable neurologically-directed movements. It is hoped that the newest class of antipsychotics will have fewer seriously harmful side effects.

Other psychiatric drugs, such as lithium (for treatment of bipolar disorder) and stimulant drugs (such as Ritalin for hyperactivity) help in the treatment of psychological disorder by managing maladaptive symptoms. Patients and therapists must resist the temptation to treat all psychological disorders with the apparent "quick fix" available through drug therapy. Biomedical therapies are not a substitute for psychological treatments, and psychotherapy is at least as effective as the available drug therapies. Often a combination of the two approaches is most effective. Biomedical therapies also include electroconvulsive shock therapy (to treat severe cases of depression, especially when the sufferers have not responded to other forms of treatment) and psychosurgery. Both of these latter methods are quite controversial, rarely used, and only then in extreme cases as a last resort. It is apparent that the best treatment for mental disorders is a combination of biomedical intervention and psychological therapy.

Due to very unpleasant living conditions for the mentally ill and the creation of the first psychotropic drugs for treatment of psychological disorders, a movement began in the middle of the 20th century to get severely mentally ill patients out of the dismal mental hospitals and into more humane, more accessible community mental health centers. This was a very promising, if overly optimistic, concept. Patients were transferred to mental health centers within communities, and many state mental hospitals were closed or had inpatient populations greatly reduced. Drugs did help control the most extreme symptoms of the severely ill individuals; however, community mental health centers have seen at best a mixed success. Severely psychologically disturbed patients need numerous, frequent, intensive services and interventions. The great need for these can and do overwhelm the mental health centers, both in terms of staff and budget. Patients "fall through the cracks," and ultimately end up among the homeless or worse. The degree of support needed from community mental health centers for the severely mentally ill is great, and currently is not fully met. Efforts to improve the depth, scope, and availability of services continues, along with attempts to better match patient needs with existing community mental health resources.

KEY TERMS

Psychotropic drugs

Antianxiety drugs

Antidepressants

Tricyclics

Monoamine oxidase (MAO) inhibitors

Selective serotonin-reuptake inhibitors (SSRIs)

Antipsychotics

Tardive dyskinesia (TD)

Electroconvulsive therapy (ECT)

Psychosurgery

Prefrontal lobotomy

Deinstitutionalization

SELF-TEST PRACTICE QUIZ

Match the following Key Terms and definitions:

1. _____ The most serious side effect from taking antipsychotic drugs; potentially disabling damage to the nervous system, particularly that function directing motor activity

2. _____ A psychological surgical procedure (now no longer used) to control violent behavior; neural connections between the frontal lobes and other brain centers are severed

a. Psychotropic drugs

b. Antianxiety drugs

c. Antidepressants

d. Tricyclics

e. Monoamine oxidase (MAO) inhibitors

f. Selective serotonin-reuptake inhibitors (SSRIs)

g. Antipsychotics

h. Tardive dyskinesia (TD)

i. Electroconvulsive therapy (ECT)

j. Psychosurgery

3. _____ A class of psychotropic drugs used to treat depression and other disorders by specifically increasing the availability of serotonin through limiting how much is reabsorbed

4. _____ Psychiatric drugs developed to treat psychological disorders by means of chemical and biological intervention

5. _____ One of the major classes of antidepressants, which are generally effective because they increase the availability of neurotransmitters by interfering with their reuptake

6. _____ A class of antipsychotic drugs developed to treat depression and other psychological disorders

7. _____ One of the major classes of antidepressants, which increases the availability of neurotransmitters related to emotional states by limiting the action of an enzyme that normally breaks down these neurotransmitters in the synapse

8. _____ Drugs used in the treatment of severe psychological disorders such as schizophrenia

9. _____ A controversial biomedical therapy for severe cases of depression where there is no real response to other forms of treatment; involves an electrical shock delivered to the head of a patient—the shock is of sufficient strength to induce convulsions

10. _____ A rarely used procedure involving surgical alterations to the brain in an effort to control dangerously psychologically disturbed behavior

11. _____ A class of psychotropic drugs developed to treat various anxiety disorders

k. Prefrontal lobotomy

l. Deinstitutionalization

12.   _____ A movement begun in the mid-20th century to get even severely psychologically disturbed patients out of mental hospitals and into community-based mental health centers

13.   The development of psychiatric drugs to treat psychological disorders has led to

    a.   the complete relief of psychological disturbances.
    b.   the ability to control the more debilitating aspects of abnormal behavior.
    c.   an increased reliance on psychotherapy as a means for treating psychological problems.
    d.   a minimization of side effects normally involved in psychological treatments.

14.   Selective serotonin-reuptake inhibitors (SSRIs) are in the _____ classification of psychotropic drugs.

    a.   antianxiety
    b.   antidepressant
    c.   antipsychotic
    d.   clozapine

15.   Antianxiety drugs act on the neurotransmitter

    a.   norepinephrine.
    b.   serotonin.
    c.   GABA (gamma-aminobutyric acid).
    d.   dopamine.

16.   How do antidepressants such as Prozac (fluoxetine) affect neurotransmitter functioning?

    a.   They reduce levels of serotonin in the brain.
    b.   They inhibit the action of the enzyme monoamine oxidase (MAO).
    c.   They make GABA receptors more sensitive.
    d.   They interfere with serotonin reuptake.

17.   Normally the brain chemical monoamine oxidase (MAO)

    a.   smoothes the flow of neural messages in the brain.
    b.   interferes with the reabsorption of serotonin and dopamine.
    c.   breaks down important mood-related neurotransmitters present in the synapses.
    d.   blocks the action of dopamine at neural sending and receiving sites.

18.   The most serious side effect to taking antipsychotic drugs is

    a.   drowsiness.
    b.   reduced sexual interest and sexual response.
    c.   motor system functioning.
    d.   permanent damage to intellectual functioning.

19.   Messages are transmitted from one neuron to the next by

    a.   interneurons.
    b.   brain chemicals.
    c.   connector neurons.
    d.   nerve impulses.

20.   A newer drug used in the treatment of schizophrenia that may have fewer side effects than traditional antipsychotics is

    a.   clozapine.
    b.   Thorazine.
    c.   Elavil.
    d.   chlorpromazine.

21. How do stimulants help individuals with ADHD?
    a. They lower the effects of dopamine in the brain.
    b. They increase serotonin levels in the frontal lobe.
    c. They decrease GABA levels in the brain.
    d. They increase dopamine activity in the frontal lobe.

22. Which statement about deinstitutionalization is NOT true?
    a. When patients are released from mental hospitals, they are typically given little or no treatment after that.
    b. It has been a significant catalyst for the growth in the community mental health movement.
    c. Critics have argued that hospitals often discharge patients who are not ready.
    d. It arose in part because of advances in using medication to treat severe mental illness.

23. In what category of drugs is Thorazine?
    a. Sedative
    b. Antidepressant
    c. Anti-anxiety drugs
    d. Antipsychotics

24. In a prefrontal lobotomy,
    a. the left brain hemisphere is severed from the right brain hemisphere.
    b. the frontal lobe is severed from lower brain centers.
    c. the thalamus is severed from the parietal and occipital lobes.
    d. both the corpus callosum and the thalamus are removed.

25. Which type of drug is used most frequently in treating bipolar disorder?
    a. Antidepressants
    b. Minor tranquilizers
    c. Lithium
    d. Stimulants

26. Tricyclics are likely to produce _____ severe side effects in comparison to selective serotonin-reuptake inhibitors (SSRIs).
    a. less
    b. about the same degree of
    c. more
    d. cannot be determined; depends on the reaction of the individual patient

27. Psychotherapy has been shown to be _____ drug therapy with regard to treating psychological disorders.
    a. more effective than
    b. at least as effective as
    c. slightly less effective than
    d. much less effective than

28. Some drugs such as Valium raise concerns because
    a. regular use can lead to physical and psychological dependency.
    b. an overdose is often deadly.
    c. they can become toxic if mixed with alcohol or other drugs.
    d. all of the above

ESSAY QUESTIONS

1. How do the different classes of psychiatric drugs work? Briefly explain how each class of drugs works on the functioning of the neurological system.

2. Name the side effects or other concerns we have with at least four of five of the drugs or other biomedical therapies mentioned in this module.

3. Based on what you have read, what do you think is the best way to treat psychological disorders? Should we stay with community-based mental health centers, or return to the traditional mental hospital for the severely disturbed?

ANSWER KEY

1. Tardive dyskinesia (TD)
2. Prefrontal lobotomy
3. Selective serotonin-reuptake inhibitors (SSRIs)
4. Psychotropic drugs
5. Tricyclics
6. Antidepressants
7. Monoamine oxidase (MAO) inhibitors
8. Antipsychotics
9. Electroconvulsive therapy (ECT)
10. Psychosurgery
11. Antianxiety drugs
12. Deinstitutionalization
13. b
14. b
15. c
16. d
17. c
18. c
19. b
20. a
21. d
22. a
23. d
24. b
25. c
26. c
27. b
28. d

SAMPLE ANSWERS TO ESSAY QUESTIONS

1. Antianxiety drugs help keep patients calm and help reduce muscle tension. Antianxiety drugs bring these results about by enhancing one of the body's brain chemicals, a neurotransmitter called gamma-aminobutyric acid (GABA). The function of GABA is to keep neural impulses in check, and keep a neural transmission from exciting activity in other nearby neurons. Specifically, the antianxiety drugs increase the sensitivity of GABA receptors.

    Antidepressants affect neurological functioning by increasing the available levels of neurotransmitters associated with emotional experience or mood states. Norepinephrine and serotonin seem to be the neurotransmitters most involved in neural communication regarding emotions. Antidepressants either interfere with, and thus limit or slow, the reuptake of these neurotransmitters (this is the function of tricyclics and SSRIs), or they reduce the action of an enzyme that breaks down these neurotransmitters once they have been released into the synapse (a synapse is the gap between one neuron and adjoining neurons where the impulse transmission becomes chemical in nature). MAO inhibitors function in this latter fashion; monoamine oxidase (MAO) is the enzyme that normally degrades norepinephrine and serotonin present in the synapse.

    Antipsychotics work by blocking the action of dopamine at the dopamine receptor sites in brain neurons. Lithium is a major mood-stabilizing drug that is used in the treatment of bipolar disorder; other mood stabilizers are used in the treatment of epilepsy. Stimulant drugs help control hyperactivity and attention problems by increasing dopamine activity in the frontal lobes.

2. Drug or other biomedical therapies are not a perfect solution to the problem of psychological disorders. Psychotropic drugs do not work for everyone, and all drugs developed thus far produce side effects. A common side effect of taking antianxiety drugs is drowsiness. Antianxiety drugs such as Valium can be dangerous or fatal if mixed with other drugs or alcohol, or taken in excessively high doses. A client taking antianxiety drugs runs the risk of developing physical or psychological drug addictions. Antidepressants can cause an uncomfortable condition called dry mouth and inhibit sexual responsiveness. Antipsychotic drugs lead to the most serious side effects; they impact motor neural system functioning and may cause permanent, irreversible damage. There is concern that there is excessive reliance on drugs to treat psychological disorders, and the side effects can be sufficiently unpleasant that many individuals stop taking medication for this reason. Both electroconvulsive therapy (ECT) and psychosurgery are very controversial procedures. They are used only as a last resort in the treatment of psychological problems that have failed to respond to other, less invasive interventions. In addition to the aversive nature of the physical procedure itself, both ECT and psychosurgery can produce complications. There is a high rate of relapse after ECT, and there may be permanent memory loss. Brain surgery can result in physical or other complications and may even result in death.

3. It is clear that the best way to treat most incidences of psychologically disturbed behavior is through a combination of both psychological and biomedical interventions. The great advantage of drug treatment is that drugs can reduce and control some of the most difficult characteristics associated with the experience of psychological disorders. Schizophrenic patients who are constantly experiencing delusions or hallucinations are a prime example. It is difficult to begin or proceed further with psychological intervention if a patient continues to hallucinate or seems unaware of his or her surroundings. A client who is severely depressed may simply be unable to concentrate during psychotherapy sessions. The point is that drug interventions can help manage the more debilitating symptoms of psychological disorders. In most cases, once these symptoms are under control, then psychological interventions such as verbal therapy sessions can begin or continue with some likelihood of success. Psychotherapy sessions will be much more effective if the emotional state of the client is under control. This stability can be facilitated through the use of mood-stabilizers (e.g., for bipolar disorder), antianxiety drugs, or antidepressants. Once a client is

not experiencing severe mood swings or bouts of depression or severe anxiety, the client is much more able to attend to the benefits available in therapy sessions. Drug therapy is not effective for everyone and results are usually acceptable but do not entirely eliminate the psychological disorder. Unlike drug treatments, psychotherapy has no unpleasant or harmful physiological side effects. There is a problem of relapse when drug treatments are used. It is best if both patient and therapist resist the notion that a drug is a panacea that will provide an instant solution to all psychological difficulties. Most likely, for long-term success, the client needs assistance with learning better life skills, better coping strategies, and better approaches to problem-solving. These gains can come about if a client also has access to quality psychotherapeutic intervention. Though community mental health centers are certainly not entirely successful, their continued support and modification is a much more humane and hopeful alternative than a step back to the former mental institution approach.

MODULE 13.3 APPLICATION: GETTING HELP

LEARNING OBJECTIVE

After you have mastered the information in this unit, you will be able to:

1.   Describe the steps people can take to find qualified mental health professionals.

OUTLINE

I.   Steps for Finding Qualified Mental Health Professionals
    A.   Get recommendations from knowledgeable sources
    B.   Check with a local medical center or clinic
    C.   Consult with available services at college or university
    D.   Contact professional organizations (such as the American Psychological Association)
    E.   Look in yellow pages of telephone directory—but use these sources with caution
    F.   Check credentials, licensing and affiliations of treatment providers
    G.   Investigate the type of therapy provided (behavioral, cognitive, or other)
    H.   Inquire regarding educational and professional background
    I.   Investigate the provider's experience in treating others with a similar problem
    J.   After initial consultation and evaluation, get a clear explanation of diagnosis and proposed treatment plan before making any commitments
    K.   Discuss costs and insurance coverage
    L.   Know policies for missed or canceled appointments
    M.   Learn details regarding any prescribed medications
    N.   Discuss any concerns, especially if the treatment recommendations do not seem appropriate to you
    O.   Consider a second opinion, especially if you are experiencing doubts
    P.   Be very cautious regarding online therapy services

SUMMARY

In this module, you learn about effective and reliable ways to find good mental health care providers. Almost anyone can call himself or herself a "therapist" or even a "psychotherapist," and many, many individuals and clinics are listed in, for example, the yellow pages. It is important to have a practitioner who is fully qualified and adheres to ethical standards when an individual is undergoing treatment for psychological disorders.

Suggestions for locating a qualified mental health professional include getting recommendations from people you know who have some knowledge and experience in the field of psychology and whose recommendations you can trust. These sources can include your physician, a local medical center, your college counseling or health center, or appropriate professional organizations. The yellow pages in your telephone directory are indeed a possibility, but consider these sources with caution and try to find another resource suggested here to confirm any possibilities. Check the licensing of the mental health professional recommended to you, and verify educational background, professional affiliations, experience, and credentials. An ethical provider will have no hesitation in sharing all of this information and more with you. Investigate the type and history of experience the mental health professional has had with your particular disorder. Clarify the therapeutic approach that will be used (behavioral, psychoanalytic, or other) and how it is expected to help the type of problem you are experiencing. Be sure you know the diagnosis and proposed treatment plan before committing to anything. An understanding of costs, applicability of insurance coverage, and policies regarding missed or cancelled sessions should be part of your discussion with the therapist. If medication is to be prescribed, find out how it will work—that is, how long it should take before you experience results and what kind of side effects are possible. If you have concerns, mention them, and do not hesitate to seek a second opinion. Be particularly cautious of therapy services offered online.

CHAPTER 13   APPLICATION EXERCISE

Think of a movie or other program you have seen where individuals with psychological disorders are portrayed. What kind of treatment did they receive? How long was therapy continued? Were satisfactory results achieved? What was the site of the mental health services like? How does this media portrayal compare to what you know of psychotherapy in real life?

Have you yourself had a psychological disorder, or do you know someone who does? What kind of treatment therapy is involved, if any? If the individual is not getting psychological help of any kind—why is that so? What are the person's objections? Has the individual had a previous experience with medication causing unpleasant side effects? Did the person have difficulty with a therapist, public stigma, the institution or mental health center, or the type of treatment involved?

If the individual (or you!) is getting help from a mental health professional, how is the course of therapy going? Does therapy consist of psychotherapy talk sessions, biomedical interventions, or both? How long is treatment expected to last? Evaluate the psychological disorder as you see it. What type of treatment might be most effective? Note what you think of the results thus far.

CHAPTER 14

Social Psychology

In Chapter 14, you learn about the influences other people have on us and that we have on them. Human beings are very social creatures. As such, having the liking and acceptance of others is important to our own psychological well-being. Because acceptance from others is important, we are willing (to a greater or lesser extent) to mold and adapt our behavior in order to fit in with guidelines and standards established by the groups of which we are members. While westernized societies (individualistic cultures as opposed to collectivist) are thought to value independency and autonomy to a great extent, in fact these cultures too are very affected by group norms and group sanctions.

Social perception involves how we come to know, understand, and think about our social environment. We form impressions of others from being exposed to them, and impressions can be formed quite quickly. If we rely too much on social schemas (a way of organizing our social perceptions), we fall into the trap of stereotyping. Stereotyping means making assumptions about others just because they are members of a particular group. In part, we do need to organize our social world so our lives run more smoothly and are manageable, but not to the point that we and others are harmed by our prejudgments.

Because we are social creatures, we are always curious about others' behavior. We make attributions for behavior, which really are explanations we come up with as to why people do what they do. We also make attributions about our own behavior. Especially in western cultures like the United States, there is a tendency to underestimate situational factors when interpreting the behavior of others. The fundamental attribution error is the tendency to make dispositional (e.g., it is due to an internal personality trait) attributions for the behavior of other people, disregarding what might be legitimate situational influences on that behavior. We develop attitudes about other persons, objects or events; sometimes these attitudes can be changed. The correspondence between attitudes that we hold and behaviors we exhibit relative to those attitudes is not as high as one might think.

Social psychology also includes our liking for other individuals. Degree of liking tends to be influenced by four factors: similarity, physical attractiveness, proximity (nearness), and reciprocity. Although we tend to match up with partners who are about as physically attractive as we are, there seem to be standards for beauty (at least for the female face, thus far) that are fairly universal.

Why do people help others? Are there times when helping is truly purely altruistic—that is, we have no thought whatsoever as to what we might get out of it (including good feelings)? This is a debatable point in social psychology. Helping others also is not as obvious a matter as it might seem. Helping may, for example, put us or loved ones at risk. The situation may be confusing (is it really an emergency?) and if others are available to help, we are actually less likely to leap into the situation ourselves because surely someone else will.

Is the human by nature aggressive? That question we cannot fully answer. There are many factors related to aggression, and since it is such a complex behavior it is assumed that a variety of factors come into play when aggression is manifested. Aggressiveness may be instinctual behavior, since at least in the past it was related to one's survival. Levels of testosterone are associated with levels of aggression, although again it is not a perfect correspondence. Aggression most clearly can be learned, particularly by means of behaviors modeled and reinforced at home. Prejudices are also passed on that way. Aggression may be the result of anger or frustration, but that is not always the case.

We are all members of groups, and our group membership (known as our group identity) is an important part of our self-concept, or psychological identity. In other words, who we are is in part defined by our relationship with others. There is a pronounced tendency to conform (and this is not at all necessarily a bad thing!) and to obey directions from individuals in authority. Classic studies on conformity (by Asch, 1956), and on obedience (by Milgram in the 1960s) demonstrate these points well. Social facilitation describes the impact of the presence of others on our performance. As long as a task is familiar and not too difficult, our performance usually is enhanced when we have an audience. Performance usually is impaired if we are trying to carry out a difficult, unfamiliar task. Conformity to a requester's demands can occur as part of sales techniques. The social psychological phenomena of consistency and reciprocity are not unknown to sales personnel, and may be used to lead buyers to make purchases even though the item or price ultimately is not what the buyer originally had in mind.

MODULE 14.1 PERCEIVING OTHERS

LEARNING OBJECTIVES

After you have mastered the information in this unit, you will be able to:

1. Define social psychology and understand the nature of social perception.

2. Identify the major influences on first impressions, and explain why first impressions often become lasting impressions.

3. Explain the role of cognitive biases in explaining behavior.

4. Describe attitudes, their acquisition, and their relationship to behavior.

5. Describe cognitive dissonance theory.

6. Explain how persuasive appeals impact attitudes.

OUTLINE

I.   Social Psychology and Social Perception
   A.   Social psychology—the study of how our thoughts, feelings, and behaviors are influenced by our social interactions with others and by the culture in which we live
   B.   Social perception—the process by which we come to form an understanding of our social environment, on the basis of three sources
      1.   Observations of others
      2.   Personal experiences
      3.   Information we receive
II. Impression Formation
   A.   Background information on impression formation
      1.   Impression formation—the process by which we form an opinion or impression of another person
      2.   First impressions can be formed in a fraction of a second according to recent research (Willis & Todorov, 2006)
      3.   Tend to be long-lasting and difficult to change although impressions may well change as people get to know you better, you never get a second chance to make a first impression
      4.   Affect how we relate to the person we have formed an impression of
   B.   Personal disclosure
      1.   More favorable impression formed of people willing to disclose personal information about themselves
      2.   Revealing too much too soon results in a negative impression

    3.   Cultural norms a factor in personal disclosure
  C.   Impressions as social schemas
    1.   Social schema or mental representation
       a)   Impression is a type of social schema
       b)   Social schema is a mental image or representation we use to understand our social environment
       c)   Information about others is filtered through the social schema
       d)   Existing schema influences how we perceive new information
  D.   Stereotyping
    1.   Preconceived ideas about groups of people – stereotypes about members of other social or ethnic groups are usually more negative than those about members of one's own group
    2.   Stereotypes can influence first impressions, either favorably or unfavorably
    3.   Stereotyping a normal cognitive activity; helps us process social input more efficiently
    4.   May be some truth in commonly held stereotypes – not necessarily accurate
    5.   Stereotyping on basis of race, ethnicity, gender, and the like is ineffective, unfounded
  E.   Self-fulfilling prophecies – what goes around comes around
    1.   Initial impression influences subsequent exhibited behavior towards that person
    2.   Behavioral message sent (perhaps unintentionally) then influences response of the other individual
III.   Attributions: Forming Personal Explanations of Events
  A.   Attribution—a personal explanation we form about the causes of behavior or events we observe
    1.   Dispositional causes—attributing behavior to internal traits
    2.   Situational causes—attributing behavior to external or environmental factors
    3.   Attributions are affected by cognitive biases (see B, C and D, below)
  B.   Fundamental attribution error
    1.   We tend to overlook situational factors when interpreting behavior of others
    2.   Tendency is to make internal attributions when interpreting behavior of others (our focus is on the actor, not the influence that the surroundings might have on the people)
    3.   Members of collectivist cultures less likely to make fundamental attribution error (less emphasis on the individual in these cultures)
  C.   Actor-observer effect
    1.   Tendency to attribute causes of our own behavior to external (situational – the exam was not fair) factors, make internal (they are not very smart so they failed) attributions regarding other people's behavior
    2.   Actor-observer effect probably due to differing perspectives (Heider, 1958)
  D.   Self-serving bias
    1.   Tendency to attribute our personal successes to our own inner traits (internal attribution) – taking credit for our own successes
    2.   Tendency to make an external (situational) attribution with regard to things that did not work out well for us – looking for excuses as to why we did not succeed
    3.   Helps to keep our self-esteem intact
    4.   Much more widespread in western than in eastern cultures
    5.   Westerners value protection of self-esteem; eastern cultures emphasize self-criticism, humility
IV.   Attitudes
  A.   An evaluation or judgment (either liking or disliking) regarding a person, object, or issue
  B.   Three components to attitudes (Crites, Fabrigar, & Petty, 1994)
    1.   Cognitions—set of beliefs

2.   Emotions—feelings of liking or disliking – emotions also include three basic components: bodily arousal, cognitions, and expressed behaviors

3.   Behaviors—what is manifested in actions; inclination to act positively or negatively

C.   Sources of attitudes

1.   Attitudes acquired from many sources in social environment

2.   Sources include parents, teachers, peers, personal experiences, and media

3.   Individuals of similar backgrounds tend to hold similar attitudes

4.   Possible genetic link to attitudes (resulting from commonality in intelligence, personality, and temperament)

5.   Environmental influences probably more important than genes

D.   Attitudes and behavior

1.   Behaviors not as closely linked to attitudes as is expected – may not carry over into behavior

2.   Research reveals modest relationship only

3.   Possibly due to great variation in situational factors

4.   Correspondence related to stability and strength of attitude; also how directly it applies to a given situation

V.   Cognitive Dissonance

A.   Maintaining consistency between attitudes and behavior

B.   Inconsistency should lead to emotional discomfort (dissonance)

C.   Several ways to reduce cognitive dissonance

1.   Change behavior to fit attitudes or beliefs

2.   Change attitudes and beliefs to better fit behaviors

3.   Explain away inconsistencies or ignore discrepancies

D.   Most common approach is to simply wait for inconsistencies to disappear ("I'll worry about it later")

E.   Need for consistency may make us vulnerable to outside manipulation

VI.   Persuasion

A.   We are constantly bombarded by messages designed to influence our attitudes

B.   Frequently involve political figures or merchandise available for purchase

C.   Relationship between appeals and possible attitude change

1.   Elaboration likelihood model (ELM)

a)   Central route to attitude change—when motivation is high, have skills and knowledge needed for careful evaluation of message

b)   Peripheral route to attitude change—when motivation low; listeners more influenced by cues not centrally related to the content of the message

2.   Variables influencing persuasion

a)   Source—greatest influence when speaker credible, likable, similar to listener

b)   Message—repeated often enough people may come to believe it, usually best to present both sides (with opposition side refuted), not appear to serve own interests – contains emotional appeal

c)   Recipient—easier to persuade people of low intelligence, low self-confidence; also when people in a more positive mood (more likely to see message in a positive light – also a good time to ask for a favor)

SUMMARY

In this module, you are introduced to the field of social psychology. Social psychology examines how the behavior of an individual is influenced by interactions with others. This module discusses factors related to the impressions we form of others, and also describes attitudes and how attitudes may be changed. Social perception concerns how we come to perceive, or have an understanding of, others. As you might guess, social perception is something of a subjective process. Impressions of others tend to be formed rather quickly, yet they may be tenacious. That is, once an impression is formed, the impression may be somewhat resistant to change. An impression is one component of our social schemas—our way of categorizing the world so that we can function more effectively within it. Thus, once an impression is formed, all future information regarding the subject of that impression is filtered through the existing schema. We may no longer interpret new experiences with that person in a completely objective manner, in part because of our expectations. Stereotypes can influence the formation of impressions because they constitute a preconceived set of beliefs about an individual simply because that individual is a member of a group. Stereotypes may bias our interpretations of another, and prejudicial behavior resulting from stereotyping is clearly wrong and unfounded.

Since humans are very social creatures, we are always trying to interpret and understand our social world. Why did that person you know glance down when you looked his way? Did your friends really enjoy your last party? To understand human behavior, we make attributions. Attributions are simply explanations as to why a behavior occurs. Attributions actually are somewhat difficult to make accurately since often we have access to only limited information. However, we usually go ahead and make attributions anyway! In part we need to, to help make our complex social world more manageable. We tend to attribute behaviors to one of two sources—either internal (we believe the behavior occurred because of a fairly stable personality trait) or external (we believe the behavior occurred because of situational, or environmental, factors). Especially in western, individualistic cultures, there is a tendency towards one kind of attribution error. This error is so pervasive in western cultures, in fact, that it is known as the fundamental attribution error. That error is the tendency to underestimate situational factors when evaluating the actions of another. When we observe behavior, the actor performing that behavior is usually the focus of our attention. The actor is much more likely to attract our attention than are other features of the environment in which the actor appears. Probably that is the reason we tend to make internal attributions. We attribute the actor's behavior to personality characteristics. Interpreting our own behavior may be another story! The actor-observer effect is an expansion on the fundamental attribution error concept. The actor-observer effect includes the fact that we also tend to attribute our own actions (at least, when they do not come out well!) to external, or situational, causes. The self-serving bias is the tendency to put what we do in the best light possible. In order to do that, we tend to make an internal attribution where we have succeeded and an external attribution where we have not.

Attitudes are how we feel about something—an object, a person, or an issue. Attitudes tend to have three components. These components include a cognitive aspect (what we believe), an emotional aspect (feelings of liking or disliking), and a behavioral aspect (what we convey through our actions). We get our attitudes from many sources. Interestingly, there may even be a genetic component linked (probably indirectly) to attitudes. Twins raised apart show more consistency in attitudes than can be explained by situational factors alone. Although we would expect the correspondence between what we believe and how we act regarding those beliefs to be quite high, in fact it is not. When attitudes and related behaviors are measured, there is only a modest correlation between the two.

In general it is important that our attitudes and our behaviors correspond. We would and should feel a little ridiculous if we verbally tout one perspective but in actual practice do another. Cognitive dissonance theory suggests that when we do this (believe one thing, manifest another), we will feel uncomfortable; this feeling of discomfort is termed cognitive dissonance (the term dissonance suggesting emotional imbalance). There are ways we can remedy this imbalance—change the behavior to fit the attitude, change the belief to fit the behavior, or introduce another concept or explanation that would help apparently reconcile the two. However, interestingly, the most likely strategy when facing cognitive dissonance is to simply ignore the experience and wait for sufficient time to pass so that the discrepancy is no longer an issue. An example, I will give up smoking when I am through college.

Since we all have many attitudes, how likely is it that an attitude will change? This module also examines attitude change as a result of attempts at persuasion. The elaboration likelihood model (ELM) helps represent what occurs when persuasive attempts are made. For an intelligent audience motivated to attend to a persuasive message, the central route to persuasion is likely to be more effective. That is, features of the message itself will be attended to, and it is best if both sides of an argument (with the opposing side refuted) are presented. If an audience is not motivated to attend to a message, is fatigued, or is distracted, the peripheral route to persuasion is more likely to be effective. Here, the audience is probably not attending very closely to actual features of the message. Rather, they are likely to be influenced by peripheral characteristics—the attractiveness of the speaker, the tunefulness of the jingle, or how engaging the setting is. Variables influencing the effectiveness of persuasion messages include factors related to the source (the speaker), the message itself, and the recipient (the listener—if he or she is listening!). Communicators who are perceived as credible, likeable, and similar to the listeners are more likely to change attitudes.

KEY TERMS

Social psychology

Social perception

Impression formation

Social schema

Stereotypes

Self-fulfilling prophecy

Attribution

Dispositional causes

Situational causes

Fundamental attribution error

Actor-observer effect

Self-serving bias

Attitude

Cognitive dissonance

Cognitive dissonance theory

Elaboration likelihood model (ELM)

SELF-TEST PRACTICE QUIZ

Match the following Key Terms and definitions:

1. _____ Interpreting the behavior of an individual as a function of external (environmental) factors

2. _____ Putting ourselves in the best light by taking credit for our accomplishments and making situational explanations for what we have not done well

3. _____ How we feel about a person, object, or issue

4. _____ How we come to understand our social world

5. _____ The tendency to evaluate an individual and attribute characteristics simply because that individual is a member of a group

6. _____ When our behavior towards another inadvertently creates or encourages the behavior we are expecting

7. _____ Interpreting the behavior of an individual as a function of internal (e.g., personality, consistent traits) factors

8. _____ A field within psychology dealing with how our thoughts, feelings and behavior are influenced by our interactions with others

9. _____ A mental representation (such as an impression) that helps us function more efficiently and effectively within our social environment

10. _____ The tendency to make internal attributions regarding others' behavior and external attributions regarding our own

11. _____ The process by which we develop an opinion or impression of another

a. Social psychology
b. Social perception
c. Impression formation
d. Social schema
e. Stereotypes
f. Self-fulfilling prophecy
g. Attribution
h. Dispositional causes
i. Situational causes
j. Fundamental attribution error
k. Actor-observer effect
l. Self-serving bias
m. Attitude
n. Cognitive dissonance
o. Cognitive dissonance theory
p. Elaboration likelihood model (ELM)

12. _____ The tendency to underestimate the impact of situational factors with regard to others' behavior

13. _____ An explanation we arrive at as to why an event or behavior occurred

14. _____ A representation of how attitude change due to persuasive messages may occur

15. _____ The feeling of discomfort we have when our beliefs or attitudes do not correspond to actual behaviors we exhibit

16. _____ Research examining the inconsistency when thoughts and behaviors do not match; the steps, if any, people may take to reconcile the discrepancy

17. The study of how we are influenced by our interactions with others and our culture is known as

   a.   social psychology.
   b.   social perception.
   c.   attribution theory.
   d.   the elaboration likelihood model (ELM).

18. An impression is a(n)

   a.   schema.
   b.   stereotype.
   c.   expectation.
   d.   attitude.

19. Once we have formed an impression, why is that impression rather resistant to change?

   a.   We tend to filter new information about a person based on the impression that already exists.
   b.   Our first impressions usually are quite accurate and there is no need to change.
   c.   Humans are by nature stubborn and resistant to change.
   d.   We have turned our focus to other more pressing issues.

20. We have heard that Ms. Albright is very warm and caring. We greet her with an attitude of great warmth, and make her welcome. Sure enough, she is just as warm and caring as others said that she was. What social psychological phenomenon is occurring here?

   a.   The central route to persuasion
   b.   The peripheral route to persuasion
   c.   The self-fulfilling prophecy
   d.   The fundamental attribution error

21. There is a very slow driver on the road in front of you. You think, "That guy must be ancient. He hasn't a brain in his head. Why do they let people like this guy on the road?" Just then there is a bend in the highway, and you see there is another, slow-moving vehicle right in front of the driver ahead of you. You have

   a.   made an external attribution.
   b.   inadvertently initiated a self-fulfilling prophecy.
   c.   committed the fundamental attribution error.
   d.   made good use of your driver education classes.

22. Which of the following statements is an example of a situational attribution?

    a. "He helped that old woman because he is a generous man."
    b. "She got into a car accident because it was raining."
    c. "She got an A on the test because she is smart."
    d. "They don't have jobs because they are lazy."

23. People who are_____ are more likely to commit the fundamental attribution error.

    a. from individualist cultures
    b. male
    c. elderly
    d. highly intelligent

24. According to Heider (1958), what is one reason that the actor-observer effect occurs?

    a. An audience tends to be fatigued and is not listening closely to the message.
    b. People with lower levels of intelligence and self-confidence are more likely to be persuaded.
    c. Attributions made about behavior may very well have to do with one's perspective.
    d. Our dispositional attributions are strengthened once we get to know the actor better.

25. There is _____ correspondence between people's attitudes and their behaviors.

    a. some
    b. very high
    c. little
    d. no

26. Generally speaking, people who _____ are more easily persuaded.

    a. have low intelligence
    b. have high self-esteem
    c. are in a bad mood
    d. none of the above

27. If an audience is reasonably intelligent, and motivated to listen to a message, persuasion is mostly likely to occur if

    a. the speaker relies on the peripheral route to persuasion.
    b. only one side of the argument is presented in detail.
    c. the message clearly presents why the alternative is beneficial to the speaker.
    d. the speaker creates the impression of being knowledgeable and trustworthy.

28. One characteristic of a message that is likely to result in attitude change, even if the information presented in the message in inaccurate, is

    a. repetition.
    b. an offer of money.
    c. clarification of the speaker's intent in presenting the message.
    d. the communication of threats, or emotionally charged content.

29. Cognitive dissonance occurs when

    a. people's behaviors are inconsistent with their attitudes.
    b. people are persuaded to change their minds about a subject.
    c. prejudice is reduced.
    d. people use the central route of information processing.

30. People are more likely to respond to a persuasive message when the communicator is

    a. similar to the audience.
    b. physically attractive.
    c. seemingly trustworthy.
    d. all of the above

ESSAY QUESTION

1. In general, with regard to impression formation, we form a more favorable impression when a person is willing to share personal information. However, too much information, too soon, has the opposite effect. Why might this be so?

ANSWER KEY

1. Situational causes
2. Self-serving bias
3. Attitude
4. Social perception
5. Stereotypes
6. Self-fulfilling prophecy
7. Dispositional causes
8. Social psychology
9. Social schema
10. Actor-observer effect
11. Impression formation
12. Fundamental attribution error
13. Attribution
14. Elaboration likelihood model (ELM)
15. Cognitive dissonance
16. Cognitive dissonance theory
17. b
18. a
19. a
20. c
21. c
22. b
23. a
24. c
25. a
26. a
27. d
28. a
29. a
30. d

SAMPLE ANSWER TO ESSAY QUESTION

1. It is true that we usually like people more if, when we first get to know them, they are willing to disclose somewhat more personal aspects and information about themselves. Perhaps this helps build a bridge between two people, and if the topic of conversation becomes a little more emotional, our emotional feelings about the entire exchange may become a bit more engaged. New social partners who disclose information that is too personal, in too great a quantity, and too soon, however, tend to elicit a more negative first impression. This occurs most probably because individuals who disclose a great deal of fairly personal information very early in social contact are perceived as being immature and less emotionally secure. They are also perceived as exhibiting poorer social and psychological adjustment than individuals who also share personal information but with more restraint.

With regard to personal disclosure, it should be remembered that some standards for disclosure are a function of cultural norms. People who are members of East Asian cultures (such as China and Japan), for example, are likely to disclose less in the way of personal information, and also to be uncomfortable with others who are highly personal, especially in the early phases of a social relationship. In such an instance, this reluctance to disclose and greater restraint regarding personal matters is more a reflection of cultural, rather than personal, characteristics.

MODULE 14.2 RELATING TO OTHERS

LEARNING OBJECTIVES

After you have mastered the information in this unit, you will be able to:

1. Discuss the major determinants of attraction.
2. Identify the three components of love in Sternberg's model of love.
3. Describe factors that are linked to helping behavior.
4. Explain prejudice and its development.
5. Describe what can be done to reduce prejudice.
6. Explain the factors that contribute to human aggression.

OUTLINE

I. Attraction
   A. Background factors in attraction
      1. Includes feelings of liking others, positive thoughts, positive actions
      2. Liking and love both topics in social psychology
      3. Attraction is not limited to romantic or sexual attraction
   B. Key determinants in attraction
      1. Similarity
         a) We are attracted to those who are like us and share our values, attitudes
         b) Similarity serves as validation for each other
         c) Common ground important but room in relationships for differences
      2. Physical attractiveness
         a) Physical attractiveness seems to be very important factor in initial attraction
         b) Gender and cultural differences exist regarding importance of attractiveness
         c) Physical appearance affects how personality and intelligence are perceived
         d) Cross-cultural similarities in standards for facial beauty

        e)   Support for matching hypothesis—that we choose those similar in attractiveness, the less attractive partner usually compensates by having greater wealth or social position than the more attractive partner

        f)   Casual sexual relationships, both men and women place a premium on the physical attractiveness of prospective partners (Li & Kenrick, 2006; Nevid, 1984; Stambor, 2006)

        h)   In our society, it also pays to be tall – literally; wvidence shows that height is associated with higher incomes (Dittmann, 2004)

3.   Proximity
        a)   Friends usually those who live (or sit in classroom) near us
        b)   Proximity increases opportunity to be exposed to, get to know, others

4.   Reciprocity
        a)   Liking those who like us back
        b)   Reciprocal interactions build upon themselves, increase liking
        c)   We may be wary of people who compliment us too quickly or seem to like us too much before they get to know us; we may suspect that they want something from us or are not very discriminating

II.   Love: The Deepest Emotion
   A.   Recently psychologists have attempted to scientifically study love
   B.   Love to be both a motive (a need or want that drives us) and an emotion (or feeling state)
   C.   Love has three basic components (Sternberg, 1988, 1997a)
      1.   Intimacy—close bond, attachment, sharing innermost thoughts and feelings
      2.   Passion—sexual desire for the other individual
      3.   Decision/Commitment—recognition and intention to support, maintain relationship
        a)   Decision and commitment need not go hand in hand – a person may acknowledge being in love but not be ready or willing to make a lasting commitment
   D.   Different components and combinations yield different kinds of love (see Table 14.1)
      1.   Intimacy + passion = romantic love – may burn brightly but soon flickers out
      2.   Intimacy + commitment = companionate love – type found in many long-term marriages; intimacy and commitment remain strong even though passion has ebbed
      3.   Passion + commitment + intimacy = consummate love – may be an ideal for many couples than an enduring reality
   E.   Relationship balanced when love triangles well matched or closely overlapping – partners are similar in the levels of passion, intimacy, and commitment

III. Helping Behavior
   A.   Background factors in helping behavior
      1.   Story of Kitty Genovese
        a)   Stabbed to death in street in Queens, New York (1964)
        b)   Thirty-eight neighbors watched, no one helped
      2.   Many helped in World Trade Center disaster
        a)   What explains help in some cases, and not others?
      3.   Prosocial behavior—behavior that is beneficial to others
        a)   Altruism—pure helping, no thought of return; some social psychologist believe that all forms of helping benefit the helper to a certain extent
        b)   Helping to benefit helper (to look good, relieve guilt)
   B.   Bystander intervention
      1.   Result of a decision-making process
        a)   Is there a need for help?
        b)   Is it a true emergency?
        c)   Decision to assume personal responsibility
        d)   What kind of help to give?

      e) Implement course of action
     2. Interpret situations in light of these factors
   C. Influences on helping
     1. Situational ambiguity—less help likely when situation is confusing; not a clear cut emergency
     2. Perceived cost—less help likely if costs (including psychological) are high
     3. Diffusion of responsibility—less help likely when more people witness, available
     4. Similarity to those in need of help—also more help for kinship members
     5. Empathy—more likely to help if able to identify or empathize with victims
     6. Facial features—helping greater to individuals with baby-face features
     7. Mood and gender
      a) More help likely when helper in a good mood
      b) More assistance still typically given to women
     8. Attributions regarding the cause of need—more help to innocent victim
     9. Social norms (prescribe behavior)—especially a factor when request is made in front of others

IV. Prejudice
   A. Background factors regarding prejudice
     1. A preconceived attitude, usually negative, without rational evaluation
     2. Cognitive, emotional, and behavioral components
      a) Cognition—biased beliefs, stereotypes
      b) Emotion—e.g., feelings of negativity, dislike
      c) Behavior—discrimination (unfair or biased treatment) based on group membership
     3. Often a disparity between voiced attitude and actual behavior
     4. Stereotypes and prejudices are resistant to change
     5. Prejudice and discrimination increase during social upheaval, and increase competition among groups
   B. The development of prejudice
     1. An outgrowth of negative stereotypes
     2. Stereotypes are learned, acquired the same way other attitudes are learned
     3. Everyone has some stereotypes—partly a cognitive, adaptive strategy
      a) In-group/out-group distinction
      b) In-group favorable, out-group negative
      c) Out-group homogeneity—seen as all alike; perceiving members of own group as being "different as snowflakes" (Nelson, 2002)
     4. Cognitive basis for prejudice—developed over thousands of generations, for survival
   C. Why some people are more prejudiced than others
     1. Learning and experience play key roles
     2. Parental influence, cognitive style, personality (e.g., authoritarian) are factors
   D. Effects of stereotyping and prejudice on stereotyped groups
     1. Racism—negative perspective solely due to racial membership
     2. Stressful, may affect physical and psychological health (of recipient)
     3. Stereotype threat—lowered, internalized expectations; self-fulfilling prophecy
   E. Reducing prejudice—contact hypothesis (Gordon Allport, 1954)
     1. Four conditions that determine whether intergroup contact will reduce prejudice—but these conditions may not always be realistic
      a) Social and institutional support—authority figures must endorse effort
      b) Acquaintance potential—opportunities available to get to know each other better
      c) Equal status—contact must be on equal footing

             d)   Intergroup cooperation—all members working together towards common goal; cooperation can foster feeling of friendliness and mutual understanding

       2.   Effort begins with what we teach children, empathy, countering prejudicial thinking

       3.   Enforcing laws against discrimination and encouraging tolerance are societal measures

V.   Human Aggression

   A.   Background factors regarding aggression

       1.   Stereotyping and prejudice can lead to more negative behaviors

       2.   Varying opinions on nature of human aggression

   B.   Explanations for aggression

       1.   Instinct

             a)   Fighting a survival mechanism (Lorenz, 1966)—to protect family, species

             b)   Instinct also leads members of prey to fight or flee, for survival

             c)   Current view is aggression too complex to be explained just on basis of instinct (probably is a combination of causes)

       2.   Biological influences

              a)   History of violent or impulsive behavior: abnormal brain circuitry?

             b)   Brain chemical serotonin the behavioral "seat belt" "emergency brake" for restraining impulses (Raine 2008)

             c)   Testosterone and aggression are related—much more aggression in males

             d)   Ancestry benefited by males who were aggressive, for hunting purposes

       3.   Learning influences

              a)   Social-cognitive approach: children learn through observation, modeling

             b)   Aggressive behavior increases if reinforced

             c)   Failed to learn alternative ways of resolving conflicts

       4.   Sociocultural influences

             a)   Consider social stressors (poverty, child abuse and neglect, unemployment, family breakdown and exposure to violence)

             b)   Children who are abused may fail to develop loving attachments, lack empathy

             c)   Attempt may be made to use aggression and violence for coercion

       5.   Alcohol use

             a)   Strong link between alcohol use and rape, homicide, domestic violence

             b)   Alcohol loosens inhibitions, restraints; affects judgment, and reduces sensitivity to punishment-related cues

       6.   Emotional influences—negative emotions may trigger aggression

             a)   Frustration—when path to goal is blocked

             b)   Anger – blow minor provocations out of proportion

             c)   Neither frustration nor anger necessarily lead to aggression

       7.   Environmental influences

             a)   Outdoor temperature shown to be a factor

             b)   Heat induces hostility, increases readiness for aggressive response to provocation – although it may decline at very high temperatures (Anderson & DeNeve, 1992; Sundstrom et al., 1996)

SUMMARY

In this module, you learn about the many social psychological factors involved in our relationships with others. Our interactions with others involve many pleasant circumstances, such as social and emotional relationships and the opportunities we take to help each other. Our relationships can also have unpleasant aspects, such as when prejudice or aggression materialize. All of these issues are studied by social psychologists, and it is hoped that as we learn more and gain more understanding about our relationships with others, the quality and harmony of interpersonal exchange may improve.

What attracts us to others? Social psychologists suggest that attraction tends to be based on four factors: similarity, physical attractiveness, proximity, and reciprocity. In general, we are most attracted to people who are like ourselves. Yes, individual differences can be interesting, but attractions are more likely to occur and be maintained when the social partners share common ground. Perhaps the reason for our attraction to others who are like us is because the characteristics in the other person validate who we are. When people spend time with each other, their attitudes can actually grow more similar. Physical attractiveness seems to be the predominant factor leading to initial attraction. There are gender and cultural differences, however. Men place more emphasis on the physical attractiveness of their partner, while women are more interested in attitude similarity or (in the Korean culture, for example) educational, occupational, or family background. The standards for what is beautiful in the human face are consistent across cultures, although there are of course some cultural variations. There also is a tendency for us to choose partners who more or less match us with regard to physical attractiveness (known as the matching hypothesis). Proximity (how close we are to others—in terms of where we live, where we sit in a classroom or office, and the like) is a distinct factor in attraction. In part, proximity gives you the opportunity to be exposed more often to another person (and vice versa!). Also, in part, we may be near others because of other similar background factors. Reciprocity means we like another person because that person has exhibited liking for us. The reaction to positive feedback from another is often, but not always, a feeling of liking in return.

Love is a relatively new topic for psychologists, and we probably will gain more sophisticated and detailed knowledge as time goes on. The leading model for love has been proposed by Robert Sternberg (1988); his view is termed the triangular model. His theory suggests that there are three components, each of which contributes to feelings of love. Different combinations of components result in different kinds of love. The basic components, according to Sternberg, are intimacy, passion, and commitment. Only consummate love consists of all three of these components. Love relationships will be most successful when partners agree (overtly or covertly) on what their love is comprised of.

Helping is a kind of prosocial behavior. Prosocial behavior means we engage in the behavior because it is beneficial to others. Do we ever truly help someone with no concern for what is in it for us? If so, this is known as altruism (Batson, 1991). We may also help because it feels good to do so, or because we hope some time to be helped ourselves in the future. The intensive study of helping, and of prosocial behavior in general, was sparked in part by a brutal death some forty years ago. This involves the story of Kitty Genovese, who was repeatedly stabbed and left to die on a street near her home. What was shocking was that she was surrounded by neighbors, who heard and saw the crime as it was being committed. No one went to help, and no one called the police until at least a half-hour had passed. By that point, she could not be revived. With so many people aware of the murder, and capable of helping, why did no one go to her aid? Yet, many people risked their lives to help others during the World Trade Center disaster. What is the difference? The answer to this question has been proposed by Bibb Latané and John Darley (1970), based on research on the topic they call bystander intervention. According to this research, bystanders must make a number of decisions, which may involve their own welfare, before they act to provide help. These five steps are (1) recognizing the need for help, (2) determining that the situation is a true emergency, (3) feeling that one's own intervention is necessary, (4) deciding on how that help will be provided, and (5) taking action to intervene. What seems to lead people to help? If the situation is confusing, or if many others are around who could provide help also, intervention is less likely. It is harder to help when we put ourselves or our loved ones at risk. We are more inclined to help those who are like us, and especially when we perceive that the person in need of help did nothing to bring on the problem. Social norms, the mood of the potential helper, and the gender of the person in need are also factors.

Prejudice and aggression are the more negative side of human behavior. Prejudice is an attitude, which may be related to stereotyping (a set of cognitions stemming from a person's membership in a particular group) and discrimination (the behavior of treating others in a biased or unfair manner simply because of their membership in a particular group). Prejudices emerge from negative stereotypes, and negative stereotypes are most likely learned. Children will imitate the behaviors and attitudes of their parents, and prejudices can be passed on in this way. There is a tendency also to see those like us as the in-group; others then form the out-group. Out-group homogeneity means we perceive "them" (the out-group) as all alike. Groups that experience prejudice and racism are hampered because they may internalize the attitudes conveyed towards them, and they are aware of the negative attitudes others hold. Prejudice among groups can be reduced by providing opportunities for all to get to know each other directly, and on an equal footing. Organizations and institutions must support the effort to reduce prejudice, and a common goal for all involved groups is helpful.

There are many explanations for aggression, and aggression is a sufficiently complex behavior that there is probably a combination of causes. Proposed explanations for aggression include instinct (it may be helpful for survival), biological influences, learned behaviors, sociocultural influences, the consumption of alcohol (which lowers inhibitions and impairs reasoning), emotional influences, and environmental influences. Aggression and violence are more likely (but will not necessarily occur) when one is angry, male, feels frustrated, and if outdoor air temperature is high. The higher rate of aggression in males may have had evolutionary significance since our male ancestors were hunters and faced risks and competition from out-group members.

KEY TERMS

Attraction

Matching hypothesis

Proximity

Reciprocity

Love

Prosocial behavior

Bystander intervention

Social norms

Prejudice

Discrimination

In-groups

Out-groups

Out-group negativism

In-group favoritism

Out-group homogeneity

Authoritarian personality

Racism

Contact hypothesis

Frustration

SELF-TEST PRACTICE QUIZ

Match the following Key Terms and definitions (note: not all Key Terms will be used):

1. _____ A preconceived attitude towards an individual or group without direct experience

2. _____ Liking that occurs as a response to behavior indicating that another likes us

3. _____ A personality type that constitutes rigid, inflexible behaviors and attitudes

4. _____ Having positive thoughts, feelings, and behaviors with regard to another

5. _____ An approach for reducing prejudice involving the opportunity for members of different groups to get to know each other on an individual basis, with equal status, support from authority figures, and ideally working towards a superordinate goal

6. _____ Groups of which we are a member or with which we identify

7. _____ The idea that we are likely to choose as partners those who are similar to us with regard to physical attractiveness

8. _____ The action of offering help to a stranger who is in need

9. _____ The tendency to perceive individuals who are not in our in-group as being all the same

10. _____ The act of treating others with bias or unfairly because they are part of a particular group

11. _____ Simply being near another individual; a factor contributing to interpersonal attraction

a. Attraction

b. Matching hypothesis

c. Proximity

d. Reciprocity

e. Prosocial behavior

f. Bystander intervention

g. Social norms

h. Prejudice

i. Discrimination

j. In-groups

k. Out-groups

l. Out-group negativism

m. In-group favoritism

n. Out-group homogeneity

o. Authoritarian personality

p. Racism

q. Contact hypothesis

r. Frustration

12. _____ A negative emotional state that typically occurs when one discovers that one's efforts at reaching or obtaining an objective are blocked

13. _____ Standards regarding what is acceptable that are held by a particular culture; there are subtle pressures on members of the culture to adhere to these standards

14. _____ Negative attitudes and behaviors directed towards individuals simply because they are members of a particular racial group

15. _____ Behavior on our part that fosters the well-being of others (it may or may not help our own outlook and well-being also)

16. Which seems to be the strongest predictor regarding whether or not you and someone you just met will date again?
    a. Similarity
    b. Physical attractiveness
    c. Proximity
    d. Reciprocity

17. When we help someone else with truly no thought or expectation as to what we might get out of it, we are said to have
    a. altruistic motives.
    b. a hidden agenda.
    c. a philanthropic personality.
    d. the reciprocity norm.

18. The first step in Latané and Darley's model of bystander intervention is to
    a. weigh the potential costs of helping.
    b. decide that a need for help exists.
    c. decide that the situation is a clear emergency.
    d. assume personal responsibility for helping others.

19. People are generally more likely to help when
    a. the individual who needs help is an older male.
    b. many others nearby are available to help as well.
    c. it is uncertain as to whether there is a true need for help or not.
    d. they are in a good mood.

20. According to Allport, several conditions must exist if intergroup contact is to lead to prejudice reduction. Which of the following is NOT one of those conditions?

    a. Authority figures need to support the initiative.
    b. People from different groups need plenty of opportunities to interact.
    c. Group members should do whatever they like, without having any sort of predetermined goals.
    d. Members of different groups need to have equal status.

21. What are the three parts of Sternberg's triangular model of love?

    a. Similarity, proximity, and reciprocity
    b. Passion, intimacy, and commitment
    c. Similarity, intimacy, and commitment
    d. Passion, proximity, and reciprocity

22. Albert Bandura (1986) demonstrated that children imitate aggressive behavior when they have seen it at home, at school, or in the media. This explanation for aggression involves

    a. instinct and emotions.
    b. biological influences, including testosterone and alcohol use.
    c. sociocultural influences.
    d. learning influences.

23. Which of the following is NOT associated with higher levels of aggression in adults?

    a. Cool temperatures
    b. Alcohol use
    c. A history of being abused as a child
    d. High levels of testosterone

ESSAY QUESTIONS

1. Did individuals who died giving aid at the World Trade Center exhibit truly altruistic behavior? Support your response.

2. Given the circumstances of the Kitty Genovese murder, we can conclude that making the decision to help is not a simple matter. Describe, referring to the research by Latané and Darley, steps we are likely to take when making the decision whether or not to intervene and provide help.

3. What are some of the reasons that may explain why humans exhibit aggressive behavior?

ANSWER KEY

1. Prejudice
2. Reciprocity
3. Authoritarian personality
4. Attraction
5. Contact hypothesis
6. In-groups
7. Matching hypothesis
8. Bystander intervention
9. Out-group homogeneity
10. Discrimination
11. Proximity
12. Frustration
13. Social norms
14. Racism
15. Prosocial behavior
16. b
17. a
18. b
19. d
20. c
21. b
22. d
23. a

SAMPLE ANSWERS TO ESSAY QUESTIONS

1. Daniel Batson and colleagues have proposed that genuinely altruistic behavior occurs when assistance is given but there is absolutely no benefit to the helper. This concept of altruism is in contrast to prosocial behavior, where indeed help is given to another but the actions may also have benefits to the person giving help. People may help because it makes them feel good, or allows them to avoid the uncomfortable guilt they would feel if a situation arose where aid was needed but they did not offer assistance. In the World Trade Center disaster, individuals not only helped other humans in need but gave their lives (surely knowingly, in some cases) to rescue fellow workers and other trapped or suffering individuals. Risking one's life does not suggest that the helper is expecting anything in return. Clearly no apparent benefit came to the helping individuals whose only "reward" was ultimately death. Although the notion of true altruism remains under debate by some, it does seem that humans will suffer or even give their lives to aid others.

2. Kitty Genovese was murdered while at least thirty-eight of her neighbors were aware of the assault and did nothing to intervene. Why did people around her not help? Latané and Darley

(1970) proposed steps one may go through when considering whether to help another individual in need or not. The first step is to decide whether there really is a need for help. That seems clear in the Genovese case. The second step is to determine whether the situation really is an emergency. In the Genovese case, that also seems clear. Step three in Latané and Darley's model is perhaps the key. That step involves assuming personal responsibility. The fourth step is to decide what one is going to do to provide help, and the fifth step is to actually put that decision to help into action. This murder took place in an urban area. We can assume the neighbors were aware that many other people were at home and available to provide help also. It appears that the neighbors did not feel a need to get involved themselves; there were plenty of other people who could do that. Another thing to consider in evaluating the response to the Genovese murder is the influence of the helping factor known as perceived cost. The murder was an assault with a knife. To provide any direct assistance was to put one's own life in danger. Still, a neighbor could have called the police. However, no one called until thirty minutes later.

3. Aggression is a very complex behavior, and there seems to be no single precipitating factor. Explanations that have been proposed for aggressive behavior include (1) that it is a survival instinct, (2) biological influences (may be related to levels of serotonin), (3) that it is a learned behavior, (4) sociocultural influences, (5) alcohol use (since alcohol tends to loosen inhibitions and impair reasoning), (6) emotional influences (particularly experiencing frustration or anger) and (7) environmental influences (incidences of aggression increase as the outdoor temperature rises). We can see some value in aggression for our ancestors in that it was literally necessary to fight off threats to home, family, and food sources. Aggression is most certainly learned. Children may learn both that aggression is an acceptable form of behavior (if it is modeled in the home) and to pick up pointers (so to speak) on how to aggress. If a youngster's aggressive acts meet with success and are not effectively discouraged, aggressive behavior is reinforced. All influences listed here are associated with the occurrence of aggression. No one influence or event always leads to aggressive behavior for all people. Yet, there is no shortage of aggression. Thus, psychologists adhere to the belief that aggressive behavior results from a combination of factors.

MODULE 14.3 GROUP INFLUENCES ON INDIVIDUAL BEHAVIOR

LEARNING OBJECTIVES

After you have mastered the information in this unit, you will be able to:

1. Explain social identity.

2. Discuss Asch's study on conformity and its implications.

3. Describe Milgram's findings on obedience, and explain why his methods were controversial.

4. Describe how the presence of others affects individual performance.

5. Discuss groupthink.

OUTLINE

I.   Background Factors Regarding Group Influence
    A.   Humans are very social creatures ("no man is an island")
    B.   Since social connections vital, interpersonal influence can be powerful
II.   Our Social Selves
    A.   Two components of psychological identity (self-concept)
        1.   Personal identity (individual identity; asking "Who am I?")
        2.   Social identity (group identity; asking "Who are we?")
    B.   Social identity more prominent in collectivist cultures

    C. Western cultures more likely to emphasize individuality, autonomy – affects many aspects of our daily behavior

    D. People have a fundamental need to belong, relating most to those who are similar

    E. Variations too within cultural boundaries

III. Conformity

    A. Fitting our behavior to prevailing social standards

    B. Lack of conformity involves risk of social disapproval

    C. Conformity to group as well as general social norms

    D. Resisting conformity pressures not as easy (even in individualist cultures) as it might seem

    E. Asch study (a social psychology classic) on conformity – recognize that we may conform more than we think

        1. All group members except one (subject participant) were collaborating with researcher

        2. Task was judging length of lines (matching to a target line)

        3. Three-fourths of participants gave wrong answer (to conform) at least once

    F. Why do some people conform more than others (even when answer obvious)?

        1. People assume the majority must be correct

        2. Concern for acceptance by group overrides desire for accuracy

        3. Easier to go along with group than disagree

        4. Other characteristics

            a) Women slightly more likely to conform than men

            b) More conformity among collectivist cultures than individualistic

            c) More conformity among individuals with low self-esteem, social shyness, especially strong need to be liked

            d) Conformity tends to decline with age (after childhood)

    G. Situational factors

        1. More conformity when behavior public than in private

        2. Conformity increases as group size increases (up to four or five people)

        3. Conformity increases when stimuli more ambiguous

        4. With dissent from anyone else in group—conformity drops sharply

        5. Note that some degree of conformity is helpful (groups run more smoothly) – can stifle individuality and independence

IV. Obedience to Authority

    A. Atrocities of Nazis during WWII raised questions

    B. Research program to test obedience created by Stanley Milgram (1960s)

        1. Participants were adult residents of New Haven (Connecticut) and surrounding area

        2. Cover story for experiment—the effects of punishment on learning

        3. "Learner" a collaborator, real participant in study was "teacher"

        4. Each wrong answer prompted increasing levels of administered shock

        5. Experimenter pressured "teacher" to continue, throw switch

        6. Sixty-five percent of participants went to "severe shock" voltage

        7. Some variation related to proximity of "teachers" to "learners"

        8. Also raised questions regarding deception, ethical treatment of participants

    C. Why do people obey immoral commands?

        1. Humans are taught from an early age to obey authority figures such as parents and teachers and not to question or second-guess them

        2. Also some impact from social comparison, difficulty stopping behavior once begun

    D. Evaluating Milgram's legacy

        1. Cannot duplicate study because of ethical considerations

        2. Does suggest inner capacity for destructiveness, blind obedience exists

        3. Perhaps more emphasis needed on personal responsibility for actions

V. Social Facilitation and Social Loafing

    A. Social facilitation
1. Working harder when in presence of others
2. Presence of others increases performance of dominant responses
3. For complex tasks, presence of others impairs

    B. Social loafing
1. Less effort expended when working as member of a group
2. Thought is other group members will pick up slack
3. Less likely to occur when individual performance is evaluated – holding each member accountable for contributions and giving public feedback of individual performance (Hoeksema van Orden, Guillard, & Buunka, 1998; Levine & Moreland, 1998)

VI. Groupthink
1. Concern to reach a consensus outweighs concern to critically evaluate issue
2. Pressure is to conform to majority opinion; debate to critically examine the issues stifled
3. Groupthink most likely to occur
    a) when members strongly attached to group
    b) external threat present
    c) strong-minded leader directs the group
4. Suggested ways to minimize occurrence of groupthink (Janis, 1982, 1997)
    a) Encourage group members to consider all alternatives, weigh all evidence
    b) Group leader should avoid stating a preference at outset
    c) Call upon outsiders to voice opinions and analyses
    d) Encourage group members or outsiders to play "devil's advocate"
    e) Subdivide group; smaller groups review issues independently
    f) Hold several group meetings and evaluate all new information before final decision is made

SUMMARY

In this module, you learn about how our membership in groups can influence us. Humans are very social creatures, and thus we value the opportunity to share social contact with others. Since we value social contact, the acceptance and opinions of others becomes important. We are influenced by others because of this need for social acceptance. We have a psychological identity (also known as a self-concept) that is derived in part from who we are as unique individuals but also in part due to the various groups to which we belong. Group acceptance and group membership, then, matters. Thus, we may be inclined to conform to views or standards of a group, even when these views are not our own. Though there are, of course, no legal sanctions against social nonconformity, there certainly are social pressures to conform and repercussions if we do not. A classic study carried out by Asch (1956) utilized the seemingly simple task of matching comparison lines to a target line. Asch began this study to investigate independence, not conformity. However, the study showed that, even among participants who did not know each other, and even when criteria for making judgments were completely clear, most participants disregarded their own evaluation and went along with inaccurate judgment of the group at least once. Greater levels of conformity are particularly likely to be found among individuals who lack self-esteem and who are especially in need of being liked and accepted by the group.

The atrocities in Nazi Germany led researchers to investigate blind obedience and inhumane deeds. Nazis stated they were "only following orders" (Elms, 1995). Beginning in the 1960s, Milgram designed research studies assessing the psychological factors involved in obedience to an authority. Milgram's classic studies involved participants who thought they were teaching another volunteer (this was the cover story). The supposed task was for the learner to match word-pair lists correctly. In fact, the "learner" was in on the study and was assisting Milgram as he carried out his research. For every wrong answer the "learner" in the study gave, the "teacher" (the only real participant in the study) was instructed to give the learner a shock. The shocks increased to a "severe shock" level. Participants were uncomfortable with administering the shock, but most continued to shock the learner when repeatedly urged by the experimenter to do so. This was the real study. Though you might not expect it, approximately two-thirds of individuals participating in the study followed orders from an authority to administer shocks all the way up to and including the "severe shock" level. This study and ones like it cannot be repeated due to ethical considerations (deception and trauma experienced by the participants, even though they found out later they were not giving shocks). However, it does shed light on the fact that, under certain conditions, people will inflict severe harm on others because they are told to do so.

Other sources of group influence include social facilitation and social loafing. Social facilitation means the presence of others usually enhances our ability to perform well. A further clarification of social facilitation indicated that the facilitating effect occurred only when the task we were faced with was one that was not too difficult or was one that we knew very well. Social facilitation increases our ability at dominant responses; performance on a task that is difficult for us will usually be impeded. Social loafing conveys the finding that members of a group tend to expend less effort on a task than they would if they were doing it alone. Social loafing will usually not occur, however, if it is made clear to group members that their individual contribution will be evaluated.

Desire to conform to the views of a group we value and the opinions of a forceful leader can lead to groupthink. Groupthink involves the process of minimizing and often withholding one's own opinions in deference to what appears to be the group's assessment. Obviously, groupthink can be a problem! Group decisions may be made that do not really reflect the best thinking of the individual group members. To help prevent groupthink, members should be clearly directed to evaluate all factors with contrasting opinions encouraged. The group should meet several times to reassess the matter, and members might meet in subgroups that would result in a greater variety of independent perspectives. The group leader should avoid stating his or her opinion at the outset. One or more individuals can be designated to play "devil's advocate," critiquing the statements, proposals, and opinions set forth by the group. Outsider perspectives should be contributed and new information welcomed.

KEY TERMS

Personal identity

Social identity

Conformity

Obedience

Legitimization of authority

Social facilitation

Social loafing

Groupthink

Compliance

Social validation

SELF-TEST PRACTICE QUIZ

From the Key Terms select that which best matches the following:

1. _____ Following the directions of another because that person is an authority figure

2. _____ A term that describes the tendency to stifle one's own opinion when feeling pressure from desirable group to conform

3. _____ A sense of pressure to adjust one's behavior or views to standards set by a group

4. _____ Our sense of who we are which results from our membership in various groups

5. _____ When the presence of others improves our ability to perform tasks well

6. _____ Our understanding of ourselves due to who we are as a unique individual

7. _____ Being inclined to go along with the request or demand of another

8. _____ Socialization leading us to accept and follow the demands of an authority figure

9. _____ Feeling more comfortable about our own characteristics because they are exhibited by others

10. _____ Doing less work because one's individual contribution to a group is not evaluated

a. Personal identity

b. Social identity

c. Conformity

d. Obedience

e. Legitimization of authority

f. Social facilitation

g. Social loafing

h. Groupthink

i. Compliance

j. Social validation

11. Getting tattoos and body piercing because your friends do it is
    a. conformity to general social norms.
    b. conformity to group or peer norms.
    c. nonconforming behavior.
    d. a reflection of practices in an individualistic society.

12. People are more likely to conform to the norms of a group if
    a. their responses are kept private from the rest of the group.
    b. they are male.
    c. they come from an individualist culture.
    d. they have low self-esteem.

13. Which statement about Stanley Milgram's research on obedience is NOT true?

    a.   Participants were more likely to obey the researcher if the "learner" was in a different room.
    b.   His research is invalid because participants quickly realized that the "learner" was not truly being shocked.
    c.   His research has been criticized on ethical grounds.
    d.   Those participants who administered severe shocks were generally very upset about it at the time.

14. In which of the following settings for Milgram's research were obedience levels HIGHER than in the original study reported?

    a.   When the research setting was moved from Yale to a commercial storefront
    b.   When "teachers" and "learners" were placed in the same room
    c.   When teachers could hear learners screaming through the walls
    d.   When teachers were instructed to ask others to administer the shock for them

15. Which of the following is a good way to decrease social loafing?

    a.   Make the group larger.
    b.   Make the task less interesting.
    c.   Provide public feedback about each member's performance.
    d.   none of the above

16. When we start to be more preoccupied with arriving at consensus within a group than with our own beliefs, intellectual assessment, and personal standards, we are experiencing

    a.   social facilitation.
    b.   deindividuation.
    c.   groupthink.
    d.   cognitive dissonance.

ESSAY QUESTIONS

1. What are some reasons that people conform? Can you think of situations where conformity is good?

2. What are some of the factors that seemed to make obedience to an authority harder to resist in Milgram's study?

ANSWER KEY

1. Obedience
2. Groupthink
3. Conformity
4. Social identity
5. Social facilitation
6. Personal identity
7. Compliance
8. Legitimization of authority
9. Social validation
10. Social loafing
11. b
12. d
13. b
14. d
15. c
16. b

SAMPLE ANSWERS TO ESSAY QUESTIONS

1. People conform because social contact is important to us. We want acceptance from members of groups to which we belong, and we are willing to modify our behavior, at least to an extent, in order to help gain that acceptance. Part of our own understanding of ourselves, and our sense of who we are, is enmeshed in our relationships with others; this is known as our social identity. Thus, being connected to others is a fundamental part of us. We conform both to the general norms of our culture and to the more specific norms or standards established (formally or informally) by the groups in which we participate. Although often not clearly spelled out, there are social sanctions and repercussions for not conforming to either cultural or group standards.

    People may conform because they assume that the group must be correct, or they conform despite their own beliefs and attitudes because acceptance by the group is extremely important. Greater levels of conformity are found among individuals who have lower self-esteem, who exhibit social shyness, and who have a very high need to be liked and accepted by the group. Many times, of course, conformity is good, and perhaps we often conform without being aware of it. If we did not all stop on the red lights and go on the green, for example, we would indeed all be in trouble!

2. In Milgram's study on obedience, participants played the role of someone teaching someone else (who was really a confederate of the researcher). Every time the learner gave a wrong answer, the teacher was instructed to administer an unavoidable shock to the learner. The cover story for the study involved research on learning—the participant may have felt that he or she was contributing to the advancement of knowledge. The experimenter running the study was visible to (in most versions of the study) and near the participants, the "learner" was not. Thus, in general, the experimenter's presence and influence was much more salient to the participants than that of anyone else. To a degree, we do like to conform in order to gain approval and acceptance from others, even strangers. The experimenter wore a lab coat and exuded the air of an authority figure.

The early versions of Milgram's research had the preeminence of Yale University as a backdrop. The "teachers" were in foreign surroundings and had to perform a task that they most certainly had never experienced before. The unfamiliarity of the situation and perhaps uncertainty as to proper ways to handle it may have led the participants to comply with authority requests more so than they might have in another situation. The obedience study began with a very low level of shock administered. These were very gradually increased with every wrong answer. Most likely results would have been different if participants were asked at the outset to administer the very highest level of "severe shock." Once the pattern of response was established, as well as the relationship among the experimenter, the "teacher," and the "learner," it was harder for the participant to stop carrying out the same kinds of behaviors. Again, because the shock gradations were increased in fairly small steps, there was no radical change in the procedure that might have provided participants with a break point at which they could stop. Relocating Milgram's study to a commercial storefront still resulted in unexpectedly high levels of obedience, but once the experimenter was removed altogether and/or the "learner" was brought in closer proximity to the "teacher," obedience dropped. Clearly we do want to remember the importance of situational factors.

MODULE 14.4 APPLICATION: COMPLIANCE: DOING WHAT OTHERS WANT YOU TO DO

LEARNING OBJECTIVE
After you have mastered the information in this unit, you will be able to:

1. Define compliance and the factors that influence it.

OUTLINE
I. Background Factors in Compliance
   A. Process of acceding to the requests or demands of others
   B. Reasons for compliance
     1. Authority
     2. Social validation—helps us interpret and direct our own behavior
     3. Consistency—in our thoughts, actions, plans
II. Sales and Marketing Strategies
   A. Those based on need for consistency
     1. Low-ball technique
       a) Agreement is made, based on advertised lower price;, buyer plans to make purchase
       b) Opportunity rescinded due to story from salesperson
       c) Buyer more likely to make another purchase because action consistent with original intention
     2. Bait-and-switch technique
       a) As with low-ball, original offer appealing, low-priced, great value
       b) Salesperson then is derogatory regarding first item, or it is unavailable
       c) Presentation is made of higher quality, available merchandise (but more expensive)
       d) Again buyer more likely to make alternative purchase—consistent with original intention
     3. Foot-in-the-door technique
       a) Original request is for very small or unobtrusive favor
       b) When compliance for small favor obtained, request on larger scale is made

      c)   People who agree to smaller requests are more likely to comply with larger ones, apparently due to the desire for consistency (Cialdini & Trost, 1998)

B.   Door-in-the-face technique—based on reciprocity principle
    1.   First request is for unreasonably large favor
    2.   Following request much less demanding, much more reasonable – which is actually what the person wanted in the first place
    3.   Help more likely when these two steps occur—helper feels more obligated since refused first request (and was relieved, grateful to have an alternative)

SUMMARY

In this module, you learn about techniques sometimes utilized by sales personnel (or even your friends!) to get you to provide assistance, make a donation, or purchase an item. Salespeople may use the low-ball technique—get you to agree to a purchase at a given price, then come back and report that that price is no longer available. Similarly, with the bait-and-switch technique, a desired item is advertised at a very good price, and the buyer comes in with the intention to purchase. The buyer is then told the original product is shoddy or unavailable. In both cases, the buyer is still more likely to make the purchase (at the higher price), since that behavior is consistent with his or her original intentions. The foot-in-the-door involves our first agreeing to a simple, small request. Research shows we are then much more likely to acquiesce to a more large-scale request because we want our behaviors to be consistent with the pattern established. The door-in-the-face technique is based on the reciprocity principle. We feel relief when an original, demanding request is rescinded and the requester appears willing to compromise. We are much more likely then to agree to a smaller, more reasonable request— we are reciprocating the requester's "kindness" at offering an alternative to the unreasonable request!

KEY TERMS

Compliance

Low-ball technique

Bait-and-switch technique

Foot-in-the-door technique

Door-in-the face technique

SELF-TEST PRACTICE QUIZ

1. Making an unreasonable demand of someone else that is refused, and then asking for a less demanding favor is known as the
    a.   foot-in-the-door technique.
    b.   door-in-the-face technique.
    c.   bait-and-switch technique.
    d.   low-ball technique.

2. Many stores like to use a sales technique in which they advertise one item at a very cheap price. When customers arrive, they find that the cheap item is sold out and are encouraged instead to buy a more expensive version. Such stores are using the
    a.   low-ball technique.
    b.   bait-and-switch technique.
    c.   foot-in-the-door technique.
    d.   door-in-the-face technique.

3.   Erica agreed to buy a car at what seemed a very reasonable price. After agreeing to this price, the dealer started adding on all sorts of extra charges. Erica fell victim to the

   a.   low-ball technique.
   b.   bait-and-switch technique.
   c.   foot-in-the-door technique.
   d.   door-in-the-face technique.

4.   Gaining compliance to a smaller request in order to gain compliance to a larger one is called the

   a.   low-ball technique.
   b.   bait-and-switch technique.
   c.   foot-in-the-door technique.
   d.   door-in-the-face technique.

ESSAY QUESTION

1.   What is the relationship between the self-serving bias and the amount of control people have over the work that they do?

ANSWER KEY

1. b
2. b
3. a
4. c

SAMPLE ANSWER TO ESSAY QUESTION

1. Research on job satisfaction indicates that most employees are happier in occupations where they have a fair degree of control over the work that they do. Typically, people who have some control over what they do at work exhibit less job-related stress and report a more positive work experience. However, it is important to not overgeneralize regarding the relationship between control in the occupational setting and job satisfaction. For workers who have a negative attributional style (e.g., they tend to blame themselves when things go wrong), having some control over what happens at the job is not a good thing. This subset of workers prefers jobs where they do not have control over what they do. Lack of control over what happens at work frees such individuals from responsibility for problems. When the individual does not feel responsible for events at work, the individual does not fall into the pattern of blaming himself or herself for things that go wrong.

CHAPTER 14   APPLICATION EXERCISE

Think of all the groups of which you are a member. Remember, the groups to which you belong do not include just your set of friends. Your family is probably a very important group, and the students who sit near you and share your classes with you are something of a group. Do you go to the gym? Are you in clubs or organizations? The people with whom you work also form a group, as does your neighborhood or residential setting. If you are not living at home, then your roommates or housemates form a group. In a larger sense, you are a member of a particular cultural and socioeconomic group.

List each group of which you are a member, formally or informally. How has your identification with each of these groups influenced who you are? How would you be different if you were not a member of that group? Do you conform to the standards of the group? Why or why not? In what ways do you conform? Lastly, how has your psychological identity been molded by your group identity?